ON THE CUSP OF CONTACT

ALASKA
BRITISH COLUMBIA
HAIDA GWAII (QUEEN CHARLOTTE ISLANDS)
CARIBOO
PACIFIC OCEAN
Fraser R
VANCOUVER ISLAND
Nootka Sound
Vancouver
FRASER VALLEY
Victoria
SCALE IN KILOMETERS
0 25 50 75
0 25 50
SCALE IN MILES
WASHINGTO

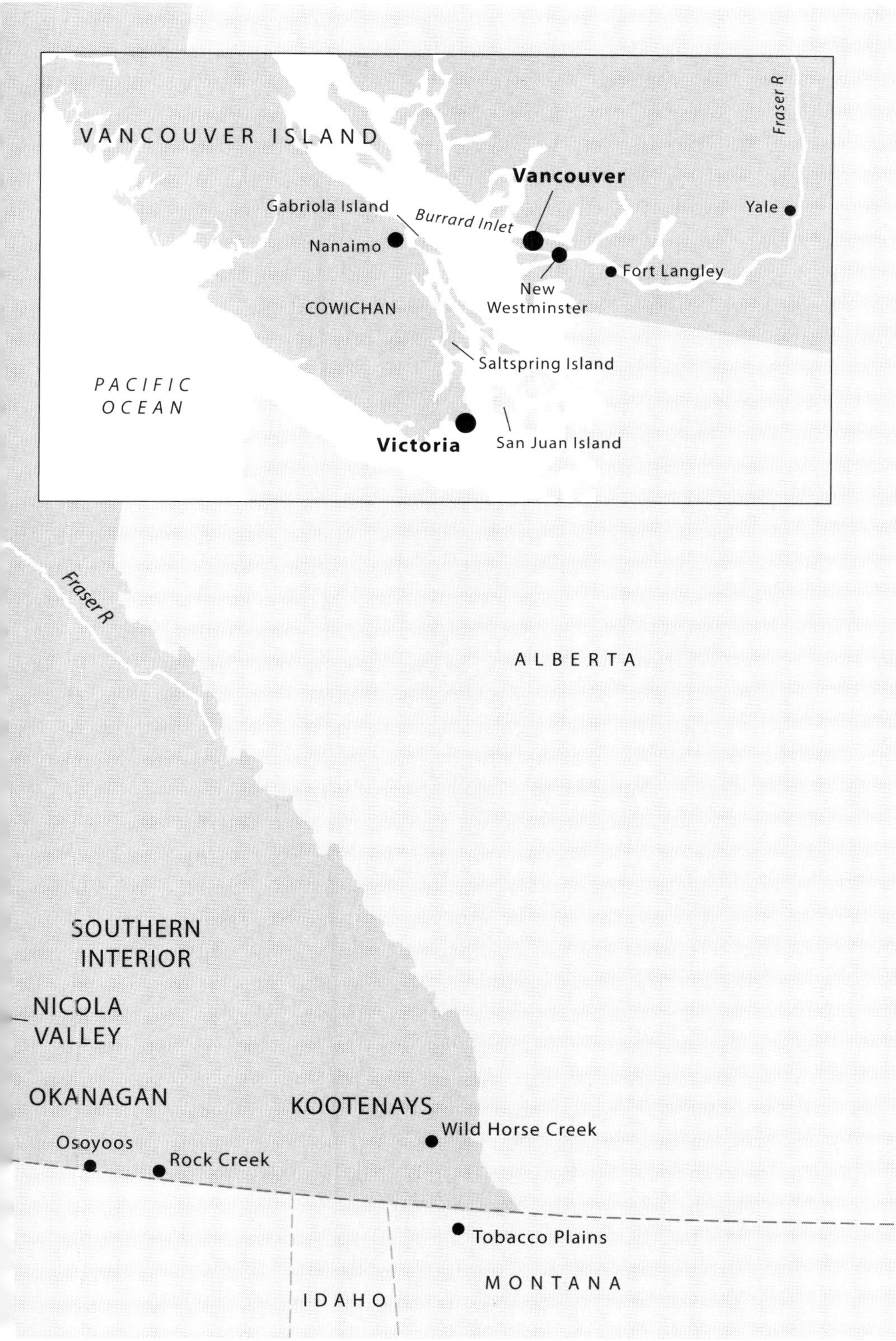
VANCOUVER ISLAND
Fraser R
Vancouver
Gabriola Island
Burrard Inlet
Yale
Nanaimo
Fort Langley
New Westminster
COWICHAN
Saltspring Island
PACIFIC OCEAN
Victoria
San Juan Island
Fraser R
ALBERTA
SOUTHERN INTERIOR
NICOLA VALLEY
OKANAGAN
KOOTENAYS
Wild Horse Creek
Osoyoos
Rock Creek
Tobacco Plains
MONTANA
IDAHO

On *the* Cusp *of* Contact

Gender, Space *and* Race *in the* Colonization *of* British Columbia

Essays by Jean Barman

Edited by Margery Fee

Harbour Publishing

1 2 3 4 5 — 24 23 22 21 20

Harbour Publishing Co. Ltd.
P.O. Box 219, Madeira Park, BC, V0N 2H0
www.harbourpublishing.com

Edited and indexed by Audrey McClellan
Cover and text design by Shed Simas / Onça Design
Map by Roger Handling
Cover image: Detail from *Entrance to Howe Sound from Mouth of False Creek* (ca. 1887) by Edward Roper, Art Gallery of Greater Victoria
Printed and bound in Canada
Printed on acid-free paper certified by the Forest Stewardship Council

Canada Council for the Arts | Conseil des arts du Canada
British Columbia Arts Council
British Columbia
Supported by the Province of British Columbia

Harbour Publishing acknowledges the support of the Canada Council for the Arts, the Government of Canada, and the Province of British Columbia through the BC Arts Council.

Library and Archives Canada Cataloguing in Publication
Title: On the cusp of contact : gender, space and race in the colonization of British Columbia / essays by Jean Barman ; edited by Margery Fee.
Other titles: Essays. Selections
Names: Barman, Jean, author. | Fee, Margery, 1948- editor.
Description: Includes bibliographical references and index.
Identifiers: Canadiana (print) 20190229039 | Canadiana (ebook) 20190229098 | ISBN 9781550178968 (softcover) | ISBN 9781550178975 (HTML)
Subjects: LCSH: Frontier and pioneer life—British Columbia. | LCSH: British Columbia—Colonization. | LCSH: British Columbia—Race relations. | LCSH: British Columbia—Social conditions.
Classification: LCC FC3811 .B34 2020 | DDC 971.1—dc23

Table of Contents

Navigating Schooling

Author's Preface

The past cannot be undone, but it can be redressed. As historians, we do this by adding new layers of understanding, principally through our writing, to the usual measures perceived to have meaning. For me, redress has meant integrating the history of Indigenous education in Canada into the scholarship long before it was fashionable to do so.[1] It has meant including everyday men and women in the *Dictionary of Canadian Biography*,[2] as the subjects of monographs and articles, and in provincial histories.[3] It has meant, in the essays that follow, changing terms I used to name Canada's first peoples to "Indigenous." In writing as I do, I have drawn on insights from politics, education, and librarianship, in which fields I have graduate degrees.

Most importantly, I was privileged to teach in a faculty of education, meaning I was not weighed down by traditional disciplinary measures of worth as to how we conceive and write about the past. Some topics, such as the everyday lives of women and of Indigenous peoples, survive in good part in human memory, and I have had the honour of many descendants sharing their families' stories and pictures with me on the understanding I would act responsibly and honestly in my use of them. I would like to think I have done so, and thank you, each and every one, for your generosity of spirit.

I am amazingly grateful to the eminent literary historian Margery Fee, who, without my foreknowledge, decided that essays I had written over the years merited re-publication as a collection, and to Audrey McClellan, Arlene Prunkl, and Rebecca Pruitt MacKenney for insightfully editing and updating the essays. My initial resistance to the project was overcome by my realization on rereading the essays, foregrounded by Margery's astute introductions, that, yes, they do matter. Indeed, the essays may matter more now than when they were first published, given changing perspectives on Indigenous women and Indigenous schooling.

—Jean Barman

Notes

1 With Yvonne Hébert and Don McCaskill, *Indian Education in Canada*: vol. 1, *The Legacy* and vol. 2, *The Challenge* (Vancouver: UBC Press, 1986 and 1987); with Marie Battiste, *First Nations Education in Canada: The Circle Unfolds* (Vancouver: UBC Press, 1995); and with Cheryl Suzack, Jeanne Perreault, and Shari Huhndorf, *Indigenous Women and Feminism: Politics, Activism, Culture* (Vancouver: UBC Press, 2010).

2 In volume 13 of *Dictionary of Canadian Biography* online, early British Columbia settler William Naukana of indigenous Hawaiian descent who had children by two or more Indigenous women; in volume 15, early British Columbia settler William Curran from the United States, who had large families with two Indigenous women in succession; and in volume 16, British Columbia writer Constance Lindsay Skinner, who made her career in New York City, and British Columbian of Indigenous Canadian and Hawaiian descent Maria Mahoi, who had large families in succession with an American whaler and with the son of an establishment Englishman and an Indigenous woman.

3 See "Selected Works by Jean Barman."

Introduction

Margery Fee

Inspired by her "Taming Aboriginal Sexuality,"[1] I started to track down Jean Barman's work. I quickly became frustrated because many of her articles could only be found in non-circulating periodicals in the library stacks. As I worked my way through the list, each volume fell open, as if by magic, at the first page of her article. Others had been there before me. This collection will free Barman fans from the stacks and the photocopier and bring some of her important work to the attention of a broader audience.

I had certainly met Jean Barman before I went to a feast at Kwantlen First Nation to welcome the nation's new babies. On arrival, I spotted Jean chatting to a small group and overheard her say, "So have you tracked those Hawaiian relatives?" She seems to be a cross between everyone's favourite auntie and Ancestry.ca. The celebration of the babies was a perfect setting for her, given her long-standing interest in how couples find each other and how children are formed by their parents, relatives, education, employment, and larger society. She has also chosen to focus her work on British Columbia, from the first arrival of Europeans—"the cusp of contact"—and through the period when it was what Mary Louise Pratt calls a contact zone. Pratt defines such zones as "social spaces where cultures meet, clash, and grapple with each other, often in contexts of highly asymmetrical relations of power, such as colonialism, slavery, or their aftermaths as they are lived out in many parts of the world today."[2]

The study of how new social formations emerge out of such contact and how men and women make lives for themselves within often stringent economic and social constraints uncovers some fascinating life stories. Barman's writing reveals "the frontier, that space between contact and settlement, where, for a brief moment, anything seems possible." These transitional moments allow for lives to break with expected narratives; often only traces of these stories survive in official histories, written "once the winners take charge."[3] Who could imagine that the granddaughter of a Chinese father and Indigenous mother would be a Gitxsan hereditary chief,[4] or that families whose members spoke Chinese, English, and an Indigenous language would flourish, or that "fluidity of relationships" might mean that one could even choose one's own father, as Sophie Morigeau may have done.[5] The federal Indian Act (1876) took Indian status from women if they married non-status men; children of such marriages were also stripped of Indian status. Despite this regulation, Barman has discovered how residential schools in the early period often admitted such non-status students to meet enrolment requirements. Nor did bureaucrats appear to notice that Chinese or Hawaiian men were welcomed, and that their families prospered, on reserve lands, or that the adult sons of white fathers were negotiating land deals for the people of their Indigenous mothers when, according to the law, such sons had no title to that land.[6] The grip of the federal regulations on Indigenous people in British Columbia was slow to tighten in the early period, and during that time things went differently, revealing that the law was based on categories that need not necessarily ever have applied.

"The West beyond the West," as Barman calls British Columbia to distinguish it from other more famous wests, is geographically, socially, and historically distinctive. As a result, any history of the province reconfigures the usual narratives of national history from the other side of the Rockies. Further, the narrower focus in this collection on those people excluded even from most provincial histories is based on much that eastern Canadian historians can no longer access. Because the far west was colonized so recently, Barman was able to talk to those who lived through some of the early history of the province or remembered stories passed down in their families, so that in this collection, archival and documentary sources are supplemented by oral history. Even today, British Columbia qualifies as remote from the national capital (a four-and-a-half-hour flight to Ottawa and a three-hour time difference). The early history of the province features San Francisco, Honolulu, and Canton (Guangzhou) rather than Ottawa, New York, London, or Paris. As Barman puts it, "Vancouver [is] a cosmopolitan city amidst one of the world's last frontiers."[7] The Indigenous peoples in British Columbia are the most linguistically and culturally diverse of any province; more than thirty Indigenous languages are still spoken here, although all the regional languages are now endangered as a result of imposed residential schooling.[8]

The territory was under the sole control of the Hudson's Bay Company (HBC) until the Colony of Vancouver Island was formed in 1849. At the lower ranks, the HBC employed mainly French Canadians, Métis, and Iroquois men from Kahnawà:ke or Oka in Quebec, but it also contracted Hawaiians and men of other ethnicities as well. This very diverse population with a strong majority of single young men meant that Indigenous women became a desirable means to consolidate trading relationships at the highest levels as well as to encourage lesser employees of the HBC to renew their contracts.[9] The HBC monopoly ended in 1858,[10] as the first of several gold rushes brought men from all over the world to the Colony of British Columbia, which was swiftly set up that year to assert British control in the face of any incursions by the United States. The two colonies united in 1866, and British Columbia joined Confederation in 1871 on the promise of a railway from eastern Canada, which finally made it over the Rockies to Vancouver in 1886. Until then, the gender imbalance persisted.

Between 1871 and 1901, settlers from Britain and continental Europe went from around 24 per cent of the population to 73 per cent, with most of that growth occurring after the railway was completed.[11] Family structures that were perfectly normal to that point suddenly were stigmatized. Transitions that were gradual in other locations took place within a few decades, rendering them more visible and more memorable.

One other important issue that makes British Columbia different from the rest of Canada is the refusal of the provincial government to make treaties with Indigenous people, despite the requirement to do so according to the Royal Proclamation of 1763. Apart from treaties on Vancouver Island, made by Governor James Douglas between 1850 and 1854, and Treaty 8 (1899), which covers the northeastern corner of the province, the province resisted treaty making until 1991, when the British Columbia Treaty Commission was established. Provincial intransigence before that date and foot-dragging after it have generated many of the important Supreme Court decisions affecting Indigenous people in the past forty years, including Calder (1973), Guerin (1984), Sparrow (1990), Delgamuukw (1997), Van der Peet (1996), Haida Nation (2004), and Tsilhqot'in (2014).

The Indigenous nations of the region forged relationships in the region's economy before settlement began in earnest, a way of life evidenced by a trade language called Chinook Jargon that permitted multilingual Indigenous people and newcomers to communicate.[12] Indigenous men worked as trappers, loggers, fishermen, miners, and packers, in canneries and sawmills, on steamers, and as traders and farmers; Indigenous women found work as servants, street traders, sex workers, and in shops, laundries, and dance halls. A few men worked as translators. The fur trade made many Indigenous communities prosperous at the same time as smallpox and other introduced diseases were taking a huge toll. Between contact in 1770 and the 1830s, these diseases killed between 60 and 90 per cent of the Indigenous population in British Columbia.[13] The result was a period of incredible loss and reconfiguration for Indigenous communities, which were faced with increasing prejudice, legal constraint, and segregation as settlement began to burgeon.

Nonetheless, as John Sutton Lutz points out, the early settler economy was dependent on the labour of Indigenous people, along with that of other racialized groups. As a result, Indigenous people retained considerable economic independence until the 1920s. In fact, Barman argues that "the principal objection to assimilation did not come from Indigenous people but rather from the dominant society. First came the demand for separation in the classroom, then more general unwillingness to allow educated young Indians into the work force."[14] Lutz expands on this, noting that Indigenous people who were denied regular employment could not fall back on traditional subsistence hunting, fishing, or foraging because of laws regulating such activities, the expansion of private property, the logging of forests, and the damming and pollution of rivers. Indigenous people who had to turn to welfare were criticized as lazy and given less than white people.[15] In other words, the assumption in many histories that First Nations people needed education to enter the workforce overlooked the fact that in the early period they were already in the workforce, albeit usually on the lowest rungs, and wanted their children to be educated to do better. Nor did this desire for education mean that they supported wholesale assimilation to the dominant culture for themselves or their children. They did not see adaptation to new circumstances as the all-or-nothing proposition that the mainstream emblematized in rituals such as Christian conversion, enfranchisement, or citizenship, rituals that marked the absolute (and implicitly required) transition from primitive to civilized, outsider to citizen. Vanishing into a homogeneous Canadianness—that was the colonizers' fantasy, albeit one that had brutal consequences, particularly for children in residential schools.

The sixteen essays collected here, published between 1995 and 2013, reflect Barman's interest in those who were at a disadvantage in white settler society, whether because of their gender, ascribed race, or social class. Here, as in other articles and books, Barman studies racialized or white working-class people who spent their lives out of the limelight in small communities, although some exceptional women did take the stage in the dance halls and at trading posts. Barman's work began with the elite, however. Her first book, *Growing Up British in British Columbia: Boys in Private School* (1984), reflects her interest in how ethnicity, gender, age, class, and education worked to form the elite men of British Columbia. The lives of such men and their wives and daughters are relatively easy to track through newspapers, histories, diaries, letters, and other official sources preserved as part of the province's history by them and their descendants in public libraries, museums, town halls, and statues or plaques in civic squares. Nonetheless, the picture she drew required interviews with 150 former students, masters, and headmasters, which provided vital background to the public record. This work laid the foundations for the more difficult work of tracking the less prominent.

Barman's interest in history broadened with the publication of the first edition of her history of the province, *The West beyond the West*, in 1991 (3rd ed. 2007). However, by this time she had also begun to work on Indigenous issues in a two-volume collaborative collection, *Indian Education in Canada*, which brought together papers by Indigenous and non-Indigenous writers. These groundbreaking volumes appeared in 1986 and asked, "Why is it only now in the late twentieth century, that Canada's aboriginal people are beginning to regain control over their children's education?"[16] A follow-up volume, *First Nations Education in Canada*, was published in 1995, co-edited with Mi'kmaq scholar Marie Battiste.[17] Only in the twenty-first century is Canada coming to grips with the consequences of past educational policies.

Barman's familiarity with mainstream history meant that she was well prepared to spot and contextualize the "anomalous" lives of the people who became the focus of much of her subsequent work. She reads against the grain of accounts usually written by white men whose main interests were economic development and the "civilization" of the new province, which entailed controlling the behaviour and curtailing the rights of women and racialized others. This work takes not only interpretative skill but also the ability to track and understand multiple sources, including fiction, drama, poetry, local history, family trees, statistical records, and oral sources. Assessing the credibility of these varied sources is also crucial.[18] This collection provides a strong awareness of how different genres allow for different perspectives on the past.

Barman regards British Columbia history from a feminist and anti-racist position. Her perspective means that she doesn't mince words, referring to settlement as "the land grab we know as settler colonialism,"[19] and the early colonial period as the one in which "Indigenous women became sexualized as prostitutes."[20] Chinese men, she writes, were "disparaged even as they were wanted" to do work white men considered "beneath their dignity."[21] A shift in educational policy from educating Indigenous students with other students for roles in mainstream society to segregated schools was justified by the supposed intellectual inferiority of Indigenous or mixed-ancestry students who had proved themselves equal or superior to their white schoolmates only a few years before. Barman blames "federal parsimony and white prejudice" for Indigenous students' poor educational results once they were segregated in residential schools—an "education" that often included physical and sexual abuse.[22] These schools, given their location and their inadequate federal funding, usually employed poorly trained teachers whose main goal was religious indoctrination. The schools essentially depended on child labour, as the pupils undertook much of the work of raising and preparing food; making, mending, and washing clothes; and cleaning and maintenance, which meant they were in the classroom for fewer hours than their public-school peers.

The jolt of Barman's blunt words reflects how quickly mainstream discourses soften and obscure such divisive moments. The history

Barman explores casts light on why so many Indigenous women have been classified as "missing and murdered," a phrase that has only entered the mainstream after decades of activism led by their grieving families.[23] And it also casts light on why, in 1988, the federal government apologized and offered redress to the Japanese Canadians removed from the west coast in the Second World War. And why, in 2006, the federal government apologized and offered redress for imposing a head tax on Chinese immigrants. And why, in 2008, it apologized and offered redress to survivors of Indian residential schools and set up the Truth and Reconciliation Commission to help educate Canadians about an almost obliterated history. And why, also in 2008, it apologized for illegally barring the Sikh passengers on the *Komagata Maru* from entry at the port of Vancouver in 1914. These incidents reflect the same racism that refused voting rights to those defined as non-white.[24] In British Columbia this refusal dated from 1871 for men of Chinese ancestry, from 1895 for men of Japanese ancestry, and from 1907 for men of South Asian ancestry (mainly Sikhs from India). In 1920, the federal government also denied men and women of these ancestries the right to vote in federal elections, a ban that extended at both the provincial and federal levels until after the Second World War.[25]

Notably, the changes in mainstream attitudes and terminology reflected in these essays even in the short period between 1995 and 2013 when they were first published are striking, and these changes continue apace. The use of terms that rarely appear now, such as "adultery" or "concubinage," in both the quotations and the text, and the shifting use of terms for Indigenous people and people of part-Indigenous descent, make clear the shifting landscape around marriage, racialization, and indigeneity in recent years. Writing about "race" is a fraught process, particularly for those of the dominant white culture. Barman is reflecting not only her own perspectives, but also those found in rapidly changing discourses on whiteness and racialization taking place in the same decades—add gender and sexuality to the mix, and the idea of retaining a perspective that will not jar some readers at some points becomes impossible. Barman supports integrated common schooling, cheers for independent women, and sees families, however constituted, as generally better places for individuals than a solo life. Her heart is often on her sleeve in ways that historians and "objective" academic writers are supposed to avoid. Barman is approving when teachers write about children whom she knows were of mixed descent without mentioning their ascribed race,[26] but of course, because she is focusing on racialization, she invariably must mention race. She faces the problem that to write about discrimination is, at some level, to re-inscribe the categories on which the discrimination is based. However, to pretend these categories and the forms of discrimination they derive from and support do not exist is to perpetuate them by promoting what Gayatri Spivak calls "sanctioned ignorance."[27]

Barman's constant shuttling between issues of individual agency and structural constraint is unusual for many historians. What happened—the historical facts—is for her always considered within a comparative and statistical framework more typical of sociology, a move in part required by what she was able to find out in answer to her questions. Statistics are crucial if we are to know anything at all about the lives of people whose traces in the public record are slight. When all that can be discovered is derived from institutional records such as the census, marriage, voting, and land title records, the specificity of individual choices recedes and structural issues come to the fore.

The focus, for example, on how racialization and gender affected the ability to find a partner or to marry and produce a family counters the still widespread belief (hope?) that people partner for love and love alone. That Barman makes it clear some of these relationships were driven not purely by choice but by pragmatism is sometimes hard to process. The desire to make a stable living, the desire for a sexual partner, and the desire for children are all fulfilled only within a net of social restrictions that are often invisible to those who have been socialized within them. Thus, the racist Social Darwinist hierarchy that put whites at the top and Indigenous people at the bottom is revealed in the marriage outcomes of men and women of mixed race. Gender played a role as well, since women did "better" than their brothers; they were more often able to marry white men at a time when white women were in very short supply. Barman describes some of the pressures that might have influenced Indigenous women's choices, which "diminish[ed] their indigeneity at a time when visible mixed race was a stigma that was virtually impossible to overcome, no matter how hard individuals worked or how well they behaved."[28] All women to some degree "disappeared" in marriage by moving into the home and taking on their husband's name, although this was truer for middle-class than working-class women. Faced with the racism of their peers, white men married to Indigenous women often "responded by hiding their Indigenous wives from view,"[29] or the women, aware that their husband's social circle would disapprove of them, chose to withdraw. Barman notes that Governor Douglas's wife, Martha, whose grandmother was Cree, was described as "suitably 'shy and modest,' essentially as knowing her inferior place and not daring to offend her racial betters."[30] Children of mixed ancestry, whether male or female, could move "up" because they were not forced to attend residential schools and therefore were usually better educated. Further, they were often less visibly "different" and thus less subject to racism.

Barman's feminist interests led to the publication of books about white women in British Columbia like Constance Lindsey Skinner (1877–1939), Emma Crosby (1849–1926), and the McQueen sisters (Jessie, 1860–1933, and Annie, 1865–1941).[31] Her knowledge of these white women's lives allowed her to articulate how they differed from the lives of mixed-race and Indigenous women, such as Maria Mahoi (c. 1855–1936), subject of Barman's *Maria Mahoi of the Islands* (2004). Ironically, she found that Indigenous women were sometimes freer to make their own choices, not only because of the different gender relations in Indigenous societies, which were often matrilineal, but also because these women could move from one social world to the other. One insight is that the women from matrilineal societies were not as used to having their freedom constrained or controlled by their fathers and husbands, the norm for settler society.[32] White women often found themselves isolated in the respectability of domestic space, far away from their families "back home" in eastern Canada or on another continent, while Indigenous women could walk or paddle home—or even hop on a convenient steamer—if they were lonely for their family, wanted to engage in traditional practices, or needed to escape domestic friction or abuse.

Barman does not romanticize these relationships, as she makes clear in many places, including in a section in her *French Canadians, Furs, and Indigenous Women in the Making of the Pacific Northwest* (2014) titled "Intimacy's Limits."[33] Such relationships were driven by compulsory heterosexuality, patriarchal ideologies, and the racism and sexism that excluded racialized people and women from entering the economy at any but the lowest levels. Some were happy; some were not. Sophie Morigeau certainly queered heteronormativity, even though Barman argues that she was exceptional only if viewed from the perspective of mainstream Victorian views on the appropriate behaviour for women. However, it is still uncomfortable to shift from hearing of individual men like Portuguese Joe Silvey, who conquered a huge array of difficulties to make a life for himself and his family, to a larger, more sociological analysis. From that perspective, Silvey recedes somewhat as an individual to a subject whose life choices—to marry an Indigenous woman, to live on an island—were driven by mainstream racism and the lack of marriageable women, factors that complicated the lives of many other men like him. We like to think we have total individual agency, or at least to think that some people do. Barman's emphasis on the biological is both rare and unsettling. That men aged over thirty—sometimes much older—had as many as a dozen children with Indigenous women less than half their age, and in some cases just out of puberty, raises other questions of power. It is hard nowadays, where families in Canada are so much smaller, to think of how these women were constrained by circumstance and biology to bear and raise so many children.

Finally, Barman shows how the single working-class white men who worked in male-dominated resource-extraction industries usually led diminished lives, in part because they were denied any chance at making a family. "Canada's poorest postal code," the Downtown East Side of Vancouver, once housed fishermen, loggers, and miners in the winters in single-room hotels surrounded by bars and dance halls. Some of these hotels remain, now crumbling, even condemned, housing single aging former resource workers, while other men like them live on the street.

The uniqueness of this region and of Barman's clear-eyed perspective explains much of the exceptional quality and appeal of her work. An additional explanation lies in her educational background. The study often crosses the boundaries between history, life writing, and sociology, and this crossing may evoke queasy feelings in readers more used to purified genres and clear disciplinary perspectives. Barman received an MA in Russian and sub-Saharan African History and Politics at Harvard; worked for a year in London for a journal analyzing stories in the daily Soviet press on Africa; and then earned a master's degree in librarianship at Berkeley. Only after that did she embark on a doctorate in the history of education, a site of interdisciplinary research. And according to Barman, her career took an unexpected turn: "I am first and foremost an archivist and professional librarian. It is those skills which make it possible for me to research and write as I have done over the years on oftentimes obscure topics."[34] When she was unable to find any trace of some histories in the written record, her skills helped track other sources, often at the insistence of determined family members who knew that evidence was there. In some cases, this digging has led to material changes to the landscape: her account of the people who were evicted from what became Stanley Park has led to the erection of a totem pole and a large sculpture carved by descendants that now memorialize their families' formerly invisible history.[35] A school in Fernie, BC, is named after Sophie Morigeau as a result of Barman's historical work. That said, as she explains, some of the people she writes about sought to disappear into the mainstream and did not foster family memory in their children: "I ponder the inequities of a past that encouraged people to forsake their heritage."[36]

The most recent essay collected here appeared first in 2013. Since then, Barman has continued her work on Indigenous issues. In *French Canadians, Furs, and Indigenous Women*, Barman points out that the region is neglected by historians in both the United States and Canada. Divided only in 1846 with the agreement that the forty-ninth parallel would form the international boundary, "whichever the country in charge, the history of the half not theirs was lost from view; that of the half acquired being tacked on to a national narrative."[37] Here the long-standing ignorance of the presence of French Canadians in the west explains the omission of these men and their Indigenous wives and families from national histories. Now these families are being widely studied, in part because of the inclusion of the Métis in the Constitution Act (1982) as one of the Aboriginal peoples of Canada. Barman argues that were it not for the presence of these settlers in the region, what is now British Columbia would likely be part of the United States.[38]

Barman's book *Abenaki Daring: The Life and Writings of Noel Annance, 1792–1869* (2016) focuses on one of the few Indigenous men to receive a higher education, at Dartmouth College in New Hampshire.[39] Up until around 1840 in eastern Canada, when the fur trade ended and settlement expanded, Indigenous men were seen as useful as interpreters, teachers, and missionaries.[40] After that, mainstream attention shifted to the control of Indigenous lands and the regulation of Indigenous lives. Although having the same excellent classical education as peers, including the politician Daniel Webster, who went on to lead prominent lives, Annance's efforts at enfranchisement were futile, despite the promise in the Indian Act that men literate in English or French and with a basic education could become equal citizens. He described his life as regulated by "the gentle and protective incubus which incapacitates me to move on the same plane and platform with my other fellow subjects of Her Majesty."[41] Historians have assumed that few men chose enfranchisement because few desired it, but Barman suggests that the Indian Department, realizing that educated Indigenous men posed a threat to its comfortable existence, may have refused to enfranchise some men. Certainly more work on the issue is warranted, including on the decision to impose enfranchisement on some Indigenous men against their will between 1920 and 1922 and again between 1933 and 1951.[42]

Iroquois in the West (2019) turns attention to Iroquois men from three communities—Kahnawà:ke (Caughnawaga), Akwesasne, and Oka—who engaged in the fur trade in the North American west, both well before and after the US-Canada border was finalized in this region in 1846. These diasporic Iroquois have been ignored in histories of the more settled communities in eastern Canada and the United States. Nor has their importance to the history of western Canada been acknowledged. Again Barman shows how Indigenous men took chances to make lives for themselves far from their birthplaces and how those who settled away from home, and their descendants, have challenged settler racism.[43]

Anyone who reads this collection straight through will spot ways in which the essays intersect and overlap. For example, a reference in "Indigenous Women on the Streets of Victoria" to what were then called "squaw dance halls" is expanded in "Taming Indigenous Sexuality" to show how Indigenous women maintained an independent stance and high standards of etiquette and decorum in dance halls, while white businessmen, city officials, and ministers of religion contended over how to regulate their behaviour for profit, votes, or moral standing. Barman describes "Indigenous Women on the Streets of Victoria" as a prequel to "Taming Indigenous Sexuality."[44] Because the essays were originally published separately, some repetition is required for the arguments to work. However, some of her repetition of particularly striking quotations or stories also serves the interests of different arguments. Readers can see how historians work with the same material by framing it in different ways to reveal different aspects of social relations marked by mainstream discrimination against Indigenous people, racialized newcomers, and most women. Not only do these essays reveal how such varied sources can be used to answer important questions about representations, attitudes, and historical events, but they also allow readers to see how articles slowly build on each other, in the process revealing how historians work: the slow and painstaking accumulation of information from primary sources, their subsequent transformation from data into narrative, and the use of that data and narrative to make important critical insights into the historical past and how we study it. This collection provides a way for graduate and undergraduate students in historical fields to start to understand how a career might unfold over time and how chance encounters with a book or an anecdote leads one to a new project. Although Barman has gone over the essays to delete some repetition and correct errors, no attempt has been made to change terms to reflect contemporary usage apart from preferring "Indigenous" over earlier synonyms. The essays themselves come out of particular historical and scholarly contexts and retain the marks of that emergence.[45]

One hallmark of Barman's practice has been to collaborate with Indigenous scholars, some of whom she supervised through their doctoral dissertations.[46] Often these intellectual relationships are as transformative of the wider intellectual and academic landscape as the publications so valued by academic colleagues. Of course, not all students agree with their supervisors, but those who go on to take a position at a research university are in a position to influence subsequent generations of students who will likely have their perspectives recalibrated in ways that reflect the supervisor's influence. Although none of the essays included here were written collaboratively, they do reflect her connections with community members. (Characteristically, Barman says that anyone mentioned in the notes should be considered a co-author.)[47]

In many ways, the history of minoritized and racialized communities, as well as women's history, still remains to be properly integrated into national and transnational histories that are both racialized and gendered in ways that need to be articulated and remedied. Jean Barman's work provides a stellar example of how this process happens, with detailed, careful archival and community work that can provide a secure foundation for others to build on.

I thank Jean for her unfailing support and add my thanks to hers for the thoughtful and painstaking editorial work done at Harbour Publishing by Audrey McLellan, Arlene Prunkl, and Rebecca Pruitt MacKenney.

Notes

1 Which appears here as "Taming Indigenous Sexuality."

2 Mary Louise Pratt, "Arts of the Contact Zone," *Profession* (Newsletter of the Modern Language Association), 1991: 34.

3 Jean Barman, *Maria Mahoi of the Islands* (Vancouver: New Star Books, 2004), 9.

4 "Beyond Chinatown," pp. 250, 254 in this volume.

5 "Sophie Morigeau," p. 182 in this volume.

6 "Race, Greed, and Something More," pp. 15–19 in this volume.

7 Jean Barman, "British Columbia and Me" (speech given on receiving the Woodcock Lifetime Achievement Award, Vancouver Public Library, June 19, 2014).

8 See Patricia A. Shaw, "Language and Identity, Language and the Land," *BC Studies* 131 (2001): 39–55.

9 On women as economic goods, see Gayle Rubin, "The Traffic in Women: Notes on the 'Political Economy' of Sex," in *Toward an Anthropology of Women*, ed. Rayna Reiter (New York: Monthly Review Press, 1975), 157–210; on elite mixed marriages, see Sylvia Van Kirk, "Tracing the Fortunes of Five Founding Families of Victoria," *BC Studies* 115/116 (1997): 148-80, and also her *Many Tender Ties: Women in Fur-Trade Society, 1670–1870* (Norman: University of Oklahoma Press, 1996).

10 The Hudson's Bay Company (HBC—sometimes jokingly rendered as "Here before Christ") was founded in 1670 and given control over the watershed of Hudson Bay, named Rupert's Land, a vast territory, most of which no British person had ever seen. As time passed, the company expanded into the Pacific Northwest, establishing Fort Vancouver in 1824 on the Columbia River in the region then jointly held by Britain and the United States. Fort Victoria was built as it became clear that the border might be drawn north of the Columbia. The Hudson's Bay Company territory was sold to Canada in 1870. See Richard Somerset Mackie, *Trading beyond the Mountains: The British Fur Trade on the Pacific 1793–1843* (Vancouver: UBC Press, 1997).

11 See chapter 12, "The Population Explosion, 1886–1914," in Jean Barman, *The West beyond the West: A History of British Columbia*, 3rd ed. (Toronto: University of Toronto Press, 2007).

12 See George Lang, *Making Wawa: The Genesis of Chinook Jargon* (Vancouver: UBC Press, 2008).

13 See Robert Boyd, "Smallpox in the Pacific Northwest: The Early Epidemics," *BC Studies* 101 (1994): 5–40.

14 "Separate and Unequal: Indigenous and White Girls at All Hallows School, 1884–1920," p. 390 in this volume.

15 John Sutton Lutz, *Makúk: A New History of Aboriginal White Relations* (Vancouver: UBC Press, 2008), 257–73.

16 Jean Barman, Yvonne Hébert, and Don McCaskill, "The Legacy of the Past: An Overview," in *Indian Education in Canada*: vol. 1, *The Legacy* (Vancouver: UBC Press, 1986), 2.

17 Marie Battiste and Jean Barman, eds., *First Nations Education in Canada: The Circle Unfolds* (Vancouver: UBC Press, 1995).

18 For example, John Jessop's personal travel diaries for the years 1872–1878 and his extensive correspondence offer an immediacy of reaction likely reflecting his views much more honestly than did the carefully crafted public reports that followed at the end of each year. See "Families vs. Schools" in this volume.

19 "Race, Greed, and Something More," p. 4 in this volume.

20 "Taming Indigenous Sexuality," p. 121 in this volume.

21 "Beyond Chinatown," p. 234 in this volume.

22 "Separate and Unequal," p. 365 in this volume.

23 See *Reclaiming Power and Place: The Final Report of the National Inquiry into Missing and Murdered Indigenous Women and Girls* (June 2019), https://www.mmiwg-ffada.ca/final-report/, accessed June 9, 2019.

24 That Hawaiian men were granted the vote and all the other rights of citizenship, such as the right to pre-empt land, makes this group an interesting test case, since they were legally equal but racialized as non-white. See "New Land, New Lives" in this volume.

25 By 1918 all women had the right to vote in federal elections in Canada except for those of Asian and Indigenous ancestry; provincially, Manitoba was the first to allow women to vote (1916) and Quebec the last (1940). Voting restrictions against Asians were lifted by 1949. The Inuit gained the federal right to vote in 1951; status Indians were only granted the federal vote in 1960. Two pacifist groups were also denied the provincial vote for a period, Mennonites (1931–1948) and Doukhobors (1931–1952).

26 "Families vs. Schools," p. 355 in this volume.

27 Gayatri Chakravorty Spivak, *A Critique of Postcolonial Reason: Toward a History of the Vanishing Present* (Cambridge: Harvard University Press, 1999), x.

28 "Island Sanctuaries," p. 292 in this volume.

29 "Lost Okanagan," p. 264 in this volume.

30 Note 7, "Invisible Women," p. 175 in this volume. See E. Pauline Johnson, "A Red Girl's Reasoning," (1893; rpt. in *Tekahionwake: E. Pauline Johnson's Writings on Native North America*, ed. Margery Fee and Dory Nason [Peterborough, ON: Broadview, 2016], 163–78.) This is a short story about Christy, whose father is a white trader and mother a Plains Indian, who marries Charlie, a white man. Johnson, the daughter of a Mohawk hereditary chief and a cultivated Englishwoman, conveys the dilemmas imposed by "mixed" ancestry, marriage conventions in both cultures, racism, and the Indian Act.

31 See Barman's *Constance Lindsay Skinner: Writing on the Frontier* (Toronto: University of Toronto Press, 2002); Jan Hare and Jean Barman, *Good Intentions Gone Awry: Emma Crosby and the Methodist Mission on the Northwest Coast* (Vancouver: UBC Press, 2006); and Barman's *Sojourning Sisters: The Lives and Letters of Jessie and Annie McQueen* (Toronto: University of Toronto Press, 2003).

32 See Lori Chambers, *Married Women and Property Law in Victorian Canada* (Toronto: University of Toronto Press for Osgoode Society for Canadian Legal History, 1997).

33 "Intimacy's Limits," in Barman's *French Canadians, Furs, and Indigenous Women: The Pacific Northwest Reconsidered* (Vancouver: UBC Press, 2014), 135–42.

34 Jean Barman, "Remarks" (on receiving the Basil Stuart-Stubbs Prize for Outstanding Scholarly Book on British Columbia, at the Irving K. Barber Learning Centre, University of British Columbia, June 9, 2015).

35 Jean Barman, *Stanley Park's Secret: The Forgotten Families of Whoi Whoi, Kanaka Ranch, and Brockton Point* (Madeira Park, BC: Harbour, 2005).

36 Barman, *Mahoi*, 6.

37 Barman, *French Canadians, Furs, and Indigenous Women*, 3.

38 Barman, *French Canadians, Furs, and Indigenous Women*, 6.

39 Dartmouth's founder, Eleazer Wheelock, used funds raised to educate Indigenous students to support white students, to the disappointment of the Reverend Samson Occom, a Mohegan who had studied with Wheelock and who had raised a considerable sum of money preaching in Britain for Indigenous education. Jean Barman, *Abenaki Daring: The Life and Writings of Noel Annance, 1792–1869* (Montreal/Kingston: McGill-Queen's University Press, 2016), 77–78.

40 See Donald B. Smith, *Mississauga Portraits: Ojibwe Voices from Nineteenth Century Canada* (Toronto: University of Toronto Press, 2013), and *Sacred Feathers: The Reverend Peter Jones (Kahkewquonaby) and the Mississauga Indians*, 2nd ed. (Toronto: University of Toronto Press, 2013) for more examples of educated Indigenous men.

41 Jean Barman, *Abenaki Daring*, 234–35.

42 See Peggy Brizinski, *Knots in a String: An Introduction to Native Studies in Canada*, 2nd ed. (Saskatoon: University of Saskatchewan Extension Press, 1993), 184–85.

43 Jean Barman, *Iroquois in the West* (Montreal/Kingston: McGill-Queen's University Press, 2019).

44 "Indigenous Women on the Streets of Victoria," in this volume.

45 Some of the many articles have images, while others have none; their uneven distribution results from the differing policies of the original journals of publication. Secondary sources in the notes have not been updated with publications appearing subsequent to the date of the original essay.

46 Barman supervised or co-supervised twenty-one doctoral students to completion, of whom ten (eight of whom were Indigenous, including Jan Hare, co-author of *Good Intentions Gone Awry*) wrote on Indigenous subjects. She also served as supervisor for many master's thesis projects, and on many graduate committees of students who were conducting such research.

47 See "Sophie Morigeau," p. 178 in this volume.

Making White Space

1

Race, Greed, and Something More

The Erasure of Urban Indigenous Space in Early Twentieth-Century British Columbia

This essay focuses on how Indigenous peoples living in what became Victoria and Vancouver were displaced from land seen as ripe for modern development by the city fathers. The Songhees (now known as the Lekwungen) occupied land across from what is now the British Columbia Legislature: their ability to not only exact financial compensation but also acquire nearby reserve land is attributed to the skills of their well-educated chief, Michael Cooper, whose father was a British lieutenant and mother a Songhees woman. His mother and other women like her had chosen to set up families with newcomer men who sometimes joined them on the reserve. The Indigenous families who lived on what is now Kits Point near Vancouver did not do so well, being forced to accept payment to leave their reserve under threat of eviction and to move onto already occupied reserve lands across Burrard Inlet. Some of the story told here is repeated in the next essay, which discusses the outcome of the Kits Point land dispute and the dispossession of those living in what became Stanley Park.

By Jean Barman. Reprinted with permission from *Making Space: Settler-Colonial Perspectives on Land, Place, and Identity*, edited by Tracey Banivauna-Mar and Penelope Edwards (London: Palgrave Macmillan, 2010), 155–73.

British Columbia was one of the last areas of North America to be caught up in the land grab we know as settler colonialism. The Canadian province's location on the northwest edge of the continent kept it isolated until the late 1700s. Another two-thirds of a century passed before newcomers began marking out land as their own.[1] Although the practice in other parts of North America had been to draw up treaties with Indigenous people to legitimize the land grab, few treaties were created in what is now British Columbia. Despite this, from the 1860s Indigenous peoples began to be shunted onto reserves, which might include the core of their traditional territory, but in no way encompassed all of it. The process was messy, often following rather than preceding newcomers' claiming of the most desirable stretches as their own. On British Columbia's shift in 1871 from a British colony to a Canadian province, the federal government assumed authority over "Indians," defined in the Indian Act as deriving legal status through an "Indian" father. As historical geographer Cole Harris details in *Making Native Space*, they received a tiny fraction of the huge province.[2]

The extent to which Indigenous peoples got a breathing space had to do with the physical character of British Columbia. The province is one of the largest political units in North America, but also one of the most difficult for outsiders to negotiate spatially. Unlike Indigenous peoples, who made use of the entire province, settlers preferred the southwestern corner, distinguished by a mild climate and ready access to the outside world. As a consequence, reserve making was less devastating than it might have been, but, at the same time,

Indigenous peoples who happened to live in the southwestern corner were increasingly targeted.

Most newcomers resided either on southern Vancouver Island in the colonial and provincial capital of Victoria, whose origins harked back to the 1840s, or in the mainland city of Vancouver, brought into being on the south shore of Burrard Inlet in the mid-1880s as the western terminus of a transcontinental rail line. While the more sedate Victoria grew modestly from 21,000 to 32,000 people between 1901 and 1911, bustling Vancouver skyrocketed from 27,000 to 100,000. No other urban centre approached their numbers.

Not just British Columbia, but the world was becoming more urban during these years. With it came, as David Sibley among others has elaborated, a strong sense of entitlement by those identifying with this major shift.[3] In Canada as elsewhere, many of the arrivals were entrepreneurs whose real or potential fortunes they linked to their city being formed in the image most profitable to themselves. As the urban historian Robert A.J. McDonald has explained, the men in charge thought they were "the boss of everything."[4] Their ambition frequently verged on greed—for profit and for the formation of urban space in their own image. In both Victoria and Vancouver it became unacceptable that Indigenous peoples should live among newcomers, even on the modest reserves to which they were confined. The spaces they occupied had to be erased.

The erasure of urban Indigenous space speaks to colonial perspectives on race, a concept that at the time was firmly anchored in human biology, most often skin tones. Australian scholar Nicholas Thomas perceptively observes that, "in retrospect, the most striking feature of colonialism in the nineteenth century seems to be its overt, pervasive, and extraordinarily confident racism."[5] The perception grew, in the words of anthropologist George Stocking, that "savages were not simply morally delinquent or spiritually deluded, but racially incapable."[6] Such thinking had profound implications for the spatial entitlements of Indigenous peoples in and around British Columbia's urbanizing spaces.

While race-based reasoning was repeatedly evoked in the two erasures, it was greed that drove them. The first half of this essay traces the ways in which race and greed interacted, and reinforced each other, in the removal of the Songhees people from their Victoria reserve in 1911 and of the Squamish from their Vancouver reserve in 1913. However powerful these two motives were, when we parse all the factors, something more emerges in respect to the Songhees erasure in particular than is usually considered in the scholarship. The second half of this essay returns to events in Victoria from the perspective of those being acted upon. While some of the Songhees were wholly Indigenous, others, including the leadership, occupied a liminal space by virtue of having Songhees mothers but newcomer fathers. Their mixed descent gave them tools to mimic the dominant society to their material advantage.[7]

While the sources on which this essay is based all originate within the dominant society and reflect a colonial perspective, they are so unselfconsciously self-confident as to make it possible to intuit, at least in part, the perspectives of those being acted upon as well as those who considered themselves the actors. The pride taken in outmanoeuvring Indigenous people caused the two principal and interdependent accounts of events—newspaper stories and the inward and outward correspondence of the federal Department of Indian Affairs—to be remarkably coherent and consistent. The story they tell is persuasive.

The erasure of Indigenous space occurred in several stages. While Victoria's origins preceded those of Vancouver in time, the interdependence that initially linked Indigenous peoples with newcomers was similar. The Songhees, also known as the Lekwungen, welcomed the first outsiders to their territory in 1843 by, according to one account, offering them a site for their proposed fur trade post in exchange for three blankets.[8] Its location encouraged the 700 or so Songhees who lived in the general area to congregate just across the harbour from Fort Victoria, creating what a fur trader's son arriving in 1850 termed an "Indian village, consisting of a double row of large houses, the shores being lined with innumerable canoes."[9] In the same year the Songhees signed a treaty with the governor of the newly established British colony of Vancouver Island, which became one of only a handful of treaties to be negotiated in British Columbia. The Songhees agreed to give up areas of land wanted by the newcomers, in exchange for which "our village sites and enclosed fields are to be kept for our own use, for the use of our children, and for those who may follow after us."[10] The Songhees reserve, 119 acres in size, came into being.

Although the city of Vancouver originated only with the completion of a rail line in the mid-1880s, the first newcomers arrived in the area two decades earlier. Just as the Songhees realized the benefits to be had from the fur trade, employment opportunities in Burrard Inlet sawmills caused some nearby seasonal sites to become permanent villages. Alongside several on the north shore of Burrard Inlet was Snauq, located south of the inlet on a parallel body of water known as False Creek. While no treaties were negotiated, Snauq was the basis for a reserve of thirty-seven acres requested in February 1868 by the forty-two persons living there under the leadership of Chief Chip-kay-um and established the next year.[11] As with the other reserves, residents did not hold land in fee simple but rather had the use of it. Half a dozen years later a reserve commission expanded what became known as the False Creek or Kitsilano reserve to eighty acres.[12]

The mutual advantage that structured relations between Indigenous peoples and newcomers disappeared in Victoria when a gold rush broke out on the adjacent mainland in 1858. Upward of 25,000 miners arrived that year, mostly through Victoria, and many thousands more over the next half-dozen years. With them came hardening attitudes toward the Indigenous population. While the Squamish were relatively unaffected, their territory lying off the routes to the gold fields, Victoria went virtually overnight from a sleepy village to a bustling emporium seeking to emulate its counterparts elsewhere in the British colonial world in its standards of propriety.

This first stage on the pathway to erasure of urban Indigenous space reflected sentiments across the colonizing world toward Indigenous peoples. A Royal Navy officer stationed in Victoria reported in 1862 how "the close contiguity of these Indians to Victoria is seriously inconvenient." In line with the supposed benevolence so much a part of racist rhetoric, removal was construed as being for the Songhees' own good: "In consequence of their intercourse with the whites—chiefly, of course, for evil—this tribe has become the most degraded in the whole island, having lost what few virtues the savage in his natural state possesses, and contracted the worse vices of the settlers."[13] As Renisa Mawani and Penelope Edmonds elaborate in their studies of the Songhees, this argument became a favourite rationale.[14] Newcomers repeatedly asserted with a straight face that Indigenous peoples should not live in proximity to themselves because some of their fellow colonials, never themselves, were bad influences.

A second justification for erasing Indigenous space also came into play. The fears of sexuality so central to colonialism were repeatedly used to justify racist perspectives.[15] Songhees women were almost inherently suspect by virtue of not accommodating to newcomers' expectations for them. Women in the public domain, considered the purview of men, must be engaged in illicit behaviour that was, by definition, sexual in nature. "The majority of the Indian women who, in consequence of the vicinity of the Reserve, are daily seen in our streets" were perforce possessed of "vicious customs."[16] In line with such thinking, "this tribe should therefore be removed."[17] The sharp sexual imbalance among newcomers due to the gold rush, and earlier the fur trade, meant that many Songhees and other Indigenous women did indeed partner with newcomer men, in some cases for the moment, in others for a lifetime.

Despite the decline of the gold rush by the mid-1860s, and with it reduction of Victoria's ambitions for urban grandeur, the Songhees reserve was never out of sight, either literally or in the pages of the local press, which found fodder in any event there for a deprecating story.[18] The consequence was several more efforts at erasure, all of which stalled. As Jeannie Kanakos has described, although both the federal and provincial governments favoured erasure, they disagreed on who had rights of ownership and thereby responsibility to negotiate.[19] One of the most determined initiatives saw local entrepreneurs seeking to acquire the reserve for a rail terminus. The economic benefit that would ensue persuaded federal authorities to authorize erasure so long as the 130 Songhees living there agreed to their proposed relocation. This they did not do.

The unwillingness of the Songhees to be erased was paralleled in Vancouver. As was the case with the gold rush in Victoria in 1858, the arrival of the transcontinental railway in Vancouver in 1886 transformed a village into a city. Since almost everyone came from somewhere else, they brought with them strong preconceptions of what a proper city should be like. Much of the enthusiasm had a "boosterish" or self-promotional quality. Residents recognized that their own well-being was directly linked to Vancouver's appeal to prospective settlers. Increasingly, Robert A.J. McDonald explains, the "people of Vancouver came to view the False Creek reserve as critical to the city's continued growth."[20] The reserve was eagerly sought by railway developers, and part of it was alienated despite the opposition of residents. These actions paled before the growing determination to snatch the reserve itself, an action the Squamish living there resisted as strongly as did the Songhees in Victoria.

As the nineteenth century became the twentieth, two critical factors tipped the balance toward erasure. The first was changing leadership on the two reserves. Chief Chip-kay-um, who had headed the False Creek reserve since at least 1868, and his counterpart Chief Sqwameyuqs, in charge of the Songhees reserve since 1864, each viewed the land in more than economic terms. On Sqwameyuqs's death in 1892, Victoria's *Colonist* newspaper described him as overseeing a "little kingdom ... from which he declared, less than a year ago, he would never be carried alive." The article related how "the old chief refused to see the question in the light the city people wanted him to, and the tribesmen stood by their ruler."[21] An official of the federal Department of Indian Affairs described how the elders were "to a man determined not to vacate the Songhees reserve which was land held and occupied by their forefathers from time immemorial and consequently dearer to them than anything they could possess."[22] Chief Chip-kay-um, who died in 1907, had a similar commitment to place. The local Indian agent reported: "Chief says that he does not want to sell the land because it belonged to his Grandfather ... He didn't want to leave this place where he was born and it is the place where his dead relatives are buried—none of the men on the place want to sell it—the Queen gave him and his people the land."[23] The two chiefs' successors would be younger men of a different generation.

The second critical factor leading to erasure was good economic times encouraging the tendency toward newcomer greed that in any case never lurked far below the surface. Indicative of the general attitude, the Victoria City Council expressed amazement to the federal Minister of the Interior in 1901 that the reserve

> located as it is almost in the centre of the city for many years and within a stones throw of the business section and of some of the best business blocks, presents a contrast so marked and repellent as to excite the wonder of every one that such a relic of barbarism should be allowed to exist in the midst of the civilized conditions of a modern city.[24]

In a debate in the Canadian Senate in 1905, the senator for Vancouver Island described the reserve's residents as "demoralized and degraded."[25]

"Prominent business men" in Vancouver were similarly determined to put the False Creek reserve to "a practical use." Such a goal was consistent with the self-confident boosterism grounded in real estate speculation that marked the rapidly growing city during these buoyant years. The initial goal of using the reserve "for public exhibition and other purposes for the general good of every citizen" became more self-interested the more it was described.[26] The refined plan for "a midsummer fair and carnival" complete with "railway, tram and water facilities" was a mildly disguised economic venture wherein "business men would reap a harvest each year from the throngs that would be visiting."[27]

In the final stage of the pathway to erasure, first in Victoria and then in Vancouver, the province's activist premier Richard McBride played a central role. Convinced that the terms by which British Columbia joined Canada in 1871 gave it reversionary rights to reserve lands no longer being used for that purpose, he pushed for negotiations. In doing so, he reflected larger sets of attitudes across Canada. Prime Minister Wilfrid Laurier pronounced in Parliament in April 1911 that, "where a reserve is in the vicinity of a growing town, as is the case in several places, it becomes a source of nuisance and an impediment to progress."[28] A month later the Indian Act was amended so that the residents of any "Indian reserve which adjoins or is situated wholly or partly within an incorporated town or city having a population of not less than eight thousand" could be legally removed without their consent if it was in "the interest of the public and of the Indians of the band for whose use the reserve is held."[29]

By the time the Indian Act was amended, the push for erasure had come to fruition in Victoria. Protracted negotiations had stalled on the question of a new reserve acceptable to the Songhees, who also held out for each family receiving a cash payment.[30] Considering that the city of Victoria and the federal government were not forceful enough to resolve matters, in the spring of 1910 Premier McBride took the lead, being joined sometime thereafter by the other two levels of government. The resulting agreement included a cash settlement of $10,000 per family. Lest there be any second thoughts, the forty-one family heads were shown the bank books to be handed over once they had physically moved to their new reserve, which they all did by the end of April 1911.[31] The agreement was speedily approved in the federal Parliament.

In the case of Vancouver, the provincial government also took the lead but overshot the mark by acting wholly on its own volition. The impetus lay in an American railway company offering the federal government $1.5 to $2 million for the reserve, which it sought for a terminal and docks. About the same time the federal Harbour Commission was eyeing it for the same purpose. The Department of Indian Affairs put the offers on hold until a Royal Commission on Indian Reserves that was then underway reported, whereupon provincial authorities acted.[32] As William Zaharoff has outlined, due process played no role, nor was federal approval sought.[33] In April 1913 the intermediary acting on behalf of the province organized a closed meeting on the False Creek reserve at which he read over a draft sale agreement that all those present signed, almost all with their mark.[34] The amount, $11,250 in total per family head, was modestly higher than that paid to the Songhees.[35] However, unlike the Songhees, they were not allocated a new reserve, but rather expected to move to one of the other Squamish reserves.

Before the sale could be finalized, news leaked of the much larger offers—about $50,000 per family head—being entertained by federal authorities. Fearful of the Squamish changing their minds, the attorney general, who represented Vancouver in the provincial legislature, took no chances. At a meeting with heads of families, he proffered cheques with the warning, according to one of the Squamish present, to "take it or you'll never get a cent."[36] Another report told of "the Provincial Government" making "threats that they would be driven off by the Police if they did not consent to sell."[37] A week later the Squamish capitulated. The attorney general met the twenty family heads at a downtown bank, where each was shown a bank book with a balance of $11,250 to be his in exchange for putting "his mark to a receipt" relinquishing any interest in the reserve. By "the stroke of 12 o'clock noon," according to a newspaper account, "the last of the band" had "accepted their bank book."[38]

The continuing roles played by race and greed were caught in two events the press reported on that fateful day. The first is captured in the image of "a squaw with a baby in her arms who stood waiting for her husband to come out of the manager's room with his bank account." Despite her looking "longingly at the comfortable seats in the bank for the use of the customers," no one invited her to sit down and "she took her baby and went and crouched for rest on the hard edge of the base of a marble pillar," whereupon "the passing throng looked down on her."[39] About the same time this mother was being relegated to the past, the provincial attorney general held a press conference looking to the future. He proclaimed how this "eyesore to the citizens of Vancouver for many years and hindrance to the development of the city" would now make "as much profit as possible for the entire province."[40] Later in the day he described in virtually the same breath how the Squamish would now be "away from the temptations of the city" and "this very valuable property ... should net us a million dollars profit." The attorney general was gleeful over what he termed "one of the best real estate transactions ever carried out in the province."[41] Greed had become a point of pride even before the Squamish actually departed. Within two days they were moved out, and their houses burned to the ground.

Unlike the Songhees erasure, title over the False Creek reserve long remained in dispute due to the province's precipitous action infringing on federal responsibility for Indigenous peoples.[42] Apart from small parcels being alienated during the 1930s for the Burrard Street Bridge and an armoury, the former reserve remained vacant apart from passing squatters. The Squamish, who amalgamated politically in 1923, argued they all needed to agree to surrender for the transfer to be legitimate, and in 1947 they did so. The province then formally conveyed the land to its federal counterpart, which, much as happened in Victoria, subdivided it into parcels for sale.[43]

The similarities between the erasure of urban Indigenous space in early twentieth-century Victoria and Vancouver, both grounded in a mixture of race and greed, obscure something more. The surrender of the Squamish reserve was based on the Songhees precedent, with the exception that the Squamish did not get a new reserve in addition to a substantial cash payout. Parsing the Victoria case, this something more comes into view. The dominant society's insistence on stereotyping Indigenous people in line with the racism of the day obscured a fundamental shift occurring on the Songhees reserve from the late nineteenth century onward. When we probe beyond the newspaper headlines as to why the Songhees did so well, compared to what might have been the outcome, we discover a counter-narrative with considerable explanatory power.

The outcome rested on two interlinked factors. The first was the identity of the Songhees chief from 1894 onward, the second the larger context out of which he emerged. Michael Cooper's accession to leadership harked back to the independent character of Songhees women that for so long distressed outsiders. Unlike the Squamish, who were bypassed by the fur trade and the gold rush, the Songhees, and in particular Songhees women, had been at the centre of these phenomena. Cooper and a growing proportion of reserve residents were part of a second generation living between two worlds, that of their Songhees mothers and also that, even if only indirectly, of their newcomer fathers.

Michael Cooper had been baptized Catholic in Victoria on April 28, 1866, aged six months, as the son of "Cooper native of England or Scotland [he was not present himself, so it is not possible to be sure of the place of his birth] and of Catherine S-kuvanit-nar, Indian woman of the Songhees tribe."[44] His father was a lieutenant in a British military unit stationed on San Juan Island adjacent to Victoria following a fracas with the Americans in 1859.[45] The arrangements were made, perhaps by his father, for young Michael to attend Catholic St. Louis College in Victoria where he received an education not unlike many of his newcomer counterparts. In 1893 Cooper was elected chief, and that December he solidified his Songhees credentials by marrying

Sara, the niece of the first Songhees chief, Freezy. Like Cooper born to an English father and Songhees mother, Sara was the widow of a Victoria sea captain from Greece named Frank Albany by whom she had five children. She would have two more with her new husband.

Cooper's election corresponded with other interracial families moving onto the Songhees reserve. Almost everyone listed on reserve censuses compiled in 1876 and 1881 had wholly Songhees names, indicating Indigenous paternal origins.[46] The Indian agent commented in 1898 on an increase in "youths and children, who, though having Songhees mothers, had white fathers who had practically deserted them."[47]

This movement likely encouraged the repeated observations as to how well residents were doing. Although concerned "they live so near the temptations of a town," federal authorities considered it would be "difficult to induce them to agree to the sale of this reserve, however good the terms offered may be," for "several have regular employment in the city."[48] The Victoria *Colonist* noted in 1898 that "throughout the Songhees reservation new fences, fresh paint and substantial additions are the order of the day," and the number of gardens was greatly increasing.[49] A year later a newspaper headline stated, "Songhees Indians Better Off in the Way of Homes Than Most People."[50]

At this point in historical time, by the terms of the federal Indian Act, only persons with status were permitted to live on reserves, and the acquisition of status demanded a father who was a status Indian, which none of these mixed-race Songhees possessed.[51] The silence in the next years' annual reports of the Department of Indian Affairs suggests that virtually everyone simply looked the other way. One of the reasons may have been that, as the reports emphasized, reserve residents were prospering, which reflected well on the department.

In the 1901 Canadian census, which required individuals to disclose mixed race, at least half of the thirty-one families enumerated on the reserve contained such persons.[52] Their diversity in backgrounds contrasted sharply with the single inheritance that had energized

Sqwameyuqs and his generation to protect land they considered to be theirs from time immemorial.

The Fridays and Kamais were in the tradition of the first Songhees chief, Freezy, named for the frizzy hair he inherited, it was said, from his Hawaiian father, one of several hundred hired to work in the fur trade.[53] Thus it was not surprising that in 1870 long-time Hawaiian fur trade employees Peter Friday and Kama Kamai wed Songhees women. The Fridays settled down on San Juan Island, the Kamais on Coal Island off southern Vancouver Island. It was likely following her husband's death in 1894 that Mary Friday returned to the Songhees reserve along with their two adult children. By then two Kamai sons were living on the reserve with their wives and children. So were members of the Fallardeau family, who the Fridays knew from San Juan Island. Mary Fallardeau, a Songhees woman there with her two sons, was the widow of a French Canadian employed in the fur trade.[54]

The others—August Gabriel, Johnny Golledge, Charles Gunion, Jimmy St. Louis, and Johnny Silva—had similar inheritances. Golledge was almost certainly the son of an establishment Englishman who was a government official before being dismissed for drunkenness and disorderly conduct, whereupon he lived for many years on the Songhees reserve where he died destitute in 1887.[55] Gabriel's French Canadian father had married Cooper's mother, making the two half-brothers.[56] Gunion's father also came from Quebec, Silva's from the Azores. Gunion and Silva had, like Cooper, been educated at Catholic St. Louis College.[57]

The situation on the Songhees reserve came to public attention when the Deputy Superintendent of Indian Affairs visited in 1906 in the hopes of securing an agreement for residents to give up their reserve. He subsequently asked the local Indian agent for "the status of Indians residing on the Songhees Indian reserve," who responded that of ninety-five persons living there, sixty-three "claim descent through the father, a person of Indian blood belonging to the band," whereas thirty-two "trace their descent through their mother belonging to the band but whose father was or is not of Indian blood or if

Indian blood not a member of the band."[58] In other words, a third of those living there, including the chief and his extended family, should not have been there by a strict interpretation of federal regulations.

By then residents were becoming even more fully integrated into the dominant economy. "Fishing, hunting, stevedore-work, farming and working in saw-mills and factories are the chief occupations," the Indian agent noted in 1906, adding that "these Indians are industrious and many of them well-off."[59] Chief Cooper exemplified the changing times, occupying a managerial position in a large Victoria company.[60] With his neatly trimmed moustache, customary dress of suit, tie, and overcoat, and educated signature, he personified a new generation of leadership consciously replicating the dominant society, by so doing gazing back at it almost as if through a mirror.[61]

Due in part certainly to his appearance, Cooper gained the trust of those seeking to acquire the reserve, which gave him a much stronger negotiating position than he would otherwise have had. He and thereby the Songhees were treated with more respect than ever were the Squamish on the False Creek reserve, who were almost all solely Indigenous by descent.[62] At the various meetings Cooper was front and centre, sometimes "speaking in his own language" to assert his Indigenous credentials. Residents' blunt refusals in 1906 of an initial offer of $1,000 and in 1908 of an upgraded $2,000 per family by a unanimous vote attest to their understanding of the dominant society and its workings.[63]

For some contemporaries, including the Deputy Superintendent of Indian Affairs who had visited Victoria in 1906, another solution came into view. The Songhees were just as rational as, or more so than, those negotiating on the other side. "They were independent of and were receiving very little assistance, if any, from the government" and so considered quite logically that "the Reserve was their own and they should be allowed to do as they pleased with it."[64] An enfranchisement act was drafted, whereby the Songhees themselves, rather than their reserve, would be erased: "Owing to their long proximity to civilization and the adoption by them of the manners, customs and means of obtaining a livelihood generally prevalent amongst persons other than Indians, the members of said band are well qualified to assume the status of white men." The reserve would be "subdivided by survey into lots and allotted to the individual members of the band" in fee simple with suitable allowance being "made for necessary streets and public places." In return the Songhees and their unmarried minor children "shall cease in every respect to be Indians" within the meaning of the Indian Act.[65]

As to the reasoning, the Deputy Superintendent pointed out to his superior how "most of the members of the band, as far as I was able to discover from personal observations and also from the records, are not by any means of full blood, but in a great many cases are scarcely distinguishable from the white population." Reserve residents were "for all practical purposes evidently capable of performing the duties of ordinary citizenship." There was in his view "no good and valid reason why they should not be placed in practically the same position in the state as white people are." Provided with the franchise and home ownership, they would become even "more self-reliant, energetic and independent."[66]

Needless to say, the Songhees did not become white. The proposal ran absolutely counter to the sentiments of the Victoria City Council, which a month later exploded in outrage. Just across the harbour from "millions of dollars worth of buildings and stocks, paved streets, electric cars, and all the appurtenances of modern city lives" stood "a row of unsightly, tumble-down, smoke-covered wood shacks ... hardly removed from its primitive condition of a hundred years ago." So far as the city fathers were concerned, "this incongruity, deformity, and impediment to the growth and commercial progress and prosperity of the City should be removed once and forever."[67] The city of its imagination came first, last, and always.

Cooper oversaw the agreement negotiated later in 1910, which swapped the reserve for another of virtually the same size, at just over 160 acres, fronting on the harbour in nearby Esquimalt and also gave a much higher payment per family—$10,000—than had been offered previously. The Songhees essentially exchanged urban space for suburban space and, by so doing, received a windfall of investment capital equivalent to $265,000 per family in today's dollars.[68] Cooper observed sometime later that the erasure succeeded whereas its predecessors had failed precisely because the government "snowed that amount of money."[69]

It was Cooper who determined eligibility for the monetary payout and relocation. Among the forty-one family heads on a list finalized with his approval, seventeen were mixed ancestry, being Cooper himself, three Fallardeaus, three Kamais, two Albanys, two Jacksons, and Friday, Gabriel, Golledge, Gunion, St. Louis, and Silva.[70] They received what many of them, particularly those who walked in two worlds, must have viewed primarily in economic terms.

Events were not lost on contemporaries. Among those querying them was the mixed-ancestry daughter of the colonial governor who in 1850 had arranged the treaty creating the Songhees reserve:

> How is it that Chief Cooper, who was born on San Juan Island, and whose father was a soldier, does not become a white man? ... How do the Albany boys, whose father was a Greek fisherman, after whose death the boys' mother married Cooper and the boys were taken to the reserve and each receive $10,000? Are they Greeks or Songhees?[71]

In an attempt to get payouts, ten self-described "fullblooded Songhees Indians" hired a lawyer, who detailed the non-Songhees inheritance of those receiving money, including the Cooper-Albany clan and the Fallardeaus, Golledges, Silvas, Gabriels, Gunions, and Kamais.[72] Yet another group who lost out claimed quite accurately that the Albany sons were "quarter breeds only, yet they are reported to have received the $10,000 payment and a portion of the new reserve," and that Chief Cooper "appears not to be an Indian at all," but was nonetheless permitted "to act as the arbiter of the rights of the individual Indians."[73] Needless to say, Cooper's will prevailed.

From the perspective of most outsiders, the Songhees continued to be Indians. Even as the payments were being distributed, federal officials waxed stereotypically that, "no matter to what use some of them may ultimately put their money or how they may let it dwindle away, their families will always have a good home."[74] A similar account of a few years later ran: "The Siwashes ["Indians" in the Chinook trading jargon] had never seen so much money before, and didn't know what to do with it. Shortly afterwards some of them were seen driving about the city in their own autos!"[75]

In reality the money was put to good use. Two years later, the Department of Indian Affairs collected receipts and examined bank accounts in order to determine just what had happened to its largesse. About 40 per cent had gone into material assets and 20 per cent each into interest-bearing deposits or loans, was cash on hand, or had been used for expenses or given to relatives. The audit concluded that, although a few had "squandered their money," overall the Songhees "have done as well, if not better, with their money than the same number of white people, at a much higher stage of civilization, would have done."[76]

Our perspectives on the past depend in good part on the approach we take. Our gaze determines what we see. With the erasures of urban Indigenous space in early twentieth-century British Columbia, the advantages to be had from a comparative perspective are balanced by parsing events. These two approaches give us complementary ways of seeing. Each has its merits. The comparative approach causes us to realize just how broadly pervasive were race and greed in erasing Indigenous space in British Columbia's two major cities. Looking more closely, we glimpse the important role played by Indigenous women in the larger course of events. Their mixed-race offspring facilitated the good deal made in Victoria that was then echoed in Vancouver.

They understood how to mimic the dominant society in dress and actions, and did so. As literary critic Homi Bhabha explains, "the *menace* of mimicry is its *double* vision which in disclosing the ambivalence of colonial discourse also disrupts its authority."[77] Granted, urban Indigenous space was erased, but not as a wholly one-sided event.

This achievement did not equate with acceptance within the dominant society. Bhabha reminds us that "the object of colonial discourse is to construe the colonized as a population of degenerate types on the basis of racial origin, in order to justify conquest and to establish systems of administration and instruction."[78] When the possibility arose that the Songhees might become legally white, it was quickly rejected at the local level. Theirs was perforce a liminal location characterized by ambivalence and ambiguity. "The ambivalence of mimicry" meant that over time they might become "almost the same but not quite."[79]

Mixed-race British Columbians living on the Songhees reserve acted nonetheless. They used their education, understandings of the ways of the dominant society, and realization of just how much their land was coveted to make the best possible deal they could for their families and for themselves. In doing so, they were not necessarily any less driven by self-interest, perhaps even by greed, than were their counterparts in the dominant society, nor should they have been. By acting, they accomplished something not easy to do within the racial confines in which they found themselves. They gazed back at the dominant society in a fashion beneficial to themselves and others on the Songhees reserve and also, a couple of years later, to their Squamish cousins.

Notes

1 It became possible to acquire land from 1859 onward on Vancouver Island and from 1860 on the British Columbian mainland by marking out up to 160 acres not being used by Indigenous peoples or otherwise designated by the colonial government, registering the claim, making certain improvements, and then paying a smallish amount per acre once it had been surveyed. See Robert E. Cail, *Land, Man, and the Law: The Disposal of Crown Lands in British Columbia, 1871–1913* (Vancouver: UBC Press, 1974), 1–18.

2 Cole Harris, *Making Native Space: Colonialism, Resistance, and Reserves in British Columbia* (Vancouver: UBC Press, 2002).

3 David Sibley, *Geographies of Exclusion: Societies and Difference in the West* (London: Routledge, 1995).

4 Robert A.J. McDonald, "'He Thought He Was the Boss of Everything': Masculinity and Power in a Vancouver Family," *BC Studies* 132 (Winter 2001–2002): 6–30.

5 Nicholas Thomas, *Colonialism's Culture: Anthropology, Travel and Government* (Cambridge, UK: Polity Press, 1994), 77.

6 George W. Stocking, Jr., *Victorian Anthropology* (New York: Free Press, 1987), 237.

7 There is no single most appropriate terminology for persons combining Indigenous and non-Indigenous descent. The terms "half-breed," "miscegenation," "mixed race," "interracial," and "hybrid" can have both biological and socially negative connotations. The broader term "mixed descent" is used by some Canadian scholars. The Canadian term "Métis," originating in the fur trade, is relevant for British Columbia only where descent originated east of the Rockies. It has acquired an ethnogenesis flavour, limiting its relevance to particular historical, geographical, and cultural settings. See Mike Evans, Jean Barman, Gabrielle Legault, and Erin Dolmage, "Métis Networks in British Columbia: Examples from the Central Interior," in *Contours of a People: Metis Family, Mobility, and History*, ed. Nicole St-Onge, Carolyn Podruchny, and Brenda Macdougall (Norman: University of Oklahoma Press, 2012), 331–67; Jean Barman and Mike Evans, "Reflections on Being, and Becoming, Métis in British Columbia," *BC Studies* 161 (Spring 2009): 59–91; and Jean Barman, "At the Edge of Law's Empire: Aboriginal Interraciality, Citizenship, and the Law in British Columbia," *Windsor Yearbook of Access to Justice* 26, no. 1 (2006), 3–22.

8 See *Colonist* (Victoria), August 22 1901.

9 J.R. Anderson, "Vancouver in 1850," typescript in BC Archives, Add. Ms. 1912, box 15/18, file 4.

10 See Dennis Madill, *British Columbia Indian Treaties in Historical Perspective* (Ottawa: Indian and Northern Affairs, 1981), 67–73; also ongoing correspondence in Department of Indian Affairs (DIA), Black series, RG 10, vol. 3689, file 13,886, microfilm reel C-10121, Library and Archives Canada (LAC), especially Alex C. Anderson, Archibald McKinlay, and G.M. Sproat to Victoria Superintendent of Songish Indians, Decision of May 4, 1878, and memo entitled Songhees Indian Reserve Question, Ottawa, December 2, 1906, which recounts the history of events from 1843 onward from a government perspective in considerable detail.

11 For a summary, see "Reasons for Judgment from the First Phase of the Trial" in *Squamish Indian Band vs. Canada*, court file T-1636-41, October 5, 2000: 20–22, 46.

12 Another reserve, occupied by the Musqueam people, was created along the Fraser River at a location that became part of Vancouver on the city's expansion in 1929 to encompass the municipalities of South Vancouver and Point Grey. Thus, while the Musqueam reserve is now within the boundaries of the city of Vancouver, it was not a consideration during the time period examined in this essay.

13 R.C. Mayne, *Four Years in British Columbia and Vancouver Island* (London: John Murray, 1862, repr. 1969), 30.

14 Renisa Mawani, "Legal Geographies of Aboriginal Segregation in British Columbia: The Making and Unmaking of the Songhees Reserve, 1850–1911," in *Isolation: Places and Practices of Exclusion*, ed. Carolyn Strange and Alison Bashford (London: Routledge, 2003), 173–190; and Penelope Edmonds, "From Bedlam to Incorporation: Whiteness and the Racialisation of Settler-Colonial Urban Space in Victoria, British Columbia, 1840s–1880s," in *Exploring the British World: Identity–Cultural Production–Institutions* (Melbourne: RMIT Publishing, 2004), online.

15 The classic study is Anne McClintock, *Imperial Leather: Race, Gender and Sexuality in the Colonial Contest* (New York: Routledge, 1995).

16 "The Removal of the Indians," *Victoria Gazette*, February 24, 1859.

17 Editorial, *Victoria Gazette*, February 24, 1859.

18 See, for instance, the small item on page 3 of the *Colonist*, September 17, 1880, describing "a dissolute woman in an utter state of nudity" making her way on foot from the Songhees reserve to "the police barracks requesting that she might be taken into custody."

19 Jeannie L. Kanakos, "The Negotiations to Relocate the Songhees Indians, 1843–1911" (master's thesis, Simon Fraser University, 1982), 51–52.

20 Robert A.J. McDonald, *Making Vancouver 1863–1913* (Vancouver: UBC Press, 1996), 217.

21 "Scomiak Is No More," *Colonist*, September 13, 1892.

22 A.W. Vowell to L. Van Koughnet, Deputy Superintendent of Indian Affairs, May 3, 1890, DIA, RG 10, vol. 3688, file 13,886, microfilm reel C-10120, LAC.

23 R.C. McDonald, Indian agent, quoted in "Reasons for Judgment," 42.

24 City Clerk, City of Victoria, to Clifford Sifton, Minister of the Interior, April 23, 1901, in DIA, RG 10, vol. 3689, file 13,886, microfilm reel C-10121, LAC.

25 William John Macdonald in Senate debate, February 23, 1905, in *Senate Debates*, 1st session, 10th Parliament, 59.

26 "Want a Grant of the Reserve," *Province* (Vancouver), May 28, 1902.

27 "Indian Reservation May Be Lost to Vancouver," *Province*, June 7, 1903.

28 Wilfrid Laurier in House of Commons debate, April 19, 1911, in *House of Commons Debates*, 3rd session, 11th Parliament (vol. 4), 7249.

29 "An Act to Amend the Indian Act," assented to May 19, 1911, online at http://epe.lac-bac.gc.ca/100/205/301/ic/cdc/aboriginaldocs/m-stat.htm.

30 See the detailed correspondence in DIA, RG 10, vol. 3688–3690, file 13,886, microfilm reels C-10120 and C-10121, LAC. The sequence of events is summarized in Kanakos, "Negotiations," 66–75.

31 "Songhees Shown Money Is in Bank," *Victoria Daily Times*, April 4, 1911; "Passing of the Songhees Reserve," *Victoria Daily Times*, April 5, 1911; and W.E. Ditchburn, Indian Inspector, to Inspector of Indian Agencies, Southwestern Inspectorate, Victoria, April 26, 1911, in DIA, RG 10, vol. 3690, file 13,886, microfilm reel C-10121, LAC.

32 "Offered Indians One and a Half Million Dollars," *Vancouver World*, April 4, 1913; telegram from the Vancouver law firm Deacon, Deacon and Wilson to Superintendent of Indian Affairs, Vancouver, April 30, 1913, and memo from W.R. White to the Deputy Minister of Indian Affairs, Ottawa, March 25, 1913, in DIA, RG 10, vol. 3741, file 28835, microfilm reel C-10121, LAC; also "Militia Want Indian Lands at Kitsilano," *Vancouver World*, April 9, 1913; "Kitsilano Indian Reserve Bargain," *Vancouver World*, April 11, 1913.

33 William Zaharoff, "Success in Struggle: The Squamish People and Kitsilano Reserve No. 6" (master's thesis, Carleton University, 1978).

34 "Red Men Took Cash from Mr. Bowser This Morning," *Province*, April 9, 1913; "Offered Indians One and a Half Million Dollars," *Vancouver World*, April 4, 1913.

35 W.E. Ditchburn, Inspector of Indian Agencies, to secretary of Department of Indian Affairs, Victoria, April 26, 1913, in DIA, RG 10, vol. 3741, file 28835, microfilm reel C-10121, LAC.

36 W.J. Bowser, quoted in "Indians Decline Bowser's Cheques," *Victoria Daily Times*, April 3, 1913.

37 Joseph Cole to W.E. Ditchburn, Indian Inspector, Vancouver, May 18, 1913, in DIA, RG 10, vol. 3741, file 28835, microfilm reel C-10121. LAC.

38 "Red Men Took Cash." One individual received $5,000 only.

39 "Red Men Took Cash."

40 Attorney General W.J. Bowser, quoted in "Red Men Took Cash."

41 "An Act of Greatest Benefit to Vancouver," *Province*, April 9, 1913.

42 House of Commons debate on the Kitsilano reserve, April 24, 1913, in *House of Commons Debates*, 2nd session, 12th Parliament (vol. 5), 8465–8500. In 1916 the Harbour Commission expropriated the property for development, which it legally had authority to do, and held it for a decade before abandoning its interest in it.

43 "Reasons for Judgment," 76. Half of the land became the present Vanier Park containing the Vancouver Museum, Planetarium, and Maritime Museum; the other five parcels became private commercial and housing developments. On this later time period see Jordan Stanger-Ross, "Municipal Colonialism in Vancouver: City Planning and the Conflict over Indian Reserves, 1928–1950s," *Canadian Historical Review* 89, no. 4 (December 2008): 541–80.

44 Church records, St. Andrew's Catholic Church, Victoria, 1849–1934, in BC Archives, Add. Ms. 1.

45 "Obsequies to Be Held," *Colonist*, January 12, 1936.

46 See Grant Keddie, *Songhees Pictorial: A History of the Songhees People as Seen by Outsiders, 1790–1912* (Victoria: Royal BC Museum, 2003), 103, and *Supplement to Songhees Pictorial* (online on the Royal BC Museum website at http://staff.royalbcmuseum.bc.ca/2013/08/29/songhees-supplement/), n.p. The census was enclosed with reports of the British Columbia Reserve Commission in DIA, RG 10, v. 3645, file 7936, microfilm reel C-10113, LAC.

47 DIA, Annual Report (1898), 215.

48 DIA, Annual Report (1887), 107.

49 *Colonist*, May 13, 1897.

50 Editorial, *Colonist*, December 20, 1898.

51 See Barman, "At the Edge of Law's Empire."

52 Songhees Band, Cowichan Agency, in 1901 manuscript census, available online through Library and Archives Canada. The exact number is impossible to determine, given that some individuals who other information indicates were wholly Songhees were enumerated as of mixed race and vice versa, due likely to the enumerator.

53 This topic is explored in Jean Barman and Bruce Watson, *Leaving Paradise: Indigenous Hawaiians in the Pacific Northwest, 1787–1898* (Honolulu: University of Hawai'i Press, 2006).

54 Church records, St. Andrew's Catholic Church, Victoria, 1849–1934, BC Archives.

55 *Colonist*, September 7, 1887.

56 Schedule B enclosed in Smith and Johnston, barristers and solicitors, to J.D. McLean, Secretary, Department of Indian Affairs, Ottawa, January 18, 1911, in DIA, RG 10, vol. 3690, file 13,886, microfilm reel C-10121, LAC.

57 See the information in Census of the Songhees Band on Songhees Reserve Made November 21–25, 1910, and Schedule B attached to Smith and Johnston to Frank Oliver, Superintendent General of Indian Affairs, Ottawa, January 18, 1911, in DIA, RG 10, vol. 3690, file 13,886, microfilm reel C-10121, LAC.

58 W.R. Robertson, Indian agent, to A.W. Vowell, Indian Superintendent for British Columbia, Duncan's Station, December 20, 1906, and January 19, 1907, in DIA, Black series, RG 10, vol. 3689, file 13,886, microfilm reel C-10120, LAC.

59 DIA, Annual Report (1906), 203.

60 Kanakos, "Negotiations," 103. According to John Sutton Lutz, *Makúk: A New History of Aboriginal White Relations* (Vancouver: UBC Press, 2008), 100, a leading salmon cannery regularly employed Cooper "to secure labour and look after the Indian help."

61 See the images in Keddie, *Songhees Pictorial*, 147, 150–53.

62 This conclusion is based on surnames and other information in Department of Indian Affairs files and on J.S. Matthews, comp., *Conversations with Khahtsahlano 1932–1954* (Vancouver: City Archives, 1955). Certainly some Squamish women had families with newcomer men, a topic explored in Jean Barman, *Stanley Park's Secret: The Forgotten Families of Whoi Whoi, Kanaka Ranch, and Brockton Point* (Madeira Park, BC: Harbour, 2005).

63 Meetings of October 13, 1906, and October 28, 1908, held on the Songhees reserve, in DIA, Black series, RG 10, vol. 3689, file 13,886, microfilm reel C-10121, LAC; and "At Deadlock over Songhees Reserve," *Colonist*, November 8, 1906.

64 Frank Pedley, Deputy Superintendent of Indian Affairs, to Frank Oliver, Superintendent General of Indian Affairs, Ottawa, December 17, 1906, in DIA, RG 10, vol. 3689, file 13,886, microfilm reel C-10120, LAC.

65 "An Act for the Enfranchisement of the Songhees Band or Indians, of the City of Victoria, in the province of British Columbia," February 1909 in DIA, RG 10, vol. 3690, file 13,886, microfilm reel C-10121, LAC.

66 Frank Pedley to Frank Oliver, Ottawa, February 19, 1906, in DIA, RG 10, vol. 3690, file 13,886, microfilm reel C-10121, LAC.

67 Lewis Hall, Mayor, and Vancouver City Council, to the Right Honourable Earl Grey, Governor General, and to the House of Commons, Victoria, March 24, 1909, in DIA, RG 10, vol. 3690, file 13,886, microfilm reel C-10121, LAC.

68 See Lutz, *Makúk*, 51–52.

69 Michael Cooper, quoted in "Bargain Made Was Excellent," *Colonist*, March 22, 1916.

70 See Census of Songhees Indians, March 12, 1910; H. Dallas Helmcken, legal council for the Songhees, to Premier Richard McBride, Victoria, October 26, 1910; Census of the Songhees Band on Songhees Reserve Made November 21–25, 1910; and "Complete List of Payments re Songhees Reserve," in DIA, RG 10, vol. 3690, file 13,886, microfilm reel C-10121, LAC.

71 Martha Douglas, letter quoted in Keddie, *Supplement to Songhees Pictorial*, n.p.

72 Smith and Johnston, barristers and solicitors, to J.D. McLean, Secretary, Department of Indian Affairs, Ottawa, November 18, 1910, and January 18, 1911, in DIA, RG 10, vol. 3690, file 13,886, microfilm reel C-10121, LAC.

73 Law firm Huntington and Jackson to W.R. Ross, July 19, 1911, and Huntington and Jackson to the Minister of the Interior, Victoria, August 22, 1911, in DIA, Black series, RG 10, vol. 3690, file 13,886, microfilm reel C-10121, LAC.

74 DIA, Annual Report (1912), 209, 274.

75 C.F.J. Galloway, *The Call of the West: Letters from British Columbia* (London: T. Fisher Unwin, 1916), 82.

76 W.E. Ditchburn to Duncan C. Scott, December 11, 1913, in DIA, Black series, RG 10, vol. 11,060, file 33-3, LAC.

77 Homi Bhabha, "Of Mimicry and Man," in *The Location of Culture* (London: Routledge, 1994), 88. Italics in original.

78 Homi Bhabha, "The Other Question: Stereotype, Discrimination, and the Discourse of Colonialism," in *The Location of Culture*, 70.

79 Bhabha, "Of Mimicry and Man," 91, 86. Italics in original.

2

Erasing Indigenous Indigeneity in Vancouver

Barman comments that "Persons who were indigenous to the area and considered it their home long before the arrival of outsiders were first removed from the land they called their own and then saw even their memory lost from view." This is the story of illegal removals to other reserves of Indigenous people from Snauq, now called Kits Point, and from Whoi Whoi and other locations in what is now Stanley Park. Part of this essay is a useful summary of Barman's book *Stanley Park's Secret: The Forgotten Families of Whoi Whoi, Brockton Point and Kanaka Ranch* (2005).

By Jean Barman. Reprinted with permission from *BC Studies* 155 (2007): 3–30.

Canada has become increasingly urban. More and more people choose to live in cities and towns. Under a fifth did so in 1871, according to the first census to be held after Canada was formed in 1867. The proportion surpassed a third by 1901, was over half by 1951, and reached 80 per cent by 2001.[1]

Urbanization has not benefited Canadians in equal measure. The most adversely affected have been Indigenous peoples. Two reasons intersect: first, the reserves confining those deemed to be status Indians are scattered across the country, meaning lives are increasingly isolated from a fairly concentrated urban mainstream; and second, the handful of reserves in more densely populated areas early on became coveted by newcomers, who sought to wrest them away by licit or illicit means. The pressure became so great that in 1911 the federal government passed legislation making it possible to do so. This essay focuses on the second of these two reasons.

The city we know as Vancouver is a relatively late creation, originating in 1886 as the western terminus of the transcontinental rail line. Until then Burrard Inlet, on whose south shore Vancouver sits, was home to a handful of newcomers alongside Squamish and Musqueam peoples who had long used the area's resources for sustenance. A hundred and twenty years later, apart from the hidden-away Musqueam reserve, that Indigenous presence has disappeared from Vancouver.

This essay traces, and reflects on, the erasure of indigenous indigeneity in Vancouver. Persons who were indigenous to the area, and considered it their home long before the arrival of outsiders, were first removed from the land they called their own and then saw even their memory lost from view. Having been unsettled, the indigenous indigeneity they personified could be erased.

Erasure had two purposes. It was an end in itself in the unsettling process whereby residents of Vancouver's most desirable Indian reserve, visible from the city's centre, were in 1913 persuaded to leave. Erasure also gave the means for the young city to assert that sense of rootedness which is at the heart of indigeneity without its having to be indigenous to Vancouver. With the totem poles erected in Stanley Park in 1923 to mark the forced removal of the last of its Indigenous residents, erasure functioned as a pathway to indigenous indigeneity's replacement by a sanitized indigeneity got from elsewhere.

Both forms of erasure served the dominant society, but in different ways. The first was intended to grow the city by opening up land for newcomer purposes; the second was more invidious, creating the illusion Vancouver was Indigenous-friendly even as it rid itself of the real thing.

Unsettling Reserve Lands

Of the two means to erasure that occurred in Vancouver, the unsettling of reserve lands was the most straightforward. The emptying of reserves was not a uniquely Vancouver or British Columbian phenomenon. When British Columbia joined Canada in 1871, "the charge of the Indians" passed to the Dominion government.[2] The Indian Act of 1876 restricted the role of the Department of Indian Affairs to Indigenous people defined as having status by virtue of male descent: to be Indian was to have an Indian father. The many women with families by newcomer men were left to their own devices, their offspring generally being termed "half-breeds," a word almost always derogatory in its connotation. Even though no treaties were signed in British Columbia (unlike elsewhere in Canada), except for small parts of Vancouver Island and the northeast corner across the Rocky Mountains, reserves were nonetheless marked out for status Indians, who were expected to reside there out of sight of the expanding dominant society.[3] The Indian Act provided for Indian agents charged with overseeing both everyday life on reserves and residential schools, which were intended to inculcate newcomer ways into offspring.

This centralization of authority in the federal government did not prevent the Province of British Columbia from coveting reserve lands for newcomer settlement. By the terms of entry into Confederation, land not legally transferred to individual owners or for reserves remained the property of the provincial government, being known as Crown land. An 1875 agreement with the federal government establishing a joint commission to confirm reserves contained a contentious clause sought by the province that "any land taken off a Reserve shall revert to the Province."[4] In other words, to the extent Indians could be persuaded to unsettle reserves, it was British Columbia that benefited.

The country was in a chipper mood at the time Richard McBride became premier of British Columbia in 1903. Convinced of the province's reversionary right to reserve lands, he pushed for the negotiations that would unsettle the province's two principal urban reserves, located in Victoria and Vancouver. In doing so, he reflected larger sets of attitudes in the dominant society. Most everyone agreed that Indians who did not use land set aside for them in ways consistent with newcomers' assumptions had no right to retain it. Urbanization caused reserves in or near cities to be especially coveted. Prime Minister Wilfrid Laurier pronounced in Parliament in April 1911 that "where a reserve is in the vicinity of a growing town, as is the case in several places, it becomes a source of nuisance and an impediment to progress."[5] A month later the Indian Act was amended so that the residents of any "Indian reserve which adjoins or is situated wholly or partly within an incorporated town or city having a population of not less than eight thousand" could be legally removed without their consent if it was in "the interest of the public and of the Indians of the band for whose use the reserve is held."[6]

Two years before Vancouver's Kitsilano reserve was unsettled, and even as the Indian Act was being amended, the Songhees had been displaced in British Columbia's capital city of Victoria. There was no reason for the Songhees to want to move, and, in fact, they did not want to do so. An official of the Department of Indian Affairs attested in 1890 that they were "to a man determined not to vacate the Songhees reserve which was land held and occupied by their forefathers from time immemorial and consequently dearer to them than anything they could possess."[7] It was the promise of easy money, backed by Premier McBride's determination and Prime Minister Laurier's consent, that changed minds. The province offered forty-one family heads $10,000 each, which was deposited in their names in a bank account with the bank book handed over once the family had moved to a new reserve at nearby Esquimalt.[8] By the end of 1911, federal legislation had confirmed the reserve's sale to the province. A visitor a couple of years later caught the prevailing sentiment: "It was an intolerable state of affairs to see such a large area in such a location lying waste, occupied only by a few Indians, and after much negotiation it was bought by the city." An unexpected consequence was, to the dismay of the dominant society, Songhees "seen driving about the city in their own autos!"[9]

Reserves were also sought elsewhere in British Columbia. Between 1913 and 1916, a Royal Commission on Indian Affairs toured the province with the goal of rectifying complaints to do with reserves. It received a torrent of proposals. Municipality after municipality requested reserve lands for supposedly higher-minded purposes ranging from public amenities like parks and exhibition grounds to industrial and residential expansion. Among their number, North and West Vancouver officials wanted the Squamish reserves on the north shore of Burrard Inlet, and the Fraser Valley communities of Sumas and Chilliwack the nearby Stó:lo reserves.[10]

Unsettling the Kitsilano Reserve

The process by which Indigenous people were unsettled in Vancouver was, as in Victoria, the final act in a one-sided drama whereby

City of Vancouver founding archivist, Major James Skitt Matthews, spent years conversing with Vancouver's Indigenous peoples about their ways of life, putting down on paper what he learned, and compiling a detailed map of one-time Indian villages and landmarks. *Conversations with Khahtsahlano 1932–1954* (Vancouver: City Archives, 1955), accessible online, includes Major Matthews's conversations and features this map on the inside back cover.

newcomers claimed the city for themselves—and only for themselves. The Squamish and Musqueam had long used the area's resources. With employment opportunities in sawmills from the 1860s onward, some sites previously seasonal in their use became more permanent villages. A map constructed by Vancouver's first archivist, Major J.S. Matthews, in the 1930s, based on conversations with elderly Indigenous and non-Indigenous residents about a time still in living memory, showed three dozen "Indian Names for Familiar Places," indicating their regular usage.[11]

Among locations mapped on the south side of False Creek, across from the future city centre, was Snauq, located under today's Burrard Street Bridge. Snauq was the basis for a reserve of thirty-seven acres requested in February 1868 by the forty-two persons living there under the leadership of Chief Chip-kay-um, and established the next year.[12] Half a dozen years later the joint Dominion-Provincial Reserve Commission expanded what became known as the Kitsilano reserve to eighty acres.

As well as this reserve on False Creek, the commission confirmed four other reserves for the Squamish on the north shore of Burrard Inlet in what would become North and West Vancouver, and a principal reserve for the Musqueam on the north arm of the Fraser River in an area that would be amalgamated into Vancouver in 1929. Due to its location on the city's periphery, the Musqueam reserve has remained relatively intact.[13]

At the time the reserve commissioners visited the reserve on False Creek in November 1876, fifteen men, fifteen women, and twelve children were living there under Chief Chip-kay-um, whom newcomers called Chief George. The federal government was convinced Indians should become subsistence farmers, so it is not surprising the commissioners' basis for approval of the reserve's expansion had to do with agriculture. They reported optimistically "about 8 acs of land partially cleared," although "¾ ac only cultivated principally vegetables."[14] They counted two horses, thirty fowls, and seven geese. Residents would later plant a cherry orchard.[15]

The Kitsilano reserve's stability is attested by Methodist missionary Charles Tate, who preached at Snauq regularly from 1872. Half a century later, he recalled his Sundays there:

> They were a hospitable lot, and I was entertained by Chief George and his band in their community house ... There was quite a settlement at Chief George's False Creek Reserve, probably a dozen houses, built of split cedar, saw boards and slabs, and the big community house; a total population, perhaps, of fifty persons all told. It was a settlement of consequence ... Old Chief George was ... a very good kind man, a fine Indian.[16]

The Kitsilano reserve, also known as the False Creek reserve and Reserve No. 6, acquired much of its appeal for residents through its access to natural resources. Chief Chip-kay-um's great-nephew August Jack Khahtsahlano, who lived at Snauq as a child during the 1880s and became a principal informant to Major Matthews, explained how not agriculture but the sea brought the Squamish there, seasonally, in great numbers. According to August Jack, Chip-kay-um was the "first man to go to Snauq; he built first house close to water" in a tiny clearing framed by the towering forest.[17] The reason for the location was the big sand bar that would later be built up as Granville Island. "The Indians had from time immemorial had a fish corral there; two converging fences of brush in the water made from hurdles of twisted vine maple fastened to sharpened stakes driven in the mud to guide the flounders and smelts into the narrow part where they were trapped."[18] Others recalled great numbers of salmon, ducks that "rose in clouds," and muskrats.[19]

The reserve's centrepiece was a longhouse made of cedar slabs with an earthen floor. According to August Jack, all around the inside about sixteen inches off the ground was "a bench or platform, about five feet wide; wide enough for two people to sleep side by side on it."[20] A Methodist minister who visited in 1894 described the longhouse as being about 150 feet long with up to four "smoke holes in the centre of the roof to let the smoke from the large fires, about three of them, which, probably at one time, burned in the centre, for there was a regular earth hearth in the middle." By then the benches along the sides had disappeared, but "several families were living around smaller fires in the corners or on the sides."[21] August Jack gave himself a naming potlatch there in about 1895:

> I give away about one hundred blankets. I buy them Hudson's Bay store on Cordova Street; two dollars each; double blankets. Then besides that I pay for eighty pound sack of flour; thirty pounds tea, and I buy dishes and spoons, give them away; down

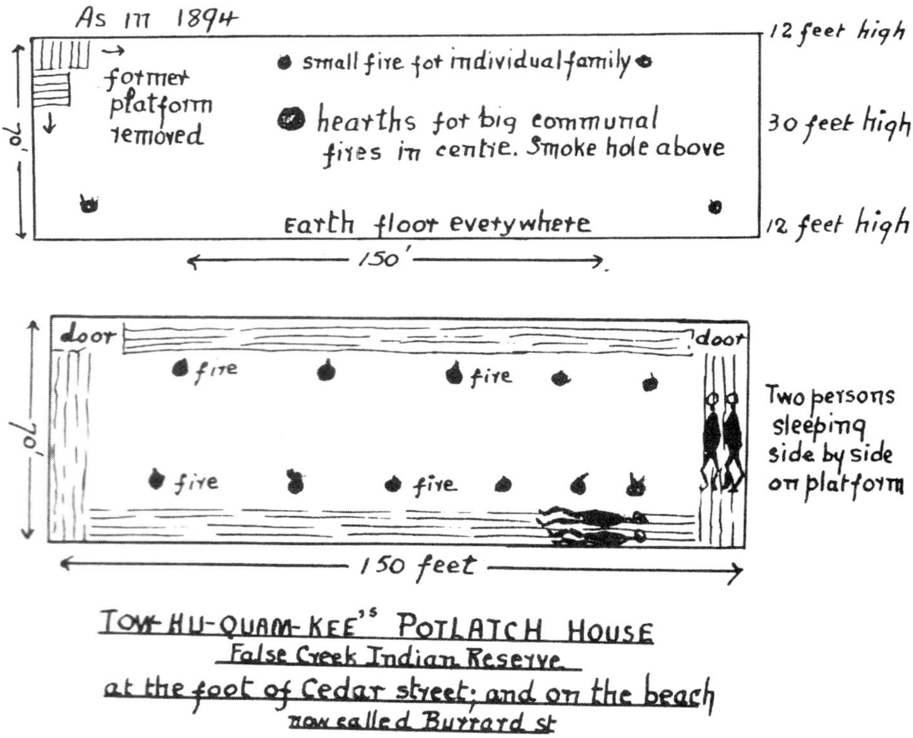

Squamish elder August Jack Khahtsahlano shared his knowledge and understanding of early Vancouver with, among others, Methodist minister George Raley, who together with Khahtsahlano sketched the interior of this longhouse located on the False Creek reserve. J.S. Matthews, *Conversations with Khahtsahlano*, 295, 56.

> at False Creek … in the big long house. [The spokesman] say this boy called by whiteman's name—August—now they going to give him his proper name, Indian name; same name his grandfather [Khahtsahlano] … Just one day celebration … Come from Squamish, Musqueam, Nanaimo. [22]

Typical of British Columbian reserves at the time, the Kitsilano reserve maintained a relatively steady population of forty-five to sixty inhabitants, most of them related through kinship or marriage.[23] August Jack explained how two members of his extended family had

Located under the south side of the present-day Burrard Bridge, the False Creek reserve, also known as the Kitsilano reserve, survived relatively intact until its "sale," so termed, in 1913. This photo taken on the reserve in 1891 depicts, from left to right, Yamschloot or Mary, Chinalset or Jericho Charlie, William Green, Peelass George, Jimmy Jimmy, and Towhuquamkee or Jack. City of Vancouver Archives, AM54-S4-: In P1.1.

houses on one side of the longhouse and two on the other side. Also living there was his stepfather Chinalset or Jericho Charlie, born about 1830, who used his large dugout canoe to freight goods between Hastings Mill (established on the south shore of Burrard Inlet in 1865), the small settlement at Gastown to the west, and logging camps.[24] Also living there was Chief Chip-kay-um's only child and her white husband, who worked as a bull puncher (i.e., he drove oxen). As recalled by an arrival of 1882, "John Beatty, and his Indian wife, lived on the reserve with old Chief George; they had a cabin on the reserve."[25]

Initially the Kitsilano reserve added a bit of colour to newcomers' everyday lives. When the Canadian Governor General, the Marquess of Dufferin, visited the young province in 1876 and his wife expressed a desire to see some Indians in their natural surroundings, she is said to have been conveyed to False Creek, where she had her hand firmly shaken by an elderly woman remembered as the "Virgin Mary."[26] A woman who lived across False Creek recalled how, "in 1891, False Creek was so quiet on a Sunday that we could hear the Indians singing at their services on the reserve as far as our place at English Bay; we used to sit on the shore and listen."[27] Reserve residents could be useful. An English woman who visited the new city of Vancouver with her husband, there to hunt game, told of hailing a canoe from the other side of False Creek: "After much calling and whistling, our Indian (William by name) came out of his house, and through [my husband] Algernon's stalking-glass we saw him packing in all haste, with the assistance of his 'clootchman' (Chinook for woman); at last he came, and we started."[28]

Vancouver's rapid growth changed attitudes. By the turn of the century it had overtaken Victoria as the province's principal city. The next decade saw the population of what was then a much smaller entity, extending south only as far as 16th Avenue, quadrupling to 100,000. An intricate system of street railways, which sometimes preceded settlement, drew attention to the reserve. So did visual proximity to the city's most exclusive residential area, the West End, with its prized beach on nearby English Bay. August Jack mused about the various houses along the shoreline of the reserve that "you could see them all from English Bay bathing beach."[29]

Increasingly, as Robert A.J. McDonald explains, the "people of Vancouver came to view the False Creek Reserve as critical to the city's continued growth."[30] In 1886 and 1902 ten of the reserve's eighty acres were alienated to the Canadian Pacific Railway to build a trestle bridge across False Creek and then a rail line passing through the reserve.[31] These actions paled before the growing determination to snatch the reserve itself. Several sets of stakeholders, or interest groups, played a role.

The first concerted attempt to acquire the Kitsilano reserve occurred in the first years of the new century, when, as described in press accounts, "prominent business men of the city" determined to put it to "a practical use" consistent with the self-confident boosterism grounded in real estate speculation that characterized Vancouver during these years. The goal of using the reserve "for public exhibition and other purposes for the general good of every citizen" became more self-interested the more it was described.[32] The refined plan for "a midsummer fair and carnival" complete with "railway, tram and water facilities" was a mildly disguised economic venture wherein "business men would reap a harvest each year from the throngs that would be visiting."[33]

While businessmen were acting in expected ways, a second stakeholder might have sided with reserve residents. Legally the federal government through the Department of Indian Affairs was the only body with authority to act, and the sole hesitation of the Indian agent for the Vancouver region to accede to the businessmen's desires had to do with the value of the reserve land, which he initially pegged at $1,800 an acre (or about $125,000), rather than the $500 an acre (or $35,000) the businessmen proposed to pay.[34]

A third possible stakeholder who might have been sympathetic to the Kitsilano reserve's Squamish residents was also apparently comfortable with their removal. According to contemporary accounts, "the Roman Catholic clergy, missionaries to the Indians, are somewhat desirous to see the Indians moved away, provided of course that the Indians are treated fairly in the transaction." The other Squamish reserves were under close Catholic oversight and much more strictly regulated according to missionaries' preferences than was the Kitsilano reserve located on the far side of Burrard Inlet and False Creek. "The missionaries look upon the reservation as nothing more or less than a hotbed of drunkenness and situated too close to the city to be a desirable residing place for their charges."[35]

A fourth set of stakeholders made its appearance just as victory seemed assured. Vancouver businessmen learned, to their consternation, that it was necessary that "the consent of the Indians interested in the land be obtained."[36] Headlines in Vancouver's leading newspaper—"Indian Reservation May Be Lost to Vancouver" and "Reservation May Be Ours"—underline the full extent to which the reserve's residents had not previously been a consideration.[37] The benign view held that, in comparison with Vancouver's rapidly growing population, there were "very few Indians living on this reservation," so that, "so far as they are concerned, a better provision could easily be made for them at some other place, just as convenient." A more critical perspective offered at a public meeting overseen by the mayor was that "the reserve as at present is of no use to any one, and is moreover an eyesore to the city and an easy resort for criminals." Vancouver business interests claimed there were "only eleven Indians on the reserve, and only about an acre and a half under cultivation."[38]

It soon became clear that this overlooked set of stakeholders had a mind of its own. Much as occurred with the Songhees reserve, the Squamish living on the Kitsilano reserve under Chief Chip-kay-um did not want to leave. Earlier, in 1901, they had refused, and now they did so again.[39] The local Indian agent reported on a meeting held there in January 1904:

> Chief says that he does not want to sell the land because it belonged to his Grandfather ... He didn't want to leave this place where he was born and it is the place where his dead relatives are buried—none of the men on the place want to sell it—the Queen gave him and his people the land.[40]

A Vancouver newspaper crisply summed up another meeting on the reserve in April 1904: "After a short consultation the Indians decided that they were unanimously opposed to selling or surrendering the reserve or any portion of it for any price or any consideration whatever."[41] Chief Chip-kay-um, who had been in charge since at least 1868 when he spearheaded the initial request for the reserve, died three years later.[42]

Following another abortive attempt in 1908–1909 to wrest the reserve away,[43] events stagnated until early 1913 when a new stakeholder took the lead. About the same time as an American railway company offered $1.5 to $2 million for the reserve, which it sought for a terminal and docks, and the federal Harbour Commission was eyeing it for much the same purpose, the province stepped in.[44] Even as the federal Department of Indian Affairs was mulling the offers but putting them on hold until the Royal Commission on Indian Reserves reported, provincial authorities acted.[45]

In a transaction culminating in early April 1913, due process played no role, nor was federal approval sought. The province's justification lay in its claim that British Columbia had reversionary rights to reserve lands. Vancouver magistrate H.O. Alexander, who was fluent in the trade jargon of Chinook, which all of the Squamish understood, acted as intermediary on behalf of the province and more particularly of Attorney General W.J. Bowser, who represented Vancouver in the legislature. According to Alexander's version of events, some reserve residents approached him about a deal similar to the one the province had negotiated with the Songhees. He thereupon organized a closed meeting on the reserve in March 1913 at which he read over in Chinook a draft sale agreement which all those present signed, almost all with their mark.[46] The amount was far less than what the Squamish had anticipated, being $11,250 per family head or about $220,000 in total.[47] Unlike the Songhees, they were not allocated a new reserve; the expectation was that they would move to one of the existing Squamish reserves on the north shore of Burrard Inlet or to others located farther north.

Before the deal could be finalized, news leaked of the much larger offers being entertained by federal authorities, which were said to come to about $50,000 per family head. Fearful of the Squamish changing their minds, Attorney General Bowser personally stepped in. At a meeting with heads of families held in the magistrate's office, he proffered cheques with the warning, according to one of the Squamish present,

> There you are. Here is your cheque with your name on it for $11,250. Take it. If you do not, you will never get a cent for your reserve.

The Squamish refused the cheques, one of them explaining:

> Mr. Bowser and Magistrate Alexander, listen to me: If you owned some property and one man came and said he would give you $11,250 for it, and another man came and said he would give you $50,000, which would you take? I think it is best for us to wait a little while until the Indian land commissioners are here.

At this point, according to this insider account, the attorney general offered what might be seen as a threat.

> When the commissioners have gone you will get nothing at all for your land, not one cent. All you will get will be a portion of land somewhere in the Squamish Valley in return for the Kitsilano reserve. Now which do you prefer, $11,250 or nothing? Here is your cheque. If you want it you can take it, and draw your money for the land; or you can leave it.

Before stalking out, the attorney general told the Squamish that they could have the money in cold hard cash the next Tuesday. "Take it or you'll never get a cent."[48] Another report based on first-hand information has "the Provincial Government" making "threats that they would be driven off by the Police if they did not consent to sell."[49]

A week later, on April 8, 1913, the Squamish capitulated. "Natives Grinned When They Became Owners of Fat Bank Accounts" is how Vancouver's principal newspaper summed up the province's victory. Early on a Tuesday morning, Bowser and Alexander met twenty "heads of families," including two women, at an "uptown bank" where $250,000 in gold was available for viewing in a vault in order to appease any doubters. Each family head was offered "a bank book, showing a balance to his account in the Canadian Bank of Commerce of $11,250," in exchange for putting "his mark to a receipt" relinquishing any interest in the Kitsilano reserve.[50] By "the stroke of 12 o'clock noon," according to a press account, "the last of the band" had "accepted their bank book."[51]

The real and psychological distance that separated the two stakeholders was caught in two events on that fateful day. The first was "a squaw with a baby in her arms who stood waiting for her husband to come out of the manager's room with his bank account." Despite her looking, according to a newspaper account, "longingly at the comfortable seats in the bank for the use of the customers," no one invited her to sit down and "she took her baby and went and crouched for rest on the hard edge of the base of a marble pillar," whereupon "the passing throng looked down on her."[52] About the same time this mother was being relegated to the past, the attorney general was holding a press conference looking to the future. He proclaimed how this "eyesore to the citizens of Vancouver for many years and hindrance to the development of the city" would now make "as much profit as possible for the entire province."[53] Later in the day he reiterated this dichotomy, describing in virtually the same breath how the Squamish would now be "away from the temptations of the city," whereas "this very valuable property … should net us a million dollars profit." The attorney general was gleeful over what he termed "one of the best real estate transactions ever carried out in the province."[54] The fear expressed in a Vancouver newspaper a week earlier that the sum the provincial government offered was "much less than their market value" had become a point of pride to the attorney general even before the Squamish had actually departed.[55] The two worlds could not have been further apart.

To ensure no minds were changed and due process did not intervene, not only was a "big scow" at the ready to tow household goods away, but the pass books were also, in the pattern of Victoria, kept by the bank until their holders physically departed the reserve within a promised day or two.[56] Vancouver newspapers had a field day, sending photographers to intrude into every aspect of what was seen as a turning point for the city. Acccunts waxed sympathetic, if stereotypically, at how "many of the young men and some of the older men, too, had been born in the waterfront shanties, and had toddled their first Siwash toddles down to the beach when the West End was still a forest." One report described how "an old, old Indian ... carrying a roll of blankets, ... only vaguely comprehended that some great change in his place of abode was happening."[57] At noon on the day of departure, magistrate Alexander gave $100 in cash to each of the family heads, ensuring that, as a newspaper put it, "easy money jingled pleasantly in their pockets." Then, as they physically departed, he and the bank manager handed over the red pass books, each already containing the $100 withdrawal.[58]

Within two days every one of the twenty-some families, totalling sixty to seventy people, had been moved out. The majority headed to reserves on the Squamish River in Howe Sound, to which they usually went in the summer as part of their seasonal economic round from their homes on False Creek.[59] Having unsettled the reserve, the city ensured most of their homes were burned to the ground.[60]

This erasure of indigenous indigeneity from Vancouver was momentous, and not just for the men, women, and children who departed. Years later a ninety-year-old woman, who at the time was a young bride living on English Bay, still remembered watching the many canoes filled with boxes and baskets pulling away from the waterfront across the water. In her recollection, "the houses they left behind were fired as they pulled away." She reflected to a great-great-niece how they must have left things behind they could not take in the boats, but everything was ashes before nightfall. It all made her "a bit angry and very sad."[61]

The deed was done. Indigenous indigeneity was erased from False Creek. One stakeholder, the province, had shortcut the process, bypassing the federal government, legally charged with the oversight of Indians. A Victoria newspaper's characterization of the unsettlement as "unjustifiable and immoral," "the greatest scandal in the history of the

Provincial government of British Columbia," and liable to "a term in the penitentiary" if undertaken by "an individual in the community" might have comforted concerned bystanders, but that was all.[62] The next days, months, and years saw rancorous name-calling, contention concerning payments to non-band members but not to reserve residents temporarily away, and arguments between the stakeholders over title to the land, none of which undid the erasure.[63] Apart from a vigorous parliamentary debate over the legality of the transaction, in which everyone agreed that the reserve had been "a blemish" on Vancouver that needed to be removed, the federal government, including the Department of Indian Affairs, did nothing to undo an action clearly infringing on federal responsibilities to the Squamish.[64]

Unlike title over the Songhees reserve in Victoria, title over the reserve on False Creek long remained in dispute. The Harbour Commission, which had had an eye on the reserve prior to the provincial action, expropriated the property for development in 1916, which it legally had authority to do, and held it for a decade before abandoning its interest in it.[65] In 1930 eight acres were alienated for the present Burrard Street Bridge, and in 1934 four acres for the Seaforth Armoury. What was left remained vacant, apart from passing squatters. August Jack lamented how, two decades after the Squamish were cajoled off the reserve, "cherry trees gone wild; there yet; all go to pieces; not look after him."[66] In another conversation with Major Matthews, August Jack described what happened: "The orchard went to ruin, the fences fell down, and the houses were destroyed. A few hops survived and continued to grow until the building of the Burrard Bridge covered them up." August Jack considered it more than a little ironic that "I received a formal invitation to be present at the opening of the great bridge as a guest of the city."[67]

Only in the last decades of the twentieth century did the land acquire its present-day appearance. The Squamish, who amalgamated in 1923 except for a minority known as the Burrard band, now the Tsleil-Waututh, argued that for any reserve's surrender to be legitimate, all the Squamish needed to agree to it. In 1947 the Squamish officially surrendered the Kitsilano reserve to the federal government, whereupon the province formally conveyed the land to its federal counterpart, which then broke it up into parcels for sale separately.[68] Half of the land became the present Vanier Park, containing the Vancouver Museum, Planetarium, and Maritime Museum; the other five parcels became private commercial and housing developments.[69]

Unsettling Stanley Park

In sharp contrast to the province's illegal but effective erasure of indigenous indigeneity from the south side of False Creek in 1913, events on the one-thousand-acre peninsula on the south shore of Burrard Inlet that would become Stanley Park were longer lived and more complex. Erasure occurred in two stages.

The first unsettling was initiated prior to Vancouver's formation in 1886 and the designation of the peninsula as Stanley Park a year later. The principal site there on archivist J.S. Matthews's map of "Indian Names for Familiar Places" was Whoi Whoi on the northeast shore. Indigenous people had long made use of Whoi Whoi, nearby Chaythoos, and other sites on the peninsula, as indicated by middens, or shell heaps, some eighty feet deep and four acres in size that were uncovered during road building around the new park in 1888.[70]

The joint Dominion-Provincial Reserve Commission charged with marking out reserves visited Burrard Inlet in November 1876. The commissioners counted fifty persons they identified as "Skwamish" in the vicinity of Whoi Whoi, including August Jack Khahtsahlano's immediate family, but refused to allocate a reserve.[71] The reason had to do with the peninsula having been supposedly set aside as a government reserve prior to British Columbia joining Canada in 1871. While no documentation has ever been located to indicate that such a reserve had been officially created,[72] the provincial government took

Today's Stanley Park was home to Indigenous peoples long before non-Indigenous newcomers decided the peninsula adjacent to the young Vancouver was theirs to do with as they pleased. Road construction two years after Vancouver's formation in 1886 uncovered middens that, being refuse heaps signalling long occupation, were destroyed out of hand. City of Vancouver Archives, SGN 91.

for granted that the peninsula had, as with Crown lands, reverted to the province on entry into Confederation.[73] Consistent with this view, a Victoria resident who in 1875 sought "to preempt 160 acres of land" on the peninsula was informed by the province that "several persons had asked for sections of land," and that "if disposed of it would be sold at public auction."[74] The commissioner appointed by the British Columbian government, who was personally sympathetic to the request, telegraphed the provincial commissioner of lands and works to ask "if the Prov Government would allow us to lay off a small reserve at this place," but received a negative response.[75]

The residents of Whoi Whoi and its vicinity were assured they "would not be made to remove in a hurry" and gradually migrated to the other Squamish reserves.[76] The last to live on the peninsula was a woman known as "Aunt Sally," sister of Chém chuk and Kwe áh jilk, enumerated at Whoi Whoi in 1876, who had a house and orchard on two acres she had fenced off near Whoi Whoi.[77] By the time Aunt Sally

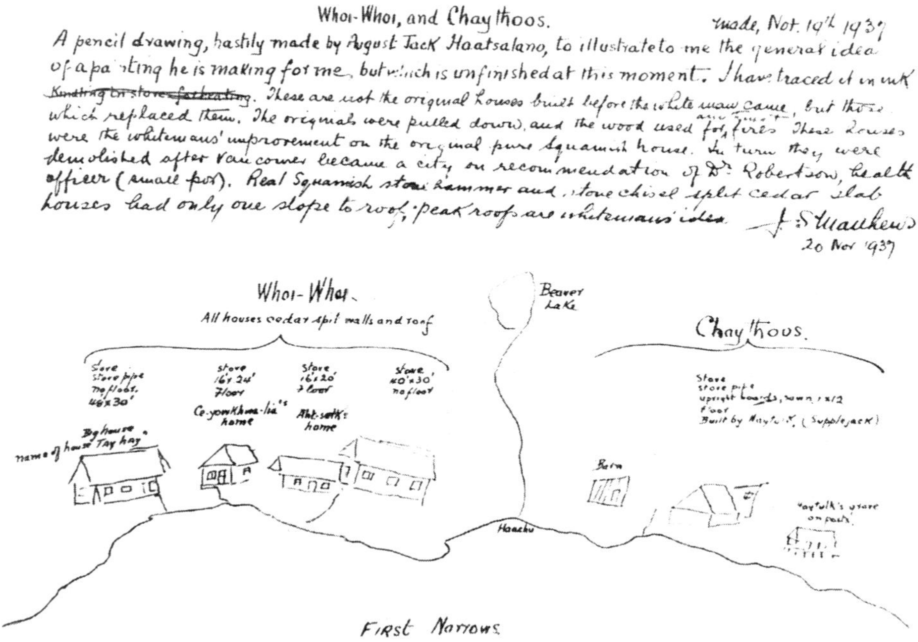

The resourceful August Jack Khahtsahlano sketched for Vancouver City archivist Major Matthews the two Indigenous villages of Whoi Whoi and Chaythoos as they existed during Khahtsahlano's childhood during the 1870s in what would become Stanley Park. City of Vancouver Archives, Add MSS 54, Stanley Park file.

died there in 1923, the name itself had been erased. For the visit to Vancouver in September 1912 of the Governor General, the Duke of Connaught, a wooden arch was erected downtown. After he departed, the leftover structure was moved to Whoi Whoi, which was henceforth known as Lumberman's Arch.

By Aunt Sally's death in 1923, which appeared to conclude the first stage in the erasure of indigenous indigeneity from Stanley Park, the second stage was underway. It had two components: one centred on legal dispossession; the other, a sleight of hand by which a sanitized indigeneity obscured the unsettling and erasure of indigenous indigeneity.

The stakeholders in this second stage shifted from the province to the municipal and federal governments, the two levels joining forces to dispossess Indigenous families who had lived on the peninsula since the early 1860s. The federal government's presence was essential, for it had by now wrested the peninsula away from the province. In 1881 the Canadian government had requested that the Colonial Office in London transfer to it all reserves acquired in British Columbia during the colonial period, when the future province belonged to Britain, that it no longer needed for military purposes.[78] Despite the British government being unable to determine that it had ever held the peninsula or, indeed, most of the other supposed reserves, it eventually decided the best course was to return whatever it might once have possessed.[79] Only in 1906 did the federal government assuredly acquire ownership of the peninsula. That year the Privy Council in London extended a ruling declaring the federal government the owner of nearby Deadman's Island.[80] Two years later the federal government gave the city a ninety-nine-year renewable lease to Stanley Park.

The target for unsettling Stanley Park was half a dozen families who had since the early 1860s lived east of Whoi Whoi on the north and south shores of Brockton Point. They consisted in the first generation of newcomer men mostly settled down with Squamish women whose families lived nearby. The women had in effect invited newcomer men they fancied onto their territory.

The Indian Act's reliance on paternal descent meant that the legally married wives were denied status as "Indians," as were their descendants through the generations. Principle and practice did not necessarily mesh. The Brockton Point families were generally considered to be Indigenous, so much so that almost all offspring in the second and third generations were as a matter of course whipped off to residential schools intended for status Indian children.[81] Much as occurred on the Kitsilano reserve with the chief's daughter, some Brockton Point offspring resided, intermittently or permanently, on the reserves established for their Squamish cousins on the north shore of Burrard Inlet. Most continued to live at Brockton Point, men longshoring on the Vancouver waterfront alongside their Squamish

Starting in the 1860s, the south shore of Brockton Point on the eastern edge of Stanley Park was home to white newcomers partnered with Indigenous women. They would continue to make their lives there until the families were dispossessed in the 1920s. This photograph by Edouard Deveille was taken in 1886. Image D-04722 courtesy of the Royal BC Museum and Archives.

relatives. The racial exception was a white couple who had been invited to settle among the families at Brockton Point after the wife nursed one of the Squamish wives back to health.

As with the Kitsilano reserve, so with Brockton Point: the press encouraged Vancouverites to see themselves as distinct from, and superior to, this Indigenous presence in their midst. Acting on a tip, a newspaper sent an investigative reporter to Brockton Point just a month after the Kitsilano reserve was emptied in April 1913. By his account:

> The wayfarer comes upon a group of about a dozen unpainted, tumble-down shacks and sheds, with one or two cottages in a better state of preservation. On the shore in the vicinity is a jumble of logs and other flotsam and jetsam of the harbor, interspersed with the remains of boats and canoes, fallen into decay

with the exception of one or two which are still in use. These shacks are surrounded by a rude fence of palings, and present, just now, an uncouth picture, with their mossgrown, ill-made roofs, some roughly shingled, some merely boarded, open in places to the sky, with rusted stove pipes thrust through gaps in the roof, in the midst of the flowering fruit trees.[82]

Now that Vancouver had a long-term lease to the park, the onus was on the Vancouver Parks Board to protect this jewel in the young city's crown. The perception that the Brockton Point families were Indigenous caused it to turn to the Royal Commission on Indian Affairs to remove them, only to be informed that they did "not come within the scope of this Commission."[83] The federal Department of Indian Affairs was beseeched. "On the peninsula which comprises the park, several groups of Indians and half-breeds have small holdings," ran the letter sent in 1919, to which came the reply that there was "only one of pure Indian blood [Aunt Sally], the balance being either half-breeds or whites" of "no particular interest" to Indian Affairs.[84]

It was four years later that the City of Vancouver managed to persuade the federal government to join in a legal suit to dispossess the families. The federal government's participation meant that the time period for which the defendants had to prove adverse possession, known commonly as squatters' rights, was raised to sixty years from the twenty required by the city. The long time period during which individuals, or others taking their place in an unbroken line of succession, had to demonstrate continuous residence in order to retain the small plots on which they were living meant most defence witnesses were elderly Squamish men and women using their own language. Their testimony asserting the families' presence at Brockton Point prior to 1863 did not persuade the judge trying the case, who then had his decision overturned by the BC Court of Appeal, which credited the witnesses. The case went to the Supreme Court of Canada, which accepted the contention of the lawyers for the city and federal

SO OLD HE FORGETS WHEN HE WAS BORN

TOM ABRAHAM, aged Squamish Indian, who is a witness for the Stanley Park squatters.

The eviction trial of Brockton Point residents in the early 1920s depended for the defence on Indigenous witnesses, including an elderly Thomas Abraham, who testified to the sixty years of residence needed to prove permanent possession. *Province*, November 6, 1923.

government that "native Indians have no idea of time" and therefore their testimony should not be credited.[85]

The Brockton Point families were unsettled. Those living on the south side of Brockton Point, whose houses were considered to spoil the view of the park from downtown Vancouver and vice versa, were forced out in 1931. Their homes were then burned to erase their presence on the peninsula. In part because the homes of the extended family living on the north side of Brockton Point were less visible to Vancouver residents, they were permitted to remain. The last member died in 1958, whereupon all evidence of their long-time presence was similarly obliterated.[86]

This final erasure of indigenous indigeneity from Vancouver was not simply an end in itself, as with the Kitsilano reserve and Whoi Whoi; rather it was the impetus to its replacement by a sanitized indigeneity got from elsewhere. Following the initial decision against the Brockton Point families in the BC Supreme Court in 1923, the Vancouver Parks Board put up four totem poles as "the first step towards the erection this year of a replica of an Indian village of the British Columbia coast

Following the BC Supreme Court's dispossession of long-time Stanley Park residents in 1923, the jubilant Vancouver Parks Board raised totem poles it had earlier acquired from the British Columbia north coast. It did so initially at Lumberman's Arch, with the poles being later moved to their present location at Brockton Point. Much as tourists still do in the present day, the Canadian all-star soccer team posed in front of the poles in 1924. City of Vancouver Archives, CVA 99-1327.

on the cleared space west of 'Auntie Sally's' cottage which adjoins the Lumberman's Arch." The proposed Indian village at the former Whoi Whoi would be named for, and honour, "the Kwagwelth Indians" of northern Vancouver Island.[87]

As to the reason for this, a Vancouver newspaper pronounced, the Kwakwaka'wakw, or Kwakiutl, together with the Haida, who were tucked even farther away from Vancouver on the Queen Charlotte Islands, were "the most advanced of all British Columbia Aboriginal tribes in culture." They were distinguished by "strong physique and higher mental capacity" and a "far higher degree of courage and intelligence than their more easy-going and pusillanimous cousins of the south."[88] The Squamish presence at Whoi Whoi and Brockton Point was overlaid with the material culture of a wholly different people who lived a safe distance from Vancouver. A few short weeks after the initial victory over indigenous indigeneity, its counterpart got from elsewhere was in place.

The Parks Board's action was not unique to Vancouver but reflected the enormous popularity during these years of romanticized indigeneity. This was an age when anthropologists, notably Franz Boas among the Kwakuitl, were making the province's Indigenous heritage fashionable in sanitized forms that did not affect the realities of newcomers' everyday lives. The passion to rehabilitate the imaginary Indian who existed prior to the arrival of outsiders was very different from coexisting with real people.

While the Indian village never came to fruition, the totem poles, subsequently relocated to Brockton Point, are a Stanley Park highlight. For residents and visitors alike, they provide an encounter with indigeneity safely removed from real life.

Reinscribing Indigenous Indigeneity

The story of indigenous indigeneity in Vancouver is not, however, over. The Kitsilano reserve was unsettled and the last families removed from Stanley Park, but that is not the end of the story. As with all erasures, however determined and intentional, faint impressions sometimes linger.

Sometimes this faint impression is relatively easy to re-erase. Such was the case with Whoi Whoi. To the consternation of the Vancouver Parks Board, on Aunt Sally's death, her daughter Mariah Kulkalem, who lived in the family home, hired a lawyer to look after her interests. She had every reason to do so. The Parks Board's attempted end run a decade earlier to get the Department of Indian

Affairs to remove the Brockton Point families had turned attention to the Kulkalem family's "long and uninterrupted occupation of about two acres of land," from which the department "fail[ed] to see how they can be removed unless they are compensated for giving up any claim to the same."[89] Aunt Sally's daughter began entertaining offers for the property, to the horror of the Parks Board. It found itself forced to dicker, and negotiated a price of $16,500 in the expectation the federal government would ante up, since it had charge of Indians. Before anything was settled, rumours began floating of a higher offer from a prospective buyer intending to build "a modern apartment house in the middle of Stanley Park."[90] The board chair took the initiative and paid Mariah Kulkalem out of his own pocket, being reimbursed a year later by the Canadian government.

A symbolic re-erasure followed. Immediately on taking possession of Aunt Sally's property in late 1925, it was noted in the minutes of the Vancouver Parks Board, "the buildings and fences were forthwith destroyed by fire and later the fruit trees were cut down and destroyed." Robert Cole, a young boy of ten living with his family at nearby Brockton Point, retained the image in his head all his life. "I watched them burn it. The fire department came down and poured gas all over it and lit it up and 'way she goes.'"[91]

More recent events have not been nearly so comfortable to those perceiving themselves as in charge. Whereas the Indigenous families who made their home on the peninsula that became Stanley Park remain erased in favour of sanitized indigeneity, deprived even of signage to recall their presence there, the Kitsilano reserve has reinscribed itself on the consciousness of Vancouver. The irregular process by which the province unsettled the reserve was never lost on the Squamish people. Initially it was a matter of money, and no one much minded when in June 2000 the Squamish negotiated with the federal government a $92,500,000 settlement of a legal action launched in 1977 over aspects of the expropriation of the Kitsilano reserve and of part of a North Vancouver reserve.[92]

Then in August 2002 the Squamish won a court case over the ten acres of land lying under the Burrard Street Bridge that had been expropriated from the reserve by the Canadian Pacific Railway in 1886 and 1902. In the late 1980s the CPR had attempted to sell the land, which, according to the original agreement, reverted to the Squamish when it was no longer being used for its designated purpose, and they had successfully sued.[93]

The reinscription of indigenous indigeneity in Vancouver in a twenty-first-century form was initiated with plans announced by the Squamish in August 2006 to generate revenue by erecting five or six large billboards, each ten by thirty feet, on its reacquired property. The billboards would be visible to everyone travelling over the Burrard Street Bridge. So were other billboards when crossing the two bridges from Vancouver to North and West Vancouver, both of which pass above Squamish reserves.[94] The Squamish explanation to Vancouverites—"I don't think a lot of people are even aware there's a reserve in Vancouver that is Squamish Nation's reserve"—was an understatement, for such an initiative was completely at odds with civic sensibilities.[95]

The consequence was a potentially major confrontation over a twenty-first-century version of indigenous indigeneity. Roadways free of billboards except when passing through an Indian reserve have become a staple of British Columbian life. In line with this perspective, the number of billboards in Vancouver shrank from some twelve thousand at one point in time to a handful, mostly in privately owned parking lots. As to the reason, one commentator explained:

> Vancouver likes to see itself as urbane, organic, green—a global model of sustainability and livability. The anti-Vegas. And the image the city has so carefully crafted for itself does not include big honking commercial billboards at the entrance to major bridges. These types of signs couldn't possibly meet

> the standards of good taste that have been artificially set in these parts.[96]

What has become clear is that the hasty erasure of indigenous indigeneity a century earlier is coming full circle in this and other ways.

Notes

1 Data taken from Canadian censuses. The exact proportions (20 per cent, 37 per cent, 56 per cent, 80 per cent) are not precisely comparable due to slightly differing definitions of urban and rural.

2 See Terms of Union, clause 13, reproduced in Robin Fisher, *Contact and Conflict: Indian-European Relations in British Columbia, 1774–1890*, 2nd ed. (Vancouver: UBC Press, 1992), 176–77.

3 On the marking out of reserves, see Cole Harris, *Making Native Space: Colonialism, Resistance, and Reserves in British Columbia* (Vancouver: UBC Press, 2002).

4 Order-in-Council, November 10, 1875, quoted in Robert Cail, *Land, Man, and the Law: The Disposal of Crown Lands in British Columbia, 1871–1913* (Vancouver: UBC Press, 1974), 204.

5 Wilfrid Laurier in House of Commons debate, April 19, 1911, in *House of Commons Debates*, 3rd session, 11th Parliament (vol. 4), 7249.

6 "An Act to Amend the Indian Act," assented to May 19, 1911, online at http://epe.lac-bac.gc.ca/100/205/301/ic/cdc/aboriginaldocs/m-stat.htm.

7 A.W. Vowell to L. Vankoughnet, Deputy Superintendent of Indian Affairs, May 5, 1890, Department of Indian Affairs (DIA), RG 10, vol. 3688, file 13,886-1, Library and Archives Canada (LAC).

8 See Grant Keddie, *Songhees Pictorial: A History of the Songhees People as Seen by Outsiders, 1790–1912* (Victoria: Royal BC Museum, 2003), 148–49. The sale of the Songhees Reserve is tracked in Jeannie L. Kanakos, "The Negotiations to Relocate the Songhees Indians, 1843–1911" (master's thesis, Simon Fraser University, 1982), and set within a larger conceptual framework in Renisa Mawani, "Legal Geographies of Aboriginal Segregation in British Columbia: The Making and Unmaking of the Songhees Reserve, 1850–1911," in *Isolation: Places and Practices of Exclusion*, ed. Carolyn Strange and Alison Bashford (London: Routledge, 2003), 173–90. See also Barman, "Race, Greed, and Something More" in this volume.

9 C.F.J. Galloway, *The Call of the West: Letters from British Columbia* (London: T. Fisher Unwin, 1916), 82.

10 Testimony, June 19, 1913, January 11, 1915, and February 5, 1916, to Royal Commission on Indian Affairs for the Province of British Columbia, Northwest Agency, Minutes of Meetings, 8–11, 134, 594–95, typescript courtesy of Coqualeetza Cultural Education Centre, Chilliwack, British Columbia.

11 Inside back cover in J.S. Matthews, comp., *Conversations with Khahtsahlano 1932–1954* (Vancouver: City Archives, 1955).

12 For a summary, see "Reasons for Judgment from the First Phase of the Trial" in *Squamish Indian Band vs. Canada*, court file T-1636-41, October 5, 2000: 20–22, 46. Newcomers spelled the chief's name as they heard it being spoken, resulting in numerous versions including Sh-praem, Chiphaim, Chupkeyim, Chipwheim, Chupnum, Chi-kay-m, Schpreme, Chprem, and Chpreame.

13 On the Musqueam reserve through time within the context of Vancouver, see Peggy Schofield, *The Story of Dunbar: Voices of a Vancouver Neighbourhood* (Vancouver: Ronsdale Press, 2007).

14 Censuses of False Creek taken November 20, 1876, enclosed with report of the British Columbia Reserve Commission, 1877, in DIA, RG 10, vol. 3645, file 7936, LAC.

15 August Jack Khahtsahlano in conversation with Major J.S. Matthews, July 16, 1940, in Matthews, *Conversations*, 114.

16 Rev. C.M. Tate in conversation with Matthews, July 1, 1932, in Matthews, *Conversations*, 158–59, 171.

17 August Jack Khahtsahlano in conversation with Matthews, May 19, 1935, in Matthews, *Conversations*, 44, also 1.

18 August Jack Khahtsahlano in conversation with Matthews, July 7, 1932, in Matthews, *Conversations*, 12; also Ayatak or Frank Charlie in conversation with Matthews, n.d., in Matthews, *Conversations*, appendix, 34.

19 Matthews, *Conversations*, appendix, 34.

20 August Jack Khahtsahlano in conversation with Matthews, May 19, 1935, in Matthews, *Conversations*, 44.

21 Rev. G.H. Raley in conversation with Matthews, May 9, 1935, in Matthews, *Conversations*, 281.

22 August Jack Khahtsahlano in conversation with Matthews, November 6, 1936, in Matthews, *Conversations*, 56.

23 See, for instance, memo, Ottawa, May 16, 1913, in DIA, RG 10, vol. 3741, file 28835-2, LAC. Also "Reasons for Judgment," 45–49, 57; and for biographies of some of the principal Kitsilano reserve residents, 50–59. The populations and familial relationships on British Columbian reserves are detailed, reserve by reserve, in Royal Commission on Indian Affairs for the Province of British Columbia, Minutes of Meetings.

24 August Jack Khahtsahlano in conversation with Matthews, August 23, 1937, in Matthews, *Conversations*, 45, also 4–5, 82, 284.

25 William Mackie in conversation with Matthews, Vancouver, September 9, 1937, revised, in City of Vancouver Archives, Add. Ms. 54.

26 Eric Nicol, *Vancouver* (Toronto: Doubleday, 1979), 45. The story may be apocryphal, given it did not make it into Marchioness of Dufferin and Ava, *My Canadian Journal 1872–78* (New York: Appleton, 1891), or *Journal of the Journey of His Excellency the Governor-General of Canada from Government House, Ottawa, to British Columbia and Back* (London: Webster and Larkin, 1877).

27 Mrs. Percy Nye in conversation with Matthews, n.d., in Matthews, *Conversations*, appendix, 34.

28 Mrs. Algernon St. Maur, *Impressions of a Tenderfoot During a Journey in Search of Sport in the Far West* (London: John Murray, 1890), 139.

29 August Jack Khahtsahlano in conversation with Matthews, May 19, 1935, in Matthews, *Conversations*, 45.

30 R.A.J. McDonald, *Making Vancouver 1863–1913* (Vancouver: UBC Press, 1996), 217.

31 "Reasons for Judgment," 15.

32 "Want a Grant of the Reserve," *Province* (Vancouver), May 28, 1902. There was at least one earlier attempt, described in L. Vankoughnet to E.D. Dewdney, Ottawa, April 18, 1889, in DIA, RG 10, vol. 3816, file 56,943, LAC. My interest in erasure, from the perspective of Vancouverites, means I have preferred contemporary press accounts as being closest to attitudes at the time, except where other sources elaborate on or contradict them.

33 "Indian Reservation May Be Lost to Vancouver," *Province*, June 7, 1903.

34 "To Secure the Indian Reserve," *Province*, June 4, 1902.

35 "Reservation May Be Ours," *Province*, October 7, 1903.

36 "Reservation May Be Ours."

37 *Province*, June 7, 1902, and October 7, 1903, respectively.

38 "To Secure the Indian Reserve."

39 The earlier refusal followed a provincial request made in May 1901 (Memo from W.R. White to the Deputy Minister of Indian Affairs, Ottawa, March 25, 1913, in DIA, RG 10, vol. 3741, file 28835-2, LAC.

40 R.C. McDonald, Indian agent, quoted in "Reasons for Judgment," 42.

41 "Indians Refuse to Vacate," *Province*, April 25, 1904.

42 "Reasons for Judgment," 50.

43 "An Election Bribe for the Citizens of Vancouver," *Province*, October 20, 1908; "City Control of Kitsalano Reserve," *Province*, November 24, 1908; "Says Ottawa Has Promised Reserve," *Province*, February 23, 1909; "Will Not Give Up Kitsalano Reserve," *Province*, March 4, 1909. Also, in 1904 eleven acres were leased to a lumber company for a fifty-year term, which would automatically terminate if the reserve was sold. (Memo from W.R. White to the Deputy Minister of Indian Affairs, Ottawa, March 25, 1913, DIA, RG 10, vol. 3741, file 28835-2, LAC.)

44 Telegram from Vancouver law firm Deacon, Deacon and Wilson to Superintendent of Indian Affairs, Vancouver, April 30, 1913, and memo from W.R. White to the Deputy Minister of Indian Affairs, Ottawa, March 25, 1913, in DIA, RG 10, vol. 3741, file 28835-2, LAC; also "Offered Indians One and a Half Million Dollars," *Vancouver World*, April 4, 1913; "Militia Want Indian Lands at Kitsilano," *Vancouver World*, April 9, 1913; "Kitsilano Indian Reserve Bargain," *Vancouver World*, April 11, 1913. In "Success in Struggle: The Squamish People and Kitsilano Reserve No. 6" (master's thesis, Carleton University, 1978), 72-75 and *passim*, William Zaharoff attributes the reserve's sale to deteriorating economic conditions among the Squamish people from 1912 onward. This perspective is too limited, given that the process had been ongoing for some time and was sped up by the emergence of competing interests; that it was the promise of ready cash that changed the minds of those actually living on the reserve; and that the Squamish more generally, centred on reserves on the north shore of Burrard Inlet, played at most a minor role in the negotiations and did not benefit from the sale.

45 "Offered Indians One and a Half Million Dollars," *Vancouver World*, April 4, 1913.

46 "Red Men Took Cash from Mr. Bowser This Morning," *Province*, April 9, 1913; "Offered Indians One and a Half Million Dollars." The ongoing interaction between Alexander, Bowser, and others seeking to profit from the sale are detailed in Zaharoff, "Success in Struggle," 79-110, based on British Columbia, Attorney General, Correspondence Inward, 1912-1916, BC Archives; and Special Committee: Kitsilano Indian Reserve, Evidence and Minutes of Hearings, in British Columbia, Clerk of the House, *Papers of the House*, 1916.

47 W.E. Ditchburn, Inspector of Indian Agencies, to secretary of Department of Indian Affairs, Victoria, April 26, 1913, in DIA, RG 10, vol. 3741, file 28835-2, LAC.

48 W.J. Bowser, quoted in "Indians Decline Bowser's Cheques," *Victoria Daily Times*, April 3, 1913.

49 Joseph Cole to W.E. Ditchburn, Indian Inspector, Vancouver, May 18, 1913, in DIA, RG 10, vol. 3741, file 28835-2, LAC.

50 "Red Men Took Cash from Mr. Bowser This Morning," *Province*, April 9, 1913. For a list of the 20 family heads as compiled by H.O. Alexander, the magistrate who arranged the sale, see Peter Byrne, Indian agent, "False Creek Indians," June 4, 1914, in DIA, RG 10, vol. 3741, file 28835-2, LAC. One individual received $5,000 only.

51 "Red Men Took Cash from Mr. Bowser This Morning."

52 "Red Men Took Cash from Mr. Bowser This Morning."

53 Attorney General W.J. Bowser, quoted in "Red Men Took Cash from Mr. Bowser This Morning."

54 "An Act of Greatest Benefit to Vancouver," *Province*, April 9, 1913.

55 "The Rights of the Red Man," *Vancouver World*, April 4, 1913.

56 "Red Men Took Cash from Mr. Bowser This Morning."

57 "Moving Today from the Kitsilano Reserve," *Vancouver Daily Times*, April 10, 1913.

58 "Moving Out from Old Home at Kitsilano," *Vancouver Daily Times*, April 9, 1913; "Moving Today from the Kitsilano Reserve."

59 Report of Peter Byrne, Indian agent, New Westminster, May 5, 1913, in DIA, RG 10, vol. 3741, file 28835-2, LAC.

60 W.E. Ditchburn, Inspector of Indian Agencies, to secretary of Department of Indian Affairs, Victoria, April 26, 1913, in DIA, RG 10, vol. 3741, file 28835-2, LAC.

61 Mary Wilkinson in conversation with Shirley Cuthbertson, who shared the conversation with Jean Barman, March 17, 2007.

62 Editorial in *Victoria Daily Times*, April 9, 1913.

63 Immediately subsequent events are detailed from a federal perspective in DIA, RG 10, vol. 3741, file 28835-2, LAC; and in "Reasons for Judgment."

64 House of Commons debate on the Kitsilano reserve, April 24, 1913, in *House of Commons Debates*, 2nd session, 12th Parliament (vol. 5), 8465-8500.

65 Enclosure with the relevant sections of the law in Maitland, Hunter and Maitland to Minister of Interior and Superintendent of Indian Affairs, Vancouver, January 8, 1915, in DIA, RG 10, vol. 3741, file 28835-2, LAC; and "Reasons for Judgment," 16. Zaharoff, "Success in Struggle," 148-79, traces the various manoeuvres concerning control over the Kitsilano reserve through time.

66 August Jack Khahtsahlano in conversation with Matthews, May 19, 1935, in Matthews, *Conversations*, 45.

67 August Jack Khahtsahlano in conversation with Matthews, July 7, 1932, in Matthews, *Conversations*, 6.

68 "Reasons for Judgment," 76.

69 "Reasons for Judgment," 15–17. The private developments were the former Molson Brewery, Parkview Towers Apartments, a shoreline Fishermen's Wharf, the Pennyfarthing condominiums, and commercial structures.

70 Major Matthews's map of Indian sites, in Matthews, *Conversations with Khahtsahlano*, inside back cover.

71 The sequence of events is described in Jean Barman, *Stanley Park's Secret: The Forgotten Families of Whoi Whoi, Kanaka Ranch, and Brockton Point* (Madeira Park, BC: Harbour, 2005), 36–41, based on DIA, RG 10, v. 3642, file 7624, and v. 3645, file 7936, LAC; RG 88, v. 494, LAC; A.C. Anderson diary, BC Archives, MS. 559; Archibald McKinlay diary, BC Archives, E/C/M21; and correspondence with Reserve Commission, BC Archives, GR 2982 and GR 294.

72 See Barman, *Stanley Park's Secret*, esp. 28 and 164–65.

73 The province's basis for this assumption lay in the British North America Act of 1867, which in Section 109 stated that all lands belonging to a province at the time of union should continue to belong to it, and in Section 117 that provinces "shall retain all their respective Public Property not otherwise disposed of in this Act, subject to the Right of Canada to assume any Lands or Public Property required for Fortifications or for the Defence of the Country." British Columbia possessed no military establishments apart from a Royal Navy base on Vancouver Island, and so all of the properties listed on an enumeration compiled by the provincial legislature in January 1873, including a "military reserve" of 950 acres (380 hectares) "south of First Narrows, Burrard Inlet," were thereafter treated as Crown land belonging to the province.

74 Joseph N. Thain to Joseph Trutch, Lieutenant Governor, Victoria, April 1, 1876, BC Archives, box 2, file 14/727/76.

75 November 16–17, 1876, entry in McKinlay diary; McKinlay and G.M. Sproat to F.G. Vernon, Howe Sound, November 27, 1876, BC Archives, GR-2982; also Sproat to A.C. Elliott, In camp, Howe Sound, November 27, 1876, and Joint Indian Reserve Commissioners to Elliott, In camp, Howe Sound, November 27, 1876, in British Columbia, Provincial Secretary, BC Archives, GR 294.

76 November 16–17, 1876, entry in McKinlay diary.

77 I am grateful to Randy Bouchard and Dorothy Kennedy for identifying Squamish names and relationships for me.

78 Report of a Committee of Privy Council, February 25, 1880, in National Archives (London), CO 42/760, and *Correspondence and Papers in Reference to Stanley Park and Deadman's Island, British Columbia* (Ottawa: S. Dawson, 1899), 7. The request was in line with the federal government's interpretation of Section 117 of the British North America Act, stating that all lands "required for Fortifications or for the Defence of the Country" belonged to the Dominion of Canada and not to the province.

79 Internal memo, Colonial Office, London, February 29, 1884, and draft minutes for Marquess of Landsdowne, March 20, 1884, National Archives, CO 42/778; also *Correspondence and Papers in Reference to Stanley Park*, 7–8. The sequence of events is described in Barman, *Stanley Park's Secret*, 85–88.

80 This case is detailed in Barman, *Stanley Park's Secret*, 163–65.

81 For specifics, see Barman, *Stanley Park's Secret*, 110–22.

82 "Have Their Home in Stanley Park," *Province*, May 10, 1913.

83 Vancouver Parks Board, minutes of meeting, July 19, 1913.

84 T.B. Jones, Barrister, to Minister of Lands, Vancouver, June 5, 1919, and W.E. Ditchburn, Chief Inspector of Indian Agencies, to Department of Indian Affairs, July 28, 1919, in DIA, RG 10, vol. 4089, file 521,804, LAC.

85 See Barman, *Stanley Park's Secret*, 216–17. The cases, including testimony and reasons given at the various levels, are detailed on 184–220.

86 See Barman, *Stanley Park's Secret*, 221–50.

87 Vancouver Parks Board, minutes of meeting, February 6, 1924; Art, Historical and Scientific Association, minutes of directors' meeting, March 11, 1924, City of Vancouver Archives, Add. Ms. 336, file 546-F-1; "Totem Poles Are Placed," *Sun* (Vancouver), February 6, 1924. The poles are described in Vickie Jensen, *The Totem Poles of Stanley Park* (Vancouver: Subway Books, 2003; rev. ed. Vancouver: Westcoast Words, 2015), and S.W.A. Gunn, *The Totem Poles in Stanley Park, Vancouver, BC* (Vancouver: Whiterocks, 1965).

88 Stephen Golder, "Indian Village in Stanley Park," *Province*, April 12, 1925, magazine.

89 W.E. Ditchburn, Chief Inspector of Indian Agencies, to Department of Indian Affairs, July 28, 1919, in DIA, RG 10, vol. 4089, file 521,804, LAC.

90 "W.C. Shelly Bought Acreage to Prevent Commercial Venture Being Launched," *Sun*, October 30, 1939; Vancouver Parks Board, minutes of meetings, November 26 and December 10, 1925.

91 Vancouver Parks Board, minutes of meeting, November 26, 1925; Robert Cole, conversation with Michael Steele in City of Vancouver Archives, Steele papers.

92 David Hogben, "Band Has No Plans Yet for the Property Expropriated for Railway 116 Years Ago," *Sun*, August 29, 2002.

93 Another decision ("Reasons for Judgment") dismissed Musqueam and Burrard claims to the Kitsilano reserve and confirmed the Squamish as the rightful former owners.

94 Nsoibh O'Connor, "Band Says Aesthetics Not Up for Discussion," *Vancouver Courier*, August 16, 2006.

95 Toby Baker, quoted in O'Connor, "Band Says Aesthetics Not Up for Discussion."

96 Gary Mason, "Squamish Billboards Debate Threatens to Get Ugly," *The Globe and Mail*, April 3, 2007.

Indigenous Women

3

Indigenous Women and Feminism on the Cusp of Contact

The essay explores three historical encounters to see how women were depicted on the cusp of contact: "As a very broad generalization, male newcomers depicted men in terms of their physicality and women in terms of their sexuality." Barman notes that "the process by which Europeans took control of virtually all the world between the sixteenth and nineteenth centuries gave men access to a huge new pool of women who were seemingly there for the taking." However, they were not always so willing to be taken. The first accounts describe contact with the "Nootka" (Mowachaht) in 1778 and following years, and note the refusal of the women to have sex with the sailors. The second accounts reference the Kwantlen women around Fort Langley, near present-day Vancouver, in the early nineteenth century. When partnered with traders who did not treat them well, some simply walked off. The final accounts concern the Indigenous women who worked in dance halls during the gold rush, who ensured that the rules of propriety governed behaviour and who would not dance with any man who had not been properly introduced to them.

By Jean Barman. Reprinted with permission from *Indigenous Women and Feminism: Politics, Activism, Culture*, edited by Cheryl Suzack, Jeanne Perrault, Shari Huhndorf, and Jean Barman (Vancouver: UBC Press, 2010), 92–108. The book received the Canadian Women's Studies Association Outstanding Scholarship Book Prize for 2012.

Indigenous women's outlooks prior to contact with Europeans are impossible to know. Archaeologists probe the material remains and anthropologists the non-material dimensions of past cultures through interviews with informants and other means. Their findings tell us quite a lot about ways of living, but very little about attitudes and perspectives prior to contact or, for that matter, on the cusp of contact.[1]

Another source exists for exploring Indigenous women's lives on the cusp of contact. Outsiders wrote about their encounters for their own purposes, and in doing so they left traces that open up possibilities. Almost all of these accounts are by men. Not only did men comprise the virtual entirety of arrivals, but the assumptions of the age whence they came meant that they considered themselves the keepers of the written word. As a very broad generalization, male newcomers depicted Indigenous men in terms of their physicality and Indigenous women in terms of their sexuality.

In a groundbreaking and seminal article entitled "The Double Standard," published in 1959, the distinguished English historian Keith Thomas analyzed the context to outsiders' attitude toward Indigenous women. In Britain and throughout much of the colonizing world, "both before and after marriage men were permitted liberties of which no woman could ever avail herself, and keep her reputation." Generally held assumptions about gender in what Thomas terms patriarchal society, being a society in which politics and the economy were male purviews, gave men sexual freedom denied to women.

Acknowledging the fundamental link that exists between gender and sexuality, Thomas considered this double standard to be but one component of "a whole code of social conduct for women which was in turn based entirely upon their place in society in relation to men."[2]

The process by which Europeans took control over virtually all the world between the sixteenth and nineteenth centuries gave access to a huge new pool of women seemingly there for the taking. Historian Stephen Garton crisply sums up this perspective in his observation that "sex was both a signifier and a practice for asserting dominance over other peoples." As he explains, "prostitution was tolerated and even accommodated by British colonial authorities as a legitimate means of regulating the sexual needs of the colonists—to protect their health, act as an outlet for natural desires and ensure social order."[3]

The unintended consequence of this attitude was considerable attention to Indigenous women in accounts from the cusp of contact. They reveal writers' perspectives on Indigenous women's behaviour, both within their own societies and in their interactions with newcomers. In the course of doing so, the various accounts hint at women's perceptions of themselves in relationship to these outsiders in their midst. The accounts tell us that, in some circumstances, Indigenous women acted independently of both Indigenous and newcomer men. Indigenous women gave the appearance of exercising agency. They took the initiative when it was in their interest to do so. We glimpse Indigenous women on the cusp of contact behaving in ways not wholly incompatible with notions of feminism.

The concept of feminism is most often employed relationally as the means by which women emancipate themselves from the subordination to men that is the hallmark of patriarchal and colonial societies. Some scholars go so far as to argue that "feminist analysis only arises in conditions of patriarchy, as a response to oppression and as a prescription for change."[4]

This limitation of the concept of feminism appears to have two principal causes. The first is the particular historical circumstances of patriarchy and colonialism in which the term came to prominence. The generation that coined the term has been reluctant to let go of the definition of it based on those experiences. The second cause is an assumption that men have always, so far as they are able, subordinated women. In this thinking, because patriarchy is assumed to be inherent to the human condition, feminism must by its very nature be adversarial.

Both of these reasons close off, rather than open up, possibilities in thinking about feminism. They discourage attention to times and places where women may have acted in ways consistent with the goals of feminism without necessarily doing so within conditions of patriarchy and colonialism. As well as being adversarial, feminism as it is usually defined is a state of mind. It emerges out of an attitude in which women take themselves seriously, value themselves as comparable or equal to men, and act accordingly.

It may be that on the cusp of contact some Indigenous women were not subordinated to men. At the least, they did not consider themselves to be. This circumstance does not make their actions any less "feminist" in the sense of their viewing themselves first and foremost as women, respecting themselves as women, and behaving accordingly in their relationships with others.

The three glimpses presented here are of Indigenous women on the cusp of contact in one of the last parts of North America attracting the attention of outsiders—British Columbia on the northwest coast. The earliest outsiders came by sea in the late eighteenth century as part of ongoing maritime expansion around the world. Others soon arrived overland in search of furs. Only in the mid-nineteenth century did a third wave of outsiders looking for gold move British Columbia from the cusp of contact to a colonial place. The three vignettes come from these three time periods.

Record keeping was taken for granted by the time the first outsiders reached British Columbia. Ships' officers and the men in charge of the land-based fur trade were tasked to record on a daily basis all and anything that came to their attention. During the gold rush, private and newspaper accounts served much the same purpose. The tedium of writing, whether by mandate or choice, about events as they occurred meant that happenings out of the ordinary sometimes received more attention than might otherwise have been the case. Encounters with Indigenous women fit into this category.

These three vignettes gleaned from the written record are in no way conclusive or definitive, nor are they necessarily representative of some larger phenomenon. They are presented much as they appear in the original documents. Our interpretations of their larger meaning will perforce differ depending on the personal backgrounds and scholarly apparatus we bring to their interpretation. However we approach the three glimpses, their telling brings us a bit closer to some Indigenous women's lives on the cusp of contact than we would otherwise come. As such, they are worth pondering.

The No-Nonsense Nootkan Women

It was the arrival of Royal Navy captain James Cook in 1778 in search of a fabled Northwest Passage across North America to facilitate British trade with Asia that first brought today's British Columbia to the attention of the outside world. The visit had two consequences. One was the almost immediate publication of accounts of Cook's travels; the other the chance discovery that sea otter pelts acquired from Indigenous peoples were much valued in China to trim garments.

Cook's month-long visit and the resulting maritime scramble for furs by entrepreneurs from Britain and, later, the United States were both centred at Nootka Sound on the west coast of Vancouver Island. The journals men kept reveal they were searching not only for the non-existent route, and then for furs, but also for local women to bed. The situation was exacerbated by many of the officers and men on board being relatively young in age, at a time in their lives when their sexuality was an especially potent force.

The generally held assumptions that Indigenous women's sexuality should satisfy male wants and that the world of work was a man's prerogative both hit a snag at Nootka Sound. As the twenty-six-year-old surgeon with Captain Cook mused, Nootkan women did not conform to stereotypes formed by "the beautiful Nymphs of the South Sea Islands."[5] After a week in the area, David Samwell lamented, "We had seen none of their young Women tho' we had often given the men to understand how agreeable their Company would be to us & how profitable to themselves."[6] It was taken for granted that, like men in the society whence the newcomers had come, Nootkan men controlled the sexuality of Nootkan women.

Samwell eventually recorded that a couple of women were "prevailed upon to sleep on board the Ship, or rather forced to it by their Fathers or other Relations who brought them on board," and thereby "received the price of the Prostitution of their Daughters."[7] It soon became obvious that something was amiss. The surgeon's assistant grew suspicious as others followed in their wake. William Ellis came to realize that at least some of the women "were not of their own tribe, but belonging to some other, which they had overcome in battle."[8]

Other observations from Cook and his officers similarly attest that Nootkan women themselves saw no reason to cavort with the visitors. Their refusal was so unexpected as to invite positive comparisons with women at home. Cook remarked in his journal that "the women were always decently cloathed, and behaved with great propriety; justly meriting all commendation for a modest bashfulness, so becoming in their sex."[9]

Men on board the next British ship to visit Nootka Sound, a trading vessel captained by thirty-three-year-old James Strange, had a similar experience. A twenty-year-old officer on board wrote that "on our arrival, when the Men were absent, which frequently happened, the Women shut us out of their houses, and Barricaded the doors with Chests and Planks." Young Alexander Walker attributed this action to the women's common sense, as he put it, to "the fears of the Women, who took this method of freeing themselves from our coarse importunities." He described how "the frequent attempts, that were made to debauch the Women, and the tempting bribes that were offered for this purpose, were with a very few exceptions constantly rejected." In his view, "the behaviour of the Women was uniformly exemplary."[10]

Strange was very impressed that the Nootkan women were not going to be bought: "As a tribute due to the Virtue & Fidelity of the female part of this Society (and indeed to the honor of the Sex in general) I cannot help Observing, that it stood the test of, & resisted bribes, which by a Comparison of local Value, I am sure could not be estimated at less then fifty thousand Pounds."[11] As had occurred during Cook's visit, according to Walker, "three or four poor wretches were produced for prostitution." He likewise concluded the women "were Captives, taken in War, and reduced to a state of Slavery."[12]

British adventurer John Meares, who arrived at Nootka Sound a couple of years later, similarly concluded about Nootkan women that "in their characters they are reserved and modest; and examples of loose and immodest conduct are very rare among them." The thirty-year-old seemed a bit astonished that "there were women in Saint George's Sound [his name for Nootka Sound], whom no offers could tempt to meretricious submissions." A bit farther north along the Vancouver Island coast, he was similarly impressed by how "no entreaty or temptation in our power could prevail on them to venture on board the ship."[13]

Nootkan women attracted attention not only for their control over their sexuality, but also for an appearance of equality with men quite different from expectations for women back home in Britain. Captain Cook wrote about the everyday behaviour of Nootkan women:

> They are as dexterous as the men in the management of their canoes; and when there are men in the canoes with them, they are paid very little attention to on account of their sex, none of

> the men offering to relieve them from the labour of the paddle. Nor do they shew them any particular respect or tenderness on other occasions.[14]

The next British seafarer to visit Nootka Sound, James Strange, who arrived in 1785 in search of sea otter pelts, made a similar observation, but went further. In his view, the Nootka "seemed to live with each other on terms the most amicable & friendly possible." He observed how, "in the married state, they appeared exemplary in love & attachment to each other."[15] To Alexander Walker, the officer on board Strange's vessel at Nootka Sound, "it would appear that the Women at Nootka are highly esteemed and treated with as much tenderness, as in the most civilized Countries of Europe." He described how "the Men were always very careful to protect the Women from our insults, whether they proceeded from violence or ignorance."[16]

Not only were Nootkan women respected by their menfolk and by themselves; they also acted accordingly. Nootkan women saw no reason why they should not participate alongside Nootkan men in the new market economy in pelts. They were also much more effective as traders than were their menfolk. Strange complained:

> The Deserved Ascendancy which the Females have over the minds and actions of their husbands, appeared accordingly in several instances to be very considerable, for my part, in my Mercantile capacity. I dreaded the sight of a Woman, for whenever any were present, they were sure to Preside over & direct all commercial transactions, and as often as that was the case, I was obliged to pay three times the Price for What in their Absence, I could have procured for One third the value.[17]

Meares's observation, made a few years later, was virtually identical in relationship to the trade for sea otter pelts, which had brought these men to Nootka. "The women, in particular, would play us a thousand tricks, and treat the discovery of their finesse with an arch kind of pleasantry that baffled reproach."[18]

These accounts challenge the easy stereotype held at the time, and into the present day, of Indigenous sexuality as a commodity. Except for women taken in war or otherwise exploited, Nootkan women on the cusp of contact controlled access to their bodies. Nootkan women also exercised power in other ways. They gave the appearance of leading somewhat independent lives in the everyday. They were confident in entering the market economy of newcomers and had no qualms about exacting as much benefit as they could from the sea otter trade.[19]

The Uppity Women of Fort Langley

During the land-based fur trade that succeeded its maritime predecessor, Indigenous women became viewed by outsiders as useful sexually for more than a single night. From 1821, the fur trade in British Columbia and across the Pacific Northwest was controlled by the Hudson's Bay Company based in London. While many of the surviving records are limited to brief factual entries, the daily post journal kept during the first several years of Fort Langley, founded in 1827 in southwestern British Columbia, is pithy.

As with ships stopping along the coast, Fort Langley was male space, managed and regulated by men in their own interests. Indigenous people were banned from the post except to trade and, in the case of men, as short-term employees. Local women were invited in, but the manner in which they responded to the invitation did not always accord with the traders' intentions for them. Like the no-nonsense women of Nootka Sound, the uppity women of Fort Langley knew their own minds.

Fort Langley's head during the late 1820s, Archibald McDonald, who was then in his late twenties, quickly realized local women's utility in acquiring pelts. One of the best means to establish "intercourse

The long-time fur trade post of Fort Langley was central both to Indigenous peoples and to non-Indigenous outsiders from the cusp of contact. Photo courtesy of Parks Canada/Fort Langley National Historic Site.

with the natives here" was using women with whom traders had sexual relationships as intermediaries.[20] He set a proposition before the post's second-in-command, thirty-year-old James Murray Yale: "The Quaintkine [Kwantlen], … being the principal Indians of the neighbourhood & [the only ones] who at all exert themselves to Collect Beaver, we have thought it good Policy in Mr. Yale to form a Connection in that family—and accordingly he has now the Chiefs daughter after making them all liberal presents."[21] This unnamed young woman whom Yale bought and bedded turned out to have ideas of her own. Initially, it was her father who acted on her behalf. He repeatedly used his new status to make demands on McDonald and Yale, and it may have been in part for this reason she decided she had had enough of being a pawn.

In the story handed down in his family, Yale returned home from two days away supervising construction of a new home for his wife and young daughter to discover that his wife had left: "Reaching his cabin he found the small Eliza wailing away to herself. Her mother was not to be seen. James knew without further thought that the thing he had feared from the first had finally come to pass."[22] The phrasing of the last sentence suggests that the departure was not of the moment or unexpected. It was rather the culmination of a long-term situation this young Indigenous woman chose to end by leaving her daughter behind in order to ensure her own freedom.

Archibald McDonald's utilization of Indigenous women to advance the fur trade went well beyond his luckless clerk. Post employees were almost all young men in their sexual prime, who were already employing various enticements to persuade local women to spend the night with them. Realizing that "those of the men that had not been lucky enough to Come in for a Chance of this kind have no inducement at all to remain at the place,"[23] McDonald devised a new policy. He permitted men who were two years into their three-year contracts "to take a woman" on a more or less permanent basis.[24] By early 1830, he reported to his fur trade superiors that "all our Men have taken Women," which "has had the effect of reconciling them to the place and removing the inconvenience and indeed the great uncertainty of being able to get them year after year replaced."[25] Men now renewed their contracts for another three years as a matter of course.

Although they were enclosed in male space, these women also inhabited a much larger Indigenous space. McDonald wrote somewhat idealistically in the post's journal that "it behooves us to ... keep these dames always within due bounds," by which he meant the post and its near vicinity.[26] The restraint McDonald assumed was women's place was, in practice, impossible. These Indigenous women were accustomed to freedom of movement, and they continued to be their own persons. When a perceived danger of attack caused them to be locked in at night, "allowed out only morning and evening for water & firewood," they "contrive to Create a little disturbance among the Indians about the beach with their batter of words."[27] A few days later, still locked up at night, the women "created a most unconscionable row among themselves, & two Couples actually proceeded to blows."[28]

Another time some of the women stole some gunpowder from a storeroom but, apart from getting it returned, the post head acknowledged "tis all we can make of it."[29] The fur traders expected deference from their womenfolk as a matter of course and were repeatedly at a loss as to how to manage uppity women. Dissatisfied women simply left; by doing so, they put men at an immediate disadvantage, for the men had either to enter Indigenous space to retrieve the women or to lose face.

In July 1829, a woman who had been "remonstrated with" by her so-called husband for talking with her mother near the gates to the post "watched her time and walked off to the [nearby Indigenous] camp." The husband wanted her back, and "after his work was over he followed her, & requested her return, which with the Concurrence of her relations and others around was positively refused under frivolous pretexts that She was not Kindly treated or entirely Secured as yet with the necessary property."[30] Reflecting colonial assumptions of male superiority, the post's head fretted over the best course of action. If this woman was not returned, there were consequences for the other men in their relationships. It would mean "the husbands are bound down never to Correct them."[31]

So Archibald McDonald acted. He described in his daily journal how he "called 5 men under arms immediately & with them proceeded to the Village when with very little gallantry in my address I ordered the lady to the Fort & acquainted the Natives that it would be best for them never to put us to Such trouble again."[32] The woman was forcibly returned, and, while we do not know for certain what happened subsequently, we get a hint of what might have occurred from a journal entry ten days later. It noted curtly, without elaboration as to whether or not it was the same woman, that "one of our men's wives decamped this morning."[33]

This glimpse of Indigenous women on the cusp of contact at Fort Langley is partial and one-sided. Even so, it suggests that women did not lose their sense of selves upon agreeing on their own accord, or after being persuaded by their families, to cohabit with newcomers. Some of these relationships were long-lived or lifelong with large families that descend to the present day.[34] Other women became uppity and, when they did so, were not afraid to act in what they perceived to be their own best interests as women and as human beings.

The Women Who Danced

The critical event moving British Columbia from the cusp of contact toward settlement was a gold rush that erupted in 1858.[35] A fur trade population numbering in the hundreds grew many times over as upward of 25,000 men rushed in from around the world in the hopes of getting rich quick. Many were experienced miners of the California gold rush, which had begun a decade earlier; others were young men in their early twenties newly arrived from homes in North America, Britain, or China. Vancouver Island had been a British colony under fur trade oversight since 1849, and the mainland now became the separate British colony of British Columbia. The two colonies would be amalgamated in 1866, and five years later British Columbia would join the new Canadian Confederation.

The most scrutinized event speaking to Indigenous women's attitudes during this rapidly changing time was the dance hall. Dance halls were an everyday feature of gold rushes, be it California in 1849, Australia in the early 1850s, or the Klondike in the late 1890s. Dance halls encouraged miners to put aside, for the moment, the hardships of the gold fields, even as they were parted from their newly got gains. The phenomenon was much the same everywhere: men paid to dance with women who were there especially for that purpose, and they were expected to treat the women to drinks.

The difference in British Columbia was that newcomer women were in such short supply that the women who danced were almost all Indigenous. The two to three dozen dance halls that sprang up during the half-dozen years of the gold rush were, as elsewhere, economic ventures intended to serve newcomer business interests. The women were the necessary sidebars to the dance halls' successful operation.

All the same, dance halls gave Indigenous women very real opportunities to exercise control in a world that, for many of them and their families, was being turned upside down by rapidly changing times. Dance halls gave women the means not only to make a bit of money but also to dress as did their newcomer counterparts. By doing so, some of them may have hoped to secure a measure of acceptance or even respectability. Indigenous women had to adopt patterns of behaviour already familiar to many of their dancing partners by virtue of their earlier participation in the Californian or Australian gold rushes. These expectations were not easy to meet, yet women appear to have done so.

The dance halls that operated in the colonial capital of Victoria on Vancouver Island, where many of the miners passed the winter months when the weather made it impossible to mine, and elsewhere did so in fairly similar fashion. Women were expected to learn cotillions, waltzes, the "Lancers," and "Julien's quadrilles," dances led by "the dulcet strains of a fiddle," by "a violin, bass viola, and a brass instrument," or perhaps only by a "fifer."[36] A participant recalled that "25 cents (about a shilling) was the entrance fee, and there was a kind of master of ceremonies who called out the figures—'first gent to the left with the left hand round, back again and turn'—'balance in a line'—it was really wonderful what a good time they all kept and how serious they all were about it."[37]

Even more important than the dances themselves was the expected behaviour between the dances, which was the most profitable aspect of the evening from the perspective of dance hall owners. A local writer described how "each man paid fifty cents for a dance, and had to 'stand drinks' at the bar for himself and his dusky partner after each."[38] A gold fields account explained how when the Quadrille was finished "Waltz up to the bar" was shouted out in a very loud voice—when every one did so at once, and we all had a drink and our partners generally took lemonade, or ginger ale. 50 cents was charged for each drink whatever it might be so one can easily understand what a good profit was made. Sometimes champagne was ordered. I should be sorry to say what it was made of but it always cost $10 a bottle.[39]

At another dance hall, according to a newspaper account, "a buff of conversation and a rush to the bar" was quickly followed by "the poppings of soda-water corks and the munchings of apples."[40]

The common means of communication was Chinook. This jargon had emerged during the fur trade out of French, English, and Nootkan, Chinookan, and other Indigenous languages.[41] Virtually everyone during the gold rush picked it up as a matter of course. A dance hall attendee recalled how the women "had learned a little English and all the men could speak Chinook more or less, which was the lingua franca."[42]

Indigenous women not only had to act suitably, they also had to dress appropriately. One account described participants as being "well and in some instances tastefully dressed," wearing "the silk dress and the dainty garter, with the air of a Parisian dame."[43] Many women sewed their own outfits. The newly arrived Anglican bishop observed at an Indigenous encampment "a woman making up a dress" for the dance house that night.[44]

Contemporary accounts indicate that women not only responded well to their new circumstances, but they also took the initiative to ensure dance halls operated as they were intended to do by those in charge. One attendee wrote, "I recollect asking one of the Kitty's in Chinook to dance with me and she drew herself up in a very dignified manner and said 'Halo introduce' which signified I had not been introduced to her! And I couldn't help laughing which made her very angry."[45] Indigenous women ensured the established rules were followed not only by themselves but also by the miners and others who sought to dance with them. By doing so, they exercised a measure of control over the new circumstances in which they found themselves.

It is critically important to disentangle these Indigenous women's resourcefulness from contemporary responses to them grounded in patriarchy and colonialism. Not unexpectedly, Indigenous women's mimicry of their newcomer counterparts became of itself cause for scorn. Postcolonial theorist Homi Bhabha, in an explanation of the fundamental nature of colonialism, comments that the women could become "the same, but not quite," almost white, but not quite.[46] The Anglican bishop had no qualms about ridiculing "the young women decked out in every sort of vulgar finery—even to the wearing of crinoline & hoops."[47]

Gender had become intertwined with race in the bishop's and others' responses. It was during these years that race became a cornerstone of colonialism. "By the middle of the nineteenth century," the respected historian of science Nancy Stepan explains, "everyone was agreed, it seemed, that in essential ways the white race was superior to non-white races."[48] Newcomers' paler skin tones became equated with a right to rule that was seemingly confirmed, in a conveniently circular fashion, by the very fact of colonialism and the unequal power relationship that had grown up between rulers and ruled.

All the same, even the most condemnatory responses, and there were many of them, sometimes incorporated an element of respect for the initiative these Indigenous women who danced took as women. An anonymous poem penned in 1862 about the women who danced in the Vancouver Island colonial capital of Victoria was intended to be satirical. It was satirical, but at the same time quite flattering in that it evoked both the fundamental shift the gold rush had facilitated for Indigenous women and the competent way in which they met the challenge of changing times.

Only three years since, in blankets,
Slovenly they rolled along,

Like old-fashioned Dutch-built vessels
    Lurching surging, in a storm.

Now Indigenous women had a very different appearance:

Sound the voice of exultation,
    Let it everywhere be known,
That the Indians round Victoria
    Almost civilized have grown.
That the squaws in radiant colors,
    Dress'd in ample crinoline,
And with graceful tread of turkeys,
    And with proud and stately mien.
Down the streets like gay gondolas
    Gliding o'er Venetian stream
Every day and in all seasons,
    May thus constantly be seen.

The reason for this change the poem's author attributed directly to the dance halls.

Now they trip the gay cotillion,
    With an elephantine prance,
In the Market Company building,
    Glide they through the mazy dance.

The rhyme attested to women's independence of character. The poem also emphasized how it was the women who ensured that dance halls operated in a respectful manner:

Without form of introduction,
    They will not allow their forms
To be clasped in waltzing graces

Or in polkas flighty charms.
Not without a Caribooite [miner]
On himself the task doth take,
To present a brother miner
Will a foot the klootchman [Chinook jargon for an
Indigenous woman] shake.[49]

The expectations dance halls put on Indigenous women were considerable, yet, contemporary accounts indicate, they largely met them. Indigenous women were amazingly resourceful in ways that speak to a self-confidence in themselves as women that is consistent with feminism.

In the event, the women who danced were undone not by the critiques levelled against them grounded in patriarchy, colonialism, and racism, but by changing times. The gold rush was in decline by the mid-1860s. Most miners departed. The handful who remained were not sufficient for dance halls to continue in operation.

Conclusion

At Nootka Sound, at Fort Langley, and in the dance halls, Indigenous women on the cusp of contact in British Columbia demonstrated a sense of autonomy apart from men that is consistent with feminism as the concept is sometimes conceived. Nootkan women and those living at Fort Langley exercised a degree of control over their sexuality and their everyday lives that was at odds with the gender assumptions Britons and others brought with them to British Columbia. It was not only in relationship to their sexuality that Indigenous women acted. They were comfortable entering the market economy outsiders introduced at Nootka Sound and in the dance halls.

In retrospect, we know these women's efforts were in vain and only served to complete the equation favoured by newcomers that, as one contemporary put it in reference to the dance halls, "they wear hoops and are prostitutes!"[50] As to the choice of that term, the historian Anne McClintock usefully reminds us, in line with Keith Thomas's double standard, how "prostitutes flagrantly demanded money for services middle-class men expected for free."[51] The equation of Indigenous women's initiative with prostitution freed men to act toward them as they would rather than as the Indigenous women's behaviour suggested they should. To a considerable extent, men have continued to treat Indigenous women as they please into the present day.

Indigenous women's easy dismissal by others should not be equated with our dismissal of the agency they appear to have employed in these three discrete circumstances on the cusp of contact. What happened elsewhere may or may not have been similar. As historical geographer Richard Phillips reminds us, "imperial sexual politics … were fundamentally situated, shaped by the material and imaginative geographies in and between which they unfolded: geographies of domination (concentrations of imperial power) and resistance (with scope for agency)."[52]

Because we are dealing with the past, we know the end of the story, so to speak. When these women acted, they did not. The attitudes displayed toward Indigenous women at that time and since then must not prevent us from considering Indigenous women, as far as possible, on their own terms within the historical contexts in which events occurred. We also know we can never retrieve the past in its entirety; rather, we only catch glimmers of it. The limited nature of the sources means we can make inferences only to a limited extent, and we are inevitably left with more questions than answers.

Indigenous women's lives on the cusp of contact, as we glimpse them in these three British Columbian vignettes, are nonetheless instructive as we reflect on the changing nature of, and possibilities for, Indigenous feminism. The distant past merits attention alongside yesterday and today.

Notes

1 Among the exceptions from a British Columbian perspective are Wendy Wickwire, "To See Ourselves as the Other's Other: Nlaka'pamux Contact Narratives," *Canadian Historical Review* 75, 1 (1994): 1–20; Louis Miranda and Philip Joe, "How the Squamish Remember George Vancouver," in *From Maps to Metaphor: The Pacific World of George Vancouver*, ed. Robin Fisher and Hugh Johnston (Vancouver: UBC Press, 1993), 3–5; and some of the essays in John Sutton Lutz, ed., *Myth and Memory: Stories of Indigenous-European Contact* (Vancouver: UBC Press, 2007), especially Lutz, "First Contact as a Spiritual Performance: Encounters on the North American West Coast," 30–45.

2 Keith Thomas, "The Double Standard," *Journal of the History of Ideas* 20, no. 2 (April 1959): 195, 210, 213.

3 Stephen Garton, *Histories of Sexuality: Antiquity to Sexual Revolution* (New York: Routledge, 2004), 130, 137.

4 Joyce Green, "Taking Account of Aboriginal Feminism," in *Making Space for Indigenous Feminism*, ed. Joyce Green (Black Point, NS: Fernwood, 2007), 21.

5 David Samwell, in *The Journals of Captain James Cook*, ed. John Beaglehole, vol. 3 (Cambridge: Cambridge University Press, 1967): 1095, also 1089. The people living at Nootka Sound refer to themselves as the Mowachaht.

6 Samwell, in *Journals of Captain James Cook*, 3: 1094–95.

7 Samwell, in *Journals of Captain James Cook*, 3: 1095.

8 William Ellis, *An Authentic Narrative of a Voyage Performed by Captain Cook and Captain Clerke*, vol. 1 (London: G. Robinson, 1782): 216.

9 James Cook and James King, *A Voyage to the Pacific Ocean*, vol. 2 (London: John Stockdale, Scatcherd and Whitaker, John Fielding, and John Hardy, 1804, orig. 1784), 258.

10 Robin Fisher and J.M. Bumstead, ed., *An Account of a Voyage to the North West Coast of America in 1785 and 1786, by Alexander Walker* (Vancouver: Douglas and McIntyre; Seattle: University of Washington Press, 1982), 85–87.

11 James Strange, *James Strange's Journal and Narrative* (Fairfield, WA: Ye Galleon Press, 1982), 84.

12 Fisher and Bumstead, *Account*, 87. In *A Narrative of the Adventures and Sufferings of John R. Jewitt* (Middleton, England: Loomis and Richards, 1816), 89, John Jewitt, who lived with the Nootka from 1803 to 1805, makes much the same point.

13 John Meares, *Voyages Made in the Years 1788 and 1789, from China to the North West Coast of America* (London: Logographic Press, 1790), 251, 149.

14 Cook and King, *Voyage to the Pacific Ocean*, 2: 258.

15 Strange, *Journal and Narrative*, 84.

16 Fisher and Bumstead, ed., *Account*, 85, 86.

17 Strange, *Journal and Narrative*, 84.

18 Meares, *Voyages*, 149.

19 Among descriptive and ethnographic accounts of the Nootka based later in time are Gilbert Malcolm Sproat, *The Nootka: Scenes and Studies from Savage Life*, ed. Charles Lillard (1868; Victoria: Sono Nis, 1987); Philip Druckner, *The Northern and Central Nootkan Tribes*, Bureau of American Ethnology, Bulletin 144 (Washington, DC: Smithsonian Institution, 1951); and Eugene Arima and John Dewhirst, "Nootkans of Vancouver Island," in *Northwest Coast*, ed. Wayne Suttles, vol. 7 of *Handbook of North American Indians*, ed. William C. Sturtevant (Washington, DC: Smithsonian Institution, 1990).

20 March 3, 1829, entry in Morag Maclachlan, ed., *The Fort Langley Journals, 1827–30* (Vancouver: UBC Press, 1998), 99.

21 November 13, 1828, entry in Maclachlan, *Fort Langley Journals*, 85.

22 James Andrew Grant, "An Unsung Pioneer: Life and Letters of James Murray Yale and his 30 years at Fort Langley," typescript, BC Archives, Add. Ms. 182, pt. 3, p. 55.

23 March 3, 1829, entry in Maclachlan, *Fort Langley Journals*, 99.

24 January 14, 1830, entry in Maclachlan, *Fort Langley Journals*, 137.

25 Archibald McDonald, Report, February 25, 1830, reproduced in Maclachlan, *Fort Langley Journals*, 222.

26 July 3, 1829, entry in Maclachlan, *Fort Langley Journals*, 118.

27 March 16, 1829, entry in Maclachlan, *Fort Langley Journals*, 101.

28 March 20, 1829, entry in Maclachlan, *Fort Langley Journals*, 102.

29 May 28, 1830, entry in Maclachlan, *Fort Langley Journals*, 149.

30 July 3, 1829, entry in Maclachlan, *Fort Langley Journals*, 118.

31 July 3, 1829, entry in Maclachlan, *Fort Langley Journals*, 118.

32 July 3, 1829, entry in Maclachlan, *Fort Langley Journals*, 118–19.

33 July 13, 1829, entry in Maclachlan, *Fort Langley Journals*, 120.

34 See Jean Barman, "Family Life at Fort Langley," in this volume. Descendants under the leadership of Lisa Pepin maintain a website entitled "The Children of Fort Langley" at http://www.fortlangley.ca/.

35 This time period is incisively probed in Adele Perry, *On the Edge of Empire: Gender, Race, and the Making of British Columbia, 1849–1871* (Toronto: University of Toronto Press, 2001).

36 "Dance-Houses," *British Colonist* (Victoria), December 29, 1861; "The Squaw Dance House," *Evening Express* (Victoria), January 20, 1864; "Police Court," *Daily Press* (Victoria), July 22, 1862; "A Relapse into Barbarism," *Evening Express*, October 15, 1863; "Fire Department," *Daily Press*, January 15, 1862.

37 Philip J. Hankin, "Reminiscences," BC Archives, Add. Mss. E/B/H19A.

38 Francis E. Herring, *In the Pathless West: With Soldiers, Pioneers, Miners, and Savages* (London: T. Fisher Unwin, 1904), 173.

39 Hankin, "Reminiscences."

40 "Squaw Dance House."

41 For a succinct introduction see Charles Lillard and Terry Glavin, *A Voice Great Within Us* (Vancouver: New Star Books, 1998).

42 Hankin, "Reminiscences."

43 "Squaw Dance House."

44 February 1, 1862, entry in Bishop George Hills diary, in Anglican Church, Ecclesiastical Province of British Columbia, Archives.

45 Hankin, "Reminiscences."

46 Homi Bhabha, "Of Mimicry and Man," in *The Location of Culture* (London: Routledge, 1994), 86.

47 August 12, 1860, entry in Hills diary.

48 Nancy Stepan, *The Idea of Race in Science: Great Britain 1800–1960* (London: Macmillan, 1982), 4.

49 Prince Albertiana, "A Civilized Song of the Solomons," *Daily Press*, March 10, 1862.

50 "Prostitution Recognized by Government," *British Colonist*, June 2, 1862.

51 Anne McClintock, *Imperial Leather: Race, Gender and Sexuality in the Colonial Contest* (New York: Routledge, 1995), 56.

52 Richard Phillips, *Sex, Politics and Empire: A Postcolonial Geography* (Manchester: Manchester University Press, 2006), 220.

4

Indigenous Women on the Streets of Victoria

Rethinking Transgressive Sexuality during the Colonial Encounter

In the years following the gold rush of 1858, "Indigenous women on the streets of Victoria were, almost by definition, 'prostitutes' or 'crones,'" a difference that depended on their effect on newcomer men. The definition of Indigenous women as essentially licentious gave these men equal licence to "seduce them with impunity, without accountability." Barman extends this insight to examine how a variety of male interests collided in discourses around Indigenous women in Victoria. These women came to sell clams, berries, potatoes, and other goods; to work as servants in hotels and private homes; to work in dance halls; and some, indeed, to work in the sex trade. The city fathers were torn between pleasing taxpayers concerned with respectability and the businessmen who saw dance halls staffed by Indigenous women as a way to keep free-spending miners in Victoria for the winter. Clergymen and missionaries, whose income depended on defending morality, revealed the most racist attitudes as they gloried in the moral superiority that they gained by depicting Indigenous women as abject victims and attacking those who did not agree with their extreme views on moral purity. Their goal was to remove these women to far-off reserves where their behaviour could be better controlled. This chapter includes a cameo appearance by Amor de Cosmos, supposed moral reformer and holder of many elected positions during the colonial period and later, including as the second premier of the province and member of the Canadian House of Commons. He appears here in a less elevated context. A policeman, finding him drunk and looking for an Indigenous prostitute, sent him home.

By Jean Barman. Original title "Aboriginal Women on the Streets of Victoria: Rethinking Transgressive Sexuality during the Colonial Encounter." Reprinted with permission from *Contact Zones: Aboriginal and Settler Women in Canada's Colonial Past*, edited by Katie Pickles and Myra Rutherdale (Vancouver: UBC Press, 2005), 205–27. Winner of Canadian Committee on the History of Sexuality Award (2006) for best article on the history of sexuality in Canada published during the past two years. Special thanks go to Chris Hanna for his research into early Victoria newspapers.

"Mary went to Victoria w[ith] Beans," William Hughes wrote on July 27, 1859, and the next day, "Mary A[arrived] from Victoria."[1] As his diary makes clear, Irishman William Hughes, his Cowichan Indian wife Mary Salslawit, and their children were engaged in a collaborative enterprise. He managed the day-to-day work on their small holding just outside of the coal mining village of Nanaimo on south central Vancouver Island, and she took charge of the commercial end. She sold not just beans, but potatoes as well, in the colonial capital of Victoria, and also in Nanaimo, to get the cash needed to support their young family at a mostly subsistence level.

All was not, however, quite so straightforward as Hughes's diary entries suggest. Each time Mary Salslawit made the trip to the capital of the British colony of Vancouver Island, she was transformed into something quite different than what she was in her everyday life. Indigenous women on the streets of Victoria were, almost by definition, either "prostitutes" or "crones." It was the presence or absence of physical desire in newcomer men that determined their identities. In the first instance, appearance, manner of dress, the way they behaved—all of the differences that separated them from the women these men knew back home—shouted out that they were willing and waiting for the first male who came along and might show them the least interest.

By repeatedly putting this image into words, newcomers gave it an authority that has survived remarkably intact to the present day. The Victoria press referred, often almost in passing, to "prostitution, so common with Northern [Indian] women," to "women have[ing] rendered the whole outskirts of the town a perfect brothel," and to how "the squaws might all be considered as prostitutes."[2] Exemplary is a lead editorial in the *British Colonist* newspaper, run by political activist Amor de Cosmos, that asserted early in 1861 how "[all the Indian] men to-day are a horde of thieves and cut-throats, and the women a community of prostitutes."[3] In a much-cited guide to British Columbia published in London in 1865, following five years' residence in Victoria, Congregational minister Matthew MacFie evoked "scenes after sunset calculated to shock even the bluntest sensibilities," "crowds of the more debased miners strewed in vicious concert with squaws on the public highway," and "hundreds of dissipated white men [who] live in open concubinage with these wretched creatures."[4] Some later descriptions are not dissimilar, as with British Columbia historian Robin Fisher's seminal *Contact and Conflict*:

> Some settlers did form temporary liaisons with Indian women, but more commonly they provided merely a temporary satisfaction of desires ... Large numbers of Indian women from the north came to Victoria annually to earn money by prostitution ... So-called "squaw dance houses," brothels, and Indian women dressed up as fine as "'White Soiled Doves' do in California" were all features of certain streets in Victoria in the early 1860's.

In Fisher's view, "prostitution was [just] another problem" among the various "social ills" besetting newcomers to Victoria.[5]

Such a perspective is far too neat and tidy to be left unexamined. Not only does it assume a single, generic definition of something called "prostitution" from a wholly newcomer perspective. It also trivializes and essentializes Indigenous women. They are, in effect, given agency, but only to do wrong. I am not so much doubting contemporary observers' credibility as I am wanting to understand what newcomers saw, why they saw what they saw, and what were the consequences for Indigenous women.

My argument has two parts. The first is consistent with the findings of a recent generation of scholars.[6] In Victoria, as in other colonial outposts around the world, Indigenous women had to be portrayed as sexually transgressive in order for men away from home and home life to be able to seduce them with impunity, without accountability. All behaviour unlike that of women whence newcomers came was equated with prostitution, with a willingness to provide sexual favours if remunerated. Women who claimed space on the streets, dared to occupy their own homes independent of men, or socialized in dance halls were particularly suspect.

The second part of my argument has not, so far as I am aware, been extensively examined by other scholars. Just as women were not alike, not all men were alike. The gratification newcomer men sought from Indigenous women differed considerably. For one set of stakeholders it was physical gratification, for another economic gain, for a third political advantage, and for a fourth a kind of moral rape. The women themselves were not pawns. They acted and they resisted. They often did so in settings where their options were far narrower than they themselves might have considered them to be.

The events themselves are not much in dispute. The northwest corner of North America comprising the present-day Canadian province of British Columbia was a fur trade outpost, loosely under British oversight, until gold was discovered on the mainland adjacent to Vancouver Island some nine years after the California rush of 1849. News of the finds transformed Victoria, near which lived the Songhees people, from a very small company town servicing the fur trade into a way station for thousands of newcomers hoping to get rich quick and be on their way. Esquimalt, the British naval port about three miles away, became the entryway for boatloads of men arriving in waves from California and elsewhere over some seven or eight years of gold fever. Hundreds of entrepreneurs brought supplies north with them to open shops. By the end of 1858 two British colonies, Vancouver Island and British Columbia on the mainland, existed side by side. Other newcomers, most often from England or British North America, serviced the two colonies as government officials, newspaper editors (such as Amor de Cosmos), and clerics (like Matthew MacFie). Victoria quickly became a bustling emporium that not only provisioned men on the way to the gold fields but also housed many of them over the winter when bad weather prevented mining, particularly as the gold rush moved north into the Cariboo region. Several thousand north coast peoples—Tsimshian, Haida, and others—were already travelling to Victoria each year to sell furs, carved goods, and their labour.[7] They continued to camp around its edges, wherever they could haul their large canoes ashore, on a seasonal basis during the gold rush years.

Such a mix of peoples gave a variety of opportunities for contact between Indigenous women and newcomers. As a close reading of newspaper accounts, government records, and other contemporary sources makes clear, Indigenous women walked the streets of Victoria and engaged in other activities for a far greater variety of purposes than what newcomers reduced to prostitution. A considerable number lived there with fur traders or miners, or as part of Indigenous families. An arrival of 1862 encountered, "scattered over the town, groups of dirty and stolid Indians, in many-colored blankets, with their squaws and little red-skins."[8] Many women, like Mary Salslawit, came to trade. Yet others, as one observer put it, were "employed as servants in our dwellings and in the culinary departments of our restaurants and hotels."[9] A poem of 1862 included a sidebar testifying to Indigenous women's workaday world on the streets of Victoria:

> Next morn the sun has risen
> Higher o'er Victoria Town,
> Whiskey shops are opening
> And shutters going down.
> Along the streets with turned-in feet,
> The squaws are kloc-kloc crying out their wares for sale.[10]

Another rhyme evoked women as "sinking under loads of berries, ... loudly crying 'klosh olilly,' fiercely shouting k-k-clams."[11] Indigenous women, in other words, had every reason to be on the streets of Victoria.

All the same, it was the word "prostitution" that won out, a term as revealing of newcomers' assumptions as it was of the women themselves. The societies from which most men came conceived the sex act as acceptable only within the confines of legal marriage and then for the purposes of procreation. Intimations of sexuality or activities perceived as encouraging sexual desire indicated a tendency toward promiscuity wholly out of tune with proper behaviour. Female sexual independence was the ultimate threat to the patriarchal family of the nineteenth century. As succinctly summed up by George Stocking, for Victorian England, "if the ideal wife and mother was 'so pure-hearted as to be utterly ignorant of and averse to any sensual indulgence,' the alternate cultural image of the 'fallen woman' conveys a hint of an underlying preoccupation with the threat of uncontrolled female sexuality."[12] Gail Hawkes, among others, describes how "prostitution provided a forum within which to express, covertly, anxieties about, and fascination with, the characteristics of women's sexuality."[13] Merely by virtue of being on the streets of Victoria, Indigenous women misbehaved, and thereby need not be treated with the same proprieties as their newcomer counterparts. These women were made, so to speak, the authors of their own destiny.

Victoria during the gold rush shared in the distinctive circumstances of colonial frontiers.[14] If unspoken and for the most part unwritten, it was generally accepted in the societies whence men came that, so long as women of their own kind were absent, Indigenous women could be used to satisfy what were perceived as men's natural needs. Differences in everyday behaviour, appearance, and skin tone conveniently confirmed that Indigenous women were not just sexually transgressive but racially inferior.[15] As Adele Perry has described in *On the Edge of Empire*, newcomer women not already taken as wives were few and far between during the British Columbia gold rush.[16] Given such circumstances, few scruples existed over what the pioneering scholar on race Philip Mason has termed "the casual use of a social inferior for sexual pleasure."[17] Indigenous women's transformation into prostitutes eliminated any sense of guilt even as it enabled satisfaction. Anne McClintock perceptively observes how "prostitutes flagrantly demanded money for services middle-class men expected for free."[18] Newcomer men did not want to need Indigenous women, but it was possible to use and abuse them as prostitutes with impunity.

The social contexts of Indigenous women's sexual contacts with newcomers varied. Some of the Songhees, Tsimshian, Haida, and other Indigenous women on the streets of Victoria had some experience with newcomers growing out of the fur trade. Its patterns of expected behaviour were, however, more predictable and less unsettling than the assumptions that arrived with the gold rush.[19] Indigenous women, moreover, came from a variety of cultural backgrounds, with distinctive notions of sexuality. In her doctoral thesis on the Tsimshian, Carol Cooper contends that "within their own societies there was little censure of Native women who engaged in sexual activity for payment."[20] Sexual relations were, Cooper explains, part of gift giving, a means to impart luck and power, and a way to cement alliances between different tribes.

Without doubt, many Indigenous women, and also some non-Indigenous women, did engage in sexual relations with newcomers outside of "marriage," in the newcomer sense of the word. The post journal from Fort Simpson noted in 1862 that "a larger number than usual of females are going to prostitute themselves."[21] A mining engineer exploring the Queen Charlotte Islands at about the same time recalled how "some Queen Charlotte women went to spend the Winter in Victoria, hoping to 'earn blankets,'" and "came back loaded with blankets, trinkets, tobacco, whiskey, and other presents, which they proceeded to distribute among their peoples."[22] Some likely did very well, as indicated by a Haida man arrested in Victoria in December 1862 for stealing $210 in gold coin from an Indigenous woman described in the press as a "prostitute."[23] There was, of course, a tremendous downside. Long-time Victoria physician John Sebastian Helmcken wrote in his memoir about how "Hyder women and men came in flocks, to go away ruined forever—Indians from the North West coast met with the same fate, from which they have never and never will recover."[24] In 1867 the *British Colonist* raised the "taboo" subject of venereal disease, lamenting "the absence of any provision" for its "relief amongst the aborigines."[25] As Cooper acknowledges, "it is hard to estimate the number of Nisga'a and Coast Tsimshian [and other Indigenous] women who engaged in prostitution, and it is impossible to know the full circumstances of their entry into this activity."[26]

Three settings were particularly scrutinized for indications of sexual transgression. The first was the streets themselves. Victoria was sited around James Bay. Government buildings were located on the south side, from where a bridge ran across the bay into Government Street. The Hudson's Bay post lay just across the bridge on the north side, set back from Humboldt Street, known familiarly as Kanaka Road because of the many indigenous Hawaiian, or Kanaka, fur trade labourers who lived there. West along the water was Wharf Street, which farther north turned into Store Street. At the junction between the two streets another bridge ran west from Victoria to the Songhees village, or reserve, located at the tip of the Esquimalt peninsula. Running inland from the trading post was Fort Street, paralleled a couple of blocks to the north by Yates, where most shops were located.

Liquor often was the impetus to labelling Indigenous women on the streets of Victoria. It was illegal to sell or give spirits to Indians.[27] Charges against men caught doing so or otherwise abusing Indigenous women were commonplace. In August 1861 "a colored man, beat a squaw on Kanaka road." The report on his arrest commented how every night in that area along the waterfront "a number of whites and blacks, who consider themselves civilized beings, delight in getting squaws drunk" and seeing them misbehave.[28] Reports tended to belittle men's victims. In February 1862 "a respectable looking man, formerly attached to the police force" of Victoria, was charged with "assaulting a miserable, sickly-looking squaw, at the old bridge, on Sunday night last." The woman claimed he "had attempted to ravish her person," after giving her a blow on her head with his fist. The police officer making the arrest stated that "beating squaws was quite a common occurrence in the neighborhood of the bridge." The judge was unusually sympathetic, remarking that "the cowardly habit indulged in by certain men of beating squaws, was becoming quite as common as it was disgraceful."[29] Women might be enticed indoors, as with a watchmaker being discovered on an autumnal night in his apartment, "*en dishabíle*, giving a squaw a drink" of liquor.[30] A magistrate observed as late as November 1866 that "it was an every day occurrence for white men to rob klootchmen," the word in the Chinook trading jargon for Indigenous women.[31]

While women could be targeted anywhere, they were especially suspect on the road running from Victoria across the bridge through the Songhees reserve to the harbour at Esquimalt. A self-styled "new settler in this Colony" described in September 1860 how "on last Sunday afternoon I walked to Esquimalt and was more deeply pained than I can find words to express, to see the road lined for a considerable distance with troops of young Indian females evidently there for the purposes of prostitution."[32] A grand jury recommended a month later "that energetic measures be taken to suppress the Indian prostitution daily going on upon the Esquimalt Road."[33] Two years later came a report that "about 30 Indian women were observed sitting by the side of Esquimalt road, ready to entrap the unwary strangers who came on the steamer Brother Jonathan."[34]

A second set of accusations was levelled against women who occupied their own "cabins" or "shanties," or resided with other women, sometimes also men, in what were termed "squaw dens" or "brothels."[35] Some of the activity so easily condemned served multiple purposes for a kind of demi-world along the waterfront that crossed racial lines in search of everyday survival and sociability. A report of July 1860 referred to "the Indian brothels on Store street and its vicinity, and in other parts of the town, used as they are for the still worse purpose of selling liquor to the Indians."[36] Many accounts are tentative, as with a report the next September that "late on Monday night a quantity of clothing was stolen from a squaw ranch on or near Broad street," just north of the fur trade post. The items "belonged to a white man, who professes to believe that one of his dusky friends took them."[37] A year later the *British Colonist* newspaper editorialized about "the state of moral degradation into which a number of the *habitues* and residents of Kanaka road have fallen." The account described how "a continual howling nightly is maintained by the drunken wretches who occupy or visit the miserable huts that have been erected along the bank of James Bay." As to the remedy: "The Indian women should be sent to the [Songhees] Reserve to live, and the white and black men who glory in keeping them proceeded against under the Vagrancy Act—for we hazard nothing in saying that very few, if any, of their number can show an honest means of obtaining a living."[38] A report to Victoria city council in September 1862 described "a number of houses of ill-fame on Humboldt street, with Indian women."[39]

Such women were almost inherently suspect at a time when females were expected to live visibly subservient to their fathers, husbands, or sons. Indicative is the court case of May 1860 against a Hawaiian named Na'hor who lived with his daughters and an Indigenous woman, likely also with others, in a house on the waterfront on Humboldt Street.[40] The police officer who instigated the charge testified: "Every time I pass the house I see five or six half breed women and Indian women and there are some half breed boys and kanakas in the same room together. I have seen both the squaws and kanakas drunk and disorderly on several occasions." A newcomer father and son testified that a young woman at Na'hor's house had, when they passed, called out to them in Chinook, "Cla-hoy-a," or "hello." The restaurant keeper for whom Na'hor worked testified on his behalf, saying Na'hor had told him he could not control his daughters.[41] Na'hor was convicted and imprisoned for two weeks.[42] A warning in a Victoria newspaper followed two years later suggesting that "the gentlemen who are in the habit of going around at a very late hour knocking at the doors of private residences in search of squaws had better be a little more careful," or they would end up in the police court.[43] The next spring the principal of the public school, located on Fort Street, made a charge of assault against his next-door neighbour, who he considered to be "the keeper of a squaw den." The principal did so in the hopes of having "the disreputable squaw harem which the prisoner kept cleared away from the neighborhood."[44] Over time, "Indian shanties" became concentrated along Humboldt Street, also on Cormorant and Fisgard Streets just north of Yates.[45] The Superintendent of Police claimed in August 1865 that "there are no less than 200 Indian Prostitutes living ... in filthy shacks."[46]

Agitation over Indigenous women on the streets of Victoria or in their own accommodations paled before a third form of activity. Dance halls were a form of sociability brought north from the California gold rush. The difference between those in San Francisco and the dance halls that sprang up in Victoria, in the mainland capital of New Westminster, and across the gold fields was, one account noted scornfully, that in California "the females were at least civilized."[47] Many believed, as did one letter writer, that "a dance hall is only a hell hole where the females are white: but it is many times worse where the females are squaws," as they were in the colonies of Vancouver Island and British Columbia.[48]

Dance halls operated in remarkably similar fashion, whatever their location. As one participant recalled: "25 cents (about a shilling) was the entrance fee, and there was a kind of master of ceremonies who called out the figures—'first gent to the left with the left hand round, back again and turn'—'balance in a line'—it was really wonderful what a good time they all kept and how serious they all were about it."[49] Among the dances led by "the dulcet strains of a fiddle," "a violin, bass viola, and a brass instrument," perhaps only by a "fifer," were cotillions, waltzes, and the "Lancers" and "Julien's Quadrilles."[50] New Westminster novelist Francis Herring described how "each man paid fifty cents for a dance, and had to 'stand drinks' at the bar for himself and his dusky partner after each."[51] This was how dance halls made their money.

> When the Quadrille was finished "Waltz up to the bar" was shouted out in a very loud voice—when every one did so at once, and we all had a drink and our partners generally took lemonade, or ginger ale. 50 cents was charged for each drink whatever it might be so one can easily understand what a good profit was made. Sometimes champagne was ordered. I should be sorry to say what it was made of but it always cost $10 a bottle.[52]

At a Victoria dance hall, "a buff of conversation and a rush to the bar" was quickly followed by "the poppings of soda-water corks and the munchings of apples."[53] As for communication, one attendee recalled that Indigenous women "had learned a little English and all the men could speak Chinook more or less, which was the lingua franca of British Columbia and Vancouver Island."[54]

Dance halls followed the miners, operating on a seasonal basis. Contemporary newspaper accounts make it possible to pinpoint their locations around Victoria. A dance hall existed from the fall of 1860 to at least early 1862 on Humboldt Street.[55] Others opened in the autumn of 1861 in the former "market building" and in at least two other locations along Fort Street.[56] In the autumn of 1863 dance halls appeared on the corner of Government and Johnson Streets, the latter paralleling Yates a block to the north, and also a bit farther away from the centre "on the flats between Fisgard street and the Gas Works ... in the immediate vicinity ... of the Esquimalt road."[57] In autumn 1864 they turned up on Johnson and Store Streets, in January and again in October 1865 on Cormorant Street, and so on.[58]

The association of dance halls with prostitution rested more on supposition than on hard evidence. The *British Colonist* asserted in December 1861: "They are sinks of iniquity and pollution. Prostitution and kindred vices, in all their hideous deformity, and disease in every form lurk there."[59] Another account ran: "Squaws reel home drunk at the dead hour of the night, in company with boisterous and scarcely less graceless white companions ... We will not say anything about the notions of refinement and taste, which these Dancing Dervishes will inculcate amongst the patrons of such halls of gaiety."[60]

The repeated condemnations of Indigenous women as sexual transgressors, be it on the streets of Victoria, in their houses, or in dance halls, gave enormous benefit to four groups of male stakeholders. Each was enabled to make use of them for their own purposes. In each case a form of gratification was sought—physical, economic, political, or moral.

Physical gratification was the most straightforward. The arrival of many thousands of men had its consequences, hence an American miner's description of that heady, first summer of 1858.

> There were over ten thousand miners in Victoria, and the Indians from up north in their large war canoes, some of which held from 75 to 100 men, were trading with the Hudson's Bay Company's stores, and the squaws got badly demoralized, and the miners

> had plenty of money to spend with them, and they gave them whiskey and there was an awful time among them, and they dressed up as fine as "White Soiled Doves" do in California.[61]

A minority of contemporaries condemned this first group of stakeholders, as in descriptions of "the lust, vice, and brutality of the deprived white men" seeking "to gratify their basest passions."[62] More often there was some attempt at justification as in this "Plea for the Dance-Houses" from the *British Colonist*:

> I think you will allow that in a town containing a large predominance of *men*, and men who, by their mode of life (even suppose them to be so inclined), are precluded from marriage, it is almost, if not totally impossible, to prevent prostitution. There is a great evil there can be no doubt; but under the circumstances I fear it is a necessary evil.[63]

As late as 1865, by which time the gold rush was moderating, there were still over four times as many newcomer men as women in Victoria.[64] Everywhere else the proportions were far more skewed.

For miners, would-be miners, former fur traders and their sons, and just plain adventurers who passed through Victoria during these years, Indigenous women offered pleasure for the moment and sometimes for longer periods of time. Their appeal is evident in the description of the "lady friend" of a man charged in court in April 1862 with "giving wine to Indians, and for haunting a house of ill-fame." She "made quite a neat little Chinook speech in his favour, and with her forensic eloquence, brilliant sallies of wit, and sparkling black eyes, exerted so profound an influence in favor of the accused, that the charge of whisky giving was dismissed."[65]

Then there was William Giles, described as "a native of one of the Western States of America," "a Caribooite, commonly known as 'Jack of Clubs,'" and "half-miner, half-sporting man."[66] Giles was fined £1 in February 1862 for being drunk "and assaulting an [Haida] Indian woman named Jenny," who was in turn fined five shillings for being drunk and disorderly.[67] Just a week later rumours began to circulate, after he had some "difficulty with Jenny," of young Giles's murder. Wintering in Victoria, he had been visiting Jenny regularly in the Haida encampment, and it was mooted her family had taken their revenge. About a hundred of Giles's social set "armed themselves with revolvers and proceeded to the encampment, where they had commenced to examine the huts, when a *posse* of Police arrived and conducted the search." Located, Jenny said "she was drunk all night and does not remember having seen Jack at all."[68] The next morning the sporting Jack-of-Clubs turned up alive and well, being shaved in a barber's chair, about the same time as Jenny was once again charged with being "drunk and disorderly."[69] Giles arrived in time to retrieve her just as the case ended, and the "next morning was seen a-drinking tea with his Jenny by his side."[70] Some such relationships made it through the winter, if not longer. Two months after the Jack-of-Clubs incident the steamer *Otter* departed for New Westminster with a load of men headed to the gold fields, an event, a Victoria newspaper reported, "much enhanced by the howling of four forlorn *clootchmen*, whose 'husbands' were aboard the steamer bound for Cariboo."[71]

A second group of stakeholders sought economic gratification from Indigenous women. Helmcken put the argument squarely: "Miners used to come to Victoria with lots of gold and exchange it for U.S. coin—this they absolutely squandered—chiefly in brothels or gin shops—so these places flourished and so did dance houses."[72] It was not just that miners patronized Indigenous women, but rather that the women's presence caused miners to be in Victoria in the first place. The London *Times* correspondent observed in November 1859 that many of the miners "would winter in Victoria did the place afford attractions which would relieve the monotony of life, ... but at present we have no places of amusement—no theaters nor 'dance houses,' which afford the miners so much pleasure and recreation."[73] A newspaper editorial acknowledged some time later:

> Without amusements Victoria is a dull place. Miners complain that they can enjoy themselves just as well at the Fraser River towns [on the British Columbia mainland] as here. Many will leave, we fear, on the next steamer for San Francisco, and money that might just as well have been spent here, will go to further enrich our American neighbours, who already enjoy the lion's share of the products of our mines.[74]

Dance halls gave the answer. The police magistrate acknowledged in December 1861 that he had been "induced to allow the Dance house to be opened to afford amusement to the miners."[75] As one observer soothed Victorians, "There are public dance-houses in San Francisco as well as in most any sea town of importance," and "this does not hurt their reputation."[76] A letter to the editor a few months later paraded dance halls' economic advantages:

> As long as they are kept open more or less of them [miners] will frequent such places, for the very reason that they have no place else to go to while away an hour or two. Miners, as a general rule, are used to an active life; but when they come down here to pass away the winter they soon become tired—having nothing to occupy their minds, and consequently they wander around and through the town in quest of excitement, and naturally hop into every hole and corner whence a little fun is to be had.[77]

It is hardly surprising that a poem written to celebrate Jack-of-Clubs's supposed murder talked about how "the town was filled with mourning ... and few they were that did repair to the squaw dance-house."[78]

Two economic interests fed off Indigenous women. The first was a handful of Victoria businessmen and government officials who invested in dance halls. The most persistent rumours pointed to Vancouver Island Attorney General George Hunter Cary, real estate agent John J. Cochrane, and other unnamed "dignitaries" as having "a high stake in the dancing house building on Fort street" constructed in the fall of 1861.[79] As each new dance hall opened, the press speculated as to who might be financing and then profiting from it.

The second group comprised small businessmen, some of them Jewish merchants who had operated along bustling Yates Street since arriving from San Francisco early in the gold rush.[80] Represented among seventy-seven "inhabitants of the City of Victoria" who in November 1862 requested that a dance hall be permitted to open over the winter was virtually every Yates Street occupation—tobacconist, newsman, grocer, clothier, boot maker, dry goods merchant, hotelier, saloon keeper. "We think it will be a benefit to the City to retain the miners here, as they all bespeak of some such place of entertainment," they wrote.[81] That autumn had, according to a contemporary's recollection, "witnessed the return from Cariboo of a large number of miners with heavy swags of gold dust [who] seemed to find difficulty in getting rid of their money."[82] The signatories were determined to capture that wealth by keeping the men in Victoria over the winter. For both investors and shopkeepers, Indigenous women were incidental but essential.

Indigenous women were also used for political advantage. These years saw a plethora of attempts to regulate and deregulate their presence on the streets of Victoria.[83] As of 1860 a law prohibited Indigenous people from remaining in Victoria after dusk, and repeated efforts were made, as indicated by the police magistrate's charge book, "to enforce it against the women" and thereby have the streets "cleared from a nuisance which has long infested them."[84] In April 1861 "orders were given to the officers of the police force, to prohibit squaws from promenading our streets after 7 o'clock, P.M., and to prevent their entering till after 6 A.M."[85] Another spate of arrests followed, but, as with most nuisance bylaws, enforcement was spasmodic.[86]

Political power became more concentrated with the incorporation of the city of Victoria on August 2, 1862, bringing into existence a mayor and council distinct from the colonial officials who had formerly been in charge.[87] A petition requesting that dance halls be permitted to operate another season hit the new council early in its mandate. The previous autumn, the police magistrate had sanctioned their opening; now it was council's decision.[88] Politics had a class dimension, one observer pointed out: "Be it remembered that citizens may have their private halls, but these assuredly are not for those miners who are unacquainted in town and who moreover might not be thought refined enough to partake in them."[89] Not only that; dance halls also served to get Indigenous women off the streets of Victoria, for which politicians could then take credit. "Yesterday [Christmas day] when no theatre nor dance-houses were open, more inebriate men were parading the streets than in preceding days" a *Colonist* writer reported, then queried: "Is dancing worse than to get beastly drunk!"[90] According to another commentator, "the falling off [of] the Indian whiskey trade is imputed to the establishment of the Dance Houses."[91]

Newspaper reports of the council meeting in November 1862 that considered the small businessmen's request for dance halls indicate general opposition among the councillors, who occupied such mid-range white-collar occupations as architect, commission merchant, clerk, and druggist.[92] "The Council generally spoke in condemnatory terms of the application, with the exception of Mr. [Richard] Lewis [architect], who thought that if conducted in a proper way, the existence of such an establishment as that petitioned for, might be of benefit to the town."[93]

In the end the matter was too hot for the council to handle. It voted unanimously to refer it to Mayor Thomas Harris, a butcher by trade, who appears to have given tacit consent to construction on the condition the buildings would be located farther away from the town centre than they had been in the previous year.[94] Very soon rumours were flying that "a dance-house is being built in the hollow near the gas-works, under the sanction of his Worship the Mayor, who our informant says, believes that the 'boys' should have an opportunity to enjoy themselves during the long winter evenings."[95] Despite opposition petitions, the first dance hall opened, its licence apparently signed by the mayor.[96] Council could no longer duck the issue. After a contentious, unresolved debate on "prohibiting persons from harboring squaws within the city limits," council in late December 1862 passed a more moderate motion "that squaw dancing houses within the city limits are a nuisance and the parties keeping such are amenable to the same penalties as are competent to be levied in the case of any other nuisance under the ordinance on nuisances."[97] In the interests of conciliating their bases of support, politicians had come full circle from the earlier nuisance bylaw whereby Indigenous women were able to be harassed merely for being on the streets of Victoria.

The fourth group of stakeholders sought moral gratification. If individuals were sometimes ham-handed, economic groups not that intrusive, and politicians unable to act decisively, the virtuous had no hesitation in using Indigenous women for their own purposes. The quest for moral gratification was the most significant in its consequences over the long run. Indigenous women had to be seduced—no, raped. They had to be overpowered, stripped of their agency and their dignity, for missionaries, clerics, and other self-styled reformers to fulfill the purposes for which many of them came to Victoria in the first place. These men's ambition knew no bounds, being grounded in a racism more strident and unforgiving than that expressed by any other stakeholder group in gold rush Victoria.

From the outset, race mattered, as evidenced in Amor de Cosmos's fiery editorials in his *British Colonist* newspaper. The absolute assurance with which he pontificated in early 1861 that Indigenous women were "a community of prostitutes" lay in his conviction that they belonged to "an *inferior* race." Indigenous peoples' "indolent habits, dishonest disposition and intellectual degradation" meant that they must give way to "a race more enlightened, and by nature and habits better fitted to perform the task of converting what is now a wilderness into productive fields and happy homes."[98]

Clerics and missionaries built on this moral fervour, often heightening the rhetoric. Indicative was a letter to the editor from Methodist minister Ephraim Evans at a time when the dance halls were causing much public debate. In his view, the only persons who could possibly support them were those "who for the sake of the paltry fees of admittance and other unavowed sources of emolument, are ready to pander to the lowest passions of their victims, regardless of the wide-spread destruction of health, morality, and public order to which they are contributing." The dance halls' clientele, he asserted, consisted of "tangle wood manufacturers, illicit traders in small wares from the Indians, receivers of goods from parties whose possessory rights are not too strictly scrutinized, light-fingered gentry who are not scrupulous as to the means of acquisition; and kindred characters [who] are not to be confounded with an honest and industrial population," in which he included most miners. As for the women, "the only female participants in these 'Terpsichorean exercises' are the lowest order of the pagan community around us, degraded by vices unknown among them before the advent of their present white associates, and diffusing abroad disease and wretchedness." Like most clerics, Evans sought Indigenous peoples' complete separation from newcomers in order to give reformers like himself the best possible opportunity to carry out their "civilizing" work, and so wrote bitterly about how "crowds of depraved women" were "harboured in the dance houses until half the night is spent and then turned out to roam at large in their drunken excitement." For Evans, "the whole system of permitting them to frequent the town, or to live in its vicinity, is radically wrong."[99]

It was the smallpox epidemic of 1862–1863, more than any other factor, that did the moral reformers' work for them. Demographer Robert Boyd has estimated that the Indigenous population along the

British Columbia north coast halved to fourteen thousand, losses being the heaviest in areas of sustained contact with newcomers. According to Boyd, death claimed seven out of ten Songhees, leaving fewer than five hundred alive.[100] The morally virtuous were quick to depict smallpox as just punishment for past wickedness, "a fit successor to the moral ulcer that has festered in our doors throughout the last four years." Unanimity quickly developed that, to quote de Cosmos's *British Colonist*, "the entire Indian population should be removed ... to a place remote from communication with the whites." The interests of economic stakeholders were dismissed: "No half-way measures can be tolerated with safety; nor no whining about Indian trade can be allowed to interfere."[101] Shortly thereafter all Indians were evicted from the city of Victoria, excepting women living with newcomers, who could apply for a permit to remain.[102] Like all regulations, this one too proved imperfect. When a Spanish sailor died in January 1863 from smallpox, the press took great pleasure in asserting that "there are strong grounds for believing that the unfortunate man caught the infection when mingling amongst Indian women at the squaw dance house."[103]

For the morally virtuous, the dance halls became the symbol of the struggle between the forces of good and evil. They continued to operate, but the moral tide had turned, led not unexpectedly by clergymen. Stakeholders seeking political gain from using Indigenous women now also lost out. The nuisance bylaw was already being used against "squaw dance-houses" or "squaw halls," as well as against individual women,[104] but never quite so determinedly as in the campaign the Reverend Evans led in the autumn of 1864. Debating the issue a couple of years earlier, one of the more moderate city councillors had argued that, if "prostitution" were to be the grounds for action, "the law must be equally enforced without respect to race or nationality."[105] The righteous had no such compunctions about using race to serve their cause. Virtually as soon as a dance hall opened on Johnson Street, Evans, who lived nearby, persuaded a couple of neighbours to join him in a nuisance suit intended to shut it down.[106] The proceedings made abundantly clear how race and moral fervour had become joined, as in a witness's claim that, while he would not mind having a dance "in a genteel manner," he "would not dance with a squaw as she is not a lady."[107] A newspaper editorial supporting the suit asserted that "it was useless for it to be contended that white men frequent squaw dance houses for the purpose of innocent recreation and enjoyment. Everyone knew that their objects were fornication and prostitution."[108] The indicting jury's verdict was telling: "We find that the house in question has been conducted as well as possible for one of its character, but that this, or any other assemblage of squaws within the city limits, is a nuisance." At the sentencing hearing, the defence lawyer pointed out the verdict's absurdity in declaring, by definition, "an assemblage of squaws a nuisance."[109]

The press coverage of this and subsequent persecutions of dance halls became increasingly shrill. No longer did Indigenous women have to be portrayed as sexually transgressive in order to be labelled as prostitutes. They were assumed to be prostitutes by virtue of being racially inferior.[110] So it is not surprising that the Victoria police noted on June 18, 1866, how "all was quiet in town last night," excepting that "Constable Hough reports that Mr. [Amor] De Cosmos came on to his beat this morning at 1 a.m. drunk, and wanted the officer to shew him where he could get a squaw."[111] Indigenous women had become so wholly sexualized that even this most fervent moral reformer now found nothing wrong with using and abusing them.

Indigenous women did not, of course, know the end of the story, however certain it might appear in retrospect. Unaware that their fate was, in the larger scheme of things, sealed, they employed a variety of means to assert their autonomy on the streets of Victoria. Numerous ethnographic studies have described gender relations along the coast as more equitable than in the societies whence newcomers came.[112] As a descendant explained to me about Mary Salslawit's husband, William Hughes, "the Indian society his wife came from was matrilineal" and "she did what she would do regardless of who she was married to."[113]

So it is not surprising that Indigenous women repeatedly fought back. In January 1862 a woman turned up at the Victoria police barracks with a "white" man by the throat, having "actually dragged him [there], to be locked up as a witness." As to the reason, "the squaw had been assaulted by a friend of the captive," who had then run away.[114] A couple of weeks later, a Tsimshian women named Jenny charged an Irishman with assault: "Jenny stated that she was very nearly killed last night by the prisoner, who came to her house and wanted her company. She refused, and he went away but came back in a little time with a knife and said he would kill her. He beat her and kicked her on the arm."[115] Even when women acquiesced, they were in no way passive. In August 1860 a Portuguese man charged that "a Hydah squaw" who he had admitted to his house "for improper purposes" had "stolen $5 from his pantaloons pocket during the night."[116]

Dance halls and other forms of socialization gave Indigenous women very real opportunities in a world that, for many of them, had turned upside down. Faced with the disruption of traditional ways of everyday life, the dance halls provided a means, not only to make a bit of money, but also to learn to dress and behave as did their newcomer counterparts, and thereby, they may have hoped, to secure a measure of acceptance and even respectability. A press description of seven, mostly north coast, women arrested in May 1860 for loitering took particular pleasure in noting how "some of their hoops [were] so large that they could scarcely get inside the railing" at the prisoners' dock.[117] Anglican Bishop George Hills noted, at an encampment of north coast peoples, "a woman making up a dress" for the dance house that night.[118] An evocation of a dance hall described its participants as being "well and in some instances tastefully dressed," wearing "the silk dress and the dainty garter, with the air of a Parisian dame."[119]

Indigenous women's mimicry became cause for scorn, but they themselves were unaware of it, at least for a time. Bishop Hills ridiculed "the young women decked out in every sort of vulgar finery—even to the wearing of crinoline & hoops."[120] A newspaper reported in

February 1861 how "a Fort Rupert and a Stekeen squaw, each wearing immense hoops and a black silk dress," had got in a fight, much to a crowd's amusement.[121] A poem penned in 1862 and intended to be satirical was in its way quite flattering in evoking the fundamental shift instigated by the gold rush:

Only three years since, in blankets,
  Slovenly they rolled along,
Like old-fashioned Dutch-built vessels
  Lurching surging, in a storm.

Now Indigenous women had a very different appearance on the streets of Victoria:

Sound the voice of exultation,
  Let it everywhere be known,
That the Indians round Victoria
  Almost civilized have grown.
That the squaws in radiant colors,
  Dress'd in ample crinoline,
And with graceful tread of turkeys,
  And with proud and stately mien.
Down the streets like gay gondolas
  Gliding o'er Venetian stream
Every day and in all seasons,
  May thus constantly be seen.

The reason for the change was attributed directly to the dance halls.

Now they trip the gay cotillion,
  With an elephantine prance,
In the Market Company building,
  Glide they through the mazy dance.

The rhyme emphasized Indigenous women's agency, making clear that they themselves played a role in how the dance halls should operate:

> Without form of introduction,
> They will not allow their forms
> To be clasped in waltzing graces
> Or in polkas flighty charms.
> Not without a Caribooite
> On himself the task doth take,
> To present a brother miner
> Will a foot the klootchman shake.[122]

An attendee at a gold field dance house made a similar observation: "I recollect asking one of the Kitty's in Chinook to dance with me and she drew herself up in a very dignified manner and said 'Halo introduce' which signified I had not been introduced to her! And I couldn't help laughing which made her very angry."[123] It was much the same in New Westminster: "A strange miner going in one night, went to one of these 'maids of the forest' and intimated his desire for the pleasure of a dance with her. She eyed him with scorn and remarked, 'Halo introduce.' He accordingly had to hunt up some one who would do him the favor."[124]

Not just in the dance halls, but more generally, Indigenous women sought to behave in a manner consistent with the clothing they could now afford. A Victoria newspaper complained in November 1861 about the poor quality of the theatre, which "answers very well nowadays as a place of assignation for squaws and their paramours."[125] A fight in the theatre a year later revealed that the occupant of the adjoining store had been given "permission to introduce favorite squaws," which he described as his "particular friends," into the "boxes situated beneath the dress circle."[126] A visitor to Victoria in the fall of 1863 saw "a sort of San Francisco melodrama" with a "nigger melody," but was even more entranced by the audience, consisting "mostly of miners & rowdies with a gully set apart for the squaws (all prostitutes ... some very pretty)."[127] In retrospect, of course, all the women's efforts were in vain and only served to complete the equation as to how, as one account put it, "they wear hoops and are prostitutes!"[128]

It is difficult to know whether the various interest groups actually had anything to fear from permitting Indigenous women to exercise agency as opposed to using them for their own purposes. The concluding lines of the 1862 poem suggest—albeit a bit tongue-in-cheek—that, at least for a brief moment in time, the dance halls in particular might have been playing a greater role than were the morally virtuous or any of the other stakeholder groups in transforming traditional ways of life.

> What a sad and sober moral,
> Are we thus compelled to draw,
> From the missionary teachings—
> From the Christian's moral law.
> Years and years of good men's efforts
> Seem thus exercised in vain,
> Fiddle and the toe fantastic
> Is the way we're to reclaim
> All the Indian tribes around us,
> From their wild and savage life,
> And we'll teach them all the fashions,
> All the voices that are rife.
> And to ... those who have an interest
> In the Market Company [dance hall]
> Will we sing our loudest paeans
> Will we chant the greatest praise,
> For their calm and Christian efforts
> Teaching squaws the Christian's ways.[129]

In the event, Indigenous women were given little opportunity to adapt to changing circumstances, being suborned to stakeholders' goals. In Victoria, as elsewhere during the colonial encounter, most Indigenous women didn't stand a chance. It is clear that many Indigenous women living around Victoria did engage in sexual activity with newcomers. It is also clear that many others put themselves in situations where, so far as newcomers were concerned, it didn't much matter whether or not they actually did so. They were sexually transgressive merely by virtue of the differences that marked them out from newcomer women. This larger set of attitudes enabled the four interest groups to make use of them with impunity. Indigenous women's identification as prostitutes, alternately as crones, obscured their many other reasons for being on the streets of Victoria, be it selling beans, as with Mary Salslawit, hawking clams, going about their everyday lives as the wives of Indigenous or non-Indigenous men, working for wages as a servant or washerwoman, or perhaps also getting a bit of cash from evenings in the dance halls. Whatever their reasons for being there, Indigenous women were harassed to the margins, for the most part off the streets of Victoria, just as they have been in most accounts of the colonial encounter.

Notes

1 July 27 and 28, 1859, entries in William Hughes, "Diary kept by William Hughes of the parish of St. Paul's, City of Dublin, commenced Jan 1, 1857," Campbell River and District Museum and Archives.

2 "The Northern Indians," *British Colonist* (Victoria), September 7, 1861; "Editorial," *British Colonist*, April 18, 1861; "City Council," *British Colonist*, December 23, 1862.

3 "Indian vs. White Labor," *British Colonist*, February 19, 1861.

4 Matthew MacFie, *Vancouver Island and British Columbia: Their History, Resources, and Prospects* (London: Longman, Green, Longman, Roberts, and Green, 1865; reprinted Toronto: Coles, 1972), 471.

5 Robin Fisher, *Contact and Conflict: Indian-European Relations in British Columbia, 1774–1890* (Vancouver: UBC Press, 1977), 113.

6 Along with other scholars, Adele Perry makes a similar point in *On the Edge of Empire: Gender, Race, and the Making of British Columbia, 1849–1871* (Toronto: University of Toronto Press, 2001), esp. 54.

7 See John Lutz, "After the Fur Trade: The Aboriginal Labouring Class of British Columbia 1849–1890," *Journal of the Canadian Historical Association* 3 (1992): 71–5.

8 R. Byron Johnson, *Very Far West Indeed: A Few Rough Experiences on the North-West Pacific Coast* (London: Sampson Low, Marston, Low, and Searle, 1872, repr. 1985), 49.

9 "The Small-Pox Among the Indians," *British Colonist*, April 28, 1862.

10 "The Murder of 'Jack of Clubs,'" *Daily Press* (Victoria), March 4, 1862.

11 Prince Albertiana, "A Civilized Song of the Solomons," *Daily Press*, March 10, 1862.

12 George W. Stocking, Jr., *Victorian Anthropology* (New York: Free Press, 1987), 199–200, 202.

13 Gail Hawkes, *A Sociology of Sex and Sexuality* (Buckingham: Open University Press, 1996), 14–15, 42.

14 On the general character of prostitution on the frontier, see Anne M. Butler, *Daughters of Joy, Sisters of Misery: Prostitutes in the American West, 1865–90* (Urbana: University of Illinois Press, 1985). California shared many characteristics with British Columbia, as described in Albert Hurtado, *Intimate Frontiers: Sex, Gender, and Culture in Old California* (Albuquerque: University of New Mexico Press, 1999); Susan Lee Johnson, *Roaring Camp: The Social World of the California Gold Rush* (New York: W.W. Norton, 2000); and Susan Lee Johnson, "'My Own Private Life': Toward a History of Desire in Gold Rush California," in *Rooted in Barbarous Soil: People, Culture, and Community in Gold Rush California*, ed. Kevin Starr and Richard J. Orsi (Berkeley: University of California Press, 2000), 316–46.

15 One of the most revealing comparisons to gold rush Victoria is found in Eileen J. Suárez Findlay, *Imposing Decency: The Politics of Sexuality and Race in Puerto Rico, 1870–1920* (Durham, NC: Duke University Press, 1999). Findlay describes "the sexual and often racial demonization of particular marginalized groups—those who refuse to fit within the prescribed limits of morality and 'decency'" (10). She explains how, "in Puerto Rico from 1870 to 1920, such repressive episodes consistently centered on racially charged excoriation of unruly plebian women, who were labeled 'prostitutes'" (10, elaborated on 81).

16 Adele Perry, *On the Edge of Empire: Gender, Race, and the Making of British Columbia, 1849–1871* (Toronto: University of Toronto Press, 2001).

17 Philip Mason, *Patterns of Dominance* (London: Oxford University Press for the Institute of Race Relations, 1970), 88.

18 Anne McClintock, *Imperial Leather: Race, Gender and Sexuality in the Colonial Contest* (New York: Routledge, 1995), 56.

19 Jean Barman and Bruce Watson, "Fort Colville's Fur Trade Families and the Dynamics of Aboriginal Racial Intermixture in the Pacific Northwest," *Pacific Northwest Quarterly* 90, no. 3 (Summer 1999): 140–53.

20 Carol Ann Cooper, "'To Be Free on Our Lands': Coast Tsimshian and Nisga'a Societies in Historical Perspective" (PhD diss., University of Waterloo, 1993), 184.

21 Hamilton Moffatt and William H. McNeill, February 2, 1862, entry in Fort Simpson Journal, Hudson's Bay Company Archives, Winnipeg.

22 Francis Poole, *Queen Charlotte Islands: A Narrative of Discovery and Adventure in the North Pacific* (London: Hurst and Blackett, 1872), 313.

23 "Haida Joe," *Victoria Daily Chronicle*, December 27, 1862.

24 Dorothy Blakey Smith, ed., *The Reminiscences of Doctor John Sebastian Helmcken* (Vancouver: UBC Press, 1975), 186–87.

25 "Our Social Evil," *British Colonist*, October 22, 1867.

26 Cooper, "'To Be Free on Our Lands,'" 182.

27 *British Columbian and Victoria Directory, 1863*, published by Howard and Barnett (Victoria: Searby and Moore), 90, refers to the Indian Liquor Act, passed on November 24, 1860, which prohibited the sale or gift of spirits to Indians, but prosecutions occurred earlier, as with "Whiskey Cases," *British Colonist*, July 24, 1860, and "An Interesting Whiskey Affair," *British Colonist*, September 22, 1860.

28 "Beating a Squaw," *British Colonist*, August 24, 1861. Charles Mitchel was sentenced to pay costs and be on good behaviour for six months.

29 "Assaulting a Squaw," *British Colonist*, February 25, 1862.

30 "An Interesting Whiskey Affair," *British Colonist*, September 22, 1860. Antoine Fassovier was fined fifty dollars.

31 "Dismissed," *British Colonist*, November 27, 1866.

32 "To the Editor," *Victoria Gazette*, September 22, 1860.

33 "Grand Jury Report," *British Colonist*, October 6, 1860.

34 "Indian Prostitutes," *British Colonist*, July 13, 1862.

35 "Serious Charge against a Policeman," *British Colonist*, June 28, 1860; "Police Court," *British Colonist*, November 8, 1862; "Assault," *Evening Express* (Victoria), January 21, 1863; Smith, *Reminiscences of Doctor John Sebastian Helmcken*, 186–87.

36 "Grand Jury Report," *British Colonist*, July 5, 1860.

37 "Robbery of Clothes," *British Colonist*, September 24, 1860.

38 "A Disorderly Neighborhood." *British Colonist*, October 14, 1861.

39 "Town Council," *British Colonist*, September 5, 1862.

40 "A Brothel," *British Colonist*, May 29, 1860.

41 Session of May 28, 1860, Court records, Victoria, in BC Archives, GR419, box 1, file 1860/69.

42 Entries in Magistrate's Charge Book, Victoria, in BC Archives, GR848. Two years later Na'hor was charged with "keeping house of ill-fame."

43 "Caution!" *British Colonist*, December 29, 1862.

44 "Ruffianly Assault," *Evening Express*, June 25, 1863. The man, named Jackson, was fined five dollars or fourteen days, but nothing else seems to have happened.

45 "Licensing Court," *Evening Express*, October 6, 1864.

46 Philip Hankin, Superintendent of Police, to Colonial Secretary, August 25, 1865, in Colonial Correspondence, BC Archives, reel 118/1992.

47 "The Dance Houses," *Daily Press*, December 22, 1861.

48 "Dance House," *British Colonist*, November 29, 1862.

49 Philip J. Hankin, "Reminiscences," BC Archives, Add. Mss. E/B/H19A. The admission fee in Victoria in 1864 was also a "twenty five cent piece." See "The Squaw Dance House," *Evening Express*, January 20, 1864.

50 "Dance-Houses," *British Colonist*, December 29, 1861; "The Squaw Dance House," *Evening Express*, January 20, 1864; "Police Court," *Daily Press*, July 22, 1862; "A Relapse into Barbarism," *Evening Express*, October 15, 1863; "Fire Department," *Press*, January 15, 1862.

51 Francis E. Herring, *In the Pathless West: With Soldiers, Pioneers, Miners, and Savages* (London: T. Fisher Unwin, 1904), 173.

52 Hankin, "Reminiscences."

53 "The Squaw Dance House," *Evening Express*, January 20, 1864.

54 Hankin, "Reminiscences."

55 "Fight at the Dance House—A Man Stabbed," *British Colonist*, April 7, 1860; "Nearly a Row," *Press*, January 7, 1862. This was the area known as Kanaka Road.

56 "The Dance House," *British Colonist*, December 20, 1861; "Rev. Dr. Evans on the Dance Houses," *British Colonist*, December 25, 1861.

57 "The Projected Dance House" *Victoria Daily Chronicle*, November 30, 1862; "The Dance House," *British Colonist*, December 1, 1862.

58 "Squaw Dance Houses," *Evening Express*, November 7, 1864; "Squaw Dance Houses," *Evening Express*, November 25, 1864; "The 'Hall of Miscegenation,'" *Victoria Daily Chronicle*, January 16, 1865; "Squaw Dance House," *Victoria Daily Chronicle*, October 7, 1865.

59 "The Dance House," *British Colonist*, December 20, 1861.

60 "The Dance Houses," *Daily Press*, December 22, 1861.

61 Herman Francis Reinhart, *The Golden Frontier: The Recollections of Herman Francis Reinhart, 1851–1869*, ed. Doyce B. Nunn, Jr. (Austin: University of Texas Press, 1962), 143.

62 "City Morals," *Victoria Gazette*, September 29, 1860.

63 "A Plea for the Dance-Houses," *British Colonist*, December 23, 1861.

64 Philip Hankin, "Population of Victoria," January 20, 1865, in Police Department (Victoria), in BC Archives, Colonial Correspondence, file 1392.

65 "Police Court," *British Colonist*, April 17, 1862.

66 "Possible Murder of a Well Known Caribooite," *British Colonist*, February 26, 1862.

67 "Assault," *Daily Press*, February 17, 1862. Jenny was also ordered to enter £5 into security for good behaviour for two months, or suffer ten days' imprisonment.

68 "Possible Murder of a Well Known Caribooite," *British Colonist*, February 26, 1862.

69 "Drunk," *Daily Press*, February 26, 1862.

70 "The Murder of 'Jack of Clubs,'" *Daily Press*, March 4, 1862.

71 "Departure of the 'Otter,'" *British Colonist*, April 24, 1862.

72 Smith, *Reminiscences of Doctor John Sebastian Helmcken*, 186–87.

73 Donald Fraser, Victoria, November 10, 1859, in *Times* (London), December 28, 1859, BC Archives, E/B/F86.

74 "Theatricals," *British Colonist*, November 8, 1861.

75 "Brawl in the Dance House," *Daily Press*, December 16, 1861.

76 "The Dance-Houses," *British Colonist*, December 23, 1861.

77 "Dance Houses—Miners Not to Blame," *British Colonist*, December 24, 1861.

78 "The Murder of 'Jack of Clubs,'" *Daily Press*, March 4, 1862.

79 Prince Albertiana, "A Civilized Song of the Solomons," *Daily Press*, March 10, 1862; "Sale of the Market Company's Property," *British Colonist*, November 13, 1861; "Theatrical Change," *Press*, January 3, 1862.

80 See Cyril Edel Leonoff, *Pioneers, Pedlars, and Prayer Shawls: The Jewish Communities in British Columbia and the Yukon* (Victoria: Sono Nis, 1978), 27.

81 "City Council," *British Colonist*, November 8, 1862. The names were checked in Edward Mallandaine, *First Victoria Directory* (Victoria: Edward Mallandaine, March 1860), and in *British Columbian and Victoria Directory, 1863*.

82 D.W. Higgins, *The Mystic Spring and Other Tales of Western Life* (Toronto: William Briggs, 1904), 227.

83 Perry, *On the Edge of Empire*, esp. 110–19. Among the secondary literature on nineteenth-century efforts to regulate prostitution, a source with some comparability to Victoria and British Columbia is Joel Best, *Controlling Vice: Regulating Brothel Prostitution in St. Paul, 1865–1883* (Columbus: Ohio State, 1998).

84 "Squaws Arrested," *Victoria Gazette*, May 9, 1860. For examples of enforcement, see entries in Magistrate's Charge Book, Victoria, in BC Archives, GR848.

85 "A Move in the Right Direction," *Press*, April 19, 1861.

86 See, for instance, "A Move in the Right Direction," *Press*, April 19, 1861; "Loitering," *British Colonist*, August 21, 1863; "Loitering," *Evening Express*, September 18, 1863; "A Female Delinquent," *Evening Express*, December 2, 1863; "Malicious Mischief," *Evening Express*, December 2, 1863; and entries in Magistrate's Charge Book, Victoria, in BC Archives, GR848.

87 See *British Columbia and Victoria Directory, 1863*, 93.

88 "City Council," *British Colonist*, November 8, 1862.

89 "The Dance-Houses," *British Colonist*, December 23, 1861.

90 "Dance-Houses Again!" *British Colonist*, December 27, 1861.

91 "Whiskey Seller," *Press*, January 20, 1862.

92 The councillors' names were checked in Mallandaine, *First Victoria Directory* and *British Columbian and Victoria Directory, 1863*.

93 "City Council," *British Colonist*, November 8, 1862.

94 "Got a License," *Victoria Daily Chronicle*, December 3, 1862.

95 "Can Such Things Be?" *Victoria Daily Chronicle*, November 16, 1862.

96 "Judge Pemberton," *Victoria Daily Chronicle*, November 23, 1862; "Got a License," *Victoria Daily Chronicle*, December 3, 1862.

97 "City Council," *British Colonist*, December 23, 1862; Victoria Council, minutes of meeting, December 22, 1862, Victoria City Archives.

98 "Indian vs. White Labor," *British Colonist*, February 19, 1861. Italics in original.

99 "Rev. Dr. Evans on the Dance Houses," *British Colonist*, December 25, 1861.

100 Robert Boyd, *The Coming of the Spirit of Pestilence: Introduced Infectious Diseases and Population Decline among Northwest Coast Indians, 1774–1874* (Vancouver: UBC Press, 1999), esp. 229.

101 "The Small-Pox among the Indians," *British Colonist*, April 28, 1862.

102 "Prostitution Recognized by Government," *British Colonist*, June 2, 1862.

103 "Small Pox," *British Colonist*, January 21, 1863.

104 "A Relapse into Barbarism," *Evening Express*, October 15, 1863; "Go In!—The More the Merrier!" *British Colonist*, February 13, 1862; "Police Court," *Daily Press*, July 22, 1862; "Nymphs of the Pave[ment]," *Evening Express*, September 20, 1864; "Another Nuisance," *Vancouver Times*, December 8, 1864; "A Caution," *Vancouver Times*, July 2, 1865; "Police Court," *Vancouver Daily Post*, January 2, 1866.

105 "City Council," *British Colonist*, December 23, 1862.

106 "Squaw Dance Houses," *Evening Express*, November 7, 1864.

107 "The Squaw Dance House Nuisance," *British Colonist*, November 8, 1864.

108 "Autumn Assizes," *Evening Express*, November 17, 1864.

109 "Court of Assize," *Vancouver Times*, November 21, 1864.

110 See "Squaw Dance House," *Evening Express*, December 8, 1864; "The Squaw Dance House," *British Colonist*, December 10, 1864; "The Squaw Dance House," *British Colonist*, December 17, 1864; "Prosecution," *British Colonist*, January 16, 1865, "Failed," *Evening Express*, January 18, 1865.

111 June 18, 1866, entry in Police Sergeant's Report Book, Victoria, in BC Archives, GR308.

112 A useful introduction to this literature is William Sturtevant, ed., *Handbook of North American Indians* (Washington, DC: Smithsonian), esp. vol. 7, *Northwest Coast*.

113 Conversation with Danny Joyce, Campbell River, July 28, 1992.

114 "A Squaw Arrests a White Man,'" *British Colonist*, January 17, 1862. The woman demanded that the man "be locked up as a witness," and "the man appeared much frightened and asked the protection of the police, which was granted until the woman had left."

115 "Assault Case," *Press*, February 24, 1862. Patrick Finnegan had resources far beyond Jenny's words, hiring an attorney, who "claimed that Finnegan belonged to a country the men of which were noted for their defence of the fair sex, and that he had only entered the house for the purpose of protecting the squaw from the fury of the Indians when he was set upon by them." The magistrate responded somewhat dryly that Finnegan was not a policeman and should not have played that role, that "the woman had marks of violence on her person." To his credit, the magistrate fined Finnegan £3 or two months' imprisonment.

116 "Promptly Dismissed," *British Colonist*, August 24, 1860. The case brought by Gregory Fernandez was dismissed.

117 "Arrest of Street-Walkers," *British Colonist*, May 9, 1860.

118 February 1, 1862, entry in Bishop George Hills diary, in Anglican Church, Ecclesiastical Province of British Columbia, Archives.

119 "The Squaw Dance House," *Evening Express*, January 20, 1864.

120 August 12, 1860, entry in Bishop George Hills diary.

121 "Squaw Fight," *British Colonist*, February 15, 1861.

122 Prince Albertiana, "A Civilized Song of the Solomons," *Daily Press*, March 10, 1862.

123 Hankin, "Reminiscences."

124 Herring, *In the Pathless West*, 173.

125 "Theatricals," *British Colonist*, November 8, 1861.

126 "The Fight in the Theatre," *British Colonist*, November 22, 1862.

127 November 25, 1863, entry in Robert Brown, "Vol. II: Journal of British Columbia Botanical Expedition—From Nov 24, 1863 to Jan 29, 1864," in BC Archives, Ms. 794.

128 "Prostitution Recognized by Government," *British Colonist*, June 2, 1862.

129 Prince Albertiana, "A Civilized Song of the Solomons," *Daily Press*, March 10, 1862.

5

Taming Indigenous Sexuality

Gender, Power, and Race in British Columbia, 1850–1900

Barman begins this essay by recounting the case of Catholic Bishop Hubert O'Connor, tried for four counts of rape or indecent assault of four young Indigenous girls three decades after the event and convicted on two of the charges. In his defence, he maintained he was a "celibate man" and that he had been seduced. The essay treats "the lineage of his attitudes in the history of British Columbia." Barman notes that most history of British Columbia is written by men and from a male perspective, one which tends either to ignore the lives of women or to depict them in ways focusing on their sexuality (or, occasionally, on their regrettable lack of sexual appeal). Given the colonial norm of female modesty and submission, those Indigenous women who exercised autonomy were invariably seen as doing so in order to get money by prostituting themselves; in order to prevent this evil, almost anything was seen as justified, from forcible return home to flogging. Barman gives a useful overview of colonial and feminist theories on the issues while situating them in a particular location with its distinctive social life. She makes clear that every aspect of traditional Indigenous life, particularly important socio-economic customs such as the potlatch, was sexualized in order to justify the "taming" not only of Indigenous women, but also of their culture.

By Jean Barman. Original title "Taming Aboriginal Sexuality: Gender, Power, and Race in British Columbia, 1850–1900." Reprinted with permission from *BC Studies* 115–16 (1997–1998): 237–66. Winner of Joan Jensen-Darlis M ller Prize, awarded by the Coalition for Western Women's History for best article on the history of women west of the Mississippi.

In July 1996 I listened in a Vancouver courtroom as Catholic Bishop Hubert O'Connor defended himself against charges of having raped or indecently assaulted four young Indigenous women three decades earlier. His assertion of ignorance when asked what one of the complainants had been wearing on the grounds that, "as you know, I'm a celibate man," encapsulated his certainty that he had done nothing wrong.[1] He admitted to sexual relations with two of the women, but the inference was clear: they had made him do it. They had dragged him down and led him astray. The temptation exercised by their sexuality was too great for any mere man, even a priest and residential school principal, to resist.

I returned home from that day, and subsequent days in the courtroom, deeply troubled. I could have been reading any of hundreds of similar accounts written about Indigenous women in British Columbia over the past century and more. This essay represents my attempt to come to terms with Bishop O'Connor and his predecessors, made more necessary on reading the National Parole Board's decision of March 1997. The board denied Bishop O'Connor parole, subsequent to his conviction on two of the charges, because "your recent psychological assessment indicates that you hold your victims in contempt," and "at your hearing today ... you maintain that ... you in fact were seduced."[2] If I earlier considered that my response to my days in the courtroom might have been exaggerated, I no longer did so. My interest is not in Bishop O'Connor's guilt or innocence in a court of law, but rather in the lineage of his attitudes in the history of British Columbia.

The more I have thought about Bishop O'Connor, the more I realize that those of us who dabble at the edges of Indigenous history have ourselves been seduced. However much we pretend to read our sources "against the grain," to borrow from the cultural theorist Walter Benjamin, we have become entrapped in a partial world that represents itself as the whole world. Records almost wholly male in origin have been used by mostly male scholars to write about Indigenous men as if they make up the entirety of Indigenous people. The assumption that men and male perspectives equate with all persons and perspectives is so accepted that it does not even have to be declared. Thus, an American researcher wanting to find out about her Indigenous counterparts discovered that "indigenous communities had been described and dissected by white men—explorers, traders, missionaries, and scholars—whose observations sometimes revealed more about their own cultural biases than about Native people. Misperceptions of Indian women were rampant because they were held up to the patriarchal model."[3]

So what happens when we turn the past on its head and make our reference point Indigenous women instead of Indigenous men? We come face to face with Indigenous sexuality or, more accurately, with male perceptions of Indigenous sexuality. The term "sexuality" is used here in its sociological sense as "the personal and interpersonal expression of those socially constructed qualities, desires, roles and identities which have to do with sexual behaviour and activity," the underlying contention being "the social and cultural relativity of norms surrounding sexual behaviour and the sociohistorical construction of sexual identities and roles."[4] English sociologist Gail Hawkes tells us that the word sexuality "appeared first in the nineteenth century," reflecting "the focus of concerns about the social consequences of sexual desire in the context of modernity." Christian dogma defined sexual desire "as an unreasoned force differentially possessed by women, which threatened the reason of man" and the "inherent moral supremacy of men." According to Hawkes, "the backbone of Victorian sexuality was the successful promotion of a version of women's sexuality, an ideal of purity and sexual innocence well fitted to the separation of spheres that underpinned the patriarchal power of the new ruling class."[5] Sexuality, as Hawkes contextualizes the term, helps us better understand the half century in British Columbia, between 1850 and 1900, when newcomers and Indigenous peoples came into sustained contact.

Everywhere around the world Indigenous women presented an enormous dilemma to colonizers, at the heart of which lay their sexuality. Initially solutions were simple and straightforward. During conquest, local women were used for sexual gratification as a matter of course, just as had been (and still are) female victims of war across the centuries. If unspoken and for the most part unwritten, it was generally accepted in the societies whence men came that, so long as colonial women were absent, Indigenous women could be used to satisfy what were perceived as natural needs. No scruples existed over what the pioneering scholar on race Philip Mason has termed "the casual use of a social inferior for sexual pleasure."[6] The growth of settler colonies changed the "rules of the game." As anthropologist and historian Ann Laura Stoler astutely observes, drawing from her research on colonial Asia, "while the colonies were marketed by colonial elites as a domain where colonizing men could indulge their sexual fantasies, these same elites were intent to mark the boundaries of a colonizing population, to prevent these men from 'going native,' to curb a proliferating mixed-race population that compromised their claims to superiority and thus the legitimacy of white rule."[7]

In British Columbia, gender, power, and race came together in a manner that made it possible for men in power to condemn Indigenous sexuality and at the same time, if they so chose, use the very women they had turned into sexual objects for their own gratification. While much of what occurred mirrored events elsewhere,[8] some aspects were distinctive. Colonizers never viewed Indigenous men as sexual threats,[9] whereas attitudes toward women acquired a particular self-righteousness and fervour. The assumptions newcomers brought with them shaped attitudes, which then informed actions. By the mid-nineteenth century Europeans perceived all female sexual autonomy to be illicit, especially if it occurred in the public sphere, considered exclusively male. Indigenous women in British Columbia not only dared to exercise agency but often did so publicly, convincing men in power that their sexuality was out of control. To the extent that women persisted in managing their own sexual behaviour, they were wilded into the "savages" that many newcomers, in any case, considered all Indigenous peoples to be.[10] That is, until Indigenous women acceded to men in power by having their sexuality tamed, they were for the taking, making it essential that, even today, interpretations of Indigenous women portray them as the keepers of tradition. As noted about American anthropological writing, "Native women are pictured as unchanging—clinging to a traditional way of life that exists outside the vicissitudes of history."[11] To avoid the image that men like Bishop O'Connor continue to project on them, Indigenous women have had to be stripped of their agency past and present.

Prostitution

Indigenous sexuality struck at the very heart of the colonial project. British historian Catherine Hall has noted, in reference to Victorian England, that "sex was a necessary obligation owed to men and not one which women were permitted to talk or think about as owed to themselves."[12] Sexual independence, or circumstances where that possibility existed, was the ultimate threat to the patriarchal family. Children were considered to belong to their fathers, who had to have the assurance that they were indeed his biological heirs. As succinctly summed up by George Stocking in his history of Victorian anthropology, "if the ideal wife and mother was 'so pure-hearted as to be utterly ignorant of and averse to any sensual indulgence,' the alternate cultural image of the 'fallen woman' conveys a hint of an underlying preoccupation with the threat of uncontrolled female sexuality." By the time Victoria came to the throne in 1837,

> the basic structure of taboos was already defined: the renunciation of all sexual activity save the procreative intercourse of Christian marriage; the education of both sexes in chastity and continence; the secrecy and cultivated ignorance surrounding sex; the bowdlerization of literature and euphemistic degradation of language; the general suppression of bodily functions and all the "coarser" aspects of life—in short, the whole repressive pattern of purity, prudery, and propriety that was to condition sexual behavior for decades to come.

Counterpoised to this stereotype were "savages," who were by definition "unrestrained by any sense of delicacy from a copartnery in sexual enjoyments."[13]

Any interpretation of events in British Columbia must adopt the language of colonialism as it was applied to Indigenous women's sexual independence. Around the colonized world the charge of prostitution, engaging in a sexual act for remuneration, was used by those who sought to meddle in Indigenous lives. Sexuality was not to be talked about openly, but prostitution and all that it implied could be publicly condemned. In other words, sexuality had to be wilded into prostitution or possibly concubinage, cohabitation outside of marriage, for it to be tamable. Hawkes traces the fervour over prostitution back to Christianity, which both gave it prominence and held out the promise for "the redemption of the prostitute, the personification of polluting and uncontrolled women's sexuality." Moving to the nineteenth century,

> Victorian sexual morality was focused on, and expressed through, the "social evil" of prostitution. Prostitution was discussed in such diverse venues as popular journalism, serious weekly reviews, medical tracts and publications from evangelical organizations devoted to the rescue of fallen women ... prostitution provided a forum within which to express, covertly, anxieties about, and fascination with, the characteristics of women's sexuality.[14]

No question exists but that Indigenous people in British Columbia viewed their sexuality differently than did colonizers. It is difficult, if not impossible, to reconstruct gender relations prior to newcomers' arrival, nor is it necessary to do so in order to appreciate the enormity of contact. The scholarship is virtually unanimous in concluding that, traditionally, marriages were arranged with goods passing to the woman's family. Intrusions of European disease, work patterns, and economic relations unbalanced Indigenous societies and tended to atomize gender relations. Women possessed opportunities for adaptation not available to their male counterparts.[15] Many of the taboos normalized and universalized by Europeans simply did not exist. If for Europeans sexuality had to be strictly controlled in the interests of assuring paternity, the link may have been less critical for Indigenous people in that the group, rather than the immediate biological family, was the principal social unit.

To grasp the rapidity with which Indigenous women became sexualized as prostitutes in colonial British Columbia, it is instructive to go back in time to another bishop, George Hills, first Anglican bishop of Vancouver Island. Arriving in Victoria in January 1860, he encountered a figurative tinderbox, a fur trade village which in just twenty months had been turned upside down by the gold rush, bringing with it thousands of newcomers from around the world, almost all of them men. Bishop Hills was almost immediately condemning "the profligate condition of the population": "the Road to

Esquimalt on Sunday is lined with the poor Indian women offering to sell themselves to the white men passing by—& instances are to be seen of open bargaining."[16] Bishop Hills's Methodist counterpart Thomas Crosby, who arrived in the spring of 1862, was similarly struck by "the awful condition of the Indian women in the streets and lanes of Victoria."[17]

What newcomers constructed as prostitution did become widespread during the gold rush, just as it had existed to some extent during the fur trade. The evidence may be largely anecdotal, but it is consistent and for some times and places overwhelming. Virtually all of the descriptions come from a colonial male perspective, but are so graphic and diverse as to leave little doubt as to the circumstances. The most visible sites were seasonal dance halls where, for a price, miners could while away "the long winter evenings" by interacting socially with Indigenous women.[18] A New Westminster resident evoked its "Squaw Dance-House" frequented by miners "hastening to throw away their hardly earned gold." Her description is graphic:

> As soon as eight or half-past struck, the music of a fiddle or two and the tramp of many feet began. Later on the shouts of drunken men and the screams of squaws in like condition made night hideous. Each man paid fifty cents for a dance, and had to "stand drinks" at the bar for himself and his dusky partner after each.[19]

Bishop Hills described "houses where girls of no more than 12 are taken in at night & turned out in the morning—like cattle."[20] Even while acknowledging dance halls' contribution to urban economies, the press repeatedly denounced the Indigenous women whose participation made them possible, as in an 1861 editorial charging that "prostitution and kindred vices, in all their hideous deformity, and disease in every form, lurk there." In their San Francisco counterparts "the females were at least civilized," but "here we have all the savagery of the ancient Ojibbeways [*sic*], with all the vice of a reckless civilization."[21] If the decline of the gold rush from the mid-1860s put an end to dance halls' excesses and dampened down excitement over prostitution,[22] the wild that was Indigenous sexuality had permeated settler consciousness.

Female Agency

Turned on their head, contemporary portrayals of Indigenous women's sexuality during the gold rush affirm their agency. Agency is by its very nature relational and interactive. Just as occurred during the fur trade,[23] and in traditional societies,[24] Indigenous women both initiated and responded to change. They scooted around, they dared, they were uppity in ways that were completely at odds with Victorian views of gender, power, and race. Some likely soon realized that, however much they tried to mimic newcomers' ways, they could not earn their recognition, so they might as well act as they pleased.[25] An Indigenous woman "dragged" the friend of a man who had assaulted her to a nearby police station "to be locked up as a witness," only to have him seek "the protection of the police, which was granted" until she left.[26] The jury in a court case against a Victoria policeman accused of "having attempted to ravish the person of an Indian squaw" was told that the verdict hinged on whether "you believe the simple evidence of the three Indian women," and, "after consulting together about one moment, [the jury] returned a verdict of 'Not guilty.'"[27] In some cases Indigenous women were encouraged or forced by the men in their lives. References abound to fathers selling their daughters, "for a few blankets or a little gold, into a slavery which was worse than death,"[28] exchanges likely viewed by some as only continuing traditional marital practice. Yet even missionary accounts hint at female agency, as with Bishop Hills's comment after unsuccessfully remonstrating with "a woman making up a dress" for the dance house that night: "Poor creatures they know these things are wrong—but the temptations are too strong."[29]

Perhaps the most telling evidence of Indigenous women's management of their sexual behaviour is the numbers who chose to live, at least for a time, with non-Indigenous men. The nature of some decisions is suggested by Crosby's account of a twelve-year-old girl who, having "refused at first to follow a life of sin," "was visited by a great rough fellow who, with his hand full of money and with promises of fine clothes and trinkets and sweets, coaxed her and finally prevailed upon her to come and live with him."[30] Although referring to a later point in time, Emily Carr's observations in her fictionalized memoirs are particularly evocative, as in a conversation between two Indigenous women whom she almost certainly knew personally: "We got a house with thlee looms, and a sink and kitchen tap. Jacob and Paul go to school with white children. Too bad you not got white man for husband, Susan."[31] Indigenous women caught in the tumultuous world that was the gold rush sometimes had to make hard decisions, whether for material goods or personal safety. In such circumstances a lonely miner's entreaties could be persuasive.

Non-Indigenous men had their own reasons for entering into relationships with Indigenous women. During the heady years of the gold rush, at least thirty thousand white men and several thousand Chinese and Black men sought their fortunes in British Columbia. Most soon departed, for the difficulties of getting to the gold fields were horrendous, but however long they stayed, their utter loneliness in a sea of men cannot be discounted. The most fundamental characteristic of non-Indigenous women in gold rush British Columbia was their paucity.[32] A Welsh miner reported back to his local cleric how "considerable value is placed on a good woman in this country."[33] An Englishman who had already tried his hand in Australia lamented:

> The great curse of the colony so far, as it must always be the curse of any colony in which such a want exists, is the absence

> of women ... there must be at least two hundred men to every woman ... I never saw diggers so desirous of marrying as those of British Columbia ... If it is one thing more than another a miner sighs for after a hard day's work, it is to see either his tent, or his log hut, brightened up by the smiles of a woman, and tidied up by a woman's hand ... The miner is not very particular—"plain, fat, and 50" even would not be objected to; while good-looking girls would be the nuggets, and prized accordingly.[34]

When a non-Indigenous man saw an Indigenous woman, what he may have perceived was not so much her indigeneity as her gender and, certainly, her sexuality.

Although some of the relationships spawned by the gold rush extended through the couple's lifetime, others were fairly transient, two persons cohabiting for a time until one or the other decided to move on. Women might end relationships, as at Lytton in 1868 where a man "lately left by his Indian wife who had had two children by him ... confesses having sown the seed he has reaped."[35] Other women simply ensured that their husbands knew they could leave if they wished to do so. An early novel depicted a saloon keeper with a "squaw wife" named Desdemona whose independent character drew on the author's long experience in British Columbia.

> All who know the habits of the squaws married to white men, especially if they lived in one of the towns, will remember the overmastering desire they occasionally developed for a return to their tribe, and a resumption of their old life for at least a time. To fish all night from a light cedar canoe, with no thoughts of the white man's scorn, to pick berries, cut and dry fish till their garments were saturated with the odour of salmon, gather roots, herbs, and the bark of trees for baskets, the rushes also for klis-klis or mats. To extract the beautiful and durable reds and blues

> from certain plants and berries, and generally to revel in God's great temple of nature.

So it was with Desdemona. "One of these calls from the wild had taken Desdemona, and when her tenase tecoup man (small white man) came in one night, the house was dark, and she and the children gone." She had "stepped into a canoe, paddled across the wide [Fraser] river, and up the salmon stream," and only when it suited her fancy did she return home to her husband.[36]

The various data encompassing personal accounts, church records, and the manuscript censuses suggest that about one in ten Indigenous women in areas of British Columbia opened up to Europeans during the colonial years cohabited at some point in her life with a non-Indigenous man.[37] Such unions' prevalence even caused the first session of the new provincial legislature, following entry into Confederation in 1871, to pass a bill, subsequently disallowed by the federal government, to legitimize children of unions between Indigenous women and non-Indigenous men whose parents wed subsequent to their birth.[38]

Taming Indigenous Sexuality

By the time British Columbia became a Canadian province in 1871, Indigenous women had been almost wholly sexualized.[39] The perception of widespread prostitution, and if not prostitution then concubinage, gave men in power a freedom to speak openly about matters which otherwise would have been only whispered.[40] Newcomers took for granted the fall as depicted in the Bible. Human nature was weak, and the biological man could easily be tempted to evil by his female counterpart, just as Bishop O'Connor considered himself to have been over a century later. It was woman's place to be docile and subservient so as not to provoke man. For all those seeking to control Indigenous peoples, women who exercised sexual autonomy were women out of control who had to be subdued, their sexuality tamed. Conversion to Christianity held the key, for "woman was always the slave or burden-bearer until the Gospel came and lifted her into her true social position," which was essentially as man's handmaiden.[41] Whether missionaries, government officials, or Indigenous men, the common perception was that the only good Indigenous woman was the woman who stayed home within the bosom of her family. And so an informal alliance developed between these three groups to refashion Indigenous women.

This tripartite alliance, wherein men in power buttressed and comforted each other, was grounded in mutual expediency and to some extent mutual male admiration. With British Columbia's entry into Confederation, responsibility for Indigenous people shifted to the federal government under the terms of the British North America Act, and it did not take long for newly appointed officials to realize the enormous benefit to be had from cordial relations with missionaries already at work across much of the sprawling province. Officially, missionaries had no status, but unofficially they became the government's foot soldiers, and its eyes and ears. Indigenous policy as it developed in British Columbia was to minimize official involvement in everyday affairs, which effectively meant letting missionaries have a free hand.[42] If disagreeing in many areas, including Indigenous people's right to an adequate land base, government officials repeatedly commended missionaries for having "taught, above all, the female portion of the community to behave themselves in a modest and virtuous manner."[43]

The other prong of the alliance to tame Indigenous sexuality crossed racial boundaries in the interests of gender solidarity and mutual self-interest. Members of the Indian Reserve Commission active across British Columbia in the mid-1870s left an extensive paper trail and repeatedly expressed approval of Indigenous "manliness" and of "the industry of the men."[44] Similarly, in missionary accounts it is almost wholly Indigenous men who are given individuality and personality.[45] Men, particularly those who emulated colonial ways, needed to have suitable spouses, and for this reason also, Indigenous women had to have their sexuality tamed.

As for Indigenous men, they were likely motivated by a shortage of women and also, for some of them, by a desire to please their colonial mentors. Reports of a shortage are sufficiently widespread across space and time to be convincing. As early as 1866 Bishop Hills observed "a scarcity of wives" among the northern Tsimshian, many of whose members camped in Victoria on a seasonal basis.[46] The Indian Reserve Commission's census of a decade later counted 1,919 Indigenous persons in the area extending from Burrard Inlet north to Jervis Inlet, across to Comox, and down through the Saanich peninsula, including the Gulf Islands; of these, 979 were adult males compared with 919 adult females, and 94 male youth compared with 84 female youth.[47] The enumerator of the southern Interior, extending from Lytton through the Nicola Valley, counted 884 adult males compared with 803 adult females and lamented "the absence of females both adults and youths—those who should have been the future mothers of the tribe."[48]

Some Indigenous men, in effect, made deals to behave in accord with missionary aspirations in exchange for getting wives.[49] Crosby described a visit to a Queen Charlotte Islands village in the mid-1880s, with "about eighty people, but not more than three or four healthy-looking women." The local men promised Crosby: "Sir, if you will come and give us a teacher, we will stop going to Victoria. Victoria has been the place of death and destruction to our people, as you see we have no children left to us. All our young women are gone; some of our young men can't find wives and more; and we wish that you could help them to get wives among the Tsimpshean people."[50]

The tripartite campaign to tame the wild of Indigenous sexuality had two principal goals. The first was to return Indigenous women back home. The second was to desexualize Indigenous everyday life, in effect to cleanse it so that the home to which women returned would emulate its colonial counterpart.

Returning Indigenous Women Home

Marriage lay at the heart of newcomers' morality and, as concluded by anthropologist George Stocking, "it is perfectly clear that 'marriage proper' meant proper Victorian marriage," whose "purpose was to control human (and especially female) sexuality, so that there might be 'certainty of male parentage.'"[51] As summed up by historians Leonore Davidoff and Catherine Hall, in England between the late eighteenth and mid-nineteenth centuries, "marriage was the economic and social building block for the middle class ... Marriage became both symbol and institution of women's containment. It was marriage which would safely domesticate the burgeoning garden flower into an indoor pot plant; the beautiful object potentially open to all men's gaze became the possession of one man when kept within the house like a picture fixed to the wall."[52]

In theory, two marital strategies could have tamed Indigenous sexuality. One was to encourage non-Indigenous men to wed their Indigenous partners, the other to return Indigenous women home to wed Indigenous men. Either would have satisfied Victorian notions of marriage, but the alliance of interests that existed among men in power combined with growing racism to ensure that the second would be favoured. As early as 1873 an agitated provincial official pointed to the federal government's responsibility for "the care and protection of the native race in this Province, [and] so long as this shameful condition of things is suffered to continue unchecked, the character of that race in the social scale is practically a delusion."[53] Reserve commissioners reported on conversations with chiefs at Nanaimo, where "the evil of concubinage of their young women with the white men around were specially pointed out."[54] By 1884 an Indian agent with an Indigenous wife and grown daughters felt able to argue, perhaps with a touch of self-interest, that "with the present state of civilization in the country and the abundance of white and educated half breed women—such a practice should be put a stop to in future."[55] Indigenous women were needed at home to service their menfolk.

For men in power, gender and race neatly dovetailed. Within the framework of social Darwinism, newcomers accepted that the races were arranged in a hierarchy with whites, not unexpectedly, on the top and Indigenous people near the bottom. Persons of mixed race ranked even lower, for, to quote a colonial visitor, "half-breeds, as a rule, inherit, I am afraid, the vices of both races."[56] Concerns grew over "a class of half-breed children ... who, under the bond of illegitimacy, and deprived of all incentives in every respect, will in course of time become dangerous members of the community."[57] During the late 1870s such fears were exacerbated when the young sons of a Hudson's Bay trader and Indigenous woman went on a murderous rampage in 1879,[58] and were given a sexual edge two years earlier when female mixed-race students at a public boarding school became pregnant by their male counterparts.[59] While some encouragement was given to non-Indigenous men to marry Indigenous women with whom they were cohabiting, this was, for the most part, done somewhat grudgingly. Petitions became a favoured means to force Indigenous women back home. The tripartite alliance developed a dynamic whereby Indigenous men signed petitions orchestrated by missionaries who then dispatched them to government officials to justify taking action.[60] Both Catholic and Protestant missionaries participated, as did Indigenous men across much of the province and numerous officials at various levels of government.

In 1885 Oblate missionaries stage-managed two identical petitions to the Governor General, affirmed with their mark by 962 Indigenous men, including at least eighteen chiefs, from across the Cariboo south through the Lower Fraser Valley, to return Indigenous women home. In the best English prose the petitioners "beg[ged] to lay before your Excellency" that a "great evil is springing up amongst our people" whereas "on a dispute between a married couple, the wife leaves her husband and goes off the Reservation, and takes up with a bad white man, China man, or other Indian, and [they] live together in an unlawful state." The men sought permission to "bring back the erring ones by force if necessary."[61] Caught up in the rhetoric to tame Indigenous sexuality, the Ministry of Justice drafted an even broader regulation for consideration by the chiefs, one that made it possible to "bring back to the reserve any Indian woman who has left the reserve and is living immorally with any person off the reserve." The proposal was only derailed due to the Ministry of Justice's suggestion, made almost in passing, that the Department of Indian Affairs should "consider before it is passed whether or not the putting of it in force will lead to riots and difficulties between the Indians and the white people and others with whom the Indian women are said to be living immorally."[62] Three of the four Indian agents consulted considered that this might well happen were chiefs given such authority. One of them acknowledged female agency in his observation that, "while in some cases the Indian woman might be brought back without trouble, it would be impossible to keep her on a reserve against her will."[63] The project was shelved, even though the Catholic bishop at New Westminster intervened directly at the federal ministerial level in an attempt to bypass the bureaucrats.[64]

The campaign to tame Indigenous sexuality by returning women home was not to be thwarted, and the Oblates were almost certainly behind a bolder petition dispatched in 1890 to the Governor General. The chiefs of fifty-eight bands, again extending from the Cariboo through the Fraser Valley, indicated by their marks that they were "much aggrieved and annoyed at the fact that our wives, sisters and daughters are frequently decoyed away from our Reserves by ill designing persons." No means existed to return "these erring women," but, even were this possible, "in most cases these women are induced to return again to their seducers." Fearing that "some of our young men who are sufferers will certainly take the law into their own hands and revenge themselves on the offending parties," the petition sought "a law authorising the infliction of corporal punishment by the lash."[65]

The advisability of "legislation, making it an offence for a white man to have sexual intercourse with an Indian woman or girl without Christian marriage," was referred to the Ministry of Justice,[66] which in this case pulled the plug. The ministry considered the legislation unnecessary, since "the laws relating to the protection of females and for the punishment of persons who seduce or abduct them, apply to Indian women as well as to white women."[67] Yet the campaign persisted, and later in 1890 the Indian agent at Lillooet urged, on behalf of "the Chiefs of the numerous Bands around here," that "a severe penalty should be imposed upon any person, not an Indian, who, harbouring an Indian woman, does not deliver her up to the Chief of the Reserve."[68]

At this point the enthusiasts may have stumbled. Acting largely independent of civil authority, the Oblates had allied themselves across much of the Interior with local Indigenous men to effect control over everyday life.[69] As one Indian agent noted in the early 1890s, although the "flogging habit has been abandoned for some years past" and fines were not so common as they once were, "considerable sums of money are annually collected by the chiefs and their watchmen for the benefit of the churches whose functionaries attend to their spiritual welfare."[70] In the spring of 1892 the Oblate missionary at Lillooet, the chief, and four other men were brought before the local magistrate, convicted, and given jail sentences for "flogging a young girl … on the report only of a fourth party" for some unspecified sexual activity. "Without investigation <u>he</u> [priest] *ordered* 15 lashes. His plea was 1st ancient customs of the Indians & 2nd necessity for such punishment in order to suppress immorality." The Indian agent who made the report considered both that the "ancient customs" were not as portrayed by the missionary and that the local men should not have been punished so severely, since they "believed the Priest to be their Commander in all Church matters—and that consequently they were obliged to obey him."[71] The incident appears to have cooled the alliance between the Oblates and local men, who "were astonished at the extent of the jurisdiction of the Courts of law, when even the dictates of a Priest should be upset and the Priest himself held accountable."[72]

The Protestants could be just as enthusiastic as the Catholics in allying themselves with local men to keep women at home and in then calling on federal officials to enforce what they could not effect by their own devices. In 1889 the Indian agent at Alert Bay, acting in concert with the local Anglican missionary, stopped a group of women from boarding a steamer to Victoria. His justification was that they "went with the avowed purpose of prostituting themselves," and he "had previously been requested by numbers of young men to prevent if possible their wives and sisters from going to Victoria."[73] Reflecting the tripartite alliance's perspective, the Indian agent considered that "nearly all the young women, whenever they leave their homes, whether ostensibly for working at the canneries or at the Hop Fields, do so with the ultimate idea of making more money by prostitution."[74] The steamboat company vigorously protested and the provincial Indian Superintendent was lukewarm, perceptively observing that "the Indian women and their friends come to Victoria, and other places, in their canoes," making their restriction practically impossible.[75] Nonetheless, the Indian agent and Anglican missionary did such a successful end run to federal officials as to persuade them to propose legislation to keep at home, by force if necessary, "Indian women from the West Coast of British Columbia, who are in the habit of leaving their Villages and Reserves by steamers and by other mode of transport with the object of visiting the Cities and Towns of that Province for immoral purposes."[76]

The proposed legislation hit a snag only after the federal Minister of Justice indicated "that there is not at present sufficient material on hand to permit of the drawing up of a Bill fully dealing with the question."[77] The minister requested the provincial Superintendent to circularize Indian agents around the province. Even though the agents would likely have found it far easier to acquiesce to expectations, they were all, apart from Alert Bay and Babine in the northern Interior, remarkably sanguine. On the west coast of Vancouver Island, the agent wrote, "I do not know of a single instance on this Coast where a young girl has been taken to Victoria or elsewhere for the purposes of prostitution."[78] His neighbour was "not aware of any Indian women belonging to the Cowichan Agency who leave their Reservations for immoral purposes."[79] In the Fraser Valley and Lower Mainland, "there are very few immoral women."[80] As for the central Interior, "the practice of Indian women leaving their Reserves for the purpose of leading immoral lives is not common in this Agency."[81] The southern Interior agent offered a general observation: "Indians are in their nature, in consequence of their training, habits and surroundings, far less virtuous than the average whites. Their morality should not therefore be judged by the standards of the white people. The Indian woman, although, as above stated, inclined to be worse in her morals, is naturally modest."[82] The North Coast agent considered that the "Indians have learned from sad experience the effects of immorality in the cities and are rapidly improving their conduct."[83] Summarizing the responses, the provincial Superintendent concluded that "the few Indian women who may be found living an immoral life in our towns and Cities are less in number as a rule than of their white sisters."[84]

Nonetheless, the depiction of Indigenous sexuality as unrestrained was too attractive an explanation for the failure of missionaries and the government to control women to be abandoned. Just three years later, in 1895, a petition signed by thirty-four men from central Vancouver Island, all but one with their marks, demanded legislation to prevent "our wives and daughters and sisters" from being "carried to Victoria for illegitimate purposes."[85] The British Columbia senator to whom the petition was addressed took its claims at face value and demanded that steps be taken to "prevent the deportation of Indian women," seeing that "Indians are wards of the government under tutelage and not qualified to manage their own affairs wisely." The senator, who simply assumed that Indigenous women's sole role was to service their menfolk, emphasized that an "increase, instead of a decrease, is much to be desired" in the Indigenous population.[86] The federal response is interesting because, rather than quoting from the Indian agents' reports in their files, officials emphasized the difficulties of securing legislation. In doing so, they revealed, perhaps inadvertently, that women were de facto having their travel restricted by local Indian agents "when requested by the husband or brother or anyone having proper authority, to stop a woman from going away, and so the men have the prevention of that of which they complain almost entirely in their own hands."[87] The sexualization of Indigenous women had far less to do with reality than with the needs, and desires, of men in power. So long as settler society perceived a need to tame Indigenous sexuality, men in power could refashion Indigenous society with impunity.

Reordering Indigenous Society

Over time virtually every aspect of Indigenous women's everyday lives acquired a sexual dimension. It was not only about returning Indigenous women home, but also about reordering the home to which they returned. Indigenous sexuality, or perhaps more accurately the fear of Indigenous women's agency, became a lens through which traditional preferences in housing, social institutions, and child care were critiqued and found wanting.

The rhetoric condemning the "big houses" inhabited by coastal peoples made explicit Victorian fears of the body and of human sexuality. It also reflected social Darwinian notions of the hierarchy of species, at the top of which lay Western societies premised on the monogamous conjugal family. The very existence of sites where more than a single family lived together was equated with immorality. No doubt existed but that, given the opportunity, men and women would act on their impulses. Davidoff and Hall have linked the subordination of women to the private home:

> Woman had been created for man, indeed for one man, and there was a necessary inference from this that home was "the proper scene of woman's action and influence" ... The idea of a privatized home, separated from the world, had a powerful moral force and if women, with their special aptitude for faith, could be contained within that home, then a space would be created for true family religion.[88]

So also in British Columbia, the single-family home became perceived as a necessary prelude to Christian conversion.

Men in power repeatedly lauded the single-family house, as in side notes on the Reserve Commission's census of Indigenous people. At Burrard Inlet: "The houses at this place have a pleasing appearance when viewed from the sea. They are mostly of the cottage style, white washed and kept cleaner in this than is usual with most Indians." In contrast, along the Fraser River: "Most of the houses of this tribe are of the primitive style. There are however several cottages kept and fitted up in a neat manner." At Cowichan on Vancouver Island: "There are a few tidy cottages—what they require is a desire and encouragement."[89] Missionaries like Crosby were even more fervent and repeatedly linked housing to sexuality: "The old heathen house, from its very character, was the hot-bed of vice. Fancy a great barn-like building, ... occupied by as many as a dozen families, only separated from each other by low partitions." The interior seemed made for naughty deeds. "Picture such a building, with no floor other than the ground, no entrance for light except the door, when open, and the cracks in the walls and the roof. Around the inside of such a building were ranged the beds, built up on rude platforms ... Is it any wonder that disease and vice flourished under such favorable surroundings?"[90] In sharp contrast stood "the Christian home." Crosby considered that "the only way to win the savage from his lazy habits, sin and misery" was to "be able and willing to show how to build a nice little home, from the foundation to the last shingle on the roof."[91]

Fear of Indigenous sexuality became frenzied in the rhetoric around the social institution of the potlatch. Missionaries led the campaign against this social activity practised across most of the province, garnering support from government officials and, over time, from some younger converted Indigenous men. Initially arguments focused on the event itself as being "demoralizing," leading to "debauchery."[92] Federal legislation banning the potlatch took effect at the beginning of 1885 but did not bring wholesale conversion to Christianity. Missionaries soon sought both allies in Indigenous men in search of wives and reasons, apart from themselves, to explain their failure to live up to their expectations for themselves.[93] The ethnographer Marius Barbeau concluded in 1921, after examining federal files on the potlatch, that, "as the Church has not succeeded in making converts to any material extent ... there must be found a scapegoat, and as the potlatch already had a bad name, it was blamed."[94]

The sexualization of the potlatch had a number of components but centred on the supposed sale of Indigenous women as wives or prostitutes to get the money to potlatch. In 1893 a Toronto newspaper reported that a group of missionaries had witnessed "blankets for potlatch procured at the expense of the virtue of women," an event the local Indian agent determined was sensationalized.[95] By the end of the century the press had become convinced that "the potlatch is the inciting cause of three-fourths of the immorality that exists among Indian women."[96] Writing shortly thereafter, the Indian agent at Alert Bay asserted the support of the younger generation of Indigenous men for his attempt to persuade his superiors in Ottawa to act against potlatching: "It looks cruel to me to see a child 13 or 14 years of age put up & sold just like sheep or a nanny goat, to a bleary eyed siwash old enough to be her grand-father, for a pile of dirty blankets, which will in turn be Potlatched to the rest of the band, and all to make the proud Father, a big Injun," rather than "let her marry a young man whom I am sure she wanted."[97] The Indian agent quoted a long-time missionary to make his point that "the girls die off and the young men for the most part cannot get wives because as a rule they have no blankets or money unless they are sons of chiefs and the others cannot get wives until they are able to command a certain sum which is so difficult as they have to compete with the older men who hold the property."[98]

The unwillingness to tolerate Indigenous women's agency was a major strand in the determination to replace familial child care with residential schools operated by missionaries under loose government oversight. Schools sought total control over pupils' sexuality, particularly that of girls. The twinned concepts of Christian marriage and the Christian home depended on young women remaining sufficiently unblemished so that they could become good wives by white Victorian standards of behaviour. The attitudes and actions of Thomas Crosby and his wife, Emma, are instructive. Crosby considered that parents, "though kind and indulgent to their children, are not capable of teaching and controlling them properly" and "something must be done to save and protect the young girls … from being sold into the vilest of slavery."[99] He noted that, "on account of the prevalence of this traffic in Indian girls, many of the early missionaries were led to establish 'Girls' Homes' for the rescue and further protection of these poor victims of this awful system."[100] The taming that went on in the Crosbys' girls' home and school, as in other residential schools across the province, left no doubt as to Indigenous agency. As remembered by a Crosby school matron in the early 1880s, the girls required "a great deal of Grace, Patience and determination, they were so obstinate and disobedient."[101]

The wildness associated with Indigenous sexuality explains attitudes toward a girl's transition from pupil to wife. Reflecting the assumptions of the day, the superintendent of the Children's Aid Society in Vancouver expressed relief that "the savage was so thin and washed out" of two young women of mixed race that they were able to find happiness with their white lovers. Yet this represented "only a glimmer of light in the darkness."[102] According to Crosby's biographer, "girls stayed at the Home until they were married, at which time a new girl would be admitted."[103] The full extent to which missionaries did not trust their charges is evident in the musings of another Crosby matron, in reference to the potential marriage of a fourteen-year-old student, that "it would seem sinful to allow such things to be mentioned if they were white girls, but here they are safer when married young."[104]

Again, the informal alliance operated. Schools measured their success by numbers of girls who

> have married Christian Indians, have helped to build up Christian homes, to civilize the people generally and to aid in developing their own neighborhood ... Instead of a young man with his friends going with property and buying a wife, as was done formerly, many of our brightest young men tried to make the acquaintance of the girls in the Home.

Women might no longer be sold by their fathers, but they were no less commodities when it came to marriage. The Crosbys, like other missionaries, put a romantic spin around what was, in effect, a good being made available to a handful of men considered suitably Christian: "There was no doubt in our minds that real, true love again and again developed between the young people who thus became acquainted. This acquaintance finally resulted in their marriage and the happy life that followed."[105]

Consequences

By the end of the nineteenth century, settler society took for granted the interpretation that men in power put on Indigenous women's agency. The ongoing frenzy over the potlatch is indicative. The press became ever more determined to expose its supposed basis in Indigenous sexuality. The headline "Indian Girl Sold for 1,000 Blankets" appeared on Vancouver streets in 1906.[106] The story makes clear that the supposed revelation about "the awful Indian practice of potlatch" originated with an Anglican missionary disgruntled by a pupil who had married someone other than the man selected for her. Later in the year both Vancouver and Ottawa newspapers trumpeted "Five Indian Girls Sold,"[107] a report that on investigation proved to be without foundation.[108] A Vancouver paper a year later headlined "Squaw Sold for $400.00 at Alert Bay to a Grizzled Chief from Queen Charlottes."[109] It turned out that while two marriages had occurred, neither involved "a grizzled chief," and the local Indian agent considered the article "very misleading."[110] The press coverage prompted a host of women's voluntary associations across the country to demand legislation to "put an end to this great blot on the Civilization and Christianity of Canada."[111] Writing in 1921, a barrister who was the son of the Indian agent at Alert Bay, and who represented Indigenous people opposed to the potlatch ban, considered that "the strongest reason for enforcing the law against the Potlatch is the question of Indian marriages ... It is also contended that women are bought and sold, [but] this is not true."[112] Had the potlatch not been so successfully sexualized, it is doubtful that opponents could have maintained its illegality into mid-century. The taming of Indigenous sexuality had become a means to an end, as well of course as an end in itself, but the effects were no less detrimental for Indigenous women.

For Indigenous women, the consequences of the ceaseless rhetoric of scorn heaped on them in the interests of men in power were enormous. Some women acquiesced and returned or remained at home, and the Crosbys delighted "in visiting around among the villages, to pick out these Christian mothers who had the privilege of the 'Home' life and training."[113] In a broad sense, Indigenous societies did come to mimic their colonial counterparts, not unexpectedly given federal policies and the material advantages to be got from doing so. An Indigenous informant explained in 1950 how "converts were sometimes termed 'made white men,' as they used different types of houses and they dressed in white men's clothes, while their heathen brothers … indulged in all of the old rituals."[114] Some women had the decision taken out of their hands. As more marriageable white women became available and attitudes hardened, numerous non-Indigenous men shed their Indigenous partners. The manuscript censuses for the late nineteenth century indicate that, while some of these women did return home and enter into new unions with Indigenous men, others scraped along at the edges of settler society.

Other women continued to dare. Many interracial unions survived the campaign to tame Indigenous sexuality, in some cases by the partners legally marrying or retreating outward into the frontier, or by simply standing their ground. The encouragement that missionaries and government officials gave to Indigenous men may have caused some women to disengage from their home communities in search of more satisfying life opportunities. To the extent that traditional patterns of gender relations gave way to male mimicry of European practices, so the social distance between the sexes may have widened. Women still married out, as indicated by the 1901 manuscript census,[115] and evoked in a Carr vignette about a woman who had "married white" and "both loved her husband and gloried in his name," for "it was infinitely finer to be 'Mrs Jenny Smith' than to have her name hitched to an Indian man's and be 'Jenny Joe' or "Jenny Tom.'"[116]

Most importantly, the campaign to tame Indigenous sexuality so profoundly sexualized Indigenous women that they were rarely permitted any other form of identity. Not just Indigenous women but Indigenous women's agency was sexualized. In the extreme case their every act became perceived as a sexual act and, because of the unceasing portrayal of their sexuality as wild and out of control, as an act of provocation. By default, Indigenous women were prostitutes or, at best, potential concubines. Their actions were imbued with the intent that men in power had so assiduously ascribed to them, thus vitiating any responsibility for their own or other men's actions toward them. Sexualization of Indigenous women's agency occurred in a context where they were already doubly inferior by virtue of their gender and race, thus virtually ensuring that any Indigenous woman who dared would become colonialism's plaything. Again, the stories are legion, be it the Okanagan Valley in the 1880s, Vancouver Island in the 1920s, the north coast in the 1960s, or Bishop O'Connor. Sometimes the accounts embody a strong element of bravado, in other cases the wish fulfillment of lonely men, but in yet others a strong dose of action, as with O'Connor.

A young Englishman who arrived in the Okanagan Valley shortly after the completion of the transcontinental railroad in 1886 exemplified a generation of newcomers who took for granted Indigenous women's sexualization: "Most of these girls were graceful, some even pretty; clear, light bronze skins with just a touch of color in the cheeks, even teeth and glossy jet black hair, that had almost a tinge of blue in it; their black eyes would be modestly cast down in the presence of white men. And sometimes a shy upward glance of coquetry—but not if there were any bucks in sight." He recalled a contemporary who, "fed up with batching, had disturbed the monastic peace of the community by taking unto himself a dusky mistress." By also sexualizing Indigenous women's agency, any sense of responsibility for this man's actions was removed. Even as his friends were deciding whether to be jealous, "he and his lady had a bad row, and realizing that his little romance was ended he fired her out, and as none of the rest of the old boys were gallant enough to take a chance on her, the lady returned to the bosom of her tribe, and once more there was peace on earth in the little community."[117]

Even persons who supported Indigenous people, as with the lawyer representing them in the 1920s against the potlatch ban, persisted in seeing women in sexual terms, considering that "contact between Indians and loggers has always been fraught with dire results—particularly to the Indian women." This assessment was in sharp contrast to his view of Indigenous men: "The Indian man in his own environment is a man of dignity, big and venerable."[118]

In a generally sympathetic account of a summer sojourn in 1966 at Telegraph Creek on the north coast, a young American made clear the full extent to which Indigenous women's agency long continued to be sexualized: "More than they would have in the old days, I'm sure, they make fun of the Indians to me ... [for] their limber-limbed promiscuity." A friend "eats supper with me, chatting about the morals of the Indian girls ('No morals at all if you scratch their stomachs a minute')." Their every action became a sexual action, thus his vignette of how "earlier in the spring a girl appeared in the store, sent by her parents, and took up the broom and began to sweep, after the historical fashion of a squaw proposing to a white man." For this young man, the wild that was Indigenous sexuality remained mythic. Noting that "in New York to dream of a woman is an unremarkable event" but "here it invests the whole night with sexual urgency," he repeatedly found himself tempted, as after "I've had a day hearing stories of ... Indian women being mounted and screwed." He resisted, but precisely because he did accept the equation of Indigenous female agency with sexuality: "Of course these Indian girls are too vulnerable to fool with, so I have only the past to keep me company in bed."[119]

Hence we come full circle to Bishop O'Connor, who at virtually the same time that this young American was imagining, acted on his impulses. Like so many men before him, he still considered himself to have been "seduced," and a full generation later remained in his heart "a celibate man." It was not his fault that Indigenous women had not been adequately tamed. I have no doubt that O'Connor considered himself to be sincere, just as I now have no doubt of the importance of newcomers' construction of Indigenous women's sexuality for understanding events during that critical half century between 1850 and 1900, when your, my, and Bishop O'Connor's British Columbia came into being.

Notes

1 This statement by Bishop O'Connor was taken up forcefully in "Reasons for Judgment," Vancouver Registry, no. CC920617, July 25, 1996.

2 National Parole Board, Decision Registry, file 905044C, March 21, 1997.

3 Jane Katz, ed., *Messengers of the Wind: Native American Women Tell Their Life Stories* (New York: Ballantine Books, 1995), 5.

4 David Jary and Julia Jary, *Collins Dictionary of Sociology*, 2nd ed. (Glasgow: HarperCollins, 1995), 590-91. It was 1914 before the *Oxford English Dictionary* got to the letter "s." All of its quotes were from the nineteenth century, and while the first definition was "the quality of being sexual or having sex," the second and third were the "possession of sexual powers or capability of sexual feelings" and "recognition of or preoccupation with what is sexual." See Sir James A.H. Murray, ed., *A New English Dictionary on Historical Principles*, vol. 8 (Oxford: Clarendon Press, 1914), 582. Interest in the concept of sexuality, and more generally in regulation of the body, mushroomed with the publication of Michel Foucault's *History of Sexuality* in 1978 (Harmondsworth, UK: Penguin), esp. vol. 1, and Peter Gay's *The Bourgeois Experience* in 1986 (Oxford: Oxford University Press), 2 vols.

5 Gail Hawkes, *A Sociology of Sex and Sexuality* (Buckingham, UK: Open University Press, 1996), 8, 14, 42.

6 Philip Mason, *Patterns of Dominance* (London: Oxford University Press for the Institute of Race Relations, 1970), 88.

7 Ann Laura Stoler and Frederick Cooper, "Between Metropole and Colony: Rethinking a Research Agenda," in *Tensions of Empire: Colonial Cultures in a Bourgeois World*, ed. Frederick Cooper and Ann Laura Stoler (Berkeley: University of California Press, 1997), 5. Although Stoler and Cooper co-wrote this introductory essay, the insight is clearly Stoler's, since it is her research on colonial Asia that is cited.

8 As diverse early examples of a similar sequence, if not necessarily interpretation, of events, see Albert L. Hurtado, *Indian Survival on the California Frontier* (New Haven, CT: Yale University Press, 1988), 169-92; and Caroline Ralston, "Changes in the Lives of Ordinary Women in Early Post-Contact Hawaii," in *Family and Gender in the Pacific: Domestic Contradictions and the Colonial Impact*, ed. Margaret Jolly and Martha MacIntyre (Cambridge: Cambridge University Press, 1989), 45-82. Sarah Carter introduces elements of a similar understanding for the Canadian prairies in "Categories and Terrains of Exclusion: Constructing the 'Indian Woman' in the Early Settlement Era of Western Canada," *Great Plains Quarterly* 13 (1993): 147-61.

9 In *Allegories of Empire: The Figure of the Woman in the Colonial Text* (Minneapolis: University of Minnesota Press, 1993), Jenny Sharpe argues that, after rebellions in India in the 1850s, accounts of the rape of colonial women (often unsubstantiated) provided the basis for racializing Indigenous peoples as inferior.

10 The concept of wildness is examined in Sharon Tiffany and Kathleen Adams, *The Myth of the Wild Woman* (Cambridge, MA: Schenkman, 1985).

11 Patricia C. Albers, "From Illusion to Illumination: Anthropological Studies of American Indian Women," in *Gender and Anthropology: Critical Reviews for Research and Teaching*, ed. Sandra Morgan (Washington: American Anthropological Association, 1989), 132.

12 Catherine Hall in *White, Male, and Middle-Class* (Cambridge MA: Polity Press, 1992), 61-62.

13 George W. Stocking, Jr., *Victorian Anthropology* (New York: Free Press, 1987), 199-200, 202.

14 Hawkes, *Sociology of Sex*, 14-15, 42.

15 Especially useful is Carol Cooper, "Native Women of the Northern Pacific Coast: An Historical Perspective, 1830-1900," *Journal of Canadian Studies* 27, no. 4 (Winter 1992-1993), which traces the seasonal migrations of north coast women to Victoria with their families and points out that what newcomers labelled prostitution sometimes simply continued traditional social structures wherein some persons were deprived of their autonomy as "slaves" (58).

16 September 24, 1860, entry in Bishop George Hills diary, in Anglican Church, Ecclesiastical Province of British Columbia, Archives. See also letter to the editor from C.T.W. in *Victoria Gazette*, September 22, 1860; and Matthew MacFie, *Vancouver Island and British Columbia* (London: Longman, Green, Longman, Roberts, and Green, 1865), 471.

17 Thomas Crosby, *Up and Down the North Pacific Coast by Canoe and Mission Ship* (Toronto: Missionary Society of the Methodist Church, 1904), 17.

18 "Can Such Things Be?" *Victoria Daily Chronicle*, November 16, 1862.

19 Francis E. Herring, *In the Pathless West: With Soldiers, Pioneers, Miners, and Savages* (London: T. Fisher Unwin, 1904), 173–75.

20 April 21, 1860, entry in Hills diary; also August 12 and September 24, 1860, and January 31, 1862, entries.

21 "The Dance Houses," *British Colonist* (Victoria), December 20, 1861.

22 In *During My Time: Florence Edenshaw Davidson, a Haida Woman* (Vancouver and Seattle: Douglas and McIntyre and University of Washington Press, 1982), 44–5.

23 On the maritime fur trade, see Lorraine Littlefield, "Women Traders in the Maritime Fur Trade," in *Native People, Native Lands: Canadian Indians, Inuit and Metis*, ed. Bruce Alden Cox (Ottawa: Carleton University Press, 1991), 173–85; and on the land-based trade, Sylvia Van Kirk, *Many Tender Ties: Women in Fur-Trade Society, 1670–1870* (Norman: University of Oklahoma Press, 1980).

24 For a case study, see Jo-Anne Fiske, "Fishing Is Women's Business: Changing Economic Roles of Carrier Women and Men," in Cox, *Native People, Native Lands*, 186–98.

25 On the larger meaning of mimicry as popularized by Homi Bhabha, see his "Of Mimicry and Man: The Ambivalence of Colonial Discourse," in Cooper and Stoler, *Tensions of Empire*, 152–60.

26 "A Squaw Arrests a White Man," *British Colonist*, January 17, 1862.

27 "Attempted Rape," *British Colonist*, August 17, 1860.

28 Thomas Crosby, *Among the An-ko-me-nums, or Flathead Tribes of Indians of the Pacific Coast* (Toronto: William Briggs, 1907), 62.

29 February 1, 1862, entry in Hills diary.

30 Crosby, *Among the An-ko-me-nums*, 63.

31 Emily Carr, *The Heart of a Peacock* (Toronto: Irwin, 1986), 96.

32 Adele Perry admirably tackles this and related topics in "'Oh I'm Just Sick of the Faces of Men': Gender Imbalance, Race, Sexuality, and Sociability in Nineteenth-Century British Columbia," *BC Studies* 105 (Spring/Summer 1995): 27–43.

33 Letter of Morgan Lewis to Rev. D.R. Lewis, New Westminster, October 29, 1862, printed in *Seren Cymru*, January 23, 1863, and quoted in Alan Conway, "Welsh Gold Miners in British Columbia during the 1860's," *Cylchgrawn Llyfrgell Genedlaethol Cymru: The National Library of Wales Journal* 10, no. 4 (Winter 1958): 383–84.

34 *Cariboo, the Newly Discovered Gold Fields of British Columbia* (Fairfield, WA: Ye Galleon Press, 1975), 7–8, 19–20.

35 May 27, 1868, entry in Hills diary.

36 Francis E. Herring, "Pretty Mrs. Weldon," in *Nan and Other Pioneer Women of the West* (London: Francis Griffiths, 1913), 122, 124–25.

37 The base used is the greatly diminished Indigenous population of about 25,000 to 30,000 following the devastating smallpox epidemic of the early 1860s. Another measure is the number of children resulting from the relationships, as indicated in "Supplementary Report" to British Columbia, Department of Education, *First Annual Report on the Public Schools in the Province of British Columbia* (1872), 38.

38 David R. Williams, *The Man for a New Country: Sir Matthew Baillie Begbie* (Sidney: Gray's Publishing, 1977), 106–7.

39 The age-linked, equally essentializing counterpart was, of course, an absence of sexuality. The Indigenous woman as drudge is discussed in, among other sources, Elizabeth Vibert, *Traders' Tales: Narratives of Cultural Encounters in the Columbia Plateau, 1807–1846* (Norman: University of Oklahoma Press, 1997), 127–31, 136, and 233–39.

40 In referring to men in power, I do not mean to suggest that non-Indigenous women were completely absent from the discourse, but I do contend that, at least in British Columbia, their voices were muted compared to those of men.

41 Crosby, *Among the An-ko-me-nums*, 96.

42 See, for example, private memorandum of Gilbert Malcolm Sproat, Indian Reserve Commissioner, Okanagan Lake, October 27, 1877, in DIA, RG 10, vol. 3656, file 9063, C-10115, Library and Archives Canada (LAC).

43 Remarks enclosed with letter from George Blenkinsop, secretary and census taker to Indian Reserve Commission, to Sproat, Douglas Lake, September 20, 1878, in DIA, RG 10, vol. 3667, file 10,330, LAC.

44 Private memorandum of Sproat, October 27, 1877; and Alex C. Anderson and Archibald McKinlay, Report of the Proceedings of the Joint Commission for the Settlement of the Indian Reserves in the Province of British Columbia, Victoria, March 21, 1877, in DIA, RG 10, vol. 3645, file 7936, C-10113, LAC.

45 Crosby, *Among the An-ko-me-nums*, esp. 206–32 and *passim*; and Crosby, *Up and Down*, *passim*.

46 May 24, 1866, entry in Hills diary.

47 Census data included with Anderson and McKinlay, Report, March 21, 1877.

48 Remarks enclosed with Blenkinsop to Sproat, September 20, 1878.

49 Such a contention is not inconsistent with Carol Devens's view that Indigenous men in the Great Lakes region more easily accommodated to missionaries' aspirations for them than did women; see her *Countering Colonization: Native American Women and Great Lakes Missions, 1630–1900* (Berkeley: University of California Press, 1992).

50 Crosby, *Up and Down*, 270–71.

51 Stocking, *Victorian Anthropology*, 202.

52 Leonore Davidoff and Catherine Hall, *Family Fortunes: Men and Women of the English Middle Class, 1780–1850* (London: Hutchinson, 1987), 322, 451.

53 Alex C. Anderson, J.P., to Sir Francis Hincks, MP for Vancouver District, Victoria, August 26, 1873, excerpted in undated memorandum of Anderson in DIA, RG 10, vol. 3658, file 9404, C-10115, LAC.

54 Anderson and McKinlay, Report, March 21, 1877.

55 William Laing Meason, Indian agent of Williams Lake Agency, to I.W. Powell, Superintendent of Indian Affairs, Lillooet, March 25, 1884, in DIA, RG 10, vol. 3658, file 9404, C-10115, LAC.

56 R.C. Mayne, *Four Years in British Columbia and Vancouver Island* (London: John Murray, 1862), 277.

57 Anderson to John Ash, Provincial Secretary of British Columbia, April 16, 1873, excerpted in undated memorandum of Anderson, in DIA, RG 10, vol. 3658, file 9404, C-10115, LAC.

58 The fullest account of the events occurring in 1879 is by a descendant: Mel Rothenburger, *The Wild McLeans* (Victoria: Orca, 1993).

59 The sequence of events at Cache Creek School in 1877 was followed closely in the Victoria press.

60 The constructed nature of all most Indigenous petitions is indicated by the alacrity with which missionaries and others warned federal officials about upcoming petitions "purporting to come from the Indians," but which were in fact being organized by an opposing religious group or others not to their liking, as with Alfred Hall, Anglican missionary, to Superintendent of Indian Affairs, Alert Bay, October 5, 1889, in RG 10, vol. 3816, file 57,045-1, C-10193, LAC.

61 Petitions of the Lillooet tribe of Indians and from Lower Fraser Indians, s.d. [summer and late fall 1885], and s.d. [summer 1885], in RG 10, vol. 3842, file 71,799, C-10148, LAC. On the Oblates' role see memo from Bishop Louis d'Herbomez, OMI, to the Governor General, s.d. [1887], in same.

62 George N. Burbidge, Deputy Minister of Justice, to L. Vankoughnet, Deputy Superintendent General of Indian Affairs, Ottawa, February 3, 1886, and enclosure, in RG 10, vol. 3842, file 71,799, C-10148, LAC.

63 W.H. Lomas, Indian agent of Cowichan Agency, to Powell, Quamichan, May 20, 1886; also draft of Vankoughnet to Powell, February 13, 1886; P. McTiernan, Indian agent at New Westminster, to Powell, New Westminster, April 9, 1886; Meason to Powell, Little Dog Creek, March 25, 1886; J.W. Mackay, Indian agent of Kamloops-Okanagan Agency, to Powell, Sooyoos [Osoyoos], May 2, 1886; and Powell to Superintendent of Indian Affairs, Victoria, June 21, 1886, in RG 10, vol. 3842, file 71,799, C-10148, LAC.

64 Memo from d'Herbomez [1887]; and Hector Langevin, Minister of Public Works, to John Macdonald, Superintendent of Indian Affairs, Ottawa, April 25, 1887, in RG 10, vol. 3842, file 71,799, C-10148, LAC.

65 Petition, New Westminster, September 1, 1890, in RG 10, vol. 3842, file 71,799, C-10148, LAC.

66 Draft from Department of Indian Affairs to Deputy Minister of Justice, December 17, 1890, in RG 10, vol. 3842, file 71,799, C-10148, LAC.

67 Draft of Department of Indian Affairs to A.W. Vowell, Indian Superintendent, Ottawa, December 26, 1890, in RG 10, vol. 3842, file 71,799, C-10148, LAC.

68 Meason to Vowell, Lillooet, August 4, 1890, in RG 10, vol. 3816, file 57,045-1, C-10193, LAC.

69 For the Cariboo, see Margaret Whitehead, *The Cariboo Mission: A History of the Oblates* (Victoria: Sono Nis Press, 1981).

70 Mackay to Vowell, Kamloops, May 24, 1892, in RG 10, vol. 3875, file 90,667-2, C-10193, LAC.

71 Meason to Vowell, Lillooet, May 14, 1892, in RG 10, vol. 3875, file 90,667-2, C-10193, LAC. The incident, its impetus in Oblate policy, and its aftermath are summarized in Whitehead, *Cariboo Mission*, 96–97. At the behest of Catholic authorities, the Governor General remitted the sentences.

72 Mackay to Vowell, May 24, 1892.

73 R.H. Pidcock, Indian agent of Kwawkwelth Agency, to Powell, Alert Bay, April 3, 1889, in DIA, RG 10, vol. 3816, file 57045, C-10193, LAC.

74 Pidcock to Vowell, n.d., in RG 10, vol. 3816, file 57,045-1, C-10193, LAC.

75 Vowell to Deputy Superintendent of Indian Affairs, Victoria, March 25, 1890, in RG 10, vol. 3816, file 57,045-1, C-10193, LAC.

76 Memorandum of Superintendent General of Indian Affairs to Privy Council of Canada, Ottawa, February 20, 1890, in DIA, RG 10, vol. 3816, file 57,045-1, C-10193, LAC.

77 John S.D. Thompson, Minister of Justice, to Governor General in Council, 1890, in RG 10, vol. 3816, file 57,045-1, C-10193, LAC.

78 Henry Guillod, Indian agent of West Coast Agency, to Vowell, Ucluelet, August 22, 1890, in RG 10, vol. 3816, file 57,045-1, C-10193, LAC.

79 Lomas to Vowell, Quamichan, November 22, 1890, in RG 10, vol. 3816, file 57,045-1, C-10193, LAC.

80 McTiernan to Vowell, New Westminster, June 23, 1890, in RG 10, vol. 3816, file 57,045-1, C-10193, LAC.

81 Meason to Vowell, Lillooet, August 4, 1890, in RG 10, vol. 3816, file 57,045-1, C-10193, LAC.

82 Mackay to Vowell, Kamloops, July 4, 1890, in RG 10, vol. 3816, file 57,045-1, C-10193, LAC.

83 C. Todd, acting Indian agent of North West Coast Agency, to Vowell, Metlakatla, October 8, 1890, in RG 10, vol. 3816, file 57,045-1, C-10193, LAC.

84 Vowell to Vankoughnet, Victoria, February 25, 1891, in RG 10, vol. 3816, file 57,045-1, C-10193, LAC.

85 Petition to Pidcock, Fort Rupert, March 8, 1895, in RG 10, vol. 3816, file 57,045-1, C-10193, LAC.

86 Senator W.J. Macdonald to Minister of the Interior, Ottawa, May 6, 1895, in RG 10, vol. 3816, file 57,045-1, C-10193, LAC.

87 Deputy Superintendent General of Indian Affairs to Vowell, Ottawa, May 20, 1895, in RG 10, vol. 3816, file 57,045-1, C-10193, LAC.

88 Davidoff and Hall, *Family Fortunes*, 115.

89 Census data included with Anderson and McKinlay, Report, March 21, 1877.

90 Crosby, *Among the An-ko-me-nums*, 49–50.

91 Crosby, *Up and Down*, 74.

92 For example, Cornelius Bryant, Methodist missionary, to Lomas, Nanaimo, January 30, 1884; G. Donckel, Catholic missionary, to Lomas, Maple Bay, February 2, 1884; Lomas to Powell, Maple Bay, February 5, 1884; and Powell to Superintendent General of Indian Affairs, Victoria, February 27, 1884, in DIA, RG 10, vol. 3628, file 6244-1, C-10110, LAC.

93 This point is supported by DIA to Powell, June 6, 1884, in DIA, RG 10, vol. 3628, file 6244-1, C-10110, LAC; and stated explicitly in E.K. DeBeck, "The Potlatch and Section 149 of the Indian Act," Ottawa, May 11, 1921, in DIA, RG 10, vol. 3628, file 6244-X, C-10110, LAC; and in C.M. Barbeau, "The Potlatch among the B.C. Indians and Section 149 of the Indian Act," 1921, in DIA, RG 10, vol. 3628, file 6244-X, C-10111, LAC.

94 Confidential memo to C.M.B., February 17, 1921, in Barbeau, "The Potlatch."

95 *Empire* (Toronto), received February 9, 1893, and letter from Pidcock, March 16, 1893, in Barbeau, "The Potlatch."

96 Crosby, *Up and Down*, 316.

97 G.W. DeBeck, Indian agent of Kwawkwelth Agency, to Vowell, Alert Bay, December 29, 1902, and E.A. Bird, teacher at Gwayasdurus, to DeBeck, Alert Bay, June 23, 1902, in DIA, RG 10, vol. 6816, file 486-2-5, C-8538, LAC.

98 Bird to DeBeck, June 23, 1902.

99 Letter from Thomas Crosby, *Missionary Outlook* 9 (1989), 100, cited in Clarence Bolt, *Thomas Crosby and the Tsimshian* (Vancouver: UBC Press, 1992), 64; and Crosby, *Up and Down*, 85.

100 Crosby, *Among the An-ko-me-nums*, 63.

101 Kate Hendry to sister Maggie, December 26, 1882, Kate Hendry Letterbook, BC Archives, EC/H38.

102 C.J. South, Superintendent, Children's Protection Act, to Secretary, Department of Indian Affairs, Vancouver, September 20, 1905, in RG 10, vol. 3816, file 57,045-1, C-10193, LAC.

103 Bolt, *Thomas Crosby*, 64.

104 October 2, 1886, entry in Agnes Knight, journal, 1885–1887, BC Archives, F7/W15.

105 Crosby, *Up and Down*, 89, 92–93.

106 "Indian Girl Sold for 1,000 Blankets," *World* (Vancouver), January 2, 1906.

107 "Five Little Girls Sold at Alert Bay Potlatch," *World*, April 4, 1906; and "Five Indian Girls Sold, Vancouver, B.C., April 6," *Journal* (Ottawa), April 9, 1906.

108 Letter of Vowell, April 16, 1906, in Barbeau, "The Potlatch."

109 "Squaw Sold for $400.00 at Alert Bay to a Grizzled Chief from Queen Charlottes," *Daily News Advertiser* (Vancouver), April 6, 1907.

110 Letter of William Halliday, July 9, 1907, in Barbeau, "The Potlatch."

111 The quotes are from Emily Cummings, Corresponding Secretary, National Council of Women, to Minister of Indian Affairs, Toronto, February 19, 1910, in RG 10, vol. 3816, file 57,045-1, C-10193, LAC, which also contains the many letters, often virtually identical in language, from the different associations.

112 DeBeck, "The Potlatch and Section 149."

113 Crosby, *Up and Down*, 92.

114 John Tate (Salaben), Gispaxloats, informant, recorded by William Beynon in 1950, in George F. MacDonald and John J. Cove, ed., *Tsimshian Narratives*, collected by Marius Barbeau and William Beynon, vol. 2: *Trade and Warfare* (Ottawa: Canadian Museum of Civilization, 1987), 207.

115 The 1901 manuscript census indicates persons' "colour" and mixed-race origins, making it possible to determine the character of individual households.

116 Carr, *Heart of a Peacock*, 110–11.

117 C.W. Holliday, *The Valley of Youth* (Caldwell, ID: Caxton, 1948), 155, 226.

118 DeBeck, "The Potlatch and Section 149."

119 June 16, 17, and 25, and July 11 and 26, 1966, entries in Edward Hoagland, *Notes from the Century Before: A Journal from British Columbia* (New York: Ballantine, 1969), 92, 96, 101, 141, 186, 250.

6

Invisible Women

Indigenous Mothers and Mixed-Race Daughters in Rural Pioneer British Columbia

Barman begins this essay by noting how the presence of Indigenous wives is ignored or obscured by historians who are focusing on the story of true (white) pioneer womanhood. The most striking finding of this piece is the different opportunities for family-making or marriage taken up by men and women of mixed ancestry: second-generation women of mixed ancestry partnered with 55 per cent white men, 40 per cent men of mixed ancestry, and 5 per cent Indigenous men, while second-generation men of mixed ancestry partnered with Indigenous women in 40 per cent of cases, women of mixed ancestry in 55 per cent and white women in 5 per cent. The difference reveals both how women of mixed ancestry could be subsumed into white society through a marriage that ensured they were under the control of their husbands, while men of the same ancestry posed a threat to the domination of white men in the new society.

By Jean Barman. Original title "Invisible Women: Aboriginal Mothers and Mixed-Race Daughters in Rural Pioneer British Columbia." Reprinted with permission from *Beyond the City Limits: Rural History in British Columbia*, edited by R.W. Sandwell (Vancouver: UBC Press, 1999), 159–79. The book won the Canadian Historical Association's CLIO Award for British Columbia in 2000. The essay has been somewhat shortened to avoid repetition with other essays in this volume.

For all the rhetoric on new ways of conceiving the past, scholarship is still dominated by a mythic pioneer woman who came from elsewhere to face the challenges of a new land. Mostly she was white, but regardless of skin tone, she brought with her a culture, a way of life, that she then transplanted onto the new landscape. To the extent that scholars have rethought the past, it has been principally to reveal and then critique such women's lives in terms of their contribution to some larger colonial enterprise. Their existence as the norm of rural pioneer life has not been questioned.

In the case of British Columbia, the mythic pioneer woman is best exemplified by Margaret Ormsby's *Pioneer Gentlewoman*, the memoir of Susan Allison, a young white woman who in the 1860s followed her husband into the remote British Columbia Interior.[1] *Pioneer Gentlewoman* followed naturally, perhaps inevitably, on earlier scholarship. The classic *Pioneer Women of Vancouver Island* was consciously intended to counter the "man's standpoint," which up to then (1928) had dominated "narratives of the exploration and development of the Pacific Northwest."[2] Dedicated to "the courage, strength of purpose and nobility of character which governed the lives of the Pioneer Women of Vancouver Island," the volume began with, and essentially concerned itself with, "white women's part in the history of the North Pacific."[3] Other studies have mostly followed in this tradition.[4]

If discussed at all, non-white women were long considered only in passing, and then as exceptions to the norm. The wives of Pacific Northwest fur traders sometimes become pioneer predecessors, often with some obscuring of their likely Indigenous or mixed-race descent.[5] Other Indigenous women have generally been interpreted as existing somewhere outside of history, as ethnographic specimens safely ensconced within some verbal museum of the past. When discussed, the emphasis has been on the ways in which they have held on to their traditional cultures and thereby, by inference, not muddied the waters of true pioneer womanhood.

Real life was more confused and messy than we might have it be. Pioneer women, the great majority of whom lived in rural settings, were not all cast in the same mould. While most likely bore some resemblance to the stereotypical image, in British Columbia, as in many other areas of North America, a considerable proportion of the women who contributed to the pioneer enterprise were Indigenous women and then their mixed-race daughters, the families of non-Indigenous, principally white, men.

These invisible women of the past are the subject of this essay. After examining factors encouraging relationships between non-Indigenous men and Indigenous women, it explores the nature and range of contact. The essay then turns to Indigenous mothers' mixed-race daughters, women whose life chances were very much affected by factors beyond their control but who yet exercised remarkable agency in fashioning their lives within the constraints imposed upon them.

Minimum numbers of rural pioneer women who were Indigenous or of mixed race can be inferred from the manuscript censuses of the late nineteenth century. British Columbia entered the Canadian Confederation too late to be included in the 1871 federal census, so the earliest numbers come from 1881. This census reveals about 1,500 mixed-race households encompassing some 6,000 individuals. About 500 of these households were first generation, being headed by a non-Indigenous man living with an Indigenous woman. Very importantly, the personal relationships existing in these 1,500 households were each sufficiently "public" to have been declared by the head of the household to the visiting enumerator, making them indicative of some unknown larger whole rather than the entirety.

The census numbers take on meaning when contextualized. The data indicate that most relationships between non-Indigenous men and Indigenous women occurred outside urban centres, where the social proprieties of non-Indigenous cultures were more rigorously upheld and expectations were stronger that men would marry "their own kind" or not at all. Of non-Indigenous men who in the 1881 census were living with an Indigenous woman, over half described themselves as farmers and another quarter were unskilled or semi-skilled labourers of various kinds, including farm labourers and loggers. The non-Indigenous adult male population of rural British Columbia was about 8,000 in 1881, rising to 16,000 by 1891.[6] If men of likely mixed race are removed from those totals, then about one in every ten to twenty non-Indigenous men were living with Indigenous women, and another larger proportion with a woman of mixed race.

The impetus to these relationships goes far beyond British Columbia or even the North American frontier generally. Wherever newcomers and Indigenous people met around the world during the vast and lengthy colonial enterprise, certain assumptions governed attitudes toward local women. If unspoken and for the most part unwritten, it was generally accepted in the societies whence colonizers came that so long as white women were absent, Indigenous women could be used to satisfy what were perceived as men's natural needs. The assumption of white racial superiority over Indigenous peoples muted scruples related to what Philip Mason has termed "the casual use of a social inferior for sexual pleasure" and then to that "social inferior" being discarded wherever other options became available with the growth of settler colonies.[7]

By the time the white male advance reached the Pacific Northwest in the late eighteenth century, any hesitation over sexual intimacy with local women had long since disappeared. As Robin Fisher, Sylvia Van Kirk, and others have perceptively argued, fur traders and local Indigenous peoples each perceived economic benefits to such couplings and foresaw advantages to their taking on some of the characteristics of a family.[8] The area to become British Columbia remained a fur trading enclave into the mid-nineteenth century, and numerous mixed-race relationships emerged between traders and local women, as they also did consequent to a gold rush beginning in 1858.

During the heady gold rush years from 1858 to 1864, well over thirty thousand white men and several thousand Chinese and Black men made their way to the Fraser River and then to the Cariboo to seek their fortune from gold. Most men soon departed, for the difficulties of getting to the gold fields were horrendous, but however long they might stay, their utter loneliness in a sea of men cannot be discounted. Contemporary accounts by gold seekers underline that the most fundamental characteristic of white women in gold rush British Columbia was their absence.

A paucity of contemporary sources makes it far more difficult to disentangle motivations from the perspective of Indigenous women. What is clear is that they did not always act in concert with their male counterparts, as the historiography of British Columbia has generally assumed through its tendency to see Indigenous peoples as a single, homogenous whole undifferentiated by gender. Given that most writers historically have been men, it has not unexpectedly been the Indigenous male who has been generalized. The scholarship had long accepted at face value contemporary white accounts written from the Victorian assumption of male superiority and male authority over females. Other sources suggest a different view, as in Anglican bishop George Hills's graphic description of a scene in a northern village in March 1860:

> I saw an Indian woman gesticulating & loudly talking—sometimes as in anger—other times in affliction ... A man before her was on the ground. It was her husband. He was intoxicated, not sufficiently but that he knew what he was about ... She was reproaching him. She was ashamed of him. She pitied him. She hated him. She feared him. She loved him. What she actually

> uttered I could not understand but the purpose was plain & all these states of feeling were evident ... She stood at a distance & scolded from afar. She relented & would come back as though to assist him home but on approach his folly created in her disgust & she could not bring herself to aid him. At length he was on his feet & made rush after her. She fled affrighted—as though she feared something more than himself.[9]

It was a short step for such a woman to turn to a non-Indigenous man.

Many Indigenous women likely soon came to the realization that, however much they tried to mimic newcomers' ways, they could not earn their recognition, so they might as well act as they pleased.[10] Thus Bishop Hills first found cause for optimism in young Indigenous women's attempts to emulate their white counterparts. In his words, "The young women begin to deck themselves in fashionable attire. I saw a young woman at the Schymsian [Tsimshian] camp [in Victoria] with a gold ring on the wedding finger. She was washing her face & really looked pleasing with black sparkling eyes & rosy cheeks."[11] The potential in such behaviour soon dawned on him, and by August of his first year he was musing to himself during a religious service at a Haida camp near Victoria: "Even alas this very gathering gave proofs of corruption. There were some of the young women decked out in every sort of vulgar finery—even to the wearing of crinoline & hoops. They were the unmarried wives of white men—& worse instances were there than even this."[12]

The social and material advantages accruing to Indigenous women willing to cross racial boundaries were likely a consideration. Describing an Indigenous acquaintance, British Columbia painter and writer Emily Carr observed: "Jenny had loved her husband and gloried in her name. It was infinitely finer to be 'Mrs Jenny Smith' than to have her name hitched to an Indian man's and be 'Jenny Joe' or 'Jenny Tom.'"[13]

Several factors specific to British Columbia, although also present on other settlement frontiers, facilitated relationships. At the level of everyday life, Indigenous populations were not nearly so alien as sometimes portrayed. Relations were generally peaceful, and many miners and settlers survived only because of local largesse. A German visiting the gold fields in 1858 reported that "many Indians lived in the neighborhood, who on the whole are on friendly footing with the Whites."[14] A guide to prospective settlers published a quarter of a century later asserted: "The intending settler may depend on finding the Indians peaceable, intelligent, eager to learn and industrious to a degree unknown elsewhere among the aborigines of America."[15] A related factor was ease of communication. Along the north coast and through much of the Interior communication was facilitated by common knowledge of the trading jargon of Chinook. Containing a large variety of non-verbal additions, including facial expressions and hand motions, Chinook facilitated conversations across races, including Indigenous women and non-Indigenous men. People talked to each other and sometimes did more than just talk.

British Columbia's historical development and its topography lent themselves to more permanency in relationships than might have occurred elsewhere. Most of the ten thousand or so non-Indigenous men who put down roots after the gold rush had run its course by the mid-1860s pre-empted land and so had to go wherever fertile patches happened to exist in a province that is mostly mountainous and very difficult of access. They survived largely on their own terms. Many had long since lost touch with family. Bishop Hills recalled a miner from Norfolk who "was very glad to talk about old England," yet "had not written for years & no letters now came to him." He had last seen his daughter, now aged sixteen, when she was two.[16] Few possessed the resources to secure a female partner from elsewhere by inviting out an old sweetheart or visiting back home. They became true pioneers in a new land.

Indigenous women remained integral to the colonial enterprise until nearly the end of the nineteenth century. The entry of the British colony of British Columbia into the Canadian Confederation in 1871 was essentially a political exercise, having, at first, little impact on non-Indigenous sexual ratios. It took the completion of the transcontinental railroad in the mid-1880s and the federal immigration campaign begun a decade later to even out these ratios. At that point, sexual couplings with Indigenous women were perceived to have become unnecessary.[17] Racial boundaries hardened as numbers of newcomers grew, particularly in urban areas. Class considerations compounded the force of race. As everyday behaviour became more public and social status more dependent on externalized expectations of behaviour into which an Indigenous wife simply did not fit, so a number of men with political or social aspirations abandoned their Indigenous wives and sometimes also their children.

The town that changed the most fundamentally was Vancouver, which in the mid-1880s grew almost overnight from a small lumbering enclave based in personal relationships to a much more impersonal railroad terminus.[18] Some local luminaries did opt for a new beginning by casting aside Indigenous spouses, but others, like Portuguese-born Joe Silvey, simply took their families off to a more remote rural location. Joe Silvey made the move to Reid Island, where daily life still depended on face-to-face interaction rather than on larger social constructs like race and class. Having arrived with the gold rush, Silvey had soon wed the granddaughter of a Musqueam chief in what has come down through time as an elaborate Indigenous ceremony. The Silveys settled in the area that would become known as Gastown, where he ran a saloon, fished, and traded with local Indigenous people and sawmill workers.[19] At the beginning of the 1870s, Silvey was left a widower with two daughters, and shortly thereafter married a Sechelt woman and moved to Reid Island.

By the end of the nineteenth century, several thousand, and perhaps many more, non-Indigenous men and Indigenous women had engaged in sexual couplings in the geographical area known as British Columbia. Some relationships were fairly transient, two persons cohabiting for a time until one or the other decided to move on. A young Englishman reflected the white perspective in his description of an incident occurring in the Okanagan Valley: "Soon he and his lady had a bad row, and realizing that his little romance was ended he fired her out. And as none of the rest of the old boys were gallant enough to take a chance on her, the lady returned to the bosom of her tribe, and once again there was peace on earth."[20] An Indigenous woman born late in the century put the female perspective to verse:

> They say Dunlevy had an Indian wife,
> But that was before my time,
> When I knew him, he had a white wife
> Who married a doctor when he died.
>
> Oh, it was hard on Indian wives, I guess,
> But they always managed
> To raise their children
> Even if their husbands finished with them.[21]

The man in question, Peter Dunlevy, was one of thousands of Americans arrived from the California gold fields.[22] As semi-fictionalized from a diary based on conversations with Dunlevy in old age, he and his fellow miners considered the taking of local women part of the young man's adventure that was the gold rush: "'It's pleasant to find beautiful women in this country,' said Dunlevey [*sic*], 'If we plan to stay where there are no other women' … he hesitated … 'well, no use to cross your bridges till you come to them.'"[23] A bit later on, a comrade asserts, "We shoulda just grabbed them wenches and if the bucks objected, we coulda cleaned up on them!"[24] According to the account, Dunlevy "mingled his Irish blood with that of the beautiful native Dene maiden and so helped to populate the Cariboo country."

The next comment likely embodied a touch of bravado, but nonetheless made the point: "His seed is scattered across the length and face of the great Cariboo. In the little villages or logging camps, among the rolling hills or in any spot where natives congregate for a rodeo or a Saturday night blowout, there you may find Dunlevey descendants."[25] As Dunlevy became established as a merchant throughout the Cariboo and Peace River areas, so he also "upgraded" his personal life by marrying in 1875 a young white woman twenty years his junior, born in San Francisco of Irish parents, by whom he proceeded to have five more children.[26]

It was not only men who ended relationships. Indigenous women sometimes walked out, taking children with them. At Lytton in 1868, "a man named Seward who has a farm nearby was lately left by his Indian wife who had had two children by him. He now says everything bad of her. He confesses having sown the seed he has reaped."[27]

Another situation was more complex. Bishop Hills described how "almost every man in Douglas lives with an Indian woman," including the local magistrate and constable. As recorded in Hills's journal under the heading "Immorality," the latter two, in that remote gold rush town, had shared the same woman after "the constable Humphreys was ordered to a distance by the Magistrate," who, in spite of his promise that Lucy and their child would be "kept safe" during the constable's absence, "violated the promise & induced the woman to come to him."[28] Bishop Hill's deceived constable, Thomas Humphreys, must have nonetheless returned to Lucy Semo, a daughter of the chief of the Chehalis, for their daughter Josephine, born in 1868, never forgot her father: "Voices linger of Father with Tommy, Eddie and I to say our prayers and sing hymns. He taught me how to watch and pray, to live rejoicing every day ... I can hear his voice yet many happy days." Then, as recalled by Josephine, "Father was sent to Victoria," this a reference to his election as a member of the first provincial assembly in 1871. Possibly, as justified by Josephine writing much later in time, her father is meant to have asked Lucy and their three children to go with him, but "she refused to join her husband in Victoria because she knew she would not be accepted there and that was why he had found a white wife."[29]

At the other end of the continuum of personal relationships were those that endured through the lifetimes of the two partners. For some men, few marital options existed, as with Hudson's Bay labourers recruited from Hawai'i, Mexican packers who came north with the gold rush, Chilean sailors jumping ship at Burrard Inlet, and Chinese come to chase gold. For many others, however, it was a matter of choice. Mixed-race families were often the first non-Indigenous settlers in rural, outlying Vancouver Island, across the Gulf Islands, and through the remote southern and central Interior. Almost all of the numerous mixed-race unions on Mayne Island were, according to the island's historian Marie Elliott, "permanent until the death of one of the partners."[30] The everyday lives of most of the five hundred families making it into the 1881 and 1891 manuscript censuses were usually little different from pioneer neighbours where both partners were white.[31]

Typical of such rural families, and among the numerous mixed-race households dotted across the Gulf Islands, were the Fords and the Currans. George Ford, born in Devonshire in 1831, was one of a dozen newly arrived young Englishman taking up land in the Comox area of Vancouver Island in 1862.[32] Working for a time for the Hudson's Bay Company at Fort Rupert, he met and married Mary James, seventeen years his junior and daughter of Fort Rupert Chief Kla Kwa Keela, who had been nicknamed Captain James because he piloted British gunboats.[33] In 1869 the Fords moved from Comox to Hornby Island, perhaps because, a descendant has mused, the growing white settlement around Comox "was not friendly to a Native and non-Native marriage." Ford, together with a friend who had also come out in 1862 and married an Indigenous woman, became the first white settlers and eventually owned almost half of Hornby between them. In 1897 the Ford farm was described as "splendid ... George Ford has several hundred of graded South Downs [sheep]—he has about a thousand

William Henry Curran, who was born in 1843 in Rhode Island and who died in 1930 in New Westminster, had two successive families, of seven children each, by Indigenous women. Photo courtesy of Iris Griffiths and Joe Warnock.

acres—200 acres are in the flat and in shape for use—besides much more pasture land. There has been a post office for about two years—he is postmaster—mail once a week—there is a public wharf and it is here where the SS Joan stops."[34] George Ford was responsible for getting the first wharf and had a sloop called the *Thistle*, purchased in Seattle, which he used to sell farm produce in the surrounding area. Between 1866 and 1884 the Fords had eight children.

William Henry Curran epitomizes the nineteenth-century wanderer who finally settled down so far from home that he had likely long since lost touch with family and childhood friends, and thereafter made life largely on his own terms. As recounted in old age, Curran left his Rhode Island home in 1857 at age fourteen to become a drummer boy in the US army.[35] Four years later he had made it to the gold rush in British Columbia, where he soon pre-empted land on Saltspring and then on Thetis Island. Curran's first wife, by whom he had seven children between 1867 and 1883, was Mary Sitkwa Whilemot, a Cowichan woman who already had two mixed-race children from an earlier relationship.

On Mary's death in 1894, Curran homesteaded around Shuswap Lake in the Interior, where he met his second wife, a local Indigenous woman named Elizabeth Toma, thirty-four years his junior. Eventually they settled on Lasqueti, where, according to a long-time islander, "the Curran home was always open to their neighbours," and seven more Curran children were born.[36] Family recollections suggest that life on Lasqueti embodied a strong sense of community. A descendant has recalled: "Everyone lived together—a version of utopia—there was great hospitality along the coast in those days—everyone looked after you—we all piled in together, lived together, ate together." The impersonality of race and class was held at bay, at least for a time.

Mary Sitkwa Whilemot, a Cowichan woman born in about 1845, had seven children with William Henry Curran before her death in 1894 on Kuper Island. Photo courtesy of Iris Griffiths and Joe Warnock.

If everyday lives of many mixed-race families were similar to those of their rural white counterparts, long-term consequences for their offspring were very different. To the extent that contemporaries, be it in British Columbia or elsewhere across the colonized world, perceived individuals as having a dual Indigenous and non-Indigenous heritage, they were almost always distinguished by some term embodying within it condemnation of the children for their parents having produced them in the first place. The North American word was "halfbreed" or "breed," excepting for French Canada with its equivalent of "métis." By the late nineteenth century such terms were almost always derogatory in their connotations.

To be "halfbreed" was to be disparaged by the dominant societies developing across the American and Canadian Wests. Several factors coalesced. In the American frontier myth premised on "manifest destiny," Indigenous peoples were perceived as the principal obstacle to settlement and to "progress." North Americans, along with their counterparts across the Western world, were becoming firm believers

Born in 1870, Ellen Curran married Irishman James Warnock, who was about four years her senior, in 1888. The Warnocks homesteaded on Galiano Island and had four children before Ellen's death in 1899. Photo courtesy of Iris Griffiths and Joe Warnock.

in scientific racism. As adapted from Charles Darwin's concept of the survival of the fittest, the theory argued that the races were arranged in a hierarchy with whites, not unexpectedly, on the top. Indigenous people were inherently inferior, so almost everyone agreed, and "halfbreeds" were akin to mongrels, almost certainly inheriting the worst features of each parent. Nineteenth-century literature repeatedly used the halfbreed as a metaphor for the settlement process. Heredity made the fictional halfbreed an object of fear whose demise, usually through death, symbolized the frontier's inevitable conquest.[37]

It was not only biological assumptions that shaped the mixed-race experience in British Columbia. So long as the province remained a sparsely populated, isolated enclave, men and women were more likely to be able to prove themselves as individuals. The completion of the transcontinental railway in 1886 attracted thousands of Canadians and Americans to the west coast province, whose non-Indigenous population soared from under 25,000 in 1881 to over 70,000 a decade later and then to 150,000 by 1901. By the turn of the century, British Columbia was sharing in the national immigration fever that cooled only with the outbreak of the First World War, by which time the province's non-Indigenous population exceeded 400,000. As "halfbreeds," together with Indigenous peoples, became increasingly dispensable in the economic life of the province, so prejudices hardened.

However much families might try to protect their offspring, both girls and boys of mixed race were constantly in danger of being stigmatized as "halfbreeds." They need not do anything in order to be disparaged, as indicated by Bishop Hills's private lament in his journal within a few short years of his arrival in 1860 that mixed-race children "usually sink into a degraded state, combining the force of the white race with the viciousness & lowness of the savage."[38]

Margaret Curran was born in 1879 and married Frederick James Warren in 1898. Born in 1864 to a sea captain from Prince Edward Island and an Indigenous, likely Haida, woman named Mary or Tutsamutsu, Warren followed his father's occupation. The Warrens had six children before Margaret's death in 1911. Photo courtesy of Iris Griffiths and Joe Warnock.

The one institution of the dominant society that could not be avoided, even in the most remote rural areas, was the school. Initially in some areas of British Columbia, children of mixed race formed the majority of pupils in local public schools. The first Superintendent of Education counted 287 school-age children scattered across the British Columbia mainland from the Fraser Valley east and north, of whom 182 were "half-castes" and 105 "white."[39] Although children of mixed race attended their local public school alongside white and some Indigenous counterparts, the correspondence of the Superintendent of Education suggests that unequal treatment was sometimes recommended. When he suggested to a local school board that the "teaching labor should be equalized by drafting boys under seven into girls dept," there were "objections raised to half breeds mixing with girls."[40] Expectations for children of mixed race soon became lower than those for white pupils. By 1876 the Superintendent was directly linking race and school achievement: "27 pupils in school nearly all half breeds and very backward."[41] "Half-breed children very unpromising, dull and stupid and apparently incapable of learning."[42]

Even where the majority of children were of mixed race and families were intact, pupils were not necessarily treated equitably. Of the fourteen children at school in the remote Lower Nicola Valley, at least twelve had Indigenous mothers.[43] Among the fathers were former gold miners German-born William Voght, who has come down in British Columbia history as "the father of Merritt," and Mexican-born Jesus Garcia, men who married Indigenous half-sisters.[44] Two of the three members of the Nicola's founding school board were married to Indigenous women.[45] Jessie McQueen arrived from the Maritimes in the late 1880s to teach at the Lower Nicola school.[46] Writing to her mother about the Garcias' "four half-breed girls," she observed that "they have attended schools for years but in spite of that they still have the squaw looks & manners." By comparison, "Tena Voght is a half breed too but she is clever & pleasant & just like white folks." In reference to two children of an Englishman and an Indigenous woman, "Sarah & John—they have the Indian features and voices, but are good, and fully as clever as any of the others, and I like them." As these and many similar observations attest, Jessie McQueen was ambivalent. Although she wrestled with the possibility, she simply could not accept children of mixed race as inherently equal to white children.

Another educational option for children of mixed race was a boarding school funded by a missionary body. Until the end of the nineteenth century, when federal officials began to discourage and then prohibit the practice, most of the residential schools ostensibly intended for "Indian" children quietly enrolled children of mixed race. In some cases, as at St. Mary's Mission run by the Oblates and the Sisters of St. Ann in the Fraser Valley, such children were somewhat conveniently labelled "semi-Indian pupils."[47] The Sisters of St. Ann, a Catholic religious order that arrived from Quebec in 1858, operated two schools, at Williams Lake in the Cariboo and at Cowichan on eastern Vancouver Island, catering to children of mixed race, as well as enrolling such pupils in their other schools in Victoria, New Westminster, and, later, Nanaimo. The Cowichan school was intended on its opening in 1864 to educate Indigenous girls but even then attracted the two mixed-race daughters of the first white settler in the Cowichan Valley, and soon an increasingly larger number, including the Ford and Curran daughters. In 1874 the twenty-one girls of mixed race attending the order's boarding school in Victoria were moved to rural Cowichan, ostensibly for space reasons, but also perhaps to cater to white sensibilities. Thereafter, until the end of the 1880s when numbers began to dwindle, that school was specifically intended for girls of mixed race, some of whose families contributed financially, other pupils being kept at the order's expense. The order's boarding school at Williams Lake educated both girls and boys, "mostly halfbreeds" but some white children, and operated from 1876 to 1888, by which time numbers of children of non-Indigenous fathers and Indigenous mothers were also declining in the central Interior.

As the Cowichan school register and family recollections attest, many rural Vancouver Island, Gulf Island, and Cariboo families enrolled their daughters for periods of time ranging from a couple of years to a dozen to receive "the advantages of a solid elementary education, half a session for school and the other half for domestic training." According to Sister Mary Theodore, who arrived in 1878 to become the British Columbia order's first historian, "those they received came from homes kept by Indian mothers and were ignorant, not only of books but also of the use of house furniture." As a result, "the sisters considered it a matter of justice to fit their wards to become intelligent, useful and competent in the middle class of citizens," acquiring the household and other white skills their Indigenous mothers could not teach them. The sisters sometimes took the initiative in attracting pupils, for "often a white man having lived with a native partner for a while, would desert her and leave her and her children to continue Indian life." In other cases, as with Josephine Humphreys, who was sent to St. Mary's Mission in 1874, daughters were parked in boarding school as soon as they were old enough when their fathers moved on to white wives. As Josephine Humphreys later put it somewhat tactfully, "faced with the necessity to place his small daughter where she would be cared for, St. Mary's was the only school at the time with accommodation."[48]

As children of mixed race grew up, be it in British Columbia or elsewhere across the North American frontier, they realized just how fully they were caught between the Indigenous world of their mothers and the settler society of their fathers. It was at this point that gender intervened, sharply differentiating the adulthoods of daughters and sons. Young men of mixed race, viewed by many of their white counterparts as a challenge to their own masculinity, were much more likely to be forced into the shadows. The uncompromising racism of the day easily ostracized mixed-race sons as "halfbreeds" since, as males, they had no choice but to exist in the public sphere. However much they tried, they simply could not emulate their fathers' lifestyles. Their indigeneity, to the extent that it was visible in physical features or in common knowledge about descent, almost always worked to their disadvantage. Mixed-race sons were pushed to the margin and, conversely, being in such a position, seemingly confirmed their inherent inferiority to white counterparts. As the 1881, 1891, and 1901 censuses testify, they had limited marriage prospects: about 40 per cent of those who had a wife were living with an Indigenous woman; 55 per cent were with persons of mixed race like themselves; only in very exceptional circumstances were they with a white woman. In the first instance, particularly, their children might well grow up illiterate or, alternatively, be slipped into an "Indian school" and grow up mostly Indigenous.

Yet, however much sons might choose to identify with their maternal ancestry, they were prohibited from participating fully in the lives of their mothers' families. The 1876 Indian Act limited the federal government's responsibility to "status" Indians, defined in patriarchal fashion. Whereas an Indigenous male marrying a non-Indigenous female both retained his status and acquired status for his spouse and offspring, an Indigenous woman marrying a non-Indigenous man lost her status, as did any children born of the union. With the passage of time the regulation was more rigorously enforced, and persons of mixed race and their families were not only ineligible to receive the social and other services accorded status Indians, including federal schooling, but were also prohibited from living on reserves.

Persons of mixed race were, moreover, not always welcome among Indigenous people. A woman of mixed race growing up among her mother's family, who were the Carrier, later observed "that was the only bad thing in those very early years of my life—some of the [Indigenous] village people, especially the children, treated me as a person apart, different in some way from themselves."[49] The frustration was summed up by a man of mixed race born at the turn of the century, who went through life as "neither one or the other": "Not white and not Indian but we look Indian and everybody but Indians takes us for Indian ... It has been a complicated world."[50]

Banned from living on reserves, even with kinfolk, yet unacceptable within the dominant society, most men of mixed race scratched out a living in the few non-racialized occupations of the day: subsistence farming, fishing, logging, cowboying. Of second-generation men located in the 1901 census, less than a third described themselves as farmers compared to over half of their fathers; another third were farm labourers, and most of the remainder were labourers of other kinds. Ironically, one of the most feasible sources of income came through bootlegging liquor to Indigenous friends and relatives, from whom it was prohibited by law. It was in this context that persons characterized as "halfbreeds" most often came to the attention of local

Indian agents, who then called ever more strongly for their prohibition from the vicinity of reserves. Without question, the Department of Indian Affairs contributed markedly through both its attitude and its actions to the construction of the "halfbreed."

Daughters had an alternative unavailable to their brothers, one that many of them took or was taken for them. They could simply disappear from the dominant society's gaze, from any consciousness of them as "halfbreeds." Their life chances were fundamentally affected by their gender. Unlike their brothers, they were inherently not a threat to the established economic order. The patriarchal character of society combined with white females' sparseness to make women of mixed race far more acceptable than their male counterparts ever were. Their sometimes strong physical appeal was no hindrance. Herman Reinhart, one of a myriad of young gold miners, recalled "a lot of half-breed and three-fourths white girls that were awful good-looking of the dark style of beauty."[51] Of second-generation women given as married in the 1901 census, about 55 per cent had a white husband, just under 40 per cent a husband of mixed race like themselves, and the remainder an Indigenous partner.[52]

The same logic that made it acceptable for men to use women, Indigenous or otherwise, for their sexual gratification allowed their mixed-race daughters to submerge their identity into that of their non-Indigenous father and, later, a husband, much as their mothers had done. Women of all races were intended to be subservient. The decreased status of women of mixed race only further reinforced white male superiority and made it even less likely that the female in a relationship would challenge the existing order of things. This imbalance of power was often facilitated by large age discrepancies between spouses. In the interests of their own and their offspring's survival in a racist society, many Indigenous and mixed-race women turned gender on its head and rendered themselves invisible.

Sometimes daughters found their own husbands; in other cases husbands were forced on them. Francis Herring, who arrived when

British Columbia was still a British colony, evoked “a good-looking halfbreed girl” sought after by a young white cordwood cutter on the Harrison River during the 1860s. Despite his “doing his best to get her to come and live with him,” Juanita refused to do so without a commitment to a Christian marriage, “unless he put upon her finger a plain gold ring, ‘same as white woman’”[53] He did not commit himself to a Christian marriage, and within the year Juanita had wed a young man of mixed race who was willing to do so.[54] In similar fashion, one Curran daughter wed a man of mixed race; the others who can be traced opted for white husbands, whereas most of their brothers did not marry or simply disappeared from family view.

Likewise, the four Ford daughters all married white men they likely chose for themselves. In sharp contrast, one of their brothers twice married Indigenous women, another lived for a time with a married woman of mixed race, and the other two fished and farmed on the margins between the white and Indigenous worlds that were increasingly dividing British Columbians. After George Ford’s death, the family’s Hornby property disintegrated, some of it being sold for taxes. Whatever the combination of factors, the family “pretty much stuck to themselves and gradually the farm just disappeared—it sold off bit by bit—and it was gone—all the animals and everything I guess—it went.”[55]

Other daughters were forced into marriage. The Sisters of St. Ann only expressed the common wisdom of a patriarchal society in their concern to see their pupils safely wed before leaving their care. As the order’s historian has phrased it, “these were evil times for unprotected girls and the nuns were loath to see their charges which they had reared so carefully, during ten, twelve or even fifteen years cast on their own resources.” Girls were frequently married from the school to men chosen for them either by the sisters or, in some cases, their fathers. The experience of Josephine Humphreys, who was married from the school at age sixteen to a fellow student, son of a Welsh sailor-cum-miner and an Indigenous woman, was in no way unique:

"Some how I was to marry a young school boy age about 21 or so & I married June 26 my 16th birthday had not talked to the man the day I was married that was the most terrible time of my life." As she recalled for a granddaughter, "the girls were lined up and the men picked their wives out." Josephine wrote to her politician father to tell him about the marriage, and he assured her in reply that "I want you to feel sure that I have not forgotten you" and that "I hope I may have it in my power, before long to do something for you and your brothers." "I shall always be glad to hear from you at any time and don't think because I sometimes forget to answer your letters that I am likely to forget you."[56] Neither did Peter Dunlevy completely abandon his mixed-race daughter, who acted as sponsor on the baptism of her father's eldest child by his new white wife. A few years later she married one of the first ranchers to take up land in the Chilcotin, a Nova Scotian fully thirty years her senior.[57]

Marriage could not entirely protect women of mixed race, and then their daughters, from the force of racism, particularly if they physically resembled their mothers. Most lived in the constant knowledge that any slip along the way would be attributed to their indigeneity and they would be doubly scorned. The situation was in some ways more invidious than would have been legal segregation. Unlike Indigenous peoples and the Chinese across North America or Black people in the United States, few explicit boundaries pertained. Indicative of the attitudes against which British Columbians of mixed race had to struggle was a teacher's comment from the early 1920s in a confidential report to the Ministry of Education that "there are mostly foreigners in the school, only two being of English parentage; nine are Japanese, the rest Finlanders, Norwegians and half breed";[58] or, from another school, "the pupils are backward being of mixed bloods."[59] Whether or not the particular individuals and their families were aware, they were being labelled and treated accordingly.

The stigma attached to being perceived as a woman of mixed race was evoked very powerfully in a play written at the turn of the century by Constance Lindsay Skinner, raised in the mixed-race community of Quesnel in the 1880s. Set in a fictionalized coastal enclave, its female protagonist was the part-Indigenous adopted daughter of a missionary couple, sent away to school in the hope of subduing the mixed-race heritage that, unbeknownst to her, she embodied in her person.[60] Precious Conroy was by descent only one-eighth Indigenous, yet, as her white counterpoint Cissie, "all befrilled in musliny innocence," proclaims, "Indian blood is Indian blood and the amount of it makes very little difference." Even Precious's ignorance could not protect her—she was in effect tainted by her "Birthright," to use the play's title.

The play's action revolves around the return of the missionary couple's biological son, Dick. He becomes infatuated with Precious, much to his father's displeasure, for "to marry a native wife—or a wife in whose veins was the least taint—would be in many cases to make him throw away a brilliant career and his standing in the community." To stop the relationship, the couple tell him about Precious's background. When Dick replies that they must be in error, his mother replies, "Mistake! It sticks out all over her. Haven't we seen it, your father and I—since she came back? It shows in everything she does, everything she says. Her way of sitting, moving, her walk, her very thoughts are Indian." Precious remonstrates, and her adopted mother retorts, "It's in your blood! You're Indian all through." Dick weakens, and in the end Precious accepts her destiny, but not before stabbing Dick to death, thus confirming the dominant society's fear of the imagined halfbreed.

It is not surprising that some women of the second generation, and even more so their sons and daughters, chose entirely to shed their mixed race. They simply put their past behind them and got on with their lives. They did not mull on what might be or what had been, but rather on what could be. In some cases children and grandchildren eventually lost any public identification with their Indigenous heritage, as with such well-known British Columbians as provincial premier Simon Fraser Tolmie, pioneer Fraser Valley schoolteacher Mary Jane Shannon, and long-time provincial Minister of Finance Mel Couvelier.[61] Where physical characteristics made it possible, many not only effectively became white but convinced their children and grandchildren that they were white and only white.

As "halfbreeds" became outcasts from the dominant society, it became easy to obliterate them from the province's history. White British Columbians from the late nineteenth century onward sought to legitimize their presence in the space they had so recently occupied, and they determined to construct British Columbia in the image of the places whence they came, and to venerate the pioneers whose sacrifices had made this possible. For male historians, their heroes' personal lives counted for little and could easily be ignored or obscured where wives had been Indigenous or part-Indigenous.[62] Most historians lived in urban areas, and rural life had in any case little import. A conspiracy of silence ensued. A daughter of ethnologist James Teit's second marriage to a white woman was particularly revealing in her comments made in old age: "Before father died [in 1922], people had said to us children, 'You know your father had a Klootchman,' meaning that he had lived with an Indian woman. Mother and father had never told us of this."[63] White women, for their part, took special pride in honouring their mothers and grandmothers who had first come to British Columbia from elsewhere, thus Lugrin's *Pioneer Women of Vancouver Island* initiated by the Women's Canadian Club of Victoria.

Indigenous mothers' and mixed-race daughters' invisibility was not only due to the willingness of the dominant society to have them disappear. As this essay has suggested, the women themselves were sometimes complicit. The uncompromising racism of the day, with its assumption of white superiority and utter Indigenous inferiority, easily ostracized mixed-race sons, since, as males, they had no choice but to exist in the public world of work. Daughters had more options, and in the interests of their own and their offspring's survival in a racist society, many rendered themselves invisible.

Acknowledgement of these pioneer women as part of our common history challenges one of the last bastions of the frontier myth. As we re-vision the rural pioneer woman in all her diversity, no better starting point exists than Susan Allison. What the editor chose not to reveal in her extensive introduction and notes to *Pioneer Gentlewoman* was that the man young Susan married in 1868, at the beginning of the memoir, and whose life with her forms the subject of the volume, had already, like so many of his contemporaries, cohabited with one or more Indigenous women. John Fall Allison, twenty years Susan's senior, had fathered upward of five children, the last born the same year that he and Susan married. John and Susan went on to have another fifteen children together.[64] Allison's earlier activity has remained common knowledge in the rural area where the Allisons lived, and was passed down to an Indigenous storyteller by one of Allison's sons by an Indigenous woman named Mary.

> This is white people stories,
> because I learned this from the white people.
> Not the white man.
> The white man tell his son,
> that's Allison—John Fall Allison.
> White man.
> He is the one that tell the stories to his son.
> His son, Bert Allison.
> His son was a half Indian and a half white,
> because his mother was an Indian.
> And his father was a white man.
> So his father told him these stories.
> But he told me—Bert Allison.
> So he told me,
> "This is not Indian stories.
> White man stories."
> You understand that?

John Fall Allison, he died in 1897.
And his wife Susan died in 1937.
So he is the one that tell the story.[65]

An adult daughter from this union was actually living in the Allison household at the time of the 1881 census, likely helping to care for her younger half-siblings. Two likely sons spent their adult years in the vicinity, marrying Indigenous women.[66] Local folklore even has one of Allison's natural grandchildren visiting her widowed step-grandmother, Susan Allison, in old age, only to be humiliated by her step-grandmother's utter unwillingness to acknowledge the relationship or even to receive her.[67] Everyday life on the frontier was far more messy and complex than our retrospective constructions would have it be, and nowhere is this likely to be more evident than with rural pioneer women.

Notes

1 Margaret A. Ormsby, ed., *A Pioneer Gentlewoman in British Columbia: The Recollections of Susan Allison* (Vancouver: UBC Press, 1976).

2 N. de Bertrand Lugrin, *The Pioneer Women of Vancouver Island, 1843–1866* (Victoria: Women's Canadian Club of Victoria, 1928), 2.

3 Lugrin, *Pioneer Women of Vancouver Island*, n.p. and 4.

4 Notably, Elizabeth Forbes, *Wild Roses at Their Feet: Pioneer Women of Vancouver Island* (Victoria: British Columbia Centennial '71 Committee, 1971); Jan Gould, *Women of British Columbia* (Saanichton, BC: Hancock, 1975); some of the essays in Barbara Latham and Cathy Kess, ed., *In Her Own Right: Selected Essays on Women's History in B.C.* (Victoria: Camosun College, 1980), and Latham and Roberta J. Pazdro, ed., *Not Just Pin Money: Selected Essays on the History of Women's Work in British Columbia* (Victoria: Camosun College, 1984); Jan Gould, ed., *Memories Never Lost: Stories of the Pioneer Women of the Cowichan Valley and a Brief History of the Valley 1850–1920* (Altona, MB: D.W. Friesen, 1986); and Marnie Anderson, *Women of the West Coast Then and Now* (Sidney, BC: Sand Dollar Press, 1993). An exception is Marilyn Ravicz, Diane Battung and Laura Buker, "Rainbow Women of the Fraser Valley: Lifesongs through the Generations," in Latham and Pazdro, *Not Just Pin Money*, 37–52.

5 The two volumes from which subsequent scholarship has drawn are Sylvia Van Kirk, *Many Tender Ties: Women in Fur-Trade Society, 1670–1870* (Norman: University of Oklahoma Press, 1980), and Jennifer Brown, *Strangers in Blood: Fur Trade Company Families in Indian Country* (Vancouver: UBC Press, 1980). Van Kirk and Brown limit themselves to the upper strata of the trade—in essence, a few hundred men—in part I suspect because archival records are fullest for such persons. An earlier study, generally ignored because of its racist and sexist rhetoric, made many of the same points, often more effectively and within

the broader context of the entire fur trade: Walter O'Meara, *Daughters of the Country: The Women of the Fur Traders and Mountain Men* (New York: Harcourt, Brace and World, 1968).

6 Figures derived from tables in Jean Barman, *The West beyond the West: A History of British Columbia* (Toronto: University of Toronto Press, 1991, with revised editions in 1996 and 2007).

7 Philip Mason, *Patterns of Dominance* (London: Oxford University Press for the Institute of Race Relations, 1970), 88.

8 Robin Fisher, *Contact and Conflict: Indian-European Relations in British Columbia, 1774–1890* (Vancouver: UBC Press, 1977); and Van Kirk, *Many Tender Ties*.

9 March 23, 1860, entry in Bishop George Hills diary, in Anglican Church, Ecclesiastical Province of British Columbia, Archives.

10 On the larger meaning of mimicry as popularized by Homi Bhabha, see his "Of Mimicry and Man: The Ambivalence of Colonial Discourse," in *Tensions of Empire: Colonial Cultures in a Bourgeois World*, ed. Frederick Cooper and Ann Laura Stoler (Berkeley: University of California Press, 1997), 152–60.

11 April 21, 1860, entry in Hills diary.

12 August 12, 1860, entry in Hills diary.

13 Emily Carr, *The Heart of a Peacock* (Toronto: Irwin, 1986), 111.

14 Carl Friesach, *Ein Ausflug nach Britisch-Columbien in Jahre 1858* (Gratz: Philosophical Society, 1875), reprinted in *British Columbia Historical Quarterly* 5 (1941): 227.

15 *The West Shore*, September 1884, 275, cited in Patricia E. Roy, "*The West Shore*'s View of British Columbia, 1884," *Journal of the West* 22, no. 4 (October 1984): 28.

16 July 7, 1860, entry in Hills diary.

17 For totals, see Table 11 in Barman, *West beyond the West*, 369.

18 The transition is well captured in Robert A.J. McDonald, *Making Vancouver: Class, Status, and Social Boundaries, 1863–1913* (Vancouver: UBC Press, 1996).

19 Information on the Silvey family draws on Major Matthews's conversations with descendants, held in City of Vancouver Archives.

20 C.W. Holliday, *The Valley of Youth* (Caldwell, ID: Caxton Printers, 1948), 226.

21 "Changes" in Jean E. Speare, *The Days of Augusta* (Vancouver: J.J. Douglas, 1973), 71.

22 Mark S. Wade, *The Cariboo Road* (Victoria: Haunted Bookshop, 1979), 237.

23 Edith Beeson, *Dunlevey: From the Diaries of Alex P. McInnes* (Lillooet: Lillooet Publishers, 1971), 51.

24 Beeson, *Dunlevey*, 92.

25 Beeson, *Dunlevey*, 14.

26 "Peter Curran Dunlevy," typescript in BC Archives, Vertical Files.

27 May 27, 1868, entry in Hills diary.

28 May 20, 1862, entry in Hills diary.

29 Quotes come from Josephine's writings, in possession of descendants.

30 Marie Elliott, *Mayne Island and the Outer Gulf Islands: A History* (Mayne Island: Gulf Islands Press, 1984), 7.

31 For a good verbal description by a granddaughter, see Debbie Suzuki, "Mrs. Byron Earnshaw," *Nicola Valley Historical Quarterly* 1, no. 4 (October 1978): 4.

32 Information on the Ford family taken principally from D.E. Isenor et al., *Land of Plenty: A History of the Comox District* (Campbell River, BC: Ptarmigan Press, 1987); Margery Corrigall, *The History of Hornby Island* (n.p., 1969), 17; Elizabeth Smith and David Gerow, *Hornby Island: The Ebb and Flow* (Campbell River, BC: Ptarmigan Press, 1988); and Margaret Nicholls, "Kamano—A Kanaka," *British Columbia Historical News* 24 (Summer 1991): 12; demographic sources; and conversations with descendants.

33 Nicholls, "Kamano—A Kanaka," 13.

34 "Hornby Island Jottings 1897," transcript in BC Archives, Vertical Files.

35 Information on the Curran family taken principally from Jean Barman, "William Curran," *Dictionary of Canadian Biography*, online; Elda Copley Mason, *Lasqueti Island: History and Memory* (Lantzville, BC: Byron Mason, 1992); demographic sources; and conversations with descendants.

36 Mason, *Lasqueti Island*, 19.

37 William J. Scheick, *The Half-Blood: A Cultural Symbol in 19th-Century American Fiction* (Lexington: University Press of Kentucky, 1979).

38 March 30, 1863, entry in Hills diary.

39 "Supplementary Report" to British Columbia, Department of Education, *First Annual Report on the Public Schools in the Province of British Columbia* (1872), 38.

40 December 5, 1876, entry in John Jessop diary, GR 1468, BC Archives.

41 December 4, 1876, entry in Jessop diary.

42 June 8, 1877, entry in Jessop diary.

43 Pat Lean, "Coutlee," *Nicola Valley Historical Quarterly* 6, nos. 2–3 (October 1983): 3 and 6. On Voght's and Garcia's background, see Pat Lean, "Garcia Story," *Nicola Valley Historical Quarterly* 6, no. 4 (May 1984): 2–3.

44 Pat Lean, "Commemorating: William Henry Voght, 'The Father of Merritt,'" *Nicola Valley Historical Quarterly* 1, no. 2 (April 1978): 1, and Lean, "Garcia Story," 2–3.

45 Pat Lean, "Commemorating," 4.

46 McQueen's letters home, from which these quotes are drawn, are divided between BC Archives and the Nicola Valley Archives.

47 Information and quotes are taken from Sister Mary Theodore's extensive writings in St. Ann's Archives, Victoria. I am grateful to the Sisters of St. Ann for permitting me to use their Victoria archives, now located in the BC Archives.

48 Quotes come from Josephine's writings, in possession of descendants.

49 Bridget Moran, *Stoney Creek Woman: The Story of Mary John* (Vancouver: Tillicum, 1988), 26.

50 Henry Pennier, *Chiefly Indian: The Warm and Witty Story of a British Columbia Half Breed Logger* (West Vancouver: Graydonald 1972), 12, 90, and 125.

51 Herman Francis Reinhart, *The Golden Frontier: The Recollections of Herman Francis Reinhart, 1851–1869*, ed. Doyce B. Nunn, Jr. (Austin: University of Texas Press, 1962), 112.

52 Because more second-generation men than women never married, the actual numbers who were intermarried in 1901 were very similar.

53 Francis E. Herring, "Nan," in *Nan and Other Pioneer Women of the West* (London: Francis Griffiths, 1913), 24.

54 Herring, "Nan," 33.

55 "Hornby Island Jottings 1897," transcript in BC Archives, Vertical Files.

56 Quotes come from the writings of Josephine's father, in possession of descendants.

57 Robin Skelton, *They Call It the Cariboo* (Victoria: Sono Nis, 1980), 172.

58 School District Information Form from Essington, March 12, 1923, in British Columbia, Department of Education, Teachers' Bureau Records, GR 461, box 2, BC Archives.

59 School District Information Form from East Gabriola, February 13, 1928, in British Columbia, Department of Education, Teachers' Bureau Records, GR 461, box 2, BC Archives.

60 Constance Lindsay Skinner, "The Birthright" ("A play in 4 acts. Copyright 1906."), typescript in box 8, Skinner Papers, Manuscripts Division, New York Public Library. The play was performed in Carmel, California, to very good notices.

61 Tolmie's mother was a "quarterbreed" descended from a Hudson's Bay fur trade family; Shannon's mother was the daughter of a Scots gold miner turned settler and a Cowichan Indian woman; Couvelier was the great-grandson of an Indigenous woman.

62 See Thomas Humphreys's obituary in *Colonist* (Victoria), August 27, 1890; Jim Nesbitt, "Old Homes and Families," *Colonist*, August 13, 1854; and miscellaneous clippings and notes in Vertical Files, BC Archives.

63 Katherine Howes and Pat Lean, "An Interview with Inga Teit Perkin, Daughter of the Noted Ethnologist James A. Teit," *Nicola Valley Historical Quarterly* 2, no. 2 (April 1979): 2.

64 Information from descendants.

65 Harry Robinson, "Puss in Boots," in his *Write It on Your Heart: The Epic World of an Okanagan Storyteller*, comp. and ed. Wendy Wickwire (Vancouver: Talonbooks/Theytus, 1989), 282–83.

66 Household 23 in Yale (Princeton) division and households 145 and 162 in Yale (Osoyoos) division in manuscript census for British Columbia, 1881.

67 The story of the visit was recounted by the woman in question in old age to the ethnologist Wendy Wickwire, it still being the cause of much distress to her.

7

Sophie Morigeau

Free Trader, Free Woman

Sophie Morigeau's life, in which she clearly had the upper hand in her relationships with men, whether sexual partners, customers, or competitors, seems exceptional. Barman locates its difference in her family history of "free trading." Although it is not clear who her father was, all of the likely candidates worked as traders outside the Hudson's Bay Company, moving freely across what became the Canada/US border to make a living. Despite Morigeau's literacy and wealth, Barman describes how she was still subject to condescension and worse because of her mixed ancestry. That said, Barman notes how some people manage to form their lives and identities in ways that resist social expectations.

By Jean Barman. Reprinted with permission from *Recollecting: Lives of Aboriginal Women of the Canadian Northwest and Borderlands*, edited by Sarah Carter and Patricia McCormack (Edmonton: AU Press, 2011), 175–95. The book won the Willa Literary Award in the area of Scholarly Nonfiction, awarded by Women Writing the West, 2012; Best Book in Aboriginal History Prize, awarded by the Canadian Historical Association, 2012; Best Scholarly and Academic Book, awarded by the Book Publishers Association of Alberta, 2012; and Armitage-Jameson Prize, awarded by the Western History Association and the Coalition for Western Women's History, 2011.

Sophie Morigeau became a legend in her own time, and even more so after her death in 1916 at the age of eighty. Her exploits as a free trader and free woman figure prominently in local histories of the region extending from eastern British Columbia into Washington, Idaho, and Montana. This woman, of mixed Indigenous and non-Indigenous descent,[1] has a lake and a school named in her honour, and archaeological digs have been conducted at the site of her nearby home outside Eureka, Montana. She is the subject of a graduate thesis and a video documentary, incidents from her life have been included in a curriculum guide, and she is a featured figure in re-enactments at the major British Columbian tourist site of Fort Steele.[2] The consequence is that any consideration of Sophie's life and times must be undertaken in a spirit of collaboration. I do so here. Everyone cited in the endnotes is in effect a co-author.

Sophie Morigeau's negotiation of an identity so out of keeping with expectations for women of her time is central to the widespread interest in her. To understand Sophie, though, we need to begin with ourselves. We all negotiate our identities throughout our lifespans. The person we are as a child is not who we become as an adult. We make decisions concerning our ways of life that alter our identities over time to a greater or lesser degree. Changes in the broader society cause us to respond in ways that make us yet again different from who we were before. Identity negotiation is fundamental to what it means to be human.

One way to understand how and why we are the persons we are in the present day is to look back at our predecessors. By doing so, we begin to appreciate the relationship between structure and agency that governs our lives. The dynamics of the society in which we are born and raised limit and create possibilities for individual action.

The ways in which we do and do not take initiative when we have the opportunity to do so have an impact, even if just a little, on that broader society. The interplay between larger structures and personal agency is in no way foretold. The process is dynamic and continually unfolding. If we think back on our own lives, we can all remember some moment when we did the unexpected. We took charge, we exercised agency, we surprised ourselves. Structure and agency jostle up against each other in every life. The ways in which they do so reveal much about the times and also about the people living there.

The life of Sophie Morigeau offers a useful entryway for probing our own negotiation of our identities and, more generally, the relationship between structure and agency. Primary sources about her are limited in number, but they are remarkably consistent and coherent in both their substance and perceptions.

Sophie Morigeau was a free woman making her life as a free trader on the borderlands of northwestern North America. Indeed, few women whose lives have survived through time succeeded with such aplomb, living as Sophie did between countries and races, and among men. Contemporaries attest that Sophie Morigeau was as fearless in her business dealings as any man, and as a woman of mixed race she used whichever identity was most profitable to her at a particular point in time.

Sophie Morigeau's negotiation of her identity throughout her lifespan represents a skillful intermeshing of structure and agency. Much of what appears extraordinary becomes ordinary when framed within the three principal structures that governed her life from her earliest years—familial fluidity, occupational flexibility, and racial stereotyping. Sophie was born and grew up in circumstances in which the character of family life was not so much determined by birth as it was constructed out of individual decisions to take responsibility for oneself and others. Ways of making a living were similarly situational and pragmatic. Familial fluidity and occupational flexibility had as their backdrop a time and place in which persons in the dominant society were distinguished by their paler skin tones and took for granted that this attribute of "whiteness," associated by them with a concept of "race" based on biological features, signified the superiority of their way of life over all others. The personal qualities, or agency, that Sophie Morigeau brought to bear in responding to these and other structures account, to a considerable extent, for her continuing appeal.

The Complexities of Sophie's Parentage

From the moment of her birth in 1836, Sophie received signals about desirable and undesirable attributes in herself and in other persons. These signals came through her family and through a whole range of formal and informal contacts. The earliest and most important lessons had to do with familial fluidity.

The identity of Sophie's mother we know with relative certainty, unlike that of her father.[3] Sophie's mother, Elizabeth, who was also known as Isabella and Lisette, is said to have been born in about 1816 at the fur trade colony of Red River, in present-day Manitoba. Sophie's maternal grandfather, William Taylor, born in 1788 in the Orkney Islands, off the northern coast of Scotland, arrived at Red River in 1815 as one of the original white settlers. Sophie's maternal grandmother, Sarah, had been born in Saskatchewan to an American trader, Peter Sabiston, and a local Cree woman. Sophie was embedded on her father's side in three kinship networks—extended families produced by trappers and traders who ranged across the large territory extending from the East Kootenays of British Columbia southeast into Montana and southwest to the trading posts of Fort Colville and Spokane House, in what is now Washington state.

Sophie's biological father was most likely Patrick Finley, making her grandfather the legendary Jacques Raphael or Jocko Finlay (the family's surname changed between generations from Finlay to Finley).

Jocko had a large family by several Indigenous women. Born in 1768 in Saskatchewan to a Scots fur trader and a Chippewa woman, Jocko advanced so rapidly in the fur trade that in 1806 he was dispatched to prepare a path through the Rocky Mountains for the westward exploration of David Thompson, a partner in the North West Company.

By then Jocko Finlay had five sons, including Patrick born in 1802 near the future Edmonton. The Finlays travelled as a family that continued to grow in size during the half-dozen years Jocko assisted Thompson in establishing several trading posts intended to cajole the Kootenai,[4] and also their Flathead neighbours to the east, into collecting furs for the company. Among the posts was Kootenai House, situated on the west side of lower Columbia Lake, south of present-day Invermere in British Columbia's Windermere Valley. Kootenai House would not survive Thompson's departure in 1812. A longer-lived post, known variously as Kootenai Falls, Kootenai Post, and Fort Kootenai was located near present-day Libby, Montana.[5]

Thompson left Jocko Finlay in charge of the recently constructed Spokane House to the south. By 1821, when the Hudson's Bay Company took over the North West Company, Jocko and his sons were free-trading in the area around Spokane. Their ability to do so was markedly assisted both by their personal ties with local Indigenous women and by the close relationships they had forged with the Kootenai, the Spokane, and other Indigenous peoples during their years with Thompson.

By the time of Jocko Finlay's death in 1828, his sons and their families were consolidating themselves into a tightly knit clan, into which Sophie was likely born in 1836. For the previous half-dozen years her father Patrick (also known as Pichina) and at least one of his brothers were spending much of their time trapping and doing odd jobs around the Hudson's Bay post of Jasper House, located north of the Kootenays on the Athabasca River. Patrick already had five children by a Flathead or Spokane woman when he briefly took up with Sophie's mother. On October 3, 1838, at Jasper House, eighteen-month-old Sophie was baptized by visiting Catholic priest Father Modeste Demers as the daughter of "Lisette, métisse," and "Pichina Flinlay, free man." By that time, her probable father had moved on to another mixed-race woman by whom he had two one-year-old daughters who were baptized the same day.[6] Living near Fort Colville and then in the Flathead area of western Montana, Patrick Finley would have four more children by this woman before fathering another six by yet another mixed-race fur trade daughter.

Patrick Finley is not the only possible candidate as Sophie's father. "Among the old-timers" in the area where she grew up, her mother is said to have lived briefly with Edward Berland, who arrived in the Kootenays from Quebec in 1818 in the employ of the North West Company.[7] Berland subsequently alternated between working as a trapper and interpreter for the Hudson's Bay Company and earning his living as a free trader in the Kootenays. Berland consolidated his links with the Finlay clan by marrying Patrick Finley's niece Louisa in 1845, into which union they each brought a child from earlier unions. Together, they had at least three more children.[8]

It was a third man that Sophie publicly acknowledged as her father by using his surname. Given the fluidity of relationships that marked the time and place, François Baptiste Morigeau may well have been her biological parent. Born in about 1789 west of Montreal, he arrived in the Kootenays in 1818 or 1819, about the same time as Edward Berland, to work for the North West Company.[9] According to family lore, "the plodding ordered existence of the French Canadian habitant did not appeal to him."[10] Whereas Berland transferred to the Hudson's Bay Company when it absorbed the North West Company in 1821, Morigeau became a free trader in the Upper Columbia area of the Kootenays.[11] Local historians consider him "the first white settler" to take up permanent residence in the East or West Kootenays.[12]

According to his son Baptiste, born in about 1840, François Morigeau's first wife was a Swampy Cree woman who, after three years and three children, "tiring of life in the mountains and longing for the open freedom of the plains," asked to be taken back home.

François obliged and then returned west with "Elizabeth or Isabella Taylor a person of mixed blood, of Scottish descent, whose home had been the Red River Settlement."[13] Their eldest child, Alexander, was baptized, at the age of three and a half, at the same ceremony at Jasper House on October 3, 1838, at which Sophie was baptized. He was christened as the child of "François Morjeau, freeman," and, like Sophie, of "Lisette, métisse."[14]

The most likely explanation for Sophie's biological parentage is that Lisette Taylor had a brief relationship with Patrick Finley while she was already living with François Morigeau, with whom she would have another eight children.[15] The other possibility is that the visiting priest who did the baptisms made a mistake. But, if so, Sophie herself was never made aware of the fact, for when she wed in a Catholic ceremony in 1852, she gave her parents as "Patrick Finley and Isabelle, now the wife of François Morigeau."[16] As a result of these complexities, virtually from the time she was born, Sophie Morigeau took familial fluidity as a given.

The Young Sophie

Sophie was born into the fur trade, not the neat and tidy trade centred on established posts but rather the itinerant world of free traders. Although they might seek paid employment as the need arose, otherwise they went where the animals were and zealously guarded their right to do so. Familial fluidity was to some extent derivative of occupational flexibility. While the Catholic Church might intervene from time to time, it was chance and circumstance, as well as human desire, that determined with whom, and in what place, individuals came together and then parted ways.

The appeal of the Kootenays, where Sophie spent her first years, related directly to the relative lack of interest in the area on the part of the Hudson's Bay Company. It ran a seasonal trade out of Fort Kootenai, sending someone in the fall to collect furs over the winter and then head back to its much larger post established in 1825 at Fort Colville, in northeast Washington.[17] Otherwise, the area was open to men like François Morigeau and Edward Berland. In 1839 Berland took charge of the Fort Kootenai winter trade for the Hudson's Bay Company, but Morigeau continued to trap on his own.[18]

Our clearest glimpse of Sophie as a child comes in September 1845, when she was nine. We see her everyday world through the eyes of Jesuit father Pierre-Jean De Smet on his passage through the Kootenays. Four years earlier, he had established a mission in the Bitter Root Valley of southwestern Montana at the behest of the local Flatheads.[19] An inveterate traveller, he set off along the Kootenay River, likely on foot, up the Idaho panhandle into present-day British Columbia. There, on the eastern shore of Columbia Lake, he encountered *"the Canadian!"*—which, at the time, generally referred to French Canadians. The Morigeau family used French as their first language, so communication posed no problem for the bilingual De Smet.[20] De Smet's lengthy description of Morigeau and his family, including young Sophie, was positively rhapsodic.

> The Canadian! Into what part of the desert has he not penetrated? The monarch who rules at the source of the Columbia [River] is an honest emigrant from St. Martin, in the district of Montreal, who has resided for twenty-six years in this desert. The skins of the rein and moose deer are the materials of which his portable palace is composed; and to use his own expression, he *embarks on horseback* with his wife and seven children and *lands* wherever he pleases ... His sceptre is a beaver trap—his *law* a carbine ... Encircled by so much grandeur, undisturbed proprietor of all the sky-ward palaces, the strongholds, the very last refuge which nature has reared to preserve alive liberty in the earth—solitary lord of these majestic mountains, that elevate their icy summits even to the clouds.[21]

A good part of De Smet's approval had to do with the great extent to which Morigeau, like Berland, acknowledged the force of Catholicism. "Morjeau (our Canadian) does not forget his duty as a Christian," he wrote. "Each day, morning and evening, he may be seen devoutly reciting his prayers, midst his little family."[22] There were some tasks that only a priest could perform, and it turned out Morigeau had travelled with his family in the direction De Smet was headed in the hopes of encountering him.

> Many years had Morigeau ardently desired to see a priest to procure for his wife and children the signal grace of baptism. The feast of the Nativity of the Blessed Virgin, this favor was conferred on them, and also on the children of three Indian families who accompany him on his migrations. This was a solemn day for the desert! The august sacrifice of mass was offered; Morigeau devoutly approached the holy table—at the foot of the humble altar he received the nuptial benediction; and the mother, surrounded by her children, and six little Indians, was regenerated in the holy waters of baptism. In memory of so many benefits a large cross was erected in the plain.[23]

Following the religious ceremonies, the Morigeaus entertained the priest royally during the few days he spent with the family. Once again De Smet's description gives insight into the young Sophie's world.

> I cannot leave my good Canadian without making an honorable mention of his royal *cuisine à la sauvage*. The first dish he presented me contained two paws of a bear ... A roast porcupine next made its appearance, accompanied by a moose's muzzle, which had been boiling all night. The latter I found delicious. Finally the great kettle, containing a sort of hotch-potch, or salmagundi, was placed in the midst of the guests, and each

> one helped himself according to his taste; there was the choice back-fat of the buffalo-cow, venison, cutlets, beavers' tails, quails, rabbits, dumplings and a substantial broth.[24]

Occupational flexibility continued to structure Sophie's life. It may have been Morigeau's religiosity, or perhaps it was a changing economy, that explains the family's move, shortly after encountering De Smet in 1845, almost four hundred kilometres southwest to Fort Colville. The Hudson's Bay post had become a major operation, with fifteen or so men stationed there regularly to trade and to run its large farming operation. Not only that, a burgeoning community of retired fur trade families had settled nearby, and there was a flourishing Catholic mission on the bluff just above the post at Kettle Falls.[25] Morigeau took up a large farm, which eventually covered 640 acres, and, in son Baptiste's words, "rose to be a man of some wealth."[26]

Perhaps for that reason Morigeau could afford to send Sophie to school at the Catholic mission, or so claims a local historian whose mother knew Sophie. In this version of events, Sophie spent five years there, where, "being mostly white," she "absorbed well the varied knowledge of courtesy, cleanliness, cooking, sewing, speech, and religion the Sisters offered," and "no doubt also found opportunity to observe the sometimes questionable trading and business tactics between red men and white at the Fort."[27]

Sophie Takes Charge

From a mission school, it was a short and all but inevitable path into marriage, and so it was for Sophie. She was married off to Jean Baptiste Chabotte, from Montreal, in a proper Catholic ceremony held on September 29, 1852. Aged twenty-four, as compared to Sophie's sixteen years, he had joined the Hudson's Bay Company four years earlier and only recently been transferred to Fort Colville. By the measure of the day, it was a good match. He was suitably employed, and she was a catch, for as one old-timer reminisced, "Lord, what a handsome woman Sophie Morigeau was in her young days!"[28]

Even in the mid-1830s, when Sophie was born, and more so by the time she became an adult, most white newcomers to North America took for granted a hierarchy of races based on physical characteristics that, very conveniently, put them on top. White folk simply assumed that they were superior to those with darker skin. While perhaps not an obvious factor until then in Sophie's life, racial stereotyping never lurked far below the surface, and the opportunity for a mixed-race woman such as herself to find a white husband was not to be eschewed. Of course, Sophie's actual descent differs depending on who her biological father was. Her mother was three-quarters white. If Patrick Finley was her father, she was three-quarters Indigenous on her father's side, and hence she was the genuine Métis or, in the parlance of the day, "halfbreed." If, as seems less likely, Edward Berland or François Morigeau was her father, she was seven-eighths white, but she was still of mixed race.

Sophie's future seemed set in the pattern of the day, and for a number of years it continued to be so. The ambitious Jean Baptiste Chabotte left the Hudson's Bay Company at the end of his contract in 1853 and took up a farm not far from the Morigeaus' son Alexander. The couple had no children, but seemed to get on until one day, sometime after 1860, the marriage was no more.[29]

In moving from wife to being a woman on her own, Sophie drew on the occupational flexibility she took for granted based on her childhood and youth. Her actions, which on one level were so unlike those of her white female contemporaries, returned her to familiar ways. What she knew best was the life of the free trader, who travelled to wherever there was a profit to be made, and she became and remained a free trader for the rest of her life. Along with occupational flexibility, she was also accustomed to familial fluidity, and this too she exercised in her decision to become a free woman.

Possibly as a symbolic move, Sophie went back to her family name and was henceforth known as Sophie Morigeau. The trade-off in asserting agency was to give up the measure of respectability she had achieved through snaring a white husband and submerging her identity in his. Just as newcomers assumed that they were inherently superior to Indigenous peoples and to all other non-white groups, they took for granted that men were superior to women. Justifying their assumptions in Christian terms, newcomers saw in Eve's willingness to bite the apple in the Garden of Eden proof that women had to be confined within the home to perform their expected role as wives and mothers. Power, be it political, economic, or domestic, lay with men. But the traditional path of submission and subordination did not suffice for Sophie.

For the rest of her life, Sophie subverted the gender divide so convenient to white males. She likely did so not only because she had the familiar structures of family fluidity and occupational flexibility on which to draw, but also because she was, quite simply, a tough woman. Because we tend not to think that women are capable of the degree of independence that Sophie achieved, we also tend to downplay their accomplishments.

Packing in the Wild Horse Creek Gold Rush

It may have been the excitement of the Wild Horse Creek gold rush of 1864 in southeastern British Columbia that attracted Sophie away from domesticity; here was a chance for independence seemingly for the taking, and she did so.

From the time of the California gold rush of 1849, men had searched ever farther north for riches. Gold was discovered on the British Columbian mainland in 1858. The Fraser River rush attracted many thousands of miners, forcing the British government to decree the mainland an official British colony duly christened British Columbia. Over the next years, the frantic search for riches extended across a much broader area.

One such new area was Wild Horse Creek, located not far from the Kootenay River, some fifty miles north of the international boundary established with the United States in 1846. The British government tried to contain the rush by constructing a new east-west trail across British Columbia, but many prospective miners came north from Montana to British Columbia across Tobacco Plains. Some stopped along the way in Montana to try their luck along the Clark Fork and Fisher Rivers or on Libby Creek.[30]

Somewhat ironically, as it turned out, the Wild Horse Creek gold rush initially gave a boost to the Kootenay fur trade such as it had not known since David Thompson arrived half a century earlier. When the first prospectors, whose numbers included one of Jocko Finlay's sons, arrived in 1863, they took their discoveries to Fort Kootenai, which the Hudson's Bay Company had by now moved north of the border. This action gave the trading post the edge in supplying the miners who would arrive the next spring.[31]

A respectable young Englishman named Michael Phillipps, who had recently joined the Hudson's Bay Company, was put in charge of Fort Kootenai.[32] Prior to his arrival, the post was manned by John Campbell, a mixed-race Hudson's Bay employee working out of Fort Colville who knew the Kootenai language.[33] On his arrival, Phillipps dispatched Campbell north to Wild Horse Creek and soon followed there himself to trade with miners. Up to then, the Kootenay fur trade had brought in about $7,000 a year, but, as Phillipps later recalled, on his first trip out, he carried gold dust worth $45,000—over six times that amount.[34] To expedite the trade with miners, Phillipps closed Fort Kootenai and opened up a new post, Fort Steele, about five miles from Wild Horse Creek.[35]

There was every reason for Sophie Morigeau to want to join in the excitement, and she did. During the gold rush, she ran her own pack trains from Walla Walla or Colville in Washington, or from Missoula in Montana, to hungry miners in the Wild Horse Creek area.[36] As a great-grandniece described it:

> Sophie Morigeau, scorning to lead the servile life expected of a squaw, and of most women who were even half white or red, initiated her own enterprise. Undismayed that no woman, either white or red, had done such a thing before, she assembled a pack string, and ran trade goods from Missoula and Walla Walla to Fort Steele, doing business with both whites and Indians.[37]

Along the way, Sophie would visit her nephews settled among the Flatheads in southwestern Montana. "On her trips to Missoula," her great-grandniece explained, "Sophie always stopped at their home on the Jocko River [named after Jocko Finlay, members of whose family lived nearby] about thirty miles west of Missoula."[38]

The excitement of the gold rush died down at the end of the decade. At that point, the new Fort Steele was no longer needed, which led to its closure and Phillipps's dismissal in 1870. The organized fur trade in the Kootenay region came to an end after six decades. It was men like Michael Phillipps, like the free trader François Morigeau before him, who moved the area toward settlement. Even while exploiting the gold rush, Phillipps accommodated himself to Kootenai people in a fashion reminiscent of the fur traders of a generation earlier. He learned the language, he took the Tobacco Plains chief's daughter Rowena for his wife, and, having acquired land on the British Columbian side of Tobacco Plains, he ranched and raised a family that eventually boasted a dozen children.[39]

Settling Down in the Windermere Valley

With the Wild Horse Creek gold rush winding down, Sophie returned to the world of her childhood, about a hundred kilometres north in the Windermere Valley, where she established her own business. According to her great-grandniece, "after the first mining boom at Fort Steele was past, Sophie set up a trading post at Windermere."[40]

Sophie's customers very likely included members of the extended family in which she was embedded. While some of them remained in the Colville area, where François Morigeau died in 1870 and Sophie's mother in 1902, others had headed to Montana or returned to British Columbia.[41] Whatever their precise biological relationship, Sophie was particularly close to one of her younger brothers, Baptiste, who married a Kootenai woman in 1881. A year later the couple named their first child after Sophie.[42]

Numerous other offspring of the fur trade intermarried. No doubt part of the reason was the familiarity that came through their fathers having worked together; another part, their shared mixed ancestry. Occupational flexibility and racial ambivalence interacted. Berland found for a second wife one of Jocko Finlay's granddaughters. François Morigeau's son Alexander partnered with Jocko Finlay's granddaughter Rosalie; Morigeau's daughter Rosalie had a large family by Berland's son John. The men that Berland's daughter Lucy and Phillipps's daughter Rowena found—John Campbell and Colin Sinclair—had first passed through the Kootenay region in 1854 as part of a mixed-race group heading west from Red River to settle near Fort Vancouver.

Clearly expecting to stay in the area, Sophie managed a feat only a handful of British Columbian women had so far dared, which was to claim land in her own name. The pre-emption, or homestead, records tell us that on June 1, 1872, Sophie Morigeau took up 320 acres on the southeast side of Lower Columbia Lake, about one mile north of its upper end.[43] For a time she carried on her trading activities from her homestead.[44]

Border Crossing

Sophie Morigeau's youth preceded nation making. The fur trade was borderless, simply because there was no border. Only in 1846 had the United States and Britain divided Sophie's home territory along the forty-ninth parallel, but the newly established border made little difference in practice. The terrain runs north and south along valleys interspersed with mountains, isolating the corridor that is the Kootenay region. At its heart is Tobacco Plains, which straddles the border.

In about 1879 or 1880, Sophie moved her trading post about eighty kilometres south, across the border, to the Montana side of Tobacco Plains to take advantage of travellers using that north-south corridor.[45] The site, not far from Eureka, was close to the area where locals grew wheat and peas, and it saw traffic between Canadian mining communities and American settlements such as Frenchtown and Missoula in Montana, and Colville in Washington. Kootenai people traded furs and other items.[46]

Sophie is said to have built herself a small cabin near the Kootenai villages.[47] According to a contemporary, it was made of very small logs that she had dragged in behind a horse and mudded on the inside, with a chimney made of sticks and clay.[48] A few years later, Sophie lost the sight of one eye when she was hit by a branch while riding.[49] Thereafter she wore an eye patch or spectacles, which apparently only added to her distinctiveness.

A member of a Canadian survey party who passed through the area in 1883, when Sophie was in her mid-forties, described two old Indian women living "in the middle of a field, in a one-room store deplete of provisions," one with a single eye.[50] An English adventurer,

Alexander Staveley Hill, who visited in September of the same year was more effusive in his journal. Sophie's reputation had gone before her, and he was "looking forward to 'Sophy's' as the place on the western side of the mountains where we should get stores and directions, and generally should be set on our road." Later the same day:

> We saw two or three log huts and Indian teepees on a knoll; Dan rode up and found it to be "Sophy's." He inquired of an old woman in green spectacles, who answered his inquiry with, "Me Sophy." So we rode up, and found that she had plenty of stores. We bought half a sack of flour, some rice, ten pound of venison, and some butter, which last was very rancid and uneatable. We made a capital supper on the venison and rice, and tinned peaches, and turned in about nine o'clock. [51]

The next day the group decided to rest, which gave the journal keeper time to photograph "the log hut and the stores and the teepees of some Kootenai Indians who were settled near, and were employed in making Indian work, mats, and generally in hunting and making themselves useful to Sophy." He described how "a Kootenai man who had lost his squaw was working for Sophy, looking after her horses and cattle, and supporting by his wages his three little children."[52]

The visitor evoked Sophie as a businesswoman: "Sophy is a person of very considerable energy—had three parties out prospecting mines, and possessed a good herd of cattle." While the journal keeper was fishing, a companion "had been away at Sophy's, baking the bread in her oven, and a confounded Indian dog had taken advantage of her deserted camp to run off with half our bacon and all our venison, and Sophy had most kindly given him a fowl to replace our loss." Sophie knew what appealed to passersby. "Our worthy friend Sophy treated our men to a good deal of whiskey."[53] The next morning as the visitors were leaving, they purchased "a good little horse from Sophy for fifty dollars for me to ride," and "Sophy gave L. and myself a special bottle of whisky for ourselves … We bought some martins' skins, and some small ermine, and some buckskins for shirts, and a few Indian things at her store."[54] Sophie knew how to do business.

At the time of the 1883 visit, as Sophie is said to have done most times, she had a man around: "Mr. Bovaris, who at that time occupied the position of husband to Sophy, had a talk to me about the Indians and their fight with the Boston men [Americans] under [General Oliver Otis] Howard."[55] Six years previous, the Civil War general had led army troops against the nearby Nez Perce under Chief Joseph. Hill added a postscript referring to his subsequent visit a year later: "Poor Bovaris! on my visit in this fall of 1884, I found that he had fallen a victim to the six-shooter of Sophy's brother in a quarrel, when too much whisky had been drunk."[56] Another version of this story has the luckless Bovaris killed by a new friend of Sophie's.[57] According to a daughter of Michael Phillipps, "the two men competing for Sophie's favor at about this time were both upstanding, fine-looking white men."[58] A local historian has noted more generally about Sophie: "She had friends and relatives in various parts of her operating area. She seldom lacked for masculine company if she so desired and had numerous men partners over the years; some outsmarted her and some merely tried, winding up extinct."[59]

Packing during Railway Construction

By now well into middle age, Sophie still could not resist the next free trading opportunity that came along. Occupational flexibility continued to structure her life. The most visible marker of changing times in the late nineteenth century was rail lines. The Canadian Pacific Railway was built in the first half of the 1880s with the goal of linking the young nation of Canada east and west in direct opposition to the landscape. Sophie did not hesitate, in the pattern of her kinfolk during her childhood, to shift her economic activity to supply rail crews. The story is told about how, during the line's construction, Sophie arrived with a pack-load of liquor for the construction camp at the rail junction of Golden in eastern British Columbia, where her brother Baptiste Morigeau was then running a general store. She was warned off by local purveyors, whereupon she took her pack train over the mountains to the boomtown of Calgary to be sold at a profit.[60]

The daughter of the store owner in the railway town of Demersville, located not far from Kalispell, Montana, recalled how, in the mid-1880s, "Sophie Morigeau made many trips to Demersville with her pack string, to stock up on supplies." Ida Gregg soon became Sophie's travelling companion, an experience the young Ida never forgot.

> I was about eleven years old at this time (about 1886) and I spent two summers with Sophie on Tobacco Plains, and travelling with her. Sophie gave me my own little cabin to live in on the Plains. We often travelled together with the pack horses over the mountain trails, forded rivers where very often the horses would have to swim, and many times we met not too friendly Indian parties—but Sophie always got her pack string home intact. Sophie was a friend to everyone and always helped the sick and needy. She had a lot of cattle, and she gave me several head for my own. She also had a cig-box full of gold coins under her mattress.[61]

Sophie went where money was to be made and packed in what was wanted, including a mowing machine and, on another occasion, a wagon. Later asked by some of the men how she ever got the wagon box there, Sophie is said to have responded acerbically, "Oh, [I] just cut a hole in the bottom of the box and hung 'er over the saddle horn."[62]

Ida Gregg's sojourn with Sophie was brought to a close by yet another man. As she explained, "At this time Sophie was married to a man named Clark; it seems to me they were married in Missoula. This Clark was very mean and selfish and it was because of him I did not live with Sophie any longer; he did not want anyone else around and I was afraid of him."[63] This partner was, however, just as luckless as his predecessor. A man who knew Sophie at the time recalled her husband as Tom Clark, who later drowned in Flathead Country.[64]

Settling Down on Tobacco Plains

Sophie Morigeau's railway construction coup in Calgary was likely her last big adventure. By now in her fifties, she settled down, to the extent she ever did, at her Tobacco Plains trading post. It may have been that a serious financial loss ended her packing career. Sophie told an acquaintance that she had entrusted her pack train and cash to a white man, who was supposed to buy goods for her in Missoula—but she never saw him again.[65] Sometime later, on October 28, 1896, Sophie filed a claim to homestead on the 160 acres on which she was almost certainly already living.[66] A neighbour recalled how "Sophie had milk cows, good horses, and range cattle."[67]

The archaeological record also attests that Sophie developed a home life. An excavation of "the trading post established by a French-Indian woman," conducted in 1967 by researchers from the University of Montana, found a stone fireplace in the house and "a Singer sewing machine patented in the middle 1880's." According to the report on the excavation, "she used perfume and enjoyed her liquor (or her husbands did), as old bottles indicate."[68]

A number of first-hand perspectives on Sophie survive from her later years. A young Englishman, who lived with the Phillipps family just north of the border, dramatized Sophie as a colourful character in a letter he wrote home in February 1888:

> I went to call on the only two ladies of Tobacco Plains ... two half breeds. The one Sophy by name, a remarkable character, and her servant Mary. They have one eye apiece.

> Sophy has just given her 13th husband notice to quit which is promptly done, her last having refused to do so, got shot for his pains. An every day occurrence on the American side, nothing is ever said. The nearest magistrate being 100 miles away.
>
> She was most affable and gave me the best dinner I have had for a long time. She manages the farm, puts up horses [and] whatever husband she has … is not allowed to interfere with anything only to do what she tells him.
>
> She goes down below 2 or 3 times a year for whisky, with which she remains tight for 2 or 3 weeks on end, until it is all gone. The Mrs. here [Rowena Phillipps] went to call one day unfortunately after … She got after her with a club and the Mrs. had to ride for her life we saw her coming back here at full gallop and P. thought the whole tribe of Blackfeet Indians were after her.[69]

Sophie entranced the Phillipps children. Daughter Susan, born in 1882, recalled in the third person how "she and her brothers and sisters—in spite of their father's orders, and in spite of the disapproval of their Kootenai mother, who had seen Sophie in some of her less presentable hours—used to ride across the line to Sophie's homestead whenever they could steal away." As to the reason:

> Sophie had a flock of big white geese on her little lake; and Sophie had a piece of one of her ribs hanging on the wall of her cabin with a pink bow tied around it, that she had amputated herself when it was broken and protruding after a run-away accident with a team and buggy. Sophie always had something good to eat in the house, and she always had a lot of Indian children clustered around—and she *liked* you, and "everybody liked Sophie."[70]

Herself of mixed race, Susan Phillipps was almost certainly aware of the ambivalence that marked Sophie's life and, by inference, her own.

> Sophie skinned the Indians in trade, and when both Indians and whites were sharing a meal with her, she had a separate washing-up place for "those dirty Indians" and made sure that they used it. She always used to tell how "Sophie and Mis' Desrosier were the only white women on the Plains" in the early nineties. Yet she was forever helping the Indians, and her undeclared pride of race as an Indian showed itself when she became dangerously angry with [a neighbour] Johanna Quirk [Cuffe] because Johanna was seen discarding some dirty candy offered by the Kootenais to their guests at one of [Catholic missionary] Father Coccola's church gatherings.[71]

Susan's comment that Sophie "skinned the Indians in trade" suggests that Sophie was a seasoned businesswoman. Another story about Sophie again points to her shrewdness as a trader:

> "They" tell how at one time she sold a stock of buckskin needles for five dollars apiece; when her Indian customers objected that one dollar was usually the top price, she solemnly explained that the white man across the mountains who made these needles had died and pretty soon, no more needles at any price. When many people arrived to take advantage of the fine fishing on Sophie's creek, she used to levy a toll charge for the privilege of fishing there; if the fisherman refused to shell out, she would simply wade into the creek and splash up and down until all the trout were scared in hiding.[72]

If Sophie had a hard-nosed streak when it came to doing business, she also sought sociability. Yet, however much she might have hoped to overcome the racial stereotyping structuring her life, she could never do so. The version of Susan Phillipps's candy story that her neighbour Johanna Quirk Cuffe told is revealing, since in this version it was Sophie herself, not the Kootenais, who was slighted:

> I had met Sophie several times ... when at the picnic following Mass by Father Coccala, Sophie had given me a few pieces of candy from a handful she was passing around. Not caring to eat it, I casually discarded it; however, my action was seen by Sophie, who became furious.

Some weeks later Johanna anxiously spotted "Sophie riding toward the house," but soon discovered that "Sophie had brought a peace offering, a moist gunny sack half full of fresh trout for 'her friend.'"[73]

A major attempt at reconciliation came for Johanna Cuffe when Sophie invited her and the local teacher, Mary Harsman, to visit Sophie on a Sunday in 1894. Johanna never forgot the memorable afternoon, whose telling underlines the racial ambiguities of the times:

> We rode across the plains to Sophie's yard which was swept clean; the steps, which faced the east, were scrubbed white as was the floor of the long log house. We sat in chairs near a home-made table covered with a spotless white cloth. Sophie, who was dressed in a light dress with a white apron, talked with us a while; she mentioned knowing some of Mary's acquaintances in the Flathead. Then she excused herself and went out to her cool spring-house to bring in a huge bowl full of fine, big strawberries she had raised. She then brought out a cake, the biggest we girls had ever seen; made in a small dishpan, it was frosted with whipped cream and egg whites. There was also a pitcher of thick cream for the berries, a pitcher of milk, and

home-baked bread and butter. She offered to make tea, but we declined. As we expressed appreciation for her hospitality, she was as gracious as any white lady could be.[74]

Structure trumped agency.

Sophie's Later Years

Sophie experienced various ups and downs during her later years. According to one account, she "was pretty well fixed by the early nineties," when the very harsh winter of 1892–1893 killed 100 of her 130 head of cattle.[75] According to Johanna Cuffe, she never had as many cattle "after the ice-crusted snows of the winter of 1892–1893, when the animals could not dig down to the grass below."[76]

As Sophie aged, she inevitably became more vulnerable. According to a man acquainted with her in her later years, Sophie had a succession of white men "living with her *and off her*." Known sometimes as her business partners, these men "broke her, and she never recovered financially."[77] Sophie's independence became a liability. On July 29, 1910, when Sophie was in her mid-seventies, the *Eureka Journal* reported that "'Old Sophia' was robbed of $300 at her home near Sophia Lake last Friday. A man named Shuman, and a halfbreed woman had been staying with Sophie for a few days and it is thought they saw the old woman go" to her money's hiding place.[78]

Sophie's world contracted. Johanna recalled how "in those days we went sometimes to [nearby] Gateway to trade, and would sometimes meet or stop to visit Sophie," but, "in later years, we saw Sophie seldom, as the railroad through Eureka eliminated trips to Gateway."[79] When Sophie became ill in 1915, at almost eighty years of age, she turned her remaining livestock, principally horses, over to a man whose wife then became her nurse.[80] On August 26, 1916, Sophie finally completed the formal acquisition of her property, which enabled her to sell it four days later.[81] Sophie Morigeau died on October 5, 1916, and was buried in Eureka, Montana.[82]

Conclusion

Sophie Morigeau has repeatedly been characterized as extraordinary for her time. Johanna Cuffe's daughter wrote what seems a very appropriate epitaph:

> Sophia Morigeau had enough strong Kootenai blood in her makeup to give her the resourcefulness and stamina her rugged life required. But she evidently decided to live her life as the white men of her day lived theirs, playing a dominant role. Hers was a colorful, zestful life, which if written in full, would outsell any modern novel.[83]

But Sophie's life is extraordinary only so far as we view it from the perspective of the white women and men of the dominant society, who could never quite accept her as their equal. When Sophie's way of life is framed within her upbringing, the extraordinary becomes ordinary.

The structures Sophie Morigeau knew as a child she took not as encumbrances; rather she used them as a base for opening up possibilities. Drawing on the familial fluidity and occupational flexibility with which she had grown up, Sophie fashioned an identity for herself that appears to have fit comfortably within these structures. What she knew best was the life of the free trader, going wherever there was a profit to be made, and, following her short marriage, that was the life she took up as a free woman.

The racial hierarchy of the day was more difficult for Sophie to reconcile. According to a local history, published in 1950 and based on conversations with many persons acquainted with Sophie in her later years, she grasped her life circumstances.

> Sophie was quick of wit and surely she learned fast in the missionary school. Indeed the social graces she was taught there she never forgot; she used to turn them on and off as occasion demanded. But the attitudes and actions of her father [referring to François Morigeau] and the other white men she knew spoke much louder than the words of the creeds of priests. Her mother was of the lesser race and of the subservient sex: on the whole the squaw was merely a red man's hired girl, or a white man's commodity—no other feminine way of life was open. Sophie aspired to be white; she aspired to be free and fearless like a man; she aspired to be shrewd and propertied.[84]

Sophie did not permit the racial stereotyping expressed toward her by others to structure her life, to keep her, if this account be believed, from acting as she would.

> To all appearances Sophie never allowed herself to become defeated—as so many are—by her mixed blood. She assumed a front that she was white, and for her patterns of living she adopted the ways of either white or Indian, whichever seemed most profitable in cash or satisfaction.[85]

In negotiating her identity, Sophie Morigeau maximized the opportunities that existed for her within the structures into which she was born. These structures guided her life, but so did the human agency she possessed in abundance. By virtue of her birth and upbringing, she was, like all of us, enmeshed in a larger set of circumstances, but she was also a person in her own right. Early on, Sophie set her sights on living on her own without having to rely on men, however much she might enjoy their company. Recollections testify that, by virtue of being her own woman, she influenced the girls of the next generation who she befriended. She impressed others around her to the extent of their writing about her in their journals or otherwise remembering her presence in their lives.

The interplay between structure and agency that marked Sophie Morigeau's life has utility for us today. No matter how different Sophie's life was from our own, we must all find ways to negotiate the tension between the structures we inherit and our individual capacity for agency. Even Sophie herself may have been surprised from time to time by her resourcefulness, by her ability to take advantage of her circumstances. Just as she affected those around her, she continues to influence all of us who are intrigued by her. Sophie's story, as told by those who knew her and those who honour her memory, contains lessons both for our own time and for scholars interested in interrogating the lives of those who lived in past times.

Notes

1 No most appropriate terminology exists to describe persons of both Indigenous and non-Indigenous descent. The words *halfbreed*, *miscegenation*, and *hybrid* have biological as well as socially negative connotations. The Canadian terms *Métis* and *métis*, originating in the fur trade, acquired legal and ethnogenesis components limiting their relevance to particular historical, geographical, and cultural settings; see Jean Barman and Mike Evans, "Reflections on Being, and Becoming, Métis in British Columbia," *BC Studies* 161 (Spring 2009): 59–91.

2 Carol Ray, "Sophie Morigeau: Trading Across the Boundaries" (master's thesis, University of Wyoming, 2001).

3 Genealogical information is taken principally from David C. Courchane, *Jocko's People: The Descendants of James Finlay and his son, Jacques Raphael Finley*, part 8 (privately printed and courtesy of the author, 1997). The Cree heritage of Sophie's mother is attested by son Baptiste Morigeau, who described himself in the 1901 Canadian manuscript census as a "Cree French breed." See Census of Canada, 1901, Yale and Cariboo, D6-North East Kootenay, Windermere, household 39.

4 For convenience I here use the American spelling, Kootenai, to refer to the Kootenai/Kootenay peoples living on both sides of the international boundary. Other spellings follow contemporary usage.

5 Olga Weydemeyer Johnson, *Flathead and Kootenay: The Rivers, the Tribes and the Region's Traders* (Glendale, CA: Arthur H. Clark, 1969), 173, 184–86; Michael P. Malone, Richard B. Roeder, and William L. Lang, *Montana: A History of Two Centuries*, rev. ed. (Seattle: University of Washington Press, 1991), 44. Other posts established by Thompson included Kullyspell House, near the mouth of the Clark Fort River in present-day Idaho, and Flathead House, also known as Saleesh House, on the Clark Fort River south of Libby, Montana.

6 Harriet Duncan Munnick, *Catholic Church Records of the Pacific Northwest: Vancouver*, vol. 1 (St. Paul, OR: French Prairie Press, 1972), 11, B105.

7 John Campbell cited in Johnson, *Flathead and Kootenay*, 24, 275; Olga Weydemeyer Johnson, *The Story of the Tobacco Plains Country: The Autobiography of a Community* (Caldwell, ID: Caxton Publishers for the Pioneers of the Tobacco Plains Country, 1950), 41.

8 Bruce McIntyre Watson, *Lives Lived West of the Divide: A Biographical Dictionary of Fur Traders Working West of the Rockies, 1793–1858* (Kelowna, BC: Centre for Social, Spatial, and Economic Justice, University of British Columbia, 2010), 1:373–74.

9 Basil G. Hamilton, "Baptiste Morigeau," 1928, typescript in Windermere Valley Museum, Invermere, incorporated into "Passing of Aged Pioneer Recalls Early History of District," *Kimberley Courier*, January 21, 1932.

10 Clara Graham, *This Was the Kootenay* (Vancouver: Evergreen Press, 1965), 62.

11 Johnson, *Flathead and Kootenay*, 275.

12 Graham, *This Was the Kootenay*, 62; Winnifred Ariel Weir, *Tales of the Windermere* (Invermere: The author, 1980), 16.

13 Hamilton, "Baptiste Morigeau."

14 Munnick, *Catholic Church Records of the Pacific Northwest: Vancouver*, vol. 1, 11, B101.

15 Morigeau family tree, Windermere Valley Museum Archives, Invermere.

16 St. Paul's and St. Regis Mission Marriage Records, 1848, Jesuit Archives, Gonzaga University, M24, 1852.

17 Johnson, *Flathead and Kootenay*, 228–30; see also "Reports from Kootenai Region," Hudson's Bay Company Archives, A.64/26, nos. 1 (1820)–56 (1871), typescripts in Fort Steele Archives, mss. 53.

18 Report 28, 1853, Chief Factors Peter Skene Ogden and Dugald Mactavish to Sir George Simpson, Vancouver, November 25, 1853, in "Reports from Kootenai Region."

19 Johnson, *Flathead and Kootenay*, 270; Malone, Roeder, Lang, *Montana*, 62.

20 On the use of the French language, see the 1901 Canadian manuscript census, Yale and Cariboo, D6-North East Kootenay, Windermere, household 39, where Sophie's younger brother, Baptiste Morigeau, listed his first language as French; also Hamilton, "Baptiste Morigeau," on how, in old age, Baptiste Morigeau had "just a sufficient accent in his words to stamp him as one of French Canadian origin."

21 Letter of September 9, 1845, in Pierre-Jean De Smet, *Life, Letters and Travels of Father Pierre-Jean De Smet, S.J., 1807–1878*, vol. 2, ed. Hiram Martin Cittenden and Alfred Talbot Richardson (New York: Francis P. Harper, 1905), 498. Italics in original.

22 Letter of September 9, 1845, in De Smet, *Life, Letters and Travels*, 2:498.

23 Letter of September 9, 1845, in De Smet, *Life, Letters and Travels*, 2:499.

24 Letter of September 9, 1845, in De Smet, *Life, Letters and Travels*, 2:499. Italics in original.

25 Marie Cuffe Shea, *Early Flathead and Tobacco Plains: A Narrative History of Northwestern Montana* (Eureka, MT: The author, 1977), 98; also Jean Barman and Bruce Watson, "Fort Colville's Fur Trade Families and the Dynamics of Indigenous Racial Intermixture in the Pacific Northwest," *Pacific Northwest Quarterly* 90, no. 3 (1999): 140–53.

26 Hamilton, "Baptiste Morigeau."

27 Shea, *Early Flathead and Tobacco Plains*, 98.

28 Charles McLean, quoted in Johnson, *Tobacco Plains Country*, 43.

29 The couple was living together at the time of the 1860 United States census.

30 Johnson, *Flathead and Kootenay*, 318.

31 Naomi Miller, "Michael Phillipps: Prominent Kootenai Citizen," in *The Forgotten Side of the Border: British Columbia's Elk Valley and Crowsnest Pass*, ed. Wayne Norton and Naomi Miller (Kamloops: Plateau Press, 1998), 29–30.

32 Report 37 from "Reports from Kootenai Region"; John V. Campbell to Charles N. Kessler, Lillooet, October 6, 1918, Montana Historical Society Archives, Small Collection 512.

33 John V. Campbell to Charles N. Kessler, Lillooet, May 12, 1918, Montana Historical Society Archives, Small Collection 512.

34 Dave Kay, "$45,000 Shipped by Pack Train," *Cranbrook Courier*, June 22, 1977.

35 John V. Campbell to Charles N. Kessler, Lillooet, October 6, 1918, Montana Historical Society Archives, Small Collection 512.

36 Shea, *Early Flathead and Tobacco Plains*, 99.

37 Mary Lozar, quoted in Johnson, *Tobacco Plains Country*, 44.

38 Mary Lozar, quoted in Johnson, *Tobacco Plains Country*, 44.

39 F.W. Laing, *Colonial Farm Settlers on the Mainland of British Columbia 1858–1871* (Victoria: n.p., 1939), 499.

40 Mary Lozar, quoted in Johnson, *Tobacco Plains Country*, 44.

41 Morigeau family tree, Windermere Valley Museum Archives; Shea, *Early Flathead and Tobacco Plains*, 98.
42 Hamilton, "Baptiste Morigeau"; Morigeau family tree.
43 Hamilton, "Baptiste Morigeau."
44 Shea, *Early Flathead and Tobacco Plains*, 100.
45 Mary Lozar, quoted in Johnson, *Tobacco Plains Country*, 44.
46 Shea, *Early Flathead and Tobacco Plains*, 99–100.
47 Johnson, *Tobacco Plains Country*, 46.
48 Frank Leonard, quoted in Johnson, *Tobacco Plains Country*, 45.
49 Shea, *Early Flathead and Tobacco Plains*, 100.
50 George Mercer Dawson, quoted in Johnson, *Tobacco Plains Country*, 45.
51 Entry for September 20, 1883, in Alexander Staveley Hill, *From Home to Home: Autumn Wanderings in the Northwest, in the Years 1881, 1882, 1883, 1884* (New York: O. Judd, 1885), 353.
52 Entry for September 21, 1883, in Hill, *From Home to Home*, 354–55.
53 Entry for September 21, 1883, in Hill, *From Home to Home*, 356–57.
54 Entry for September 22, 1883, in Hill, *From Home to Home*, 357–58.
55 Entry for September 21, 1883, in Hill, *From Home to Home*, 355.
56 Entry for September 21, 1883, in Hill, *From Home to Home*, 357.
57 Johnson, *Tobacco Plains Country*, 45.
58 Susan Phillipps McGuire, quoted in Johnson, *Tobacco Plains Country*, 46.
59 Shea, *Early Flathead and Tobacco Plains*, 99.
60 Johnson, *Tobacco Plains Country*, 45.
61 Ida Gregg Berry, quoted in Johnson, *Tobacco Plains Country*, 46.
62 Sophie Morigeau, quoted in Johnson, *Tobacco Plains Country*, 48.
63 Ida Gregg Berry, quoted second-hand in Johnson, *Tobacco Plains Country*, 46.
64 Charles N. Edwards, quoted in Johnson, *Tobacco Plains Country*, 47.
65 Addie Brock, quoted in Johnson, *Tobacco Plains Country*, 46.
66 Ray, "Sophie Morigeau," 15.
67 Johanna Quirk Cuffe, quoted in Shea, *Early Flathead and Tobacco Plains*, 101.
68 Shea, *Early Flathead and Tobacco Plains*, 100.
69 Frederick Norbury to Coni, Tobacco Plains, February 10, 1888, BC Archives, ms. 877.
70 Susan Phillipps McGuire, quoted in Johnson, *Tobacco Plains Country*, 47. Italics signify underlining in the original.
71 Susan Phillipps McGuire, quoted in Johnson, *Tobacco Plains Country*, 47.
72 Johnson, *Tobacco Plains Country*, 47.
73 Johanna Quirk Cuffe, quoted in Shea, *Early Flathead and Tobacco Plains*, 101.
74 Johanna Quirk Cuffe, quoted in Shea, *Early Flathead and Tobacco Plains*, 100–101.
75 Johnson, *Tobacco Plains Country*, 48.
76 Johanna Quirk Cuffe, quoted in Shea, *Early Flathead and Tobacco Plains*, 101.
77 Charles N. Edwards, quoted in Johnson, *Tobacco Plains Country*, 48. Italics in original.
78 *Eureka Journal*, July 23, 1910, quoted in Shea, *Early Flathead and Tobacco Plains*, 101.
79 Johanna Quirk Cuffe, quoted in Shea, *Early Flathead and Tobacco Plains*, 101; and in Johnson, *Tobacco Plains Country*, 49.
80 Johanna Quirk Cuffe, quoted in Johnson, *Tobacco Plains Country*, 49.
81 Ray, "Sophie Morigeau," 15.
82 Ray, "Sophie Morigeau," 23, 101.
83 Ray, "Sophie Morigeau," 102.
84 Johnson, *Tobacco Plains Country*, 43–44.
85 Johnson, *Tobacco Plains Country*, 48.

Finding Solace in Family and Place

8

Family Life at Fort Langley

This essay tracks the families of those men who worked at Fort Langley as "servants" for the Hudson's Bay Company on three-year contracts. They were primarily French Canadians, Kanakas (Hawaiians), and "English, Scots and men of mixed descent, including Iroquois from eastern Canada and Cree from Red River." Their wives were mainly Kwantlen and Cowichan. Permitted to partner with local women only after two years of services, these men's alliances were intended to encourage them to take up another three-year contract with the company. This business tactic succeeded, although some men had difficulty coping with wives who were not used to submission and who left when not well treated. Nonetheless, even after the closure of Fort Langley, the families remained and descendants of these families still live in the area.

By Jean Barman. Reprinted with permission from *British Columbia Historical News* 32, no. 4 (1999): 16–23.

We each bring to the fur trade our particular sets of assumptions. I long conceived of it as a man's game in which, to use the clichés of an earlier day, "tough-minded" Scots, "easygoing" voyageurs who always seemed to be singing as their canoes sped along, and "obliging" Kanakas more or less hung out together in the wilderness.[1] There is nothing wrong with these images, so long as we use them as a starting point and realize that much more also went on, including family life.

Context

To understand the origins of family life, generally and at Fort Langley, we have to reflect on the fur trade as a whole and to recognize, most importantly, that it was a business. The Hudson's Bay Company, which ran the fur trade across the Pacific Northwest by the time of Fort Langley's establishment in 1827, was a private enterprise out to make a profit. The goal was to persuade local Indigenous people to trade furs for goods at an exchange rate low enough to make a profit when these furs were turned into products of desire, ranging from trimming for clothing to beaver hats.

The fur trade worked only so long as Indigenous societies remained reasonably intact. Local people had both to be able to continue to hunt and trap and to want the goods that fur traders had to offer with no or few options for acquiring them. This meant that trading posts like Fort Langley and the two or three dozen others scattered across the Pacific Northwest during the first half of the nineteenth century were, by their very nature, isolated dots within an Indigenous world. Once gold was discovered along the Fraser River and the gold rush broke out in 1858 the world of the fur trade essentially collapsed.

Some posts continued in operation for a time, as did Fort Langley, but as pale reflections of what they had once been. The arrival of thousands of newcomers gave local people new choices that unbalanced the fur trade and also the Indigenous societies themselves.

Most of the jobs in the fur trade were in no way glamorous or romantic. What they demanded was hard brute labour. Furs had to be traded, packed, and transported out and new trade goods brought in. Foodstuffs had to be raised or acquired. Other commodities that might be usefully sold had also to be packaged to be shipped out, as, for instance, salmon in barrels. All the same, it is the officers whom we have most often equated with the fur trade. In particular, the few published studies we have about family life, notably *Many Tender Ties* by Sylvia Van Kirk and *Strangers in Blood* by Jennifer Brown, are really only talking about officers and their families.[2]

Each post had just one or two men known as officers, who were generally English or Scottish in background, literate, in the fur trade as a career, and what we might think of as gentlemen. The other dozen to two dozen men stationed at Fort Langley or at any of the other Pacific Northwest posts at any one point in time were what the HBC called servants. These were men hired on three-year contracts who were usually of very modest background and generally illiterate.

About 120 men worked at Fort Langley between 1827 and 1858, of whom no more than eight or ten were officers or clerks. The two most important were Archibald McDonald, there from 1828 to 1833, and his successor, James Murray Yale, from 1833 through mid-century. It was McDonald and then Yale who lived in the "Big House," in the case of McDonald with his wife, Jane Klyne, and growing family. All of the other hundred-plus men at Fort Langley were contract employees, who divided roughly equally into three groups. The first were French Canadians, the second indigenous Hawaiians known as Kanakas, and the third a combination of Englishmen, Scots, and men of mixed descent, including Iroquois from eastern Canada and Cree from Red River.

This then was Fort Langley, an isolated dot in an Indigenous sea where a gentleman officer, possibly with a clerk to assist him, oversaw a dozen to two dozen illiterate men of diverse backgrounds and language whose brute labour made the difference between profit and loss, and hence the future career prospects of the officer in charge.

Origins of Family Life

Family life came about because, quite simply, it served the economic self-interests of the fur trade and, more specifically, of Fort Langley, and also the self-interests of the Indigenous peoples all around them. Kwantlen, Musqueam, Nanaimo, and Cowichan peoples regularly passed by Fort Langley as they went up and down the Fraser River, sometimes in the hundreds.[3] It is only to be expected that they would be curious about this strange new place in their midst and were soon jostling with each other for best advantage. What better way to get access than to have someone trustworthy on the inside? Given that these newcomers were mostly men alone, without women, who better than a daughter or a sister?

McDonald, as the officer in charge during Fort Langley's early years, was just as eager as were local peoples to establish ties in order to encourage more furs to be offered. The interplay between the two sides, how each sought to manipulate the other, becomes visible by looking at this first test case, so to speak.

It was in November 1828, just over a year after Fort Langley's establishment, that McDonald made a suggestion to his young clerk, James Murray Yale, which he reported in his journal: "The "Quaintkine [Kwantlen], … being the principal Indians of the neighbourhood & [the only ones] who at all exert themselves to Collect Beaver, we have thought it good Policy in Mr. Yale to form a Connection in that family—and accordingly he has now the Chiefs daughter after making them all liberal presents."[4]

At first, events seemed to be unfolding to the newcomers' advantage. However, within two weeks it became clear that both Yale and McDonald had been taken in. The Kwantlen chief calmly informed them that he was under claim of "heavy damages for giving away his daughter in marriage to Mr. Yale [when she] was already the lawful wife (in their way) of a Scatchad [Skagit]."[5] A day later the chief's brother got into the act. He sought to benefit from the confusion by turning up at the post "with a grand total of ten and three or four Young Girls to dispose of them in marriage if he can." As if this were not enough, within the day "it turns out they [these new women being offered up] are all married wives & of course all negotiations with the men broke off."[6]

Even this was not the end of the story. Yale became caught between the fur trade's interests and sexual desire. The woman's appeal is evident in the reference in a Yale family history, based on stories originating with Yale himself, to her "laughter, that prodigal laughter so characteristic of the generously proportioned squaws and lissome maidens of the Indian race in his own haunts, laughter such as few white men hear, melodious ripples from the midst of the groups of Indian maidens in the village."[7] Thus, a week after being turfed out on discovering that she was twice "married," "Mrs. Yale Came home again."[8]

Soon the tide turned once more. Just weeks later, so the post journal recorded, "Mr. Yale has found means to get rid of his Lady that has Cost So much goods."[9]

Then Yale reversed himself yet again and the Kwantlen chief Nicamous, to quote the journal, "brought back his Daughter in Consequence of her husband regretting having given her Conge [discharge] Some days ago."[10]

It was the Kwantlen chief's turn to press his advantage. Less than two weeks later he turned up at Fort Langley to claim his reward for bringing the couple back together. "Without much ceremony [he] asked his daughter for [a] Blanket & she just as unceremoniously walked in[to the store room]—took it out, & with a pin buckled it on round his neck." Such audacity was more than McDonald could tolerate, so "with Still Less Ceremony [he, McDonald] took the liberty of removing it & told Master Nicamous to be off with his own good new, white Blanket."[11] The woman likely stuck with Yale, for in March 1830 the post journal noted the birth of a "young daughter" to "Mrs. Yale."[12]

This little drama made clear to McDonald that desire could easily spin out of control. Realizing the situation, local people became ever more determined to gain entry to the post through their women, as McDonald recorded: "Ever since the fields are Cleared of the potat[o]es—Swarms of women & Children are daily Sauntering about Collecting what they can and this unavoidably leads to a meeting with our men, who rather Seek than avoid it."[13] The very next day some of the men requested permission, which McDonald rejected as "impudent," "to go out and Stop for the night" in the nearby camp.[14] Worse yet, during the New Year festivities heralding 1829, the post journal recorded, "the drunken Sot [Quebecker Louis] Delanis had Contrived to haule [*sic*] one of the Quaitline [Kwantlen] damsels up by a port hole in one of the Bastions."[15]

McDonald became determined to wrest control of the situation and, as we can read in the Fort Langley journal, established a system whereby cohabitation became less an end in itself than the first stage of family life. Men were permitted to make "a formal application for wives,"[16] a policy that worked because it also suited the interests of Indigenous fathers, who had to indicate their willingness by accepting gifts comparable to, or better than, what they would have required of an Indigenous suitor. Thus, when "one of our men Pierre Therrein [a Quebecker] was allowed to take a wife out of the Aiskimnum's [Chinook chief's] family—He gave a Gun & 4 Blkts."[17]

Each union was also recognized within the post, likely encouraging greater stability than would otherwise have been the case. As noted in the journal, "one of the Engages—[Quebecker] Louis Ossin is allowed to take a woman from the Camp & each man had a half pint liquor on the occasion in the evening."[18] The Kwantlen chief whose daughter was cohabiting with Yale soon also had his sister ensconced within the post. Hence, when "Como—an Owhyhee [Hawaiian], & one of our best men here is married to the Sister of Nicameus—the Quaitline [Kwantlen] Chief—all hands had a half pint & a hop [evening of dancing] on the occasion."[19] Another time, "Annawuskum McDonald [an Iroquois and] our [kitchen] Servant, having taken a woman last night, our people were treated with a decent Ball on the occasion, which, with other moments of relaxation they have, Seem to make them think that they Cannot be much happier in any other part of the Country."[20]

This observation reveals McDonald's second reason for encouraging family life and that was to keep this disparate lot of men satisfied and to make them want to stay at Fort Langley once their three-year contracts expired. McDonald understood that "those of the men that had not been lucky enough to Come in for a Chance of this kind have no inducement at all to remain at the place." As he put it, "to reconcile the bucks to Fort Langley without Some indulgence of this nature is utterly out of the question—to leave them to prowl about in the [Indian] Camp would be the worst policy of all—What remains for us, then, is to make the best & wisest Selection [of a woman that] we Can for every man."[21]

McDonald very cleverly linked permission to have a wife to a willingness to continue in the company's service. A man had to have been "Engaged [by the company] for two years" to be "allowed to take a woman."[22] The timing was clearly intended to encourage contract renewal for another three-year term so as not to be separated from a new found love. The policy worked. McDonald reported in 1830 how "it has had the effect of reconciling them to the place and removing the inconvenience and indeed the great uncertainty of being able to get them year after year replaced from the Columbia." "All our [fifteen] Men have taken Women."[23]

Although no journals survive after 1830, we do have glimpses of subsequent events. The report from one of the first visiting Catholic missionaries, in 1843, stated that all of the "about twenty men ... employed there" have "wives and children after the fashion of the country."[24]

We can also trace the men as individuals. By putting together HBC records with baptisms and marriage records of visiting priests, we get some idea of what happened. Just over half of the men left within two years of arriving at Fort Langley, not surprising given the difficult working conditions of the fur trade. What is more surprising is that the other half stayed on longer, sometimes much longer.

TABLE 1
Men Who Worked More Than Two Years at Fort Langley (1827–1859)

*=Wife/Number of known children	Name	Years	Total years		Afterward
*5	ANNANCE, F. NOEL	27–30	3	French Canadian	returned home
*8	Arquoitte, Amable	27–30	3	French Canadian	to Williamette, OR
	Boisvert, Louis	27–30	3	French Canadian	to Williamette, OR
*	Kennedy, John	27–30	3	Brit/Scot	died
*7	MacMILLAN, JAMES	27–30	3	Brit/Scot	returned home
*2	Piette, Francois	27–30	3	French Canadian	to Cowlitz, WA
*11	Plamondon, Simon	27–30	3	French Canadian	to Cowlitz, WA
*	Therrien, Pierre	27–30	3	French Canadian	died
*4	Ossin, Louis	27–31	4	French Canadian	to Williamette, OR
*6	Farron, Dominique	27–35	8	French Canadian	to Cowlitz, WA
*5	McDonald, Anawiscum	27–34, 40–42	9	Brit/Scot	to Cowlitz, WA

*=Wife/Number of known children	Name	Years	Total years		Afterward
*3	Como	27–39	12	Hawaiian	to Fort Vancouver, WA
*4	Charles, Pierre	27–40	13	French Canadian	to Cowlitz, WA
*3	Satakarata, Louis	27–45	18	French Canadian	to Victoria
*4	Piopio (Peeopeeoh)	27–52	25	Hawaiian	stayed in Fraser Valley
*3	Pepin/Magice, Etienne	27–	33	French Canadian	?
*14	McDONALD, ARCHIBALD	28–33	5	Brit/Scot	to Quebec
*2	Oniaze, Etienne	28–37	9	French Canadian	to Fort Vancouver, WA
*4	Delonie, Louis	28–41	12	French Canadian	to Cowlitz, WA
*3	YALE, JAMES MURRAY	28–	31	Brit/Scot	to Victoria
*	Tai i	30–48	18	Hawaiian	died
*2	Wavicareerea	30–53	23	Hawaiian	stayed in Fraser Valley
*?	Rendall, James	31–46	15	Brit/Scot	returned home
	Hereea	33–37	4	Hawaiian	died
*1	Brown, William	32–33, 35–39	5	Brit/Scot	returned home
*3	Brousseau, Basil	33–34, 36–	23	French Canadian	stayed in Fraser Valley
*	Peeannau, Joe	37–50	13	Hawaiian	to Victoria
*5	Vautrin, Xavier	37–52	15	French Canadian	to Cowichan
*7	Minie, Frederic	38–43	5	French Canadian	to Victoria
*1	McPhail, Angus	38–46	8	Brit/Scot	to Victoria
*8	Fallardeau, Narcisse	38–	20	French Canadian	stayed in Fraser Valley
*	Laowala	39–48	9	Hawaiian	died
*7/8	Allard, Ovid	39–53, 58–	15	French Canadian	stayed in Fraser Valley
*1	Bell, John	40–53, 56–57	14	Brit/Scot	died
*	Taheenou	41–47	6	Hawaiian	returned home
*2	Borabora, George	41–52	9	Hawaiian	to Victoria

*=Wife/Number of known children	Name	Years	Total years		Afterward
*3	Mokowhehe	42–47	5	Hawaiian	returned home
*7	Holland, George	43–46	3	Brit/Scot	returned home
	Willing, Augustin	43–	15	French Canadian	to Boundary Commission
*3	Ohier	45–56	11	Hawaiian	stayed in Fraser Valley
*1	Cromarty, William	45–	13	Brit/Scot	stayed in Fraser Valley
	Kekapalale	47–54	7	Hawaiian	?
*3	Robertson, Samuel	47–	11	Brit/Scot	stayed in Fraser Valley
*3	Apnaut/Ohulu, Peter	48–49, 50–55	6	Hawaiian	stayed in Fraser Valley
*2	Kekoa	48–55	7	Hawaiian	?
*3	Dease, Napoleon	50–54	4	Brit/Scot	died
*1	Ayotte, Firmin	50–	8	French Canadian	to Victoria?
*7	Latrielle, Alexander	51–58	7	French Canadian	?
*7	Danneau, Antoine	53–56	3	French Canadian	to Victoria
	Dionne, Cyprien	53–	5	French Canadian	?
	Taylor, James	53–	5	Brit/Scot	stayed in Fraser Valley
	Wavicareerea, Robert	53–	5	Hawaiian	stayed in Fraser Valley

CAPITALIZED SURNAME = officer; Lowercase surname = ordinary employee

Table 1 lists the men who stayed at Fort Langley more than two years and hence were able to take a wife and likely began a family. What we see is that most of them did so. Fort Langley retained a strong core of men, in part at least because of the opportunity for family life. It is not surprising then that a report from the Hudson's Bay Company noted in 1839 how "the several branches of business carried on at this Post [of Fort Langley] continue in a flourishing state," and another report a year later that "the business is going on in the most prosperous manner."[25] The head of the Hudson's Bay Company across North America enthused in 1841 how Fort Langley "has for a length of time been a very well regulated post."[26] In sum, family life originated at Fort Langley and was continued as a policy, not for sentiment or romance, but because it was good business.

Nature of Family Life

For all of its prevalence, family life was never easy at Fort Langley. It had to fit into the nooks and crannies. Men worked from early morning until sunset for five and a half days each week.[27] Apart from McDonald in his "Big House," men got no perks for their families. As he noted in his journal, "provisions for them they have none, save what they derive from the regular and ample allowance to themselves."[28] The son of a long-time servant recalled that "all the employees of the company had quarters inside the fort."[29] Where relationships acquired a sense of permanence, some men built private dwellings outside of the walls.[30]

Flexibility and accommodation were essential on both sides for unions to survive. Newcomer men could not simply take the assumptions about masculinity and femininity that they brought with them whence they came and make them work at Fort Langley. Their women could simply disappear back into Indigenous space. They possessed far more freedom than did the men, who were obliged by contract to stay put for a specified period of time. Even McDonald conceded that, "like all Indians, their attachment to their own lands and friends keeps them for ever on the wing to be back again."[31]

It took McDonald and the other men at Fort Langley some time to learn that women could not be made to submit. Unhappy women simply left, forcing the male either to enter Indigenous space to retrieve her or to lose face. To take just one example from the journals, a woman who had been "remonstrated with" by "her husband" for talking with her mother near the gates "watched her time and walked off to the camp." The man she was living with wanted her back. And so, "after his work was over he followed her, & requested her return, which with the Concurrence of her relations and others around was positively refused under frivolous pretexts that She was not Kindly treated or entirely Secured as yet with the necessary property."[32]

For a time it seemed as if newcomers' might would triumph. Reflecting contemporary assumptions of male superiority, McDonald fretted that if the women were allowed to persist, "the husbands are bound down never to Correct them." So he rationalized that what this woman really wanted was, and I quote, "an opportunity of gratifying her paramour & when Convenient return to the Fort & to the arms of her outwitted husband." On that basis McDonald "called 5 men under arms immediately & with them proceeded to the [Indian] Village when with very little gallantry in my address I ordered the lady to the Fort & acquainted the Natives that it would be best for them never to put us to Such trouble again."[33] The victory was short-lived, for just ten days later the post journal noted curtly, without elaboration, that "one of our men's wives decamped this morning."[34]

More than any other factor, it was the arrival of children that forged long-term relationships. The Hawaiians were the earliest to establish family life. Their leader was Piopio, who had in 1824 been one of the men dispatched to prospect for a suitable location for what became Fort Langley, and who in 1827 was one of the two dozen sent to construct the new post. Piopio was among the first to cohabit. A daughter, Aglace Paiva, was born in 1827,[35] followed quickly by a son known as Mayo,[36] and a few years later by Sophie, who was baptized during the Catholic priest's first visit in 1841 as the "natural daughter of Pehopuho and a Kwoithe [Kwantlen?] woman."[37] When Fort Langley moved about three miles upriver in 1840, Piopio and the other Hawaiians continued to live at the original site with their families, commuting to work.

Similarly, the post journal noted on July 2, 1828, how "one of the fair Laddies [sic] of the Fort presented her Husband wi[t]h a Son & heir, He being the first born in this quarter (I mean among the whites)."[38] The next March, "At a few minutes past midnight, a Girl was born to [Quebecker Simon] Plemondon.[39] A couple of months later it was "Mrs. Annance" who gave birth. And so on.

Family life never overcame larger divisions grounded in status, religion, language, and ethnicity and race, or indeed the differences in rank that the women themselves embodied. There was never a single family life at Fort Langley, apart from brief moments in time. Christmas was one of the few occasions when the women cohabiting with Hawaiians, and thereby deemed inferior, were permitted into the post. Even then, one year they got into an almost immediate confrontation with "the women who were married to white men, were related to the chiefs," and considered themselves superior. According to the son of one of the French Canadians: "The Kanaka women were accused of passing remarks about their white sisters and then from one imaginary insult or slight the fight was on. There was no prancing or sparring. It was run and grab for the hair of the head. A regular tug-of-war ensued. Finally they were separated by their husbands and all was peace and quietness."[40]

There were three times each year—Christmas, New Year's, and the fur trade brigade's arrival in the summer—when, to quote the Yale family history, "the obligations of business ceased to regulate seniority of rank and trade."[41] Christmas was not just for squabbling; it also strengthened family life: "In the afternoon of Christmas Day the men's wives were invited to the big hall where they were given two or three 'shots' of wine after which their baskets (they were told to bring them) were filled with cookies, cranberries and blueberry jam and ships biscuits."[42] On New Year's day there was dancing: "The men, and in succession the women were received into the Hall & treated with just enough of the 'Oh be joyful' ... so that we could all again meet in the evening with propriety"[43] for a "merry reel,"[44] but "without any indecent frolick."[45]

The strength of family life at Fort Langley is most visible in the accounts of outsiders, who often used racist rhetoric to explain away what they observed rather than having to take it seriously. In his description of the dance held in 1858 to mark the brigade's arrival, a Maritime gold miner admirably evoked the sense of community that for brief moments did bind together the families of Fort Langley:

> To this ball I received an invitation, which I, with much pleasure attended, and was not a little surprised at seeing the company composed of so heterogeneous a kind. There were English, Scotch, French, and the Kanackas present, and their offspring, and all so thoroughly mixed with the native Indian blood, that it would take a well versed Zoologist to decide what class of people they were, and what relation they had to each other; though that will cause you but little surprise when you are informed that almost all the Co's. wives are the native squaws, their children, which are called half breeds, as a general thing, being fair, docile and intelligent. The ball was conducted with the best possible decorum. The music was sweet, from the violin, and the dancing was performed in the most graceful manner, by the Indians and the half breeds, who took a very prominent part of that occasion.[46]

Legacies of Family Life

Family life did not disappear just because the fur trade fell into decline. We all too often think of settlement, be it in the Fraser Valley or elsewhere in British Columbia, as beginning with the gold rush. This was most certainly not the case. Table 1 summarizes the subsequent lives of the men who remained at Fort Langley more than two years. What the lives tell us, most importantly, is that family life at Fort Langley counted. A few men returned home, almost certainly by themselves, but most looked for an intermediate place where they could continue to live satisfactorily with their wives and children. Many of the first families went to earlier places of newcomer settlement in the Pacific Northwest, such as the Willamette Valley in the Oregon Territory or to Cowlitz in the future Washington state.

Wherever they headed, families to some extent turned inward. They settled in clusters. To understand the reasons, we need to keep in mind the thousands of newcomers from Britain, the United States, and elsewhere who flooded into the Pacific Northwest during these years. We need to remind ourselves of the attitudes that many of them had toward persons perceived as different from themselves. It was not just the Maritime gold miner who ridiculed Fort Langley's fur trade families. The Anglican cleric who held religious services at Fort Langley during the early settlement years came close to ridicule in his observation: "Very unsatisfactory was the state into which many of the Hudson's Bay employés had degenerated: living insulated, from boyhood often to gray hairs, amongst debased savages, they had married squaws, and their half-bred offspring but too often were mere degraded savages like the mother."[47]

If growing racism forced families to look inward for marriage partners, other aspects of changing times worked to their benefit. Children, as well as some members of the first generation, who wanted to settle near Fort Langley were given a very important economic boost by the pre-emption policy put in place for the British Columbia mainland at the beginning of 1860. Men could take up 160 acres, even if the land were not yet surveyed. Men employed at Fort Langley, and some of their sons, were in a particularly advantageous position both because of proximity and due to the nature of their jobs. As recalled by one of Yale's daughters, "the men of the fort, with some Indian lads, used to go to Langley Prairie to cut the grain which they had sown in the Spring."[48] They had in effect received an apprenticeship in farming, including insider knowledge as to the most fertile land. Table 2 lists some of the fur trade families who settled in the Fraser Valley, including information on which families pre-empted.

All the families and clusters of families settling in the Fraser Valley have their own story to tell, and I can only sample each of the principal ethnic groups here.

William Cromarty, who arrived from the Orkneys as head barrel maker in 1844, took pains to give his family a sense of security.[49] If technically a servant, he likely enjoyed a certain status above the rank and file. For some time there had been complaints that the barrels used to export Fraser River salmon were leaking, whereas they had to be airtight for the fish to arrive edible at its destination, and Cromarty was an experienced cooper.[50] He settled down virtually immediately and remained with Salum'mia until her death in 1869.[51] Son William was born in about 1846, followed by seven other children.[52] In 1852 Cromarty requested and was given permission to purchase a cow, by which time he had his own house located "just outside the western wall."[53]

Narcisse Fallardeau joined the Hudson's Bay Company from Quebec in 1837 and spent his entire career at Fort Langley. Almost immediately he settled down with a Kwantlen woman,[54] possibly named Ellen.[55] Catherine was born in 1839,[56] followed by five more daughters and also two sons who died young.[57] Fallardeau's position as Yale's cook and servant allowed his family to live in the kitchen of the Big House. The eldest Fallardeau daughter, Catherine, was wed to Fort Langley blacksmith James Taylor in the summer of 1858.[58] As for her sisters, three white newcomers, "products of the Fraser River Gold Rush," so an acquaintance recalled, "married halfbreed sisters who were of the old Feledew family."[59]

The Hawaiian cluster, headed by Piopio, particularly benefited from the pre-emption legislation. They were already formed into a cluster. When the daughters of Piopio reached adolescence, they were,

TABLE 2
Fur Trade Continuity into the Second Generation in the Fraser Valley

ALLARD, Ovid	Sennie + David Hamburger/Yale Jason + Seraphine of Port Townsend Lucy + *Kenneth MORRISON
BROUSSEAU, Basil	Marie + *Peter Baker Basil Jr. + Sarah Pierre
*CROMARTY, William	*William + Lucy of Cheam Elizabeth + *Henry Dawson James + Annie Cliton *David Mary + *Joseph Hairsine Samuel + Caroline Garner
xDEASE, Napoleon	Mary + Godfrey McKay
*EMPTAGE, William	William Jr. + Sarah Elkins
*FALLARDEAU, Narcisse	Catherine + *James TAYLOR Harriet + Daniel Kilcup-US Louisa + Henry West-US Matilda + George Rehberger-US Rose + James Ibbotson Mary + William Worley
*Lacroix, Michel (New Caledonia)	Michel + Mary Dixon Gabriel + Sarah Jane Wells Joseph + Annie James Helen + Alonzo Baker Mary Louise + Gabriel Galland/George Newton
*PIOPIO	*Joseph MAYO Sophia + *Peter APNAUT/*William Nelson Paiva + OHIER Henry Pound + Margaret
*Robertson, Robert (New Caledonia)	*Andrew Robertson Charlotte + Frank Owens Mary + Joseph Garner Barbara + Henry Garner Andrina + Charles Robert Garner
*ROBERTSON, Samuel	Mary + *Thomas Shannon Donald + Mina Rehberger James + Christine Yates
WAVICAREERA	*Robert WAVICAREERA + Marguerite Sta-ei-els

Surname capitalized = Worked at Ft Langley; * = Early land pre-emption; x = Died before settling not unexpectedly, partnered with Kanakas working at Fort Langley.[60] When contracts expired, enough of them had not renewed so that by 1857 sufficient "free Kanakas" were living around Fort Langley for the Hudson's Bay Company to request that the "seven able men among their number" help transport an especially large load of goods.[61]

Then came disruption. The land on which the Hawaiians had informally settled near the original site of Fort Langley was surveyed and auctioned off in the fall of 1858 for a townsite named Derby, which many expected to become the capital of the new mainland colony brought into being by the gold rush.[62] Although dispossessed, the Hawaiians held on. A government official who stopped by in January 1859 found still there "a large body of Kanakas—a mixed race half Indian half Sandwich Islanders."[63] In the spring of 1859 Governor James Douglas was petitioned by Piopio, who stated that he "had cleared and had been in occupation of a piece of land there, from which he was ejected when the site of the town, of which it formed a part, was decided upon."[64] Piopio wanted forty-seven acres on the other side of the Fraser River as reparation and wanted it now so that he could plant the year's crops.

The pre-emption legislation of 1860 allowed the Hawaiians to acquire the land that they sought. Almost immediately, on January 23, Piopio's son-in-law "Peter Apponette" took up 160 acres, and I quote from the pre-emption document, "situated on the north bank of the Fraser River opposite the town of Derby, bordered on the east by a Creek (name unknown) the said claim to have a frontage of 33 chains on the river 48 back."[65] Just a month later, on February 23, Piopio's son "Magno Papu [Mayo Piopio]" followed suit, as did other Hawaiians. The group's continuing presence is attested by Piopio's grandson being elected to the Maple Ridge council in 1879.[66]

Lest you think all of this was so very long ago, in March 1999 I had the pleasure of visiting with Piopio's great-great-grandson and of hearing him tell me how, when he was a small boy, his great-grandmother, Piopio's daughter Sophie, would "sit with us and tell us stories about Hawai'i [and how] it was all sunshine." Listening, I was transported back in time almost two hundred years, for these were almost certainly stories that Sophie Apnaut Nelson, born in 1830, had herself heard as a child from her father about his life in Hawai'i before he sailed to North America and became part of the adventure that was Fort Langley.

Family life at Fort Langley is not so distant from us as we might sometimes want to believe. We have a rich and diverse human heritage all around us that, in the case of Fort Langley's fur trade families, stretches back almost two centuries, yet is very much part of who we are today as British Columbians.

Notes

1 See James Andrew Grant, "An Unsung Pioneer: Life and Letters of James Murray Yale and His 30 Years at Fort Langley," p. 82 and *passim*, typescript, BC Archives, Add. Ms. 182, pt. 3.

2 Sylvia Van Kirk, *Many Tender Ties: Women in Fur-Trade Society, 1670–1870* (Norman: University of Oklahoma Press, 1980), and Jennifer S.H. Brown, *Strangers in Blood: Fur Trade Company Families in Indian Country* (Vancouver: UBC Press, 1980).

3 For instance, June 26, July 20, and October 21, 1828, entries in Morag Maclachlan, ed., *The Fort Langley Journals, 1827–30* (Vancouver: UBC Press, 1998), 66, 69, 81.

4 November 13, 1828, entry in Maclachlan, *Fort Langley Journals*, 82.

5 November 25, 1828 entry in Maclachlan, *Fort Langley Journals*, 86.

6 November 26, 1828 entry in Maclachlan, *Fort Langley Journals*, 87.

7 Grant, "An Unsung Pioneer."

8 December 5, 1828 entry in Maclachlan, *Fort Langley Journals*, 88.

9 December 20, 1828, entry in Maclachlan, *Fort Langley Journals*, 90.

10 January 5, 1829, entry in Maclachlan, *Fort Langley Journals*, 92.

11 January 13, 1829, entry in Maclachlan, *Fort Langley Journals*, 93.

12 Jamie Morton, *Fort Langley: An Overview of the Operations of a Diversified Fur Trade Post 1848 to 1858 and the Physical Context in 1858* (Ottawa: Microfiche Report Series, Canadian Parks Service, Environment Canada, 1980), 214.

13 November 26, 1828, entry in Maclachlan, *Fort Langley Journals*, 87.

14 November 17, 1828, entry in Maclachlan, *Fort Langley Journals*, 87.

15 January 1, 1829, entry in Maclachlan, *Fort Langley Journals*, 91.

16 November 26, 1828, entry in Maclachlan, *Fort Langley Journals*, 87.

17 January 20, 1829, entry in Maclachlan, *Fort Langley Journals*, 94. Wording from "Fort Langley Journal," transcribed by Winnifreda Mcintosh, January 9, 1963, in BC Archives.

18 February 28, 1829, entry in Maclachlan, *Fort Langley Journals*, 99.

19 March 7, 1829, entry in Maclachlan, *Fort Langley Journals*, 100; also "two more of our men took wives from the Indian Camp" in May 23, 1829, entry (114), and "another one of our men took to himself a wife" in September 18, 1829 (128).

20 November 18, 1829, entry in Maclachlan, *Fort Langley Journals*, 131; also Etienne Pepin being given permission in January 14, 1830, entry (137), and Maclachlan, *Fort Langley Journals*, 23.

21 March 3, 1829, entry in Maclachlan, *Fort Langley Journals*, 99–100.

22 January 14, 1830, entry in Maclachlan, *Fort Langley Journals*, 137.

23 McDonald, Report, February 25, 1830, reproduced in Maclachlan, *Fort Langley Journals*, 222.

24 Notice no. 5, January 1843, cited in *Notices and Voyages of the Famed Quebec Mission to the Pacific Northwest, Being the correspondence, notices, etc., of Fathers Blanchet and Demers, together with those of Fathers Bolduc and Langlois* (Portland: Champoeg Press for the Oregon Historical Society, 1956), 104.

25 James Douglas to Hudson's Bay Company, Fort Vancouver, October 14, 1839, and John McLoughlin to George Simpson, Fort Vancouver, March 20, 1840, cited in E.E. Rich, ed., *The Letters of John McLoughlin, Second Series, 1839–44* (Toronto: Champlain Society, 1943), 215, 231.

26 George Simpson to Hudson's Bay Company, Fort Vancouver, November 25, 1841, in Glyndwr Williams, ed., *London Correspondence Inward from Sir George Simpson 1841–42* (London: Hudson's Bay Record Society, 1973), 74.

27 Jason O. Allard, "Reminiscences," *Province* (Vancouver), October 25, 1924, quoted in appendix C in Mary Cullen, *The History of Fort Langley, 1827–96*, Occasional Papers in Archaeology and History 20 (Ottawa: Parks Canada, 1979), 90.

28 McDonald, Report, February 25, 1830, reproduced in Maclachlan, *Fort Langley Journals*, 222.

29 Allard, "Reminiscences," in Cullen, *History of Fort Langley*, 90; also Morton, *Fort Langley*, 258.

30 Morton, *Fort Langley*, 258.

31 March 3, 1829, entry in Maclachlan, *Fort Langley Journals*, 99.

32 July 3, 1829, entry in Maclachlan, *Fort Langley Journals*, 118.

33 July 3, 1829, entry in Maclachlan, *Fort Langley Journals*, 118–19.

34 July 13, 1829, entry in Maclachlan, *Fort Langley Journals*, 120.

35 "The Naming of Kanaka Creek," typescript, BC Archives, citing Jason Allard's reminiscences, also in BC Archives, EC A1, 5A.

36 "The Naming of Kanaka Creek," citing Denys Nelson, *Fort Langley, 1827–1927* (Vancouver: Art, Historical and Scientific Association of Vancouver, July 1927), 21.

37 Harriet Duncan Munnick, *Catholic Church Records of the Pacific Northwest. Vancouver*, vol. 1 and 2, and *Stellamaris Mission* (St. Paul, OR: French Prairie Press, 1972), 1:66–67.

38 July 2, 1828, entry in Maclachlan, *Fort Langley Journals*, 67.

39 March 12, 1829, entry in Maclachlan, *Fort Langley Journals*, 100; also June 24, 1829, entry concerning "Mrs. Annance" (117).

40 Allard, "Reminiscences," in Cullen, *History of Fort Langley*, 90.

41 Grant, "An Unsung Pioneer."

42 Allard, "Reminiscences," in Cullen, *History of Fort Langley*, 90.

43 November 13, 1828, entry in Maclachlan, *Fort Langley Journals*, 82.

44 The dance is described only in the January 1, 1830, entry in "Fort Langley Journal," transcribed by Mcintosh.

45 January 2, 1830, entry in Maclachlan, *Fort Langley Journals*, 136.

46 C.C. Gardner to editor of *Islander*, March 17, 1858, cited in Morton, *Fort Langley*, 230.

47 William Burton Crickmer, "Story of the Planting of the English Church in Columbia," *Christian Advocate and Review*, s.d., 780, in Vancouver Public Library.

48 Aurelia Manson, "Reminiscences of Old Langley," appendix B in Cullen, *History of Fort Langley*, 89.

49 Morton, *Fort Langley*, 259 and 261, and genealogical materials in possession of Christy Wong.

50 Morton, *Fort Langley*, 285.

51 Verbal information from Christy Wong.

52 British Columbia manuscript censuses for 1881, NWS, family 198, and 1891, NW (11), family 255, and birth certificate of Samuel Cromarty in possession of Christy Wong. Mary and David were named in the will of William Cromarty, April 15, 1875.

53 John Gibbard, "Early History of the Fraser Valley, 1808–1885" (master's thesis, University of British Columbia, 1937), 112–13.

54 Typescript enclosure in Deann Cleveland to Jean Barman, Armstrong, early spring 1995, in author's possession.

55 Deann Cleveland to Jean Barman, Armstrong, April 8, 1995, in author's possession.

56 Donald E. Waite, *The Langley Story Illustrated: An Early History of the Municipality of Langley* (Altona, MB: D.W. Friesen, 1977), 265.

57 Cleveland to Barman, in author's possession.

58 Typescript enclosure in Cleveland to Barman, in author's possession.

59 Robert Emmett Hawley, *Skqee Mus or Pioneer Days on the Nooksack* (1945; Bellingham, WA: Whatcom Museum of History and Art, 1971), 178.

60 "The Naming of Kanaka Creek," citing Jason Allard's reminiscences in BC Archives.

61 James Douglas to James Murray Yale, July 1, 1857, cited in Morton, *Fort Langley*, 159.

62 Morton, *Fort Langley*, 258; and Cullen, *History of Fort Langley*, 61.

63 January 1859 entries in Arthur Bushby journal, cited in Morton, *Fort Langley*, 288.

64 Richard Moody to Douglas, April 1, 1859, BC Archives, Colonial Correspondence, film 915/26, cited in Morton, *Fort Langley*, 288.

65 F.W. Laing, *Colonial Farm Settlers on the Mainland of British Columbia 1858–1871* (Victoria: n.p., 1939), 99.

66 Sheila Nickols, ed., *Maple Ridge: A History of Settlement* (Maple Ridge: Municipal Hall, 1972), 33; and Waite, *The Langley Story Illustrated*, 102.

9

Beyond Chinatown

Chinese Men and Indigenous Women in Early British Columbia

Here Barman examines thirty documented marriages or common-law relationships between Chinese men and Indigenous women in British Columbia outside the Chinatowns of Victoria and Vancouver. This means that at least one in six Chinese men who at the end of the nineteenth century "engaged in intimacy leading to family formation" did so not with a Chinese woman but with an Indigenous woman. The widespread image of Chinese bachelors living in urban areas is complemented by new evidence.

By Jean Barman. Reprinted with permission from *BC Studies* 117 (2013): 39–84. This essay responds to the Chinese Canadian graduate students who over the years sought to persuade me to publish on the topic. I thank them for doing so, and Senator Isabel Eva Quan Dyck and Lily Chow for their encouragement. In appreciation for writing the essay, I was awarded a Queen Elizabeth Jubilee Medal, 2012.

The Chinese presence in early British Columbia is still largely equated with Chinatowns, where men, who made up almost all arrivals, existed in their personal lives separate from the larger society, and family life was limited mostly to a small handful of merchants with Chinese wives. Attention to men beyond Chinatown allows for a more nuanced approach, one in which some men were less constrained by tradition and more likely to make their own way in their personal as well as their work lives.

A close examination of multiple sources reveals a very different pattern of intimacy among some Chinese men living in the BC hinterland than among their countrymen in Chinatowns. Taking such persons into account, one in six Chinese men who, through the end of the nineteenth century, engaged in intimacy leading to family formation did so not with a Chinese woman but with a local Indigenous woman. While some such encounters have been noted, they have not been gathered together or interrogated.[1] The thirty relationships introduced here speak to Chinese men's initiative and resourcefulness in early British Columbia and Canada, alongside that of the Indigenous women in their lives.

Not without reason, Chinese men have been most often equated historically with Chinatowns modelled on familiar ways. Unwanted by a dominant society cheered to have them out of sight, they considered themselves away from home only for the short or medium term, with little need to break away from tradition. Most arrivals came from the Pearl River delta, a densely populated rice-growing area of Guangdong province in south China not far from the British colony of Hong Kong. A shortage of land gave priority to increased productivity. Irrigation and fertilization required capital, provided by young men going abroad to work and sending money home. The social structure was based in the extended family, which meant men could leave secure in the knowledge that their families, including wives if they were married, would be cared for until they returned, either to die or possibly only for a visit.[2] Initially most went to southeast Asia, but increasingly the west coast of North America beckoned—initially California, with its gold rush beginning in 1848, and then British Columbia with its rush a decade later.[3]

The first wave of four thousand or more Chinese arrived in British Columbia in search of gold from 1858 onward. A second wave originated with upward of fifteen thousand men hired in the early 1880s to construct the British Columbian portion of the transcontinental Canadian Pacific Railway. A census taken on the eve of the British colony of British Columbia's joining the rest of Canada in 1871 enumerated fifteen hundred Chinese, comprising one in seven of the non-Indigenous population.[4] In 1891, the nine thousand British Columbians born in China accounted for one in eight; by 1901, the fifteen thousand, accounted for one in ten (Table 2).[5] Only toward the end of the nineteenth century did some Chinese cross the Rockies. In 1891, 98 per cent of the Canadian total of persons born in China lived in British Columbia, down to 86 per cent by 1901.[6]

Chinese British Columbians long continued to be almost all men, not unexpectedly so given the circumstances of their migration. The 53 Chinese women present in 1871 made up 3 per cent of the total number. An 1885 count located 59 "married ladies," two-thirds of them living in the provincial capital of Victoria, and 72 "prostitutes," together accounting for just over 1 per cent of the total (Table 1).[7] As of 1902, Victoria housed 92 wives, and the rapidly growing rail terminus of Vancouver 27 wives, being 3 and 1 per cent respectively of the totals.[8] Even though fewer than 10 per cent of the three thousand men living in Victoria at the turn of the century were merchants, two-thirds of the city's 92 Chinese wives were so partnered, as were two-thirds of the 27 in Vancouver.[9] Inferring from these figures, the total number of Chinese wives in British Columbia by the turn of the century was likely somewhere around 150.

TABLE 1
Chinese in British Columbia, 1885

Region	Men	"Married ladies"	"Prostitutes"	17 and under	Total	Percentage of Chinese by region
Victoria	1,559	41	34	133	1,767	16.9%
Other Vancouver Island	925	8	4	32	969	9.2%
New Westminster	1,577	4	7	92	1,680	16.0%
Railway construction	3,510	0	0	0	3,510	33.5%
Other mainland	2,528	6	27	5	2,556	24.4%
Totals	10,099	59	72	262	10,482	

Source: *Report of the Royal Commission on Chinese Immigration: Report and Evidence* (Ottawa: The Commission, 1885), 363-65.

TABLE 2
British Columbians Born in China, 1901

Census region	Total non-Indigenous	Born in China	Percentage of total population	Percentage of Chinese population
Greater Victoria	23,355	2,915	12.5 %	20.0 %
Other Vancouver Island	21,429	2,558	11.9 %	17.5 %
Vancouver and north coast	33,109	2,803	8.5 %	19.2 %
New Westminster and Fraser Valley	20,592	2,556	12.4 %	17.5 %
Fraser Canyon, Cariboo, Kootenays	51,223	3,744	7.3 %	25.7 %
Totals	149,708	14,576	9.7%	

Source: Census Canada, 1901.

The more the Chinese population increased, the more attitudes toward it hardened.[10] The basis for this lay in the broad acceptance in Britain and beyond of the belief that fundamental differences between persons were based on physical features. This perversion of Charles Darwin's *On the Origin of Species*, published in 1859, argued that human beings, as distinguished by skin tones and other outward characteristics, were biologically arranged in a hierarchy. Persons perceiving themselves as "white" not unexpectedly put themselves at the top, their superiority seemingly confirmed by the Industrial Revolution and colonizing exploits. The consequence was Chinese men were disparaged even as they were wanted. The economic conditions whence they came made them willing to submit, at least outwardly, to their circumstances so long as employment was to be had—this being in good part jobs their white counterparts considered to be beneath their dignity to perform. Gold mining and rail construction were complemented by coal mining, market gardening or farming, resource-sector jobs, and the seasonal industry of salmon canning. Others worked as laundrymen, tailors, cooks, and household servants known as houseboys, or ran small stores and restaurants.

This ethos encouraged and legitimized legal as well as informal discrimination. In 1874 and 1885, the right to vote in British Columbia and Canada, respectively, was removed from persons Chinese by origin or descent, which meant they could not enter the professions of law, medicine, pharmacy, or accountancy; seek government employment; take up government land; or enjoy other privileges linked to the franchise. Canadian prime minister John A. Macdonald defended these actions on the grounds that the Chinese have "no British instincts or British feelings or aspirations, and therefore ought not to have a vote."[11] Also in 1885, a fifty-dollar head tax was imposed on new arrivals from China. This was doubled in 1900 and raised three years later to five hundred dollars. In 1923, the federal government prohibited Chinese immigration altogether. The franchise would be returned only in 1947, the same year the immigration ban was repealed, although it would take another two decades for Canadian immigration policy to become non-discriminatory.

For all these reasons, Chinatowns exercised enormous appeal. There men formed family, clan, and home district associations and political societies, which provided both social services and venues for such familiar leisure activities as gambling and opium smoking.[12] The largest Chinatowns were in Victoria on Vancouver Island and New Westminster on the mainland, both entryways to the gold fields, and from the mid-1880s in Vancouver.[13] A number of smaller counterparts were similarly self-sustaining, although it was also the case that any conglomeration of Chinese men, however informal, was liable to be so labelled.[14] As well as giving protection, Chinatowns served to isolate men from other ways of life, even when, as for some of them, their jobs took them farther afield.[15]

Chinatowns did not, however, represent the entirety of Chinese migrants' experiences in early British Columbia. Some had to rely much more on their own resources. Principal among them were the many men who mined for gold long years after most whites departed. The 1870 census indicated that, whereas the majority of the 8,500 whites lived on Vancouver Island, over three-quarters of the 1,500 Chinese were on the mainland. Excluding railway workers hired later on, a quarter or more continued to reside on the Mainland wherever the search for gold extended itself (Tables 1 and 2).[16] Early on, a fellow miner praised Chinese tenacity:

> This much-enduring and industrious race are generally to be found in little clusters, at work upon diggings deserted by the whites ... and will, doubtless, at the end of the year, by means of their frugality, save more than their white brother is likely to, in spite of his higher gains ... It is the fashion on the Pacific Coast to abuse and ill-treat the Chinaman in every possible way; and I really must tell my friends ... they are hard-working,

sober, and law-abiding—three scarce qualities among people in their station.[17]

No aspect of everyday life better illustrates the distinctiveness of Chinese men in early British Columbia than do pathways to intimacy. An alternative to arriving with a wife in tow, as did some merchants who came north from California, was to get one from home. The process was difficult, expensive, and time-consuming. Not only did most men first have to repay the cost of transportation even as they were fulfilling their obligation to remit money back home, but their wages were often less than half those of whites in the same job, all of which delayed their ability to send for a wife from China. While men who had left wives behind might return from time to time for conjugal visits, most such women never made it to Canada due to lack of resources, obligations in China, or immigration restrictions.[18] Other men turned to Chinese prostitutes, whose presence in early British Columbia (Table 1) echoed the larger society, which, as a consequence of the gold rush and, earlier, the fur trade, also contained many more non-Indigenous adult men than women.[19]

Whereas the overwhelming majority of Chinese men equated intimacy with intimacy with a Chinese woman, a minority were less inhibited, sometimes partnering with an Indigenous woman in what might become a long-term stable relationship. Such relationships might appear unexpected, given the general assumption of the day, asserted in 1885, that "Indians and Chinese" did not mix "a great deal."[20] This approach is short-sighted, if for no other reason than, in numerous areas of emigration during these same years (including Malaysia, Philippines, the Hawaiian Islands, the West Indies, and Cuba), Chinese men, as also explained in 1885, "intermarried with the native races."[21] One of the very few contemporaries to acknowledge Chinese-Indigenous unions in early British Columbia was an Englishman, resident since 1859, whose construction of pack trails and surveying took him into the hinterland, and who explained in 1879 to a federal committee on Chinese labour and immigration how "a good many [Chinese men] live with Indian women," of which relationships, in the absence of Christian marriage, he disapproved.[22]

Thirty relationships between Chinese men and Indigenous women can be glimpsed in early British Columbia in censuses, vital statistics, school and church records, contemporary accounts, family stories, and the research of scholars such as Lily Chow and Naomi Miller (Table 3). While the number is not large in itself, it is considerable when compared with the likely five times as many Chinese men, or about 150, who up to the turn of the century partnered with a Chinese woman. In other words, one in six Chinese men in early British Columbia who engaged in intimacy leading to family formation did so with an Indigenous woman. The proportion is almost certainly higher, given the ambiguity and disregard surrounding newcomer-Indigenous relationships more generally; dismissive attitudes toward both Chinese and Indigenous British Columbians; most unions' locations in the hinterland; low literacy levels in English among Chinese men and Indigenous women, making for few first-hand accounts; and common use of shortened names for Chinese men, making it difficult to track single individuals through time.[23]

Snippets here and there speak to physical attraction, which, if it did not in most instances result in intimacy, might in other circumstances have done so. One family tells a story about leading Vancouver entrepreneur Wing Sang. Employed in the early 1880s as a bookkeeper on rail construction, he made regular stops "in Yale for apple pie served by a young Native girl." On one such occasion he was informed that he was just in time for the announcement of an engagement. "Afraid that his love of apple pie served by a pretty young woman had given the wrong impression, he made a hasty departure. It wasn't that he didn't want a wife—he did—but he wanted a Chinese wife with Chinese values."[24] A local history recalls Hong Hing, who was, like so many others, born in Canton, the English name for today's Guangzhou, the capital city of Guangdong province.[25] From about 1916 a merchant in

TABLE 3

Summary of Relationships between Chinese Men and Indigenous Women in Nineteenth-Century British Columbia

Man's Name	Born	BC Location	Occupation	Beg. Year
Ah Chin	1848	Lytton	Farmer	1878
Ah Ching	1830	Yale	Farmer	1881
Ah Ching	——	Yale	Railway worker	1880s
Ah Choong	1833	Victoria	Not given	1865
Ah Chu	1850	Princeton	Miner	1901
Ah Chung/Ah Chin Yun	1842	Lytton	Farmer	1879
Ah Lean	1841	Osoyoos	Miner	1881
Ah Lem	1834	Osoyoos	Miner	1877
Ah Louis	——	Yale	Cook	1879
Ah Lum	1843	Omineca	Miner	1880s
Ah Lum/Chin Lum Kee	1835	Rock Creek	Storekeeper	1870
Ah Sing	1856	Yale	Labourer	1877
Ah Wee Kong On	1840	Lytton	Storekeeper	1872
Ah Yuen	——	Seabird Island	Farmer	1874
Bow Dung	1829	New Westminster	Baker	1870
Charley Chung	1844	Hope	Rancher	1879
Chi Chum	1830	Cache Creek	Teamster	1866
Chong Sing	1868	Clinton	Cook	1898
Chow Ah Lock	1850	Omineca	Miner	1899
Chu Jaw	1839	Osoyoos	Miner	1876
Chung Moon	——	Rock Creek	Miner/farmer	1871
Ku Tong	1842	Hope	Baker	1889
Lee Lee	1863	Princeton	Laundryman	1901
Louis Sing	1864	Nicola Valley	Houseboy	1896
Nuy Wah	1841	New Westminster	Restaurant keeper	1875
Yaow/Yow	1850	Port Essington	Contractor	1888
Unnamed	——	Chilliwack	Not given	1892
Unnamed	——	Chehalis	Restaurant keeper	1883
Unnamed	——	Tashme	Rancher	1880s
Unnamed	——	Yale	Houseboy	1895

Woman's Name	Origin	Born	Principal sources
Mary	Indigenous	1861	1881 census
Kitty	Indigenous	1820	1864 land record/1881 census/stories
Unnamed	Hope	——	Recollection
Mary Seminoo	Cowichan	1848	1865 marriage
Lupel	Similkameen	1850	1901 census
Lucy	Indigenous	1862	1881/1891 censuses
Ah On	Indigenous	1862	1881 census
Mary	Indigenous	1861	1881 census
Annie Quyanak	Boston Bar	——	1879 marriage
Esther Joseph/Nos Oep	Gitxsan	——	1901 Indian census/Lily Chow
Lucy/Squeetlewood	Stó:lo	1854	1891 census/stories/Naomi Miller
Annie	Indigenous	1851	1891 census
Unnamed	Indigenous	——	1880 school record/1881 census
Lucy Aleck	Popkum	——	1890s school records/Hilary Blair
Sarah Anne	Indigenous	1858	1881 census
Susan Qoswqusclet	Hope	1865	1880 marriage
Mary	Indigenous	1845	1881/1891 census
Gusta Qualt	Chilcotin	1878	1898 marriage
Josephine Alexander	Carrier	——	Lily Chow
Susanne	Indigenous	1859	1881 census
Emily	Rock Creek	——	Written recollection
Susan	Indigenous	1865	1891 census
Julie	Similkameen	1885	1901 census
Alice Shî shîatko	Lytton	1872	1896 marriage
Mary	Indigenous	1851	1881 census
Alice	Indigenous	1869	1891 school record/1901 census
Unnamed	Skowkale	——	1895 missionary account
Unnamed	Indigenous	——	1885 recollection
Unnamed	Indigenous	——	Oral recollection
Unnamed	Indigenous	——	1896 missionary account

Chemainus on Vancouver Island, Hong Hing was "known to make a 'Nelson's Eye' [a wink] at pretty Indian maidens who frequented his premises. His attention to the Indian ladies filled his store with sweaters, toques and sox, of which he made a specialty, with elaborate displays."[26]

While cause and effect in Chinese men's unions cannot be demonstrated, it is highly suggestive that, whereas virtually all of the men living proximate to or in an organized Chinatown appear to have restricted themselves to Chinese women, not all those at a distance did so. The thirty glimpses examined here contain three possible exceptions. In 1865, in a Methodist ceremony in Victoria, thirty-two-year-old Ah Choong, born in Hong Kong, wed a seventeen-year-old Cowichan woman named Mary Seminoo, both then living in the city.[27] The other two unions survive in the form of 1881 census entries from the New Westminster area. Fifty-two-year-old baker Bow Dung lived with twenty-five-year-old Sarah Anne; their son Fat Ah, aged nine, who was attending school; and two-year-old daughter Mun Gaw. Forty-year-old restaurant keeper Nuy Wah lived with thirty-year-old Mary and their daughters Iow Sun, aged five, and Ah Win, one. The 1881 census does not include origins, but given the women's ages and births in British Columbia, it is almost certain they were Indigenous.

Many of the Chinese men partnering with Indigenous women in early British Columbia were gold miners. Typical was Chin Lum Kee, known as Ah Lum. A variety of sources, ranging from census records to interviews by Imbert Orchard with Ah Lum's daughter Lillian Martha Ban Quan and daughter-in-law Beryl Lum to extensive research by historian Naomi Miller, make it possible to know quite a lot about him.[28] According to Lillian, Ah Lum was born in Canton, "got off the boat at San Francisco," and walked north to the original heart of the gold rush in the Fraser Valley, where he ran a store servicing miners and carried the mail. In about 1870 the twenty-five-year-old partnered with sixteen-year-old Squeetlewood, known as Lucy, recalled as belonging "to a tribe of Indians at Chilliwack" in the eastern Fraser

Valley, thus being Stó:lo. Sometime after gold strikes at Rock Creek in the southern Interior, the couple started packing in goods and then opened a store to supply settlers and miners with "groceries, hardware saddles whatnot, anything for horses." Back to Lillian: "There was about a hundred Chinese placer miners on the sluice boxes at Rock Creek, and white people ... It was very nice and quiet." That was not all Ah Lum did to support his seven children, who were born at two-year intervals: "In 1886 my father was the first guy to cook for the Mounties at Fort McLeod [in southern Alberta]. I don't know how he got that job. He was home in Rock Creek and they must have called him to cook." A placer miner visiting Rock Creek in 1892 recalled: "Quite a number of Chinamen were strung out along the creek washing gold. Dick Ah Lum also had a store nearby, and kept numerous chickens, ducks and geese. He was married to an Indian woman, and their eldest children were about grown up."[29]

Sometime after daughter Lillian settled in the Kootenays with her miner husband Chu Ban Quan, who had travelled from Canton to San Francisco in 1868 and mined his way north, her parents followed her there. Ah Lum and Lucy moved to booming Cranbrook, where they opened a grocery store; then on to Fort Steele, where they ran a butcher shop. Then, as Lillian put it, Ah Lum's Chineseness caught up with him: "He got old and he quit. Father left for China in 1911, went home to die." According to Naomi Miller, before he did so, Ah Lum burned his shop records to signify he forgave his debtors in anticipation of his death. His versatile widow, who lived another four decades, raised sheep and chickens and took in washing.

Even such a long-lived union as that of Ah Lum and Lucy was not without its tensions and contradictions. His partnering decision was pragmatic, being expeditious and inexpensive compared to the acquisition of a woman from China, but these factors did not necessarily make it right from his perspective. Indicative of Ah Lum's ambivalence, the family did not associate with Lucy's family: "We just go by Chilliwack. We don't know who mother's relatives are. We don't see no Indians around. We don't mix with them." Another descendant explained in old age how they were never to admit to either their Chinese or their Indigenous descent.[30] It was also the case that, in everyday life, the family accommodated to their circumstances: "Mother was a very nice lady, she talked to us in her language and father talked to us in Chinese."[31]

Very importantly, Ah Lum's and Lucy's offspring were sufficiently comfortable with their upbringing to make their lives across a spectrum of possibilities. Lillian slid into a traditional union: "You know how the Chinese are, they marry young ... They picked a husband for you. I was in grade 8 ... My marriage was arranged. He was 45 and I was 16." While one sister married a Chinese man who had a market garden near Fort Steele, another opted for the American who was the local blacksmith. Learning packing skills from their parents, all three sons became expert with horses and worked as guides. One felt comfortable partnering with an Indigenous woman, a second apparently did not marry, a third opted for a white woman. Having taken his father home to die, son George was meant to return with a wife from China. He did not do so, instead marrying a young Englishwoman he met while he and a brother were in charge of pony and trail rides at a major hotel at Lake Louise in the Rockies, where she worked. From her perspective, when she was interviewed in old age, it was a match made in heaven, for "I loved the western life." As for their seven children, "they are nurses and teachers and everything."[32]

The gold-mining enclave of Rock Creek nurtured at least one other Chinese-Indigenous union. Chung Moon and "Emily an Indian woman" from Rock Creek had a daughter, Ah Lan, born in 1872. In attempting, at age forty, to get a copy of her birth certificate from the provincial government, Ah Lan provided considerable information about her family and herself.[33] Chung Moon had, according to his daughter, been a "gold miner and farmer." When Ah Lan was ten, her mother had died. Five years later, in about 1887, she and her father moved to New Westminster for a year and then to Victoria. Two years later, Ah Lan married, "according to Chinese custom," Leng Tung Hai, who had arrived in British Columbia in about 1873, worked in a sawmill, and then had a market garden. His daughter settled, Chung Moon returned to China, where he died a year later.

Fifty kilometres west of Rock Creek lies Osoyoos. There, as of 1881, three Chinese miners were living with Indigenous women in a Chinese-run hotel or boarding house also containing some thirty unattached Chinese miners. Forty-year-old Ah Lean was partnered with nineteen-year-old Ah On, who, despite her name, was described as Indigenous. Ah Lem, aged forty-seven, and Mary, aged twenty, were the parents of three-year-old Pauline. Forty-two-year-old Chu Jaw and twenty-two-year-old Susanne were the parents of Agatha, aged four, and Julia, two. As most Chinese men were, all three were enumerated as Buddhists. The women were, not unexpectedly, given that missionaries were early arrivals in the region, put down as Catholics. The unions gave such men, along with their children, access to Indigenous worlds as well as to the Chinese milieu that, as of 1881, they lived in every day. Very possibly in order to visit them, an Indigenous child, living across the border in the United States during the last decade of the nineteenth century, recalled how "one trip that my parents seldom failed to make each year was ... to S'oo-yoos Lake, British Columbia, in the country of the Upper Okanagan." As to the reason: "Some Chinese men had settled" there "to placer mine for gold and had taken native wives."[34]

While women's Indigenous identities are often not given in the census or elsewhere, the majority were almost certainly local, which would have encouraged sociability. Two literate Chinese men who arrived in Canada in 1881, which suggests they came as railway labourers, were by 1901 living about a hundred kilometres west of Osoyoos at Princeton with local Similkameen women. Thirty-eight-year-old Lee Lee, a Buddhist, was running a laundry with sixteen-year-old Catholic Julie, while placer miner Ah Chu, also a Buddhist, was living with a Catholic woman named Lupel. Indicative of the broad brush strokes sometimes accorded such persons in the census, Ah Chu and Lupel were both recorded as born in 1850. Not only did such men acquire a new entryway to sociability, along with intimacy leading to family life; they got a helpmate useful in the everyday, particularly valuable to men like Lee Lee who were providing services.

Two hundred kilometres northwest of Princeton, at Cache Creek, lived Chi Chum with his "Indian" woman named Mary and their children, Nancy Fa, born 1867, Soot Fa, born 1871, and Chon Win, born 1877. In both 1881 and 1891, Chi Chum was a teamster who drove oxen, and Mary, fifteen years his junior, undoubtedly assisted him in managing the numerous boarders the couple took in. Storyteller Annie York, a Yale woman of mixed Indigenous and non-Indigenous descent born in 1904, related a similar account passed down from her mother: "Somewhere around Tashme [near Hope] that Chinaman had a ranch and all the Indians stopped there and stayed overnight. And the same on the way back. And the Chinaman had a half-Indian daughter. I don't remember her name. My mother said she [was] a pretty girl. The Chinaman lived with an Indian woman. He raised pigs for the miners, smoked them."[35]

Such families' everyday comfort with each other is attested by a young English adventurer who trekked across southern British Columbia in the mid-1880s. Morley Roberts in his *The Western Avernus*, published shortly thereafter, recounts his travels along the Fraser River to Chehalis:

> Then to Harrison River, bright and clear and blue, a Fraser tributary, and dinner at a Chinaman's restaurant, where we had a plentiful and well-cooked meal served by the owner himself, who spoke good English to us, Chinese to his pig-tailed compatriots, and fluent Chinook [Pacific Northwest trading jargon] to his Indian wife, who held in her arms a curious child with the characteristics of both Indian and Chinaman stamped unmistakenly upon it. The father admired it immensely, and was,

it seemed, very fond of his wife, who, for her part, was stolid and undemonstrative, as most pure-bred Indians are.[36]

The modestly flattering description stands out given that, in the view of his critics, Roberts's "discussions of native people and the Chinese are blinkered by racism."[37]

Chinese men partnered with Indigenous women who lived near the gold rush's origins were the most likely to find themselves subject to outsider scrutiny.[38] The school board at Hope in the eastern Fraser Valley was livid in 1876 over "Chinaman houses" occupied by them and "their squaws" on land sought for a new building.[39] At Lytton, a hundred kilometres to the north, a public school and a nearby Chinese-Indigenous family comfortably co-existed. Its new teacher was so valued that in the fall of 1880, parents sent her a letter of appreciation together with a seventy-five-dollar collection including five dollars from Ah Wee Kong On.[40] The 1881 census described him as a storekeeper born in China in about 1840, and the father of eight-year-old Ah Kow.

Two other couples were also in the Hope-Lytton area in 1881. Thirty-five-year-old Lytton farmer Ah Chin and his twenty-year-old "Indian" wife Mary were the parents of two-year-old Ten Fee. Ah Chin was Buddhist; Mary and their son were Anglican. A twenty-year-old Anglican "Indian" woman named Lucy and a year-old girl named Hydah were living in the same household as Lytton farmer Ah Chung, a forty-year-old Buddhist, and two Chinese labourers possibly in his employ. A decade later, Lucy, now described as twenty-eight, was living with forty-eight-year-old farmer Ah Chin Yun, almost certainly the Ah Chung of a decade earlier and now also an Anglican. Unlike her, he was literate. Testifying to the solidity of some Chinese-Indigenous unions, their children as of 1891 were Susan, aged ten; son Ko Kee, aged seven; and Jenny and son Coke An, both aged five.

Schools were not the only outside entity impinging on Chinese-Indigenous unions. While aimed principally at Indigenous peoples, the long-lived missionary presence going back to the earliest years of the gold rush caught up some Chinese men in its wake. One goal was their conversion from Buddhism to Christianity, as with Lytton farmer Ah Chung, who by 1891 had become Anglican like his wife, Lucy. The other goal was Christian marriage, encouraged by the presence of St. John's Anglican Church at Yale in the Fraser Canyon, where, in 1879, Yale cook Ah Louis wed Annie Quyanak from nearby Boston Bar. Describing himself as a farmer's son born in Canton, Ah Louis signed the marriage document in Chinese with a sure, literate hand. A year later, thirty-six-year-old Hope rancher Charley Chung, a labourer's son born in Canton, who similarly signed the church register in Chinese, wed fourteen-year-old Susan Qoswqusclet, daughter of a local chief.[41] Whoever was meant, at about this time the Anglican bishop described proudly in his memoir how he "married an Indian girl to a Chinaman" at Yale.[42] In similar fashion, in 1895, the Anglican order whose sisters ran All Hallows School at Yale rejoiced over the "marriage of one of the newly-made Christians [being Indigenous people baptized as adults] to a Christian Chinaman, who was in domestic service at the Mission House."[43] The 1891 census recorded thirty-six-year-old Buddhist labourer Ah Sing living at Yale with forty-year-old Indigenous woman Annie, along with Jimmy, thirteen, and Emma, nine, who, like their mother, were described as Anglican.

Visiting periodically from his base in New Westminster, the Anglican bishop not only encouraged conversions and married one or more Chinese-Indigenous couples, but also made use of their services. Annie York told of how, when the bishop first arrived at Yale in 1879, he was looked after by a Chinese man who lived nearby with his Indigenous wife. Ah Ching "housed and fed him."[44] Annie's cousin, born in 1911, described being taken care of as a child by an elderly Chinese railway labourer, also named Ah Ching, who hailed from north of Hope.[45] When the child fell seriously ill, Ah Ching cooked a blue jay for him, which he recalled as the toughest thing he ever ate.[46] Indicative of the caution necessary in dealing with multiple sources, a Chinese man, also named Ah Ching, appears as a farmer along with his wife, Indigenous Kitty, in the 1881 census. Ah Ching and Kitty were already aged fifty and sixty, respectively. Going back even further, in 1861 a Chinese man named Ah Ching pre-empted from the government 160 acres (65 hectares) near Yale; by the time he acquired the land outright in 1871, he had constructed a house with a cellar, put in a 1.4-hectare garden, and planted 250 apple trees.[47] This Ah Ching was not alone in taking up land. More than half a dozen similarly enterprising Chinese men who had arrived with the gold rush did the same in that general area prior to Chinese people being legally precluded from acquiring land through pre-emption.[48]

The Methodists were not far behind the Catholics and Anglicans in chasing souls. Enumerated at Hope in 1891 were forty-nine-year-old Methodist baker Ku Tong, twenty-six-year-old Methodist Susan, who was Indigenous, and their year-old son Ah Tong. Five years later, in a Methodist ceremony, Louis Sing from Canton, a thirty-two-year-old Methodist houseboy employed in the Nicola Valley 140 kilometres to the northeast, wed Anglican Alice Shi̓ shi̓atko, aged twenty-four and probably a Lytton woman.[49] It is unclear under whose religious auspices, if any, thirty-year-old Chong Sing, a cook at 150 Mile House, near the long-established mining town of Williams Lake, wed twenty-year-old Gusta Qualt, a Chilcotin woman, two years later.[50] Other services were sometimes sought. A Methodist minister described an 1895 visit to Chilliwack to a "Chinaman's whose little boy died this a.m. as result of scalding ... I spoke as well as I could to the mother (Indian) & all & prayed with them. On the wall there was a Buddhist shrine. There were 3 Chinese present. Got back after dark." Even though the next day's entry grumbled over the failure of his efforts at conversion, he clearly had not given up. "Buried half-breed (Chinese-Indian) boy at Skowkale. Heathen Indian & Chinese & Xtian sermon."[51]

Even as they were courted by missionaries, Chinese men were also reminded from time to time that they and the Indigenous women in their lives were not wanted. In about 1874 a man known as Ah Yuen built a house on Seabird Island, located in the Fraser River between Chilliwack and Hope, established a garden, partnered with a local Popkum woman, Lucy Aleck, and began a family that would reach five children.[52] Ah Yuen's troubles began in 1879 when, apparently oblivious to his presence, the federal Department of Indian Affairs reserved the fertile island for seven named Indigenous groups including Popkums. Six years later the chief of one of the other groups persuaded government officials to evict Yuen, who was soon back, supported by his Popkum father-in-law, to claim the landholding by virtue of having annually paid taxes on it.[53] In 1891, by which time the property comprised nine cleared hectares, three houses, and 220 mature fruit trees, Ah Yuen was killed while blasting stumps. The Department of Indian Affairs ruled two years later, in line with federal policy, that by virtue of marrying a non-Indigenous man, Lucy Aleck had lost her Indian status and thereby her right to remain on what was a reserve. However, as a special consideration, she was allowed to remain as long as she did not remarry.

For all the whims of federal policy, the widowed Lucy raised Ah Yuen's and her children as Indigenous. In 1894 she enrolled ten-year-old Frederick at newly opened Coqualeetza Industrial School for Indian Boys in nearby Chilliwack, whose records described his father as "Chinaman" now dead.[54] Frederick remained there seven years, playing in the school band and being taught farming, which he thereafter pursued back on Seabird Island. In a list of Seabird's dozen family heads, compiled during the hearings of a Royal Commission on Indian Affairs in 1914, Fred Yuen was described as a Popkum having a wife and two children, a house, and fifteen acres under cultivation, with another five cleared—the second-largest holding on the island.[55] No reference was made to Fred Yuen being of Chinese descent in the commission's meetings with Seabird residents or with the local Indian agent. Yet a list compiled four years later, which included among Seabird's twenty-five family heads both Fred and his brother Henry, described as Popkums, they were indicated to have settled there in 1879, clearly on the property their Chinese father had claimed.[56]

Relationships in the far corners of British Columbia may have proceeded more on their own terms, with less outside interference. In April 1891, provincial education authorities requested a "list of the white and half-caste children living within the bounds of the Port Essington School District with a statement of their ages." Included among those still too young to go to school but expected to do so in due course were "Sam Yow," aged two, and "Baby Yow," three months, both described as "Mother Indian, Father Chinaman."[57] The 1901 census of this north coast community gave the father as fifty-one-year-old Yaow, who came to Canada in 1873, naturalizing as a British subject in 1890 and living with a thirty-two-year-old "Indian" named Alice and their four children—Sam (twelve), Joe (nine), Mary (eight), and George (four). Yaow was Buddhist, the others Methodists. The three oldest were attending school, with the two oldest speaking Chinese, "Indian," and English as their first languages.

Yaow described himself in the census as a "contractor," earning eighty dollars by working just three months in the past year. In other words, he had charge of recruiting other Chinese to work in one of Port Essington's three salmon canneries making cans; butchering fish; and soldering, cooking, and packing the filled cans. As explained at about this time:

> The contracts are made with boss Chinamen who hire their own help in their own way ... The contractor makes an advance of $30 to $40 to each Chinaman at the opening of the season to induce him to come. The contractor furnishes the provisions, where chiefly his profits are made. At the end of each month what he has supplied is made up and charged *pro rata* to the men in his employ. At the end of the season, if the run is short, the contractor may lose money on his contract.[58]

Even though Yaow's income fluctuated with the seasons and over the years, he had sufficient status for his children both to be pre-enrolled and to attend the local public school.

The 1901 census also included an Anglican household headed by Nos Oep Ah Lum, who described herself as a Gitxsan woman and the mother of Peter, Tony, and Thomas Ah Lum, who were Gitxsan and Chinese with Gitxsan as their first language. Because the family was enumerated in the Indian component of the federal census, no ages were given. This information is consistent with historian Lily Chow's story of Ah Lum, an Omineca gold miner born in 1843 who came to Canada in 1858, partnered with a Gitxsan woman whose English name was Esther Joseph, and very profitably interspersed winter trapping with summer mining.[59]

Shortly after their mother Esther's death in about 1910, when the youngest child, Gwen, was nine, Ah Lum determined to return home to China. He wanted to take Thomas and Gwen along, but the two children did not want to go and so stayed behind to be raised by Esther's sister. The circumstance created its own tensions. Gwen's daughter Charlotte Sullivan, later a Gitxsan hereditary chief, explained to Lily Chow how the children perforce learned to value their double inheritance. "My mother did not have a very pleasant life in the native community. She was often looked down [upon] because she had mixed blood in her veins. Regardless, she was a very strong woman and held her head up high." For his part, Ah Lum did not want his children to forget him. As well as a small faded photograph that he left behind of a round-faced man with a bald head, he wrote regularly from China: "Whenever my mother and uncles received a letter from their dad, they were excited and eager to know what he wrote. But they could not read Chinese characters, so they usually took the letter to grandpa's Chinese friends in Hazelton or in Smithers who would translate the letter for them."

Lily Chow has also written about Chow Ah Lock, who arrived in British Columbia in the 1860s, aged seventeen, and mined for a dozen years before heading to the Omineca in the province's far northwest corner, where he both ran a pack train transporting goods and continued to mine so successfully he eventually had a lake, creek, and mining site named after him.[60] Chow Ah Lock settled down with a local Indigenous woman named Josephine Alexander. They had a son, David, born in 1900 to whom his father gave the Chinese name Chow Sai Yoke, Chow being his own proper surname.

In another indication of the ways in which relationships worked themselves out in the everyday, Chow Ah Lock's son grew up speaking both his father's southern Guangdong dialect of Taishanese and Gitxsan from his mother. Chow Ah Lock and Josephine's granddaughter Julie Alexander, who, when she shared her family's story with Lily Chow, still yearned for the Chinese food he used to make for them, recalled: "Both my grandparents worked very hard in the early days. My grandmother attended to the horses and worked in her own garden. In the summer she went to the bush to look for wild berries and cabbages. In winter, both of my grandparents trapped animals for fur on their trap line." One of the stories told about Chow Ah Lock has him travelling to Vancouver in 1913, loaded with gold dust and nuggets, with the intention of being naturalized as a British subject. However, on seeing streetcars, electric lights, and motor cars for the first time, he hastened back to his wife and son. In 1937, several years after Josephine's death, Chow Ah Lock, like many of his contemporaries, returned to China so he could be buried in his homeland. It may have been that Chow Ah Lock's and, earlier, Ah Lum's example encouraged half a dozen or more Chinese men in the Omineca similarly to partner with local Indigenous women in the first years of the twentieth century.[61]

Not only did many more unions similar to those described here almost certainly exist in early British Columbia, but they also continued throughout the twentieth century and into the present day, with all the stresses, as well as the satisfaction, that accompanied earlier ones.[62] A son born in 1943 to a well-established Chinese farmer in the southern Interior—a man who had been unable to bring his wife over from China—recalled his father repeatedly admonishing him as a child to pay no attention to his Indigenous mother, who was "just around" and who was, from the perspective of others, a household servant.[63] A descendant of an early Chinese restaurant owner from the gold rush era reflected on how various people she knew, "if you [went] back a couple of generations," were of Chinese descent. "But I also remember dad saying that you could have a Chinese for a good friend but you don't marry them."[64] Recollections are sometimes fragmentary, as with a self-termed "British Columbia half breed logger" in the Fraser Valley, who described the woman he married in 1924 as "a Harrison River [Chehalis] Indian except there is just a little Chinese in her some where back a piece."[65]

However many Chinese-Indigenous unions there were by the end of the nineteenth century, those about which we can know something testify to Chinese men's and Indigenous women's enterprise and determination. Chung Moon, the two Ah Lums, the almost certainly two Ah Chings, and the others did not cease to be Chinese by virtue of so partnering, and the women in their lives were not any less Indigenous. Men were not stultified by the single partnering option of a Chinese woman, which, for most of them, would have been unobtainable. The alternative of an Indigenous woman was both expedient and practical. It took most men some time to consider the possibility. Many were in their mid-thirties or forties by the time they did so, a decade and a half or two decades older than the Indigenous women with whom they partnered, who were very much of a child-bearing age. Ah Lum and Lucy at Rock Creek had seven children together, Ah Yuen and Lucy Aleck on Seabird Island five, Ah Lum and Esther Joseph in the Omineca at least four, and Yaow and Alice at Port Essington four. While most relationships survive only as snapshots in time, they speak to family stability. Morley Roberts's vignette of his Chehalis meal describes the satisfaction couples took in each other and in their offspring.

Chinese men who partnered with Indigenous women gained, together with intimacy and family life, an entryway into the place with which they cast their lot, more so than would have been the case if they had restricted their sociability to a Chinatown. Opportunities were used, as with Ah Ching taking up land in those early years before the Chinese were legally prohibited from doing so. Ah Lum and Lucy took advantage of the gold discoveries at Rock Creek to pack in goods and open a general store that serviced whites alongside Chinese and Indigenous people, as almost certainly did Lee Lee and Julie's Princeton laundry. The Port Essington school board enumerated Chinese-Indigenous offspring as a matter of course, and a Lytton teacher welcomed a Chinese father's contribution to a collection in her honour. Chinese-Indigenous couples appear, overall, to have accommodated to their white neighbours, including missionaries.[66] They were not, as with Ah Yuen and Lucy Aleck on Seabird Island, to be cowed.

At the same time, it was not necessarily easy to live at the intersection of two strong and self-contained ways of being. While the three Osoyoos families enumerated in 1881 appear to have fraternized with Indigenous counterparts across the border, Ah Lum of Rock Creek did his best to prevent his children from having contact with their mother's family, even as she taught them her language along with the Chinese they learned from their father. Neither forgot who they were and whence they came. For all of the longevity of their unions, four of the Chinese men about whom most is known turned inward with gathering age. Ah Lum and Lucy had been together over four decades at the time he, in his daughter's words, "went home to die." Three widowers acted similarly at the cost of leaving children behind: Ah Lum's namesake after over half a century away, Chow Ah Lock in Omineca after an even longer time, and Chung Moon of Rock Creek after two decades or more.

Offspring of Chinese-Indigenous unions variously made their way as adults. Chung Moon and Ah Lem at Rock Creek had no compunction arranging the marriages of their daughters, Ah Lan and Lillian, to Chinese men. Yet one of Lillian's sisters opted for an American blacksmith, and a brother for an English woman after conveniently not returning with a Chinese wife after taking his father home to die. In the other direction, despite her Chinese descent being held against her, Ah Lum's and Esther Joseph's granddaughter at Omineca was a Gitxsan hereditary chief.

Comprising a likely one in six of the total number of unions in which Chinese men are recorded as having been engaged in early British Columbia, these relationships encourage us to rethink the Chinese presence. None of these accounts are complete, yet together they tell a new story. Some men living beyond Chinatown acted differently than did their urban counterparts. They took a chance, as did the women in their lives. From the perspective of the British Columbia mainstream, such families did not exist, an attitude that served them well. It is, in other words, precisely because the unions are so difficult to retrieve historically that they may have endured as well as they did.

Whatever the topic that snares our interest, we need to be open to possibilities: in this case to an alternative so obvious it should not have slipped from view. The two groups—Chinese men and Indigenous women—were both outsiders to the dominant society, meaning their lives went largely unrecorded so long as they occurred out of view. Be they in Chinatown or in the hinterland, Chinese men were for the most part unseen outside of the workplace. It was assumed they were single, which most of them were. If they were otherwise, it did not much matter. But it does matter as soon as we consider Chinese men and Indigenous women of the past on a par with ourselves, whose lives are worthy of interrogation, rather than as objects beyond our gaze and understanding. What is evident from these glimpses is that some Chinese men were not nearly so uniform in their behaviour as has generally been thought. Men were no less Chinese, and Indigenous women no less Indigenous, by virtue of taking the future into their own hands. Living beyond the constraints and the pressure toward conformity in Chinatowns, some Chinese men, together with the Indigenous women in their lives and the couples' families, struck out on their own in this new place called British Columbia.

Notes

1 In order of publication, Naomi Miller, "The Lum and Ban Quan Families," *British Columbia Historical News* 21, 2 (Spring 1988): 19–20; Lily Chow, *Sojourners in the North* (Prince George: Caitlin, 1996), 108–11; Hilary Kathleen Blair, "Settling Seabird Island: Land, Resources, and Ownership on a British Columbia Indian Reserve" (master's thesis, Simon Fraser University, 1999), 39–43, 68, 72, 74, 93–94, 105, 120–23, 126; Lily Chow, *Chasing Their Dreams: Chinese Settlement in the Northwest Region of British Columbia* (Prince George: Caitlin, 2000), 4–5; Dexter Friesen, "Canada's Other Newcomers: Aboriginal Interactions with People from the Pacific" (master's thesis, University of Saskatchewan, 2006), 82–84; Eleanor Yuen, "Are You Who You Think You Are? A Study of Chinese Canadian Name Forms," on https://circle.ubc.ca/bitstream/handle/2429/12575/Chinese_Canadian_name_forms.pdf?sequence=1 (accessed November 16, 2019); and John Belshaw, *Becoming British Columbia: A Population History* (Vancouver: UBC Press, 2009), 152, 246n30, drawing with permission on my research notes.

2 *Report of the Royal Commission on Chinese and Japanese Immigration* (Ottawa: S.E. Dawson, 1902), 8, 33–34, 37, 236.

3 See, among other sources, Madeline Yuan-yin Hsu, *Dreaming of Gold, Dreaming of Home: Transnationalism and Migration between the United States and South China, 1882–1943* (Stanford: Stanford University Press, 2000).

4 There were 8,500 white and 450 Black people. "Report of the Population of British Columbia ... 1871," in G.P.V. Akrigg and Helen B. Akrigg, *British Columbia Chronicle, 1847–1871: Gold and Colonists* (Vancouver: Discovery Press, 1977), 404.

5 The respective Census Canada totals were 8,910 and 70,870 in 1891, and 14,576 and 149,708 in 1901. While the number of British Columbians born in China would expand by over a third to 21,500 in 1921, their proportion of non-Indigenous British Columbians fell to one in twenty-five due to the mass immigration characterizing Canada as a whole in the early twentieth century.

6 The Canadian totals of persons born in China were 9,129 in 1891 and 17,043 in 1901. The proportion living in British Columbia would fall to just under 60 per cent by 1921.

7 *Report*, 1885: 363–65.

8 *Report*, 1902: 12–13, 22. The precise numbers of men were 3,187 and 2,053. Chinese women would be enumerated separately in the federal census in 1911, when the 415 women comprised 2 per cent of the almost 20,000 British Columbians born in China, approaching 4 per cent a decade later.

9 *Report*, 1902: 12–13. On merchants, see Timothy J. Stanley, "'Chinamen, Wherever We Go': Chinese Nationalism and Guangdong Merchants in British Columbia, 1871–1911," *Canadian Historical Review* 77, no. 4 (December 1996): 475–504; Paul Yee, "Business Devices from Two Worlds: The Chinese in Early Vancouver," *BC Studies* 62 (Summer 1984): 44–67, and "A Chinese Business in Early Vancouver," *BC Studies* 69/70 (Spring/Summer 1986): 70–96; and Frances Hern, *Yip Sang and the First Chinese Canadians* (Victoria, BC: Heritage House, 2011).

10 For a contrary, sympathetic white child's perspective, see John Norris, *Wo Lee Stories* (New Denver, BC: Twa Corbies, 1997), 5–17, 111–21, esp. 118 on the sole time the family's Chinese neighbour was allowed into their living room.

11 John A. Macdonald in the House of Commons, 1885, quoted in Peter Ward, *White Canada Forever: Popular Attitudes and Public Policy toward Orientals in British Columbia*, 3rd ed. (Montreal/Kingston: McGill-Queen's University Press, 2002), 41.

12 The British East India Company began to smuggle opium into China in 1773 in an effort to force trade concessions from China. By the mid-nineteenth century Britain, the United States, and other European countries, as well as Japan and Russia, had forced the Chinese to open trade to them.

13 As of 1885, Victoria housed 1,767 Chinese and New Westminster 1,680; in 1902, Victoria housed 3,263 and Vancouver 2,080. See *Report*, 1885: 363–65; *Report*, 1902: 12–13.

14 Particularly useful in this respect is David Chuenyan Lai, *Chinatowns: Towns within Cities in Canada* (Vancouver: UBC Press, 1988), 34–51.

15 This point is well made in Patrick A. Dunae, John S. Lutz, Donald J. Lafreniere, and Jason A. Gilliland, "Making the Inscrutable, Scrutable: Race and Space in Victoria's Chinatown, 1891," *BC Studies* 169 (Spring 2011): 51–80.

16 Eventually the search extended virtually everywhere, given that, as a technical report put it sometime later, "gold is very generally distributed over the entire area of the Province of British Columbia." See John B. Galloway, *Placer-Mining in British Columbia* (Victoria: British Columbia Department of Mines, 1931), 10. On early gold finds in respect to the presence of Chinese miners, see Chow, *Sojourners in the North*; and Ying-ying Chen, "In the Colonies of Tang: Historical Archaeology of Chinese Communities in the North Cariboo District, British Columbia (1860s–1940s)" (PhD diss., Simon Fraser University, 2001), 143–55.

17 R. Byron Johnson, *Very Far West Indeed* (London: Sampson Low, Marston, Low, and Searle, 1872), 76–78.

18 Most general accounts ignore Chinese women altogether, with the possible exception of merchants' wives, or treat them summarily in passing. Among the exceptions are Tamara Adilman, "A Preliminary Sketch of Chinese Women and Work in British Columbia 1858–1950," in *Not Just Pin Money: Selected Essays on the History of Women's Work in British Columbia*, ed. Barbara K. Latham and Roberta J. Pazdro (Victoria: Camosun College, 1984), 53–78; Yuen-Fong Woon, "Between South China and British Columbia: Life Trajectories of Chinese Women," *BC Studies* 156/157 (Winter/Spring 2007–2008): 83–107; and the earlier autobiographies in *Jin Guo: Voices of Chinese Canadian Women* (Toronto: Women's Press, 1992), 17–45. For more recent vignettes of family life, see Brandy Liên Worrall, ed., *Finding Memories, Tracing Routes: Chinese Canadian Family Stories* (Vancouver: Chinese Canadian Historical Society of British Columbia, 2006), and *Eating Stories: A Chinese Canadian and Aboriginal Potluck* (Vancouver: Chinese Canadian Historical Society of British Columbia, 2007). For examples of Chinese men's unions with Chinese women outside the major Chinatowns, see Marie Elliott, *Gold and Grand Dreams: Cariboo East in the Early Years* (Victoria: Horsdal and Schubart, 2000), 113–15, also 84–85, 110; Chow, *Sojourners in the North*, 46; W.M. Hong, *And So That's How It Happened: Recollections of Stanley Barkerville 1900–1975* (Barkerville, BC: privately printed, 1978), 11–13; and Lily Hoy Price, *I Am Full Moon: Stories of a Ninth Daughter* (Victoria, BC: Brindle and Glass, 2009).

19 On Chinese prostitution see Renisa Mawani, *Colonial Proximities: Crossracial Encounters and Juridical Truths in British Columbia, 1871–1921* (Vancouver: UBC Press, 2009), 105–20; Anthony B. Chan, *Gold Mountain: The Chinese in the New World* (Vancouver: New Star, 1983), 80–84; Chen, "In the Colonies of Tang," 329–33; Woon, "Between South China," 89–92; ongoing accounts in the Victoria *Colonist* newspaper, online at http://www.britishcolonist.ca/ (accessed November 16, 2019); and for comparisons, Albert Dudley Gardner, "Two Paths One Destiny: A Comparison of Chinese Households and Communities in Alberta, British Columbia, Montana, and Wyoming, 1848–1910" (PhD diss., University of New Mexico, 2000), 187–95, 218, and *passim*; and Benson Tong, *Unsubmissive Women: Chinese Prostitutes in Nineteenth-Century San Francisco* (Norman: University of Oklahoma Press, 1994).

20 *Report of the Royal Commission on Chinese Immigration* (Ottawa: The Commission, 1885): xxvi; also Adele Perry, *On the Edge of Empire: Gender, Race, and the Making of British Columbia, 1849–1871* (Toronto: University of Toronto Press, 2001), 48–78; and Mawani, *Colonial Proximities*.

21 *Report*, 1902: 235; also *Report*, 1885: cxiii, cxxix. According to the Chinese consul in British Columbia in 1885, "in Cuba, fully seventy-five per cent, have married native women" (*Report*, 1885: 41).

22 Edgar Dewdney in "First Report of Select Committee on Chinese Labour and Immigration" (May 14, 1879), in *Journals of the House of Commons of the Dominion of Canada*, 1st session, 4th Parliament (vol. 13), appendix 4, a4-48.

23 Renisa Mawani notes several early court cases concerning Chinese men selling liquor to Indigenous people, who were legally prohibited from having such access, but does not extend the contact into the personal relationships that might have ensued. See Mawani, *Colonial Proximities*, 121–25, 152–62. Although individually enumerated in the early Canadian censuses, difficulties in communication and also lack of interest meant Chinese names were routinely simplified, occupations identical for pages on end, and ages rounded off to a convenient 0 or 5. Many of the men brought in to work on the railway were simply called Ah, which was not a surname but rather an informal prefix, much like the English-language suffix turning John into Johnny. More generally, Ah was routinely put before some small part of the actual name. See Census Canada information for 1881, 1891, and 1901, available online at various sites. On aspects of naming, see Yuen, "Are You Who You Think You Are?" Two important initiatives intended to counter these limitations are the Vancouver Public Library's Chinese-Canadian Genealogy website at https://guides.vpl.ca/ccg/home, and head tax and other records and information available online through Library and Archives Canada.

24 Hern, *Yip Sang*, 16–17.

25 Of the six of thirty unions described here where men's origins were noted, principally in marriage records, five were from Canton.

26 Ning Chang, "The Life Style of Hong Hing," in *Memories of the Chemainus Valley*, comp. Lillian Gustafson (Victoria: Chemainus Valley Historical Society, 1978), 293. For a rare vignette of everyday Chinese-Indigenous sociability, see Sing Lim, *West Coast Chinese Boy* (Montreal: Tundra Books, 1991), 5–8.

27 Pre-Confederation Marriage Records, 1858–1872, British Columbia Archives, GR-3044.

28 Interview with Lillian Martha Ban Quan by Imbert Orchard, November 5, 1964, BC Archives, T0822; interview with daughter-in-law Beryl Lum by Imbert Orchard, November 1, 1964, BC Archives, T0898; Miller, "The Lum and Ban Quan Families," 19–20; and letter from Naomi Miller, November 17, 1991.

29 Harry D. Barnes, "Reminiscences of the Okanagan and Boundary Districts, 1891–1900," *Okanagan History* 13 (1949): 97.

30 Naomi Miller named Lucy in print as Lucy Williams, "daughter of the packer at Hope," which she later explained privately (letter, November 17, 1991) was because the family did not like to admit to their background.

31 Interview with Quan.

32 Interviews with Quan and Lum.

33 File attached to British Columbia, Vital Statistics, birth registration, 72-09-038396, BC Archives, GR2965.

34 Jay Miller, ed., *Mourning Dove: A Salishan Autobiography* (Lincoln: University of Nebraska Press, 1990), 20.

35 Annie York in Andrea Lynne Laforet, "Folk History in a Small Canadian Community" (PhD diss., University of British Columbia, 1974), 297.

36 Morley Roberts, *The Western Avernus* (1887; Westminster: Archibald Constable, 1896), 156.

37 Jeremy Mouat, "Morley Roberts in the Western Avernus," *Pacific Northwest Quarterly* 93 (Winter 2001–2002): 31, 36n44.

38 See Jiwu Wang, *"His Dominion" and the "Yellow Peril": Protestant Missions to Chinese Immigrants to Canada, 1859–1967* (Waterloo: Wilfrid Laurier University Press, 2006).

39 J.A. Bowes to John Jessop, Superintendent of Education, September 10, 1876, in BC Superintendent of Education, Inward Correspondence, BC Archives, GR 1445.

40 Commendation to A[delaide] Bailey, teacher at Lytton, December 27, 1881 [*sic*, 1880], in BC Superintendent of Education, Inward Correspondence, BC Archives, GR 1445.

41 "St. Johns, Yale, Register of baptisms, marriages, and burials, August 28, 1859–April 24, 1895," Anglican Archives, Vancouver School of Theology, University of British Columbia.

42 Herbert H. Gowen, *Church Work in British Columbia* (London: Longmans, Green, 1899), 17.

43 *East and West* (Winter 1896): 428.

44 Annie York in Andrea Laforet and Annie York, *Spuzzum: Fraser Canyon Histories, 1808–1939* (Vancouver: UBC Press, 1998), 119.

45 Annie York, Richard Daly, and Chris Arnett, *They Write Their Dream on the Rock Forever: Rock Writings of the Stein River Valley of British Columbia* (Vancouver: Talonbooks, 1993), 30.

46 Arthur Urquhart in Laforet and York, *Spuzzum*, 126.

47 F.W. Laing, *Colonial Farm Settlers on the Mainland of British Columbia 1858–1871* (Victoria, 1939), 227.

48 According to Laing, *Colonial Farm Settlers*, Kim Sing and Ah Wah took up 50 and 37 acres respectively near Lytton in 1867 (239), Ah Ky 160 acres near Lillooet in 1867 (242), Ah Gin 160 acres near Alkali Lake in 1867 (282), Ah Chee and Ah Kye 10 and 160 acres respectively near Lillooet in 1868 (242), Long Tie 320 acres near Lillooet in 1872 (266), and Nam Sing 160 acres near Lillooet in 1876 (281).

49 British Columbia, Division of Vital Statistics, marriage registrations, BC Archives, GR2962, no. 96-09-169150.

50 British Columbia Division of Vital Statistics, marriage registrations, BC Archives, GR2962, no. 98-09-175273.

51 June 26 and 27, 1895 entries in Ebenezer Robson diary, in BC Archives, PR-1654.

52 The family's story is recounted in Blair, "Settling Seabird Island," 1, 27, 39–41, 104, 120–26. The seven Indigenous groups to which Seabird was allocated were the "Popkum, Skawits, Ohamil, Ska-wāh-look, Hope, Union Bar, and Yale" (1).

53 This point is made in Friesen, "Canada's Other Newcomers," 83, based on Department of Indian Affairs files.

54 Coqualeetza school register, United Church Archives, Vancouver School of Theology, University of British Columbia.

55 Meeting with the Seabird Indian Band, November 23, 1914, in *Evidence Submitted to the Royal Commission on Indian Affairs in the Province of British Columbia: Lytton Agency* (Victoria: The Commission, 1913–16), 16–18.

56 "Residents of Seabird Island—12 December 1918," compiled by the Indian agent, in Blair, "Settling Seabird Island," 122.

57 D. Jennings to S.D. Pope, April 13, 1891, in BC Superintendent of Education, Inward Correspondence, BC Archives, GR 1445.

58 *Report*, 1902: 155.

59 Chow, *Chasing Their Dreams*, 4–5; also conversations with Lily Chow.

60 Chow, *Chasing Their Dreams*, 4; Chow, *Sojourners*, 108–10; conversations with Chow.

61 Chow, *Sojourners*, 110.

62 As examples, the marriages in 1915 and 1916 respectively, in the Catholic church in Fort St. James, of fifty-five-year-old Buddhist Fort St. James cook Ah Ye, born in Hong Kong, and twenty-year-old Eugenie Sansgelau, a Catholic Carrier woman, and of twenty-seven-year-old Catholic Fort St. James cook Chen Tie, known as Charles, to a twenty-one-year-old Catholic Carrier named Celestine, recorded in British Columbia, Division of Vital Statistics, marriage registrations, BC Archives, GR2962, no. 15-09-158937 and 16-09-179358. For more recent unions, see the documentary "Cedar and Bamboo" (Vancouver: Chinese Canadian Historical Society of British Columbia, 2010); and Dorothy Christian, "Articulating the Silence: Filmmaker Dorothy Christian Breaks the Secrecy Between Native-Chinese Relations," *ricepaper* 9, 3 (Fall 2004): 22–31.

63 Personal communication.

64 Personal communication.

65 Henry Pennier, *Chiefly Indian: The Warm and Witty Story of a British Columbia Half Breed Logger* (West Vancouver: Graydonald, 1972), 12.

66 Of the fifteen women whose religious affiliations are in the records, five each were Catholic and Anglican, one Catholic-become-Anglican, four Methodist. Three of the men described themselves as Methodist, two Anglican, and twelve Buddhist, as likely were the others.

10

Lost Okanagan

In Search of the First Settler Families

Here Barman points out how much of the history of the Okanagan begins with a series of claims concerning white settlers: the first white woman and the first white child born there become markers of an origin that, as she also points out, obscures an entire generation of settlement by white men who partnered with Indigenous women, sometimes abandoning them or keeping them secluded as incoming white settlers disparaged such relationships. However, other such relationships proved stable and happy.

By Jean Barman. Reprinted with permission from *Okanagan History* 60 (1996): 8–20.

The annual reports of the Okanagan Historical Society, now *Okanagan History*, are unequalled for their commitment to local history. Since 1926, long-time residents and newcomers have shared their knowledge and insights in print. No other area of British Columbia has received as much attention, for so long a period of time, as the Okanagan Valley. Presumably, then, everything to be known should be known. However, our sense of what counts as history changes over time. Some topics are always more inviting or acceptable than others.

One of the most fundamental assumptions about the settlement of the Okanagan Valley has been its identification with whiteness. From the very beginning, whiteness counted. Oblate Father Charles Pandosy, whose arrival in 1859 initiated non-Indigenous settlement, enthused almost immediately, "Already we have a white family near us—it is probable that others will present themselves before winter, or at least at the beginning of the season."[1] White firsts have been repeatedly lauded in the annual reports of the Okanagan Historical Society. For example, "Susan Allison was the first white woman to live on the west side of Okanagan Valley ... She and Mrs. Eli Lequime, who lived across the lake at the Mission [Okanagan Mission], were the only white women at that time, in the entire Valley."[2] It is not just white women but also their children who have been celebrated, for therein lies the essence of family life. The victor as the "first white child born in the Okanagan," and even "the first white child born in the interior of British Columbia," is generally considered to have been Gaston Lequime, born in December 1861.[3]

Increasingly, I have pondered whether whiteness of the type just described—the whiteness of a woman and then the whiteness of her child—is so absolutely essential to settlement. Do settler families have to be all white? If not, then a lost Okanagan awaits retrieval from obscurity, for settlement in the Okanagan during the 1860s and 1870s very often—indeed most often—originated with an Indigenous woman cohabiting with a white man.

Until the arrival of railroads in the mid-1880s, and thus ready access to the Okanagan Valley, numbers of newcomers were very small. Nearly all of them were men, for the difficulties of getting there almost completely excluded white women. In any case, white women were in short supply more generally across British Columbia, as compared with the thousands of men who had arrived with the gold rush beginning in 1858. The provincial voters' list for the years 1874–1878, legally restricted to non-Indigenous men who were British subjects by birth or naturalization, contained just sixty-nine names spread across the Okanagan south through the Similkameen. These men divided into two types. The Oblates encouraged settlement by French speakers like themselves, most of whom were very ordinary in their lifestyles. The first gold commissioner reported in 1862 that the settlers clustered around the Oblates at Okanagan Mission were all "paupers, comparatively speaking."[4] The second group differed in being English-speaking, generally better educated and wealthier, and more dispersed in settlement.[5]

For both of these groups of men, the utter loneliness of being alone, all alone, sometimes became overwhelming. Glimpses that survive embody a strong element of pathos. Tom Ellis came out from Ireland in 1865 with the appropriate letters of introduction indicating considerable personal status and soon secured a government position. For the first few months he kept a journal, and its entries underline that loneliness rather than frontier survival most troubled him. August 11, 1865: "Have been alone for ten days and am so tired of this solitude, with nothing to do. I would not mind so much if I had a good book to read." August 19, 1865: "I am thinking a good deal of home [Ireland] today, as I do most days, especially when I am here and alone."[6] A daughter recalled how Ellis once passed three months without speaking to another white person. She emphasized how important it was to have a wife, and a suitable wife: "Like most men, my father did not go far without the aid of a woman, one who was truly his companion and helpmate."[7] Translated, she meant a white wife, and Ellis secured one from Ireland in 1872.

While Ellis could afford to go back home to find a mate, for others the wait was too long or the possibility too remote. In some cases, as with Cyprian Lawrence, a Quebec packer who accompanied the Oblates north from Washington Territory in 1859, men were married before they arrived. Indeed, it was Lawrence's wife, Theresa, described as "a Flathead Indian who, being devoted to Fr. Pandosy, had resolved to face exile with him," who was responsible for their coming in the first place.[8] Frenchman François Ortolan, who arrived in 1862, also had a Flathead wife.[9] John McDougal was among a small number of prairie Métis who settled at Okanagan Mission. Married to an Indigenous woman while working for the Hudson's Bay Company at Fort Kamloops, he had visited the Okanagan with pack trains from the early 1840s, and in 1861 pre-empted land. German-born Frederick Brent represented another strand of the small community growing up around the Mission; discharged from the US army, he arrived in 1865 and was soon operating a grist mill as well as farming. Brent's wife was an Indigenous woman named Mary Ann. Most Mission settlers of the 1860s and 1870s had Indigenous wives and relatively stable relationships. Just over a third of the sixty-nine voters of the mid-1870s lived around Okanagan Mission, and about half of them had children bearing their surname by Indigenous women.

As for the second group—those with generally greater resources—Duane Thomson in his doctoral thesis succinctly contrasted their marital circumstances with those of Okanagan Mission families:

> In the 1860s, due partially to the sexual imbalance in the population, most of the married white males had chosen Aboriginal wives. Many others, perhaps most others, men such as J.C. Haynes, C. O'Keefe, J.F. Allison and C.F. Houghton, lived with

> Aboriginal women on a more or less permanent nature. While many were eventually rejected by their common-law husbands, it cannot be denied that Aboriginal-white relations exhibited a degree of intimacy.[10]

Of voters living beyond Okanagan Mission in 1874–1877, at least a third had children by Indigenous women to whom they had bequeathed their surname.

Two measures reveal just how extensive were liaisons with Indigenous women, particularly among the more successful of the second group. Thomson calculated the thirteen wealthiest Okanagan settlers as of 1879, and half of them—Haynes, O'Keefe, Allison, Houghton, Forbes Vernon, Francis Richter, and possibly one other—had children with their surname by Indigenous women.[11] A second measure is the five settlers whom the Civil War general William Tecumseh Sherman considered worth visiting when he passed through the British Columbia Interior in grand style in 1884. Crossing over the border at Osoyoos, his entourage came first "to the residence of Judge J.C. Hayne [*sic*], the British collector of customs," and shortly thereafter to the house of "Mr. Kreuger [*sic*], a German." Next mentioned in the official report was the ranch of "Mr. Richter," and a bit later "Price's mill, the site of an old Hudson Bay trading post." Then came "Allison's ranch," where special note was made of his "rosy-cheeked English" wife.[12] All five of these men had children bearing their surname by an Indigenous woman.

As economic circumstances improved, so the pressures for men in this second group to discard an Indigenous partner in favour of her white counterpart became enormous. Described by a female contemporary as an "unmistakable gentleman,"[13] Henry Shuttleworth pre-empted land in in the 1870s; when he was looking for a teaching job a decade later, he complained to the Superintendent of Education "that for some reason or other you cannot give me the appointment of Teacher." Obviously reflecting attitudes more generally, Shuttleworth

Born in 1825 in Leeds, Yorkshire, early Okanagan settler John Fall Allison had a family by a local Indigenous woman before marrying a white woman half his age lauded for being one of the first white women to live in the Okanagan Valley. Photo courtesy of John Fall Allison's great-granddaughter, Lori Thomas.

continued: "I suppose it is because I have an Indian Woman but I can assure you and if necessary also prove to you that I am lawfully married to her."[14] The Superintendent replied only that someone else had been hired.[15]

Other men responded by hiding their Indigenous wives from view. Irishman E.J. Tronson, who pre-empted land on the eastern side of Okanagan Lake in 1868, became a very respectable businessman in the budding community of Vernon. He had at least six children by his Indigenous wife, Nancy.[16] C.W. Holliday, a young Englishman arriving there in 1889, did not know what to make of Tronson, perceiving him to be "a courtly-groomed old gentleman ... but to see him in church looking rather like a saintly old patriarch you would never have suspected ... that on his ranch he maintained an Indian wife and a large half-breed family; a quite separate establishment, none of them ever appeared in public with him."[17]

Men with pretensions to respectability found it increasingly difficult to withstand the pressure. Given the publication of Susan Allison's memoir, edited by the premier British Columbia historian Margaret Ormsby, John Fall Allison becomes perhaps the best known of the men who changed partners.[18] According to one account passed down through his first family, he had five children by three different Indigenous women. In 1868, at the age of forty-three, he married

Susan Moir, just half his age, by whom he then had a second family. Others following his example generally also chose a white woman much younger than themselves.

One of the most enduring relationships was between Francis Richter, a German who in 1865 homesteaded in the Similkameen Valley, and an Indigenous woman named Lucy.[19] Together they had five sons, and clearly got on well. Their son Joseph recalled his childhood fondly:

> When I was little coal oil was brought 70 miles from Hope on the backs of horses. It was used sparingly. My mother made candles in a special mold and after the cotton wick was threaded it was filled with our own tallow. She made soap from waste fat and lye. Some of our clothing was made from buckskin traded with Indians. Mother fashioned [it] into coats, shirts and pants. Take it from me. Buckskin garments are warm, soft and comfortable.
>
> I suppose that today most people would think that our early days were rough. We worked hard, we had everything we needed. We were a closely knit, affectionate family, self-sufficient, yet depending on one another, each respecting the other's worth under the guidance of wise parents. I shall never forget those early ranch days. The valley was all ours.[20]

The son of one of Francis Richter's close friends the Loudons, who lived just across the border in Loomis, Washington, remembered this time period similarly: "Richter took good care of his Indian wife, Lucy, and his sons ... That Lucy respected him as well as loved him was clearly demonstrated one time in a near tragedy that had a humorous ending." Richter ended up struggling in deep water while crossing the Similkameen River at near flood state, and it was Lucy who reached him with a fence rail: "She pulled him to safety then beat him soundly with the rail for risking his life unnecessarily!"[21]

Nonetheless, even the Richter relationship crumbled. Guy Waring, an acquaintance of the late 1880s, recalled how Richter, who he described as "the only rich squaw man I knew in those days … confessed to me privately one day" that Lucy "had a penchant for entertaining friends and relatives" while he was away.

> But he had chosen to solve the problem by picking out another Siwash woman and inviting her to live in the house with him, along with his Indian wife, who never again dared to entertain lest her rival, who was very fond of Richter, might make trouble. This strange design for living of course resulted in such bitter feeling between Richter and his wife so that eventually he had to let her send his Siwash mistress away.[22]

Whether or not such incidents contributed, the relationship ended in 1894. Aged fifty-six, Richter offered to escort the Loudons' daughter, aged just seventeen, to Victoria to school, and the two returned married to each other. Richter did, however, make accommodation for his first wife of over a quarter of a century and ensure that their sons were provided with their own ranches. His new brother-in-law recalled: "Immediately after his marriage to my sister, Richter established a home for Lucy and provided for her as long as she lived. She never wanted for anything, according to my mother and father … Lucy, the Indian wife, died in about 1903 or 1904 in the cabin she lived in on the original Richter Ranch."[23] In the interim, Richter fathered six more children by his second wife.

While relationships might unravel, particularly among this second group, their human consequences in the form of mixed-race children remained part of the texture of everyday lives. While increasingly unacknowledged publicly, their fates became intertwined with their white half-siblings. Three examples—Haynes, Kruger, and Allison—make the case.

John Haynes, who like Tom Ellis arrived with the requisite letters of introduction needed to get a government position, served as customs collector at Osoyoos from 1860 to his death in 1888, as well as operating a ranch.[24] Haynes had at least three children by a Colville woman named Julia. The story long circulating was that he kept a "separate little log house for his Indian 'wife'" just a few yards away from his bachelor quarters in the government building at Osoyoos.[25] Then in 1868, Haynes, aged thirty-seven, married a young white woman less than half his age. After her death in childbirth, he married a second white woman.[26]

Publicly, Haynes now had only a white wife and family, but privately his two families intermingled. Waring recalled visiting Haynes in about 1886. "In August I decided to pay a surprise visit to Mr. Haynes, an educated Irishman who had the first house across the British line. He was a lifetime Justice of the Peace, a Gold Commissioner and the local Customs Officer. In British Columbia these were dignified positions and everybody regarded Mr. Haynes as an important man." The physical setting confirmed Waring's judgment of Haynes's status:

> The Haynes ranch was large, and the house was beautifully built of logs and covered with dressed lumber ... We arrived just in time for supper, ... Mr. Haynes, a man of about forty-five, received us warmly and extended us the hospitality of his home. Mrs. Haynes proved a very delightful hostess, and her husband's half-breed daughters, who acted as waitresses and housemaids, were all very attractive.[27]

All the same, Haynes's first family disappeared from the public record, and his white daughter Hester is generally considered to have been "the eldest daughter of Judge Haynes."[28]

Theodore Kruger, born in Hanover when it was still under the British Crown, came to British Columbia with the 1858 gold rush and in 1866 took over the Hudson's Bay Company store at Osoyoos.[29] Kruger had at least two children, Matilda and Billy, by an Indigenous woman before his marriage in 1873, at the age of forty-four, to a sixteen-year-old just arrived from Denmark.[30] During the 1880s, Matilda Kruger worked for the Haynes family, as recalled by one of Haynes's white

German-born Similkameen rancher Francis Xavier Richter had five sons by an Indigenous woman named Lucy before moving on to a white successor who was aged seventeen compared to his fifty-six years. Standing in back left to right are Charles, Hans, and William; in front left to right Edward and Joseph. Doug Cox collection.

daughters: "Matilda had been with us for three years. She was Mr. Kruger's native daughter and mother's right hand. 'Splendid' ... tall, slight, lovely, olive skin, nut brown hair, ... and she could do anything."[31] If this was the private Kruger daughter, in public Matilda did not exist. The same Haynes daughter who penned these lines referred with equal ease to "Theodore Kruger and his eldest daughter, Dora," this being a child by his Danish wife.[32]

With John Fall Allison, the erasures were more thorough, even though the two families also mingled on an everyday level. At the time of the 1891 manuscript census, the Allison household at Princeton included John and Susan, thirteen children aged two to twenty-one, and also his mixed-race daughter Lily, aged twenty-eight.[33] Shortly thereafter, Lily married John Norman, a nearby farmer born in France, and the Allisons' twelve-year-old daughter Caroline served as bridesmaid. Yet when Margaret Ormsby edited Susan Allison's memoir in the mid-1970s, no reference was made, either in the text or the introduction, to Allison's first family. A white Allison grandson interviewed on tape in 1977 reiterated that "no, he did not have a family when he first came into the area, and he went back out to Hope, he met my grandmother ... and returned to the valley with her ... there were 13 children in the Allison family."[34]

The mixed character of early settlement was perhaps most visible in the classroom. Okanagan Mission Public School opened in 1875.[35] Two of its three trustees—Frederick Brent and William Smithson—had Indigenous wives.[36] Smithson was an Englishman come with the gold rush who had briefly taught school and then settled at Okanagan Mission in the early 1870s with his Indigenous wife. The school's record book reveals that at least fifteen Okanagan settlers enrolled mixed-race offspring, in some cases at considerable sacrifice through boarding them with local families.

At first school officials were optimistic: "Considering that nearly all the children were ignorant of English when school was opened, wonderful improvement has certainly been made."[37] Visiting geologist George Dawson commented in 1877 that "there is a school with about 20 scholars (all half breeds) some of whom we met on our way to the mines, with lunches & books, neatly dressed."[38] Over time, assessments became less complimentary in ways that likely lowered the expectations put on children and thereby their opportunities to learn. The teacher in 1883 reported: "With one exception the pupils are halfbreeds, & speak better Chinook & Indian than English, & those who have a French father speak French, Indian & Chinook at home, & English only when at school, consequently their written English is very inferior." Children's obligations outside the school became linked to their mixed race: "Two more are obliged to reside at home & cook as their mother (a native) has been visiting her tillicums ["friends" in the Chinook jargon]." The same teacher noted the difficulty of sending reports home: "There are several children in the first book [reader] to whom I do not give reports, some whose guardian is a native woman, uneducated."[39]

In 1884 a second school opened at Priest's Valley, soon to become Vernon.[40] Again, two of the three trustees—Edward Tronson and Alfred McNeil—had mixed-race families, and almost all of the pupils were of mixed race, including members of the Tronson, McNeil, Houghton, and Brewer families.[41] Prairie-born McNeil, who farmed and packed, was likely a prairie Métis, as was his wife, Jane. An early justice of the peace in the North Okanagan, Anglo-Irish Charles Houghton had two children by an Indigenous woman before becoming a member of Parliament in 1871, pursuing a military career, and in 1879 marrying a daughter of Vancouver Island coal mining magnate Robert Dunsmuir. Charles Brewer was an American rancher married to an Indigenous woman named Jenny. The sole white pupils were siblings from Oregon being cared for by Price Ellison, the third trustee and a bachelor who very soon wed the school's teacher.[42] From the teacher's perspective, race helped explain the school's lack of success: "They are all half breeds but three, and do not make as rapid progress as White children, because they do not understand the language well. They are accustomed to Indian talk at home, and most of them could not speak English when they started to school."[43]

Two years later, in 1886, residents of the nearby Coldstream Valley requested their own school. Again, it was men with mixed-race families who took the lead. Keefer wrote the letter, and signatories included Stephen Lambert and Vincent Duteau. The three families supplied ten of the fourteen school-age children.[44] German-born Keefer was married to Mary; Lambert, born in Manitoba and likely a Métis, to a woman named Mary; and Quebecker Duteau to Amelia.

Schools differentiated pupils by race, perhaps as much subtly and indirectly as openly and overtly. The children of the Okanagan's first families learned young that their lives would be different from those of their white counterparts. It is impossible to know which was hardest to bear—the subtle discrimination in the school, the scorn of newcomers, or the very denial of their existence by members of their own families. New arrivals' uncaring words, undoubtedly repeated time and again at dinner parties and in drinking establishments, are expressed openly in two local memoirs.

Guy Waring, an American living just across the international border during the late 1880s, was convinced he had Indigenous women pegged:

> As Justice of the Peace I also acted as confidant in cases involving domestic difficulties between white settlers and Siwash girls, many of which proved very amusing. Virtue, of course, practically did not exist among the Indian women of the Okanagan. Even when caught in the very act of adultery, of simple fornication with a white, the incident rarely resulted in a loss of caste, but was considered rather a monstrous joke by all.

Waring disparaged anyone who, in his words, "kept a squaw," "had his will with a squaw," or "took to himself a comely squaw as a mistress—this being a common custom of the time and locality."[45]

C.W. Holliday, a young Englishman who arrived at about the same time as Waring, was infatuated by "a spirit of adventure, and a desire to get away from the cramping and uncomfortable respectability of what we call civilization, to where they had freedom and space to move around in and do what they felt like doing." Like Waring, Holliday defined freedom in his own image, one that did not much respect Indigenous women or families of mixed race. Referring to Okanagan Mission, he ruminated that

> the mixture of white-Indian sometimes had produced rather unfortunate results. Occasionally they were the offspring of men of education and breeding and would be a strange mixture of two distinct personalities in the same individual—a savage and irresponsible strain from their Indian ancestors and the polished manners acquired from the white father. You might, one day, meet a dark, good-looking chap, quiet and well-bred, who would talk to you as well, or possibly better than many educated Englishmen, and a day or two later see the same lad whooping 'er up with a bunch of Siwashes on the rancherie. And the women were much the same, most of them were decidedly good-looking, and they had charming manners—in fact, the

young ones were most attractive; they had what we now call "it," that made them easy to get on with.[46]

As for Indigenous women, Holliday recalled a contemporary who, "fed up with batching, had disturbed the monastic peace of the community by taking unto himself a dusky mistress." Even as his friends were deciding whether to be jealous, "he and his lady had a bad row, and realizing that his little romance was ended he fired her out." What happened next indicates the great extent to which Indigenous women were viewed as distinct from white women, effectively disposable at will: "And as none of the rest of the old boys were gallant enough to take a chance on her, the lady returned to the bosom of her tribe, and once more there was peace on earth in the little community; Bill was received again into the fold and friendly relations were resumed all round."[47]

Only snatches survive of how mixed-race children reacted to their growing and perhaps overwhelming patronization and disparagement. Rarely did individuals have the courage to speak out publicly, as Maria Houghton, daughter of a one-time member of Parliament, did repeatedly in the Okanagan Historical Society reports. She described her parents' relationship in decidedly romantic terms: "Father fell in love and married a young Indian princess, grand-daughter to the great N'kwala. It was Chief N'kwala in person that married his granddaughter, Sophie N'kwala to my father. It must have been in 1868 or 1869." When her father went off to Ottawa, Maria and her brother "were left with our grandmother." Without going into detail, she recalled that her mother's "two younger brothers and sister died of tuberculosis," and "my mother, Sophia N'kwala died of a broken heart soon afterwards."[48]

Houghton took pride in having grown up between her two heritages and being taught the stories of her mother's family: "In an Indian tribe they pick one sober child with a good memory and train them to remember the story of their family and their ancestors. I was chosen for this."[49] Neither did Maria's father forget her. She recalled how, in 1893, "I left the Okanagan Valley to go to live with my father, Col. Houghton." This circumstance is described very differently in Holliday's memoir:

> I remember one girl, the daughter of an army officer who had spent part of his younger days ranching in the Okanagan. Later on he was attached to the Governor General's staff, and sent for his daughter—who in the meantime had been growing up with her half-breed friends and relatives—to join him in Ottawa, where she was educated and became a society belle at the vice-regal balls and such-like doings in the capital. And then I think her father died; at any rate she came back to the Okanagan, and soon dropped right back into the old half-breed ways.[50]

At least in her writings, Maria Houghton was able to reconcile the two aspects of her heritage. She was passionate in defence of persons of mixed race like herself:

> They seem to possess a certain mental aloofness, a freedom and independence and judgment which makes them different from the whites, pure blood; and these qualities make for leadership among men. The half breed will either live entirely to himself, or, if he takes part in community life at all, he is apt to forge to the front. These men are in a sense "well-born." They on one side of the house at least, have descended from a race of men who for many generations never knew what it was to receive a command from another and feel that they were under compulsion and bound to obey that command. Always they were free men, and, they say, blood will tell.

Houghton was, at the same time, aware that her views were not generally shared: "This is an aspect of Canadian history which seems to have been strangely overlooked, viz., the natural aptitude of men of mixed Indian and white blood, for public office, and for leadership."[51]

If few descendants of the Okanagan's first settler families were as eloquent as Maria Houghton, they nonetheless made clear, in a range of venues, that they would not easily be erased. According to a local historian writing in 1927, Johnny McDougal's family gained "a high reputation as skilled guides and trappers, that has lasted to the present time." It is within this tradition that, "to illustrate the family pride; a story is told of one of the younger generation who replied when asked if he was a half-breed, 'No, sir, I'm a McDougal!'"[52]

In much the same tradition is an Allison story that still circulates among local Indigenous people, as narrated by Salish elder Harry Robinson:

> The white man tell his son,
>   that's Allison—John Fall Allison.
> White man.
> He is the one that tell the stories to his son.
> His son, Bert Allison.
> His son was a half Indian and a half white,
>   because his mother was an Indian.
> And his father was a white man.
> So his father told him these stories.
> But he told me—Bert Allison.
> So he told me,
>   "This is not Indian stories.
>   White man stories."
> You understand that?[53]

With the coming of the transcontinental railway in 1886, the Okanagan familiar to us today began to emerge. New arrivals soon swamped the first generation of settlers. The more successful of the first settlers were already consolidating their holdings, and their large ranches were then bought up by entrepreneurs with even greater financial resources. As irrigated fruit growing gained in appeal, so the big holdings were subdivided and sold off. Among the most enthusiastic purchasers were British immigrants, exemplified by men like Guy Waring and C.W. Holliday. They, together with Canadians from the prairies and elsewhere, created new communities and ways of life. Canadian poet Charles Mair, who settled at Okanagan Mission in 1892, epitomized some newcomers' attitudes in his observation that "the primitive people are Siwash Indians, half-breeds, ancient, uncouth farmers who packed in with ponies 30 years ago from the Coast," but "there are good people, too, and numbers of nice old country families."[54] The foundation of the Okanagan Historical Society in Vernon in 1925, and the appearance of its first report a year later, confirmed the valley's transformation.

The consequence was a lost Okanagan. The glimpses and snatches offered here underline that the past, just like the present, is always being constructed in our own image. We select the heroic firsts that we recognize at least in part to validate ourselves and who we are. We want the comfort and security of others like ourselves being parts of our pasts. When we write, we consciously and unconsciously make it so. While we laud the first white men who came to the Okanagan Valley, we obscure or ignore the Indigenous women with whom they cohabited and the children born of these relationships, and replace them with the first white women and children. By making Whiteness the criteria, we erase an entire generation of settlement.

All of us need constantly to rethink our pasts. We are all victims of assumptions about what counts as history and what should not be revealed. Certainly, we cannot tell all, for there is simply too much to tell. It is very important, just as it always has been, that we maintain confidences and protect sensibilities. At the same time we need to be aware that by protecting some sensibilities we are silencing other voices. All of us, each and every one, must strive to ensure that there are no more lost Okanagans.

Notes

1 Father C.M. Pandosy to Father D'Herbomez, L'Anse au Sable, October 9, 1859, quoted in F.M. Buckland, "The Establishment of Okanagan Mission," Okanagan Historical Society [OHS], *Report* 1 (1926): 9. I am especially grateful to the late Dorothy Fraser of Osoyoos for sharing her husband's research notes and encouraging me to write on this topic.

2 Alice Allison Wright, "Mrs. John Fall Allison," OHS, *Report* 14 (1950): 125.

3 Clinton A.S. Atwood, "First White Child Born in the Okanagan," OHS, *Report* 11 (1945): 75.

4 Assistant Gold Commissioner W.G. Cox to William Young, August 24, 1862, cited in Duncan Duane Thomson, "A History of the Okanagan: Indians and Whites in the Settlement Era, 1860–1920" (PhD diss., University of British Columbia, 1985), 28.

5 Thomson, "History of the Okanagan," 28, 254–55.

6 Thomas Ellis, diary, cited in Kathleen W. Ellis, "Tom and Mina Ellis," OHS, *Report* 14 (1950): 102.

7 Ellis, "Tom and Mina Ellis," 102, 104, also 105.

8 Denys Nelson, "Father Pandosy, O.M.I.," OHS, *Report* 2 (1927): 15.

9 F.M. Buckland, "Settlement at L'Anse au Sable," OHS, *Report* 2 (1927): 17.

10 Thomson, "History of the Okanagan," 348–49.

11 Thomson, "History of the Okanagan," 254.

12 J.C. Tidball, "Report of Journey Made by General W.T. Sherman in the Northwest and Middle Parts of the United States in 1883," in *Report of the Secretary of War*, 1883, no. 1, part 2, vol. 1, 231–42, cited in Hester E. White, "General Sherman at Osoyoos," OHS, *Report* 15 (1951): 57, 59.

13 August 29, 1895, entry in Julia Bullock-Wheeler diary, Keremeos Grist Mill Archives.

14 Henry H.D. Shuttleworth to C.C. McKenzie, Superintendent of Education, Hope, March 1, 1884, in BC Superintendent of Education, Inward Correspondence, BC Archives, GR 1445.

15 C.C. McKenzie to Henry H.D. Shuttleworth, n.d., in BC Superintendent of Education, Outward Correspondence, BC Archives, GR 450.

16 1891 manuscript census, Yale (Priest's Valley), household 1.

17 C.W. Holliday, *The Valley of Youth* (Caldwell, ID: Caxton, 1948), 175–76.

18 Margaret A. Ormsby, ed., *A Pioneer Gentlewoman in British Columbia: The Recollections of Susan Allison* (Vancouver: UBC Press, 1976).

19 1891 manuscript census, Yale (Osoyoos), household 187.

20 Joseph Richter, cited in Eric D. Sismey, "Joseph Richter," OHS, *Report* 34 (1970): 13–15.

21 Richard J. Loudon, "An Odyssey: The Loudon Family in Retrospect," family memoir in the possession of Richard Loudon, Yuma, 75.

22 Guy Waring, *My Pioneer Past* (Boston: Bruce Humphries, 1936), 197.

23 Loudon, "Odyssey," 76.

24 George J. Fraser, *The Story of Osoyoos, September 1811 to December 1952* (Penticton: Penticton Herald, 1952), 75.

25 Conversation of Hamilton Laing with Allan Brooks, recounted by Allan Brooks, Black Creek, February 23, 1993.

26 Kenneth Lindsay, cited in Jean Webber, "Fur Trading Posts in the Okanagan and Similkameen," *Okanagan History* 57 (1993), 17; Fraser, *Story of Osoyoos*, 77; and Hester E. [Haynes] White, "Charlyne Haynes," OHS, *Report* 16 (1952): 37–38.

27 Waring, *Pioneer Past*, 188, 192.

28 D.K. Stewart, G.B. Latimer, and H.H. Whitaker, "Penticton Street Names Honouring Old-Timers," OHS, *Report* 15 (1951): 199.

29 Mrs. Chrestenza Kruger, "Early Days at Osoyoos," OHS, *Report* 3 (1929): 7.

30 Fraser, *Story of Osoyoos*, 92.

31 Hester E. White, "Reminiscences of Early Days," in Fraser, *Story of Osoyoos*, 200.

32 Hester E. White, "On Okanagan Lake in 1888: Four Days in Captain Shorts' Boat," OHS, *Report* 18 (1954): 45.

33 1881 manuscript census, Yale (Princeton), household 23.

34 Interview with Harold Allison, July 21, 1977, tape no. 3153, BC Archives.

35 Thomson, "History of the Okanagan," 99.

36 F.M Buckland, "Okanagan School," OHS, *Report* 2 (1927): 22.

37 June 12, 1876, entry in John Jessop diary, BC Archives, GR 1468.

38 George Dawson, July 4, 1877, journal entry, in Douglas Cole and Bradley Lockner, ed., *The Journals of George M. Dawson: British Columbia, 1875–1878* (Vancouver: UBC Press, 1989), 343.

39 R[richard] S. Hanna, teacher at Okanagan Mission, to C.C. McKenzie, Superintendent of Education, Okanagan Mission, October 30, 1883, in BC Superintendent of Education, Inward Correspondence, BC Archives, GR 1445.

40 Mrs. Price Ellison, nee Sophie O. Johnson, teacher at Okanagan, to S.D. Pope, Superintendent of Education, Okanagan, May 2, 1885, in BC Superintendent of Education, Inward Correspondence, BC Archives, GR 1445.

41 Mrs. William Brent [Maria Houghton], "The Priest's Valley School," OHS, *Report* 2 (1927): 27.

42 Edna Oram, *The History of Vernon, 1867–1937* (Kelowna: Sandhill, 1985),105; and Mrs. Price Ellison, nee Sophie O. Johnson, to S.D. Pope, February 3, 1885, in BC Superintendent of Education, Inward Correspondence, BC Archives, GR 1445.

43 Mrs. Price Ellison, nee Sophie O. Johnson, to S.D. Pope, May 2, 1885, in BC Superintendent of Education, Inward Correspondence, BC Archives, GR 1445.

44 Petition to S.D. Pope, Superintendent of Education, Coldstream, February 7, 1886, in BC Superintendent of Education, Inward Correspondence, BC Archives, GR 1445.

45 Waring, *Pioneer Past*, 30, 38,196.

46 Holliday, *Valley of Youth*, 121, 207.

47 Holliday, *Valley of Youth*, 146–47, 155, 207, 226.

48 Mary Houghton Brent, "Indian Lore," OHS, *Report* 30 (1966): 105, 111.

49 Brent, "Indian Lore," 105.

50 Holliday, *Valley of Youth*, 207.

51 Mrs. William Brent [Maria Houghton], "The Indians of the Okanagan Valley," OHS, *Report* 4 (1930): 25.

52 Buckland, "Settlement at L'Anse au Sable," 16–17.

53 Harry Robinson, "Puss in Boots," in *Write It on Your Heart: The Epic World of an Okanagan Storyteller*, comp. and ed. Wendy Wickwire (Vancouver: Talonbooks/Theytus, 1989), 282.

54 C. Mair to George Denison, Kelowna, October 6, 1892, in Duane Thomson, "Charles Mair's Letters from the Okanagan," OHS, *Report* 42 (1978): 60–67.

11

Island Sanctuaries

Early Mixed-Race Settlement on Gabriola and Nearby Coastal Islands

Barman here tracks over 1,500 relationships in British Columbia between 1840 and 1900 between newcomer men and Indigenous women. Of these, seventy families resided on Saltspring, Gabriola, and other Gulf Islands. She argues that the stability and visibility of these families are due to the autonomy possible on these islands with limited interference from outsiders, who generally, if white, assumed their superiority. The islands further supported autonomy because of their accessibility to sources of income, such as markets for farm produce, and because of their proximity to Indigenous in-laws. The children in these families grew up together, sometimes married each other, and were at least to some extent protected from the racism common in other places in British Columbia.

By Jean Barman. Reprinted with permission from *Shale* 2 (March 2001): 1–13.

The past can be approached from a variety of perspectives. Some of us are insiders who share in the experiences that interest us. Others are outsiders who may be equally interested but lack the insights that come from participation in the experiences themselves. The best history grows out of a combination of perspectives, as I have discovered over the past number of years while attempting to give meaning to early Indigenous mixed-race settlement across British Columbia. By this I mean the personal relationships that developed during the nineteenth century between Indigenous women and newcomer men. I am well aware that my sense of what happened on Gabriola and nearby coastal islands, and elsewhere in the province, is partial. It is my hope that by sharing what I have learned with local communities, our common understanding will be enriched and given deeper meaning.

Beginnings

The impetus to personal relationships between Indigenous men and newcomer men on Gabriola and nearby coastal islands, as well as across British Columbia, lay in two principal events of the nineteenth century—the fur trade and the gold rush.

During the first half of the nineteenth century, newcomer men came on contract to the Pacific Northwest to work in the fur trade. Many soon returned home, but others stayed on, often settling near their last place of employment. One of the main reasons they did so was that they had established personal relationships with local Indigenous women. By virtue of their doing so, those in charge got better access to furs and other resources; men were comforted during long winter nights; and Indigenous families gained a privileged position in respect to these newcomers in their midst.

The second phase of mixed-race relationships had its impetus in the gold rush, beginning on the Fraser River in 1858 and extending by the early 1860s north into the Cariboo. Many thousands of men—and they were almost all men—came to get rich quick, or so they thought. Politically, the effect of the gold rush was to transform what was still an Indigenous place into a politically defined entity increasingly under the control of newcomers. Vancouver Island had been, since 1852, a British colony run by the Hudson's Bay Company; now the mainland also became a British possession. Most newcomers left almost as soon as they came, for the difficulties of getting to the gold fields were horrendous, and the chances of actually striking it rich very small, but a number decided to stick around. The most important factor that encouraged them to do so was the opportunity to pre-empt 160 acres before the land was surveyed. Once improvements were made, they only had to pay a nominal fee in order to acquire outright ownership of the land.

These men who stayed did not have the same encouragement as fur traders had to cohabit with local women, but two reasons encouraged some of them to do so. The first was the desire for a home of their own. Many already had their share of adventure. Here was an opportunity to make their own destiny, and they wanted a woman at their side. The second reason was the gender imbalance in British Columbia. Newcomer women were in very short supply. Throughout the nineteenth century, there were two or three newcomer men for every newcomer woman. As a consequence, many men, just as had their fur trade predecessors, turned to local women, who in turn had their own reasons for deciding whether or not to cohabit with them. The social upheaval created by the gold rush and the pre-emption policy forced many Indigenous women to go out into the world and fend for themselves. In other cases, just as in the fur trade, families saw strategic advantages to allying their daughters with the newcomers in their midst.

These relationships formed by the fur trade and the gold rush took many forms. The ones that interest me are the fifteen hundred or so that I've been able to trace between 1840 and 1900, particularly those among them where children were sufficiently acknowledged by their father to be given his surname.[1] Such ties are difficult to disentangle. Most of their participants were fairly ordinary people, who were far less likely to have their lives officially documented than were the handful of men at the top. Just as importantly, these relationships were, from their beginnings, tainted by racism. Almost all white newcomers accepted the notion of a hierarchy of the races, which conveniently put themselves on top. Indigenous people were doubly disparaged, being darker in complexion and non-Christian, and thus "uncivilized." Newcomers' quest for the land on which Indigenous peoples made their lives heightened racist rhetoric, which then became a very convenient basis for dispossession.

On the islands off the British Columbia coast, including sizeable Gabriola, I have located some seventy relationships, just under one in twenty of the total number. This may sound small, but it takes on greater meaning when we realize that, in general, I know more about these families than is usual among my fifteen hundred. Many of the island families left a trace, and did so because, I want to suggest, they occurred in circumstances conducive to their longevity. My sense is that two aspects of coastal islands—accessibility and autonomy—were critical to their becoming sanctuaries for mixed-race families.

Accessibility

I see accessibility as having three aspects. The first is islands' geographical accessibility to the men themselves. The second is access to their wives' families—their in-laws. The third aspect is accessibility to other clusters of population and thereby to the cash economy. Each of these three, I think, encouraged family stability.

Accessibility to Outsiders

As to geographical accessibility, the coastal islands are hard to avoid. Most Hudson's Bay Company employees and miners came up the coast to Victoria. If heading to trading posts, such as Fort Langley, or to the gold fields, they then made their way across the Strait of Georgia to the mainland. Not only were the islands themselves visible along the way, but so were their small patches of arable grassland among the forests. Almost every one of the seventy or so persons I've traced described themselves in the census, or in their marriage papers, as a farmer. These men may have done numerous things to make a living, including logging, fishing, and lighthouse keeping, but a farmer was what, in their heart of hearts, they wanted to be. The islands gave them an opportunity to own a piece of land of their own.

Some of the earliest reports of coastal island inhabitation by newcomers living with Indigenous women come, not unexpectedly given its large size and apparent lack of an Indigenous population, from Saltspring Island. Anglican bishop George Hills, on his way by boat to Nanaimo in September 1860, wrote about a stop on Saltspring: "Several settlers met us. I visited most of the log houses which are built on each lot … There are 16 settlers mostly young men. Nearly all are living with Indian women."[2] Hills approved of men's initiative, but when he held a service in one of the houses, his sermon topic was the prodigal son. A Methodist minister who visited the north end of Saltspring the next March was less sanguine. "Nine men now in the settlement … five are living with Indian women in a state of adultery, some have families from such connections. One man has committed this degrading course since I was here last."[3] Some men squatted for a time before pre-empting or purchasing land. Others with more political acumen took advantage of the legislation, so much so that land on Saltspring began to be taken up in 1861, just a year after it became possible to do so. Clusters of newcomers soon grew up in three areas: on the west side of Burgoyne Bay, around Fulford Harbour on the south end of the island, and on the north end, each with its own distinctive character. Altogether, I've traced about two dozen mixed-race families living on Saltspring during the nineteenth century.

The second-largest island cluster after Saltspring, numbering seventeen by my count, grew up on Gabriola near Nanaimo. Here June Lewis-Harrison's wonderful local history, *The People of Gabriola*, gives a guide to what happened.[4] A somewhat different phenomenon was at work than on Saltspring. The Hudson's Bay Company began to diversify away from furs in the middle of the nineteenth century. One of the most promising directions lay in coal. A failed attempt to mine at Fort Rupert on northern Vancouver Island was followed by a successful one at Nanaimo. A general assumption exists that all the miners were brought out from England with families. Many were, but others came on their own. As these men of a more independent disposition began to settle down, some of them sought more than simply a job underground. Again, the key lay in island accessibility.

Several newcomer men made their way to Gabriola in the early 1860s. Among them were Irish miners Robert Gray and Thomas Degnan. Gray is said to have jumped ship at Nanaimo; Degnan to have got there after a stint in the US army that took him west to Oregon to fight "Indians." The story goes that Gray and Degnan, on a day off from work in the mines, paddled in their canoes the four or five hours it took to get to the "big island" they could see across the harbour. One version of the story has them being invited to do so by a young Indigenous woman whose family lived on Gabriola, or Descanso as it was then sometimes called.[5] In 1862 or 1863, the two settled there.

Like Saltspring, Gabriola was big enough that clusters of settlers could live essentially independently of each other. Four other ambitious Nanaimo men, Thomas Jones, John Caufield, Alexander McFarlane, and Richard Chapple, pre-empted land at about the same time that Gray and Degnan arrived. Magnus Edgar and Thomas McGuffie got there even earlier, pre-empting land on the southern shore of Gabriola on the same day in October 1862. Edgar arrived from the Shetland Islands in 1851 in the employ of the Hudson's Bay

Company and then, like so many others, worked for a time in the coal mines at Nanaimo, as did McGuffie, who hailed from Ireland.[6]

Others who had, or would soon have, a similar relationship joined these early settlers. Englishmen John Kemp and Henry Heath were on Gabriola from at least 1866 and 1868 respectively. Two other Nanaimo labourers, Josiah Foster and Robert Dombrain, soon arrived, as did Englishmen William Jeffries and Fletcher Ambrose. Theodore LeBoeuf from Quebec followed in 1874, as did Englishman Jonathan Martin, who had earlier pre-empted land in the Cowichan Valley and on Saltspring. That spring an article in the *Nanaimo Free Press* claimed that "though not above seven miles on its longest line, and two or two and a half on its broadest," Gabriola contained seventeen settlers "in constant occupation of their claims and hard at work."[7] Almost two-thirds of that number had Indigenous wives and young families. Following at a later date would be John Silva from Portugal, who had been living not far away on Mayne Island.

The reasons Silva, and perhaps others of the ten men with mixed-race families I have located on Mayne, abandoned the island had to do with its location. As historian Marie Elliott explains, Mayne's accessibility was for a time its undoing.[8] The route that Indigenous people long used in travelling from Vancouver Island to the Fraser River ran through Active Pass, which divides Mayne from Galiano Island, and the high volume of traffic through the pass put settlers there in danger. Following the killings of settlers from Mayne in 1863, the Royal Navy was called upon to enact justice. The result was the bombardment of the Lamalcha people living on the south end of nearby Kuper (now Penelakut) Island, a sad event that Chris Arnett has skillfully chronicled in his book *The Terror of the Coast*.[9] Only the most determined newcomers persisted on islands near Active Pass.

The other twenty or so mixed-race relationships were scattered across the other coastal islands. Whatever the location, the pattern was much the same. Newcomers, largely of a single generation, being born in the first half of the 1830s, with comparable life experiences, usually of youthful adventure culminating in the gold rush, found the idea of having a place of their own enormously attractive.

Accessibility to Wives' Families

Another aspect attracting men to coastal islands was accessibility to in-laws. Some men settled down first, then found a wife. Most found a wife, then settled nearby. In either case, proximity to women's families counted, not surprising perhaps, given the character of everyday life and also sometimes the great age differentials. Women were usually just past puberty at the time they began to cohabit with men sometimes twice their age. Accessibility to wives' families meant that women were more satisfied, their menfolk tutored in necessary skills, and families given a stronger sense of place than they would otherwise have.

Proximity to their wives' families may have spurred on several of the early Gabriola settlers. Degnan, Gray, Kemp, Martin, and later Silva lived with Cowichan women, named or more likely renamed, respectively, Jane, Margaret, Lucille, Helen, and Louisa; Dombrain, Jeffries, and Ambrose with Sechelt women called Lucy, Ellen, and Mary; and Foster with a Squamish woman named Jane.

At the time Degnan and Gray headed off to Gabriola in 1863, they were already cohabiting with local women—Degnan with a Cowichan chief's daughter Jane Janimetga, who may have been the woman leading them to the island—and beginning families by them. Their marriages did not, however, go equally well. Degnan had a lifelong union with Jane and their nine children. As well as farming on Gabriola, Gray manned the lighthouse on tiny Entrance Island northeast of Gabriola, which brought in some needed cash—six hundred dollars a year. Eventually his wife tired of doing all the work on the Gabriola homestead and left, taking their youngest son with her. Accessibility to wives' families gave a freedom of action that mostly brought families together, but could also drive them apart.

Many of the early settlers on Gabriola not only lived with local women but were legally married to them, or would soon be so, a measure of commitment shunned by some of their contemporaries across British Columbia also cohabiting with Indigenous women. Robert Dombrain, who pre-empted land on Gabriola in 1870, had wed a Sechelt woman named Lucy in an Anglican ceremony in Nanaimo in 1865, two years after the birth of their son James. Henry Heath proudly described himself as "farmer of Gabriola Island" when he married Mary Whiam in 1868 in the Methodist Church in Nanaimo, where two years later Josiah Foster wed Jane "of the Squamish tribe." John Kemp had his first child in 1866 by a Cowichan woman named Lucy, whom he married in an Anglican ceremony in Nanaimo in 1872 and by whom two more daughters and two sons would be born before her death in 1882.

In several cases, wives' origins were more distant. Theodore LeBoeuf, Thomas McGuffie, and Richard Chapple all had Tongass wives—that is, women from the Alaska panhandle—respectively Maria, Adeliza Jane, and Mary. Chapple had already fathered one or two daughters by Kanshek, or Mary, whom he married in an Anglican ceremony shortly after pre-empting land on Gabriola in 1863.[10] There would be another daughter and three sons before Mary's death a decade later in a boating accident.[11] McGuffie became the father of Annie Jane in 1861. At least five more children were born to him and Adeliza Jane by the time they wed in an Anglican ceremony in 1873.[12] LeBoeuf wed Maria in a Catholic ceremony in 1867.

As the departure of Robert Gray's wife indicates, women were in no way passive partners. Indeed, they often paved the way by teaching their husbands essential skills. The grandson of an early Saltspring settler recalled how his grandmother gave her husband a canoe, taught him to paddle and catch fish, took him to visit her people, and "always spoke the Cowichan dialect" with him so that he learned to understand and speak it fluently.[13] This grandson explained how his grandmother's brother, sister, and the rest of her family would come to Saltspring each summer to dig clams, which they dried in racks on the beach, and then threaded on strings made of cedar bark.[14]

Women, too, sometimes exchanged services, with one newcomer daughter recalling how "there was Mrs. Degnen (the older Mrs. Degnen), a lovely woman who could speak very little English and my mother used to make out her grocery list for her."[15] It was almost certainly the same Jane Degnan who served as midwife on the south end of Gabriola. A newcomer son recalls his mother working with Marie LeBoeuf, the Tongass wife of Theodore:

> [My mother, Elizabeth Eastham] knew the LeBoeufs. She knew them when she was young. [She] went with Mrs. LeBoeuf and went around as a washerwoman, washing clothes in other people's houses. She used to arrive at seven in the morning in the other people's houses and the water would be ready and she would wash all the clothes for the family. Ten hours a day … non-stop … that's how she made a living.[16]

Accessibility to Markets

The coastal islands were accessible not just for men and their wives, but also to markets for agricultural and other products. The same ease of access that encouraged settlement made it possible to get to markets and thereby gain access to the cash economy. Some of the early Gabriola settlers, like Degnan, planted orchards, soon discovering that while some varieties of apples produced in abundance, peaches were not feasible. The Degnan farm also became known for its spring lamb, sold door to door in Nanaimo.[17] At first, Thomas Degnan used a dugout canoe to get to Nanaimo, but in 1871 he acquired the first of several steam launches given the name of *Patsy*.[18] Richard Chapple constructed his own wharf in the fall of 1883 and that Christmas offered suckling pigs for sale in Nanaimo.[19] Ten years later he took there what the local newspaper described as "a quantity of Rose potatoes, the largest and finest brought to the city this season."[20] As well as growing foodstuffs for the Nanaimo market, Theodore LeBoeuf, who also worked as a carpenter, built barns in the Nanaimo area almost as easily as he did on Gabriola.[21] So it went for other families as well, in each case facilitating economic survival and thereby family stability.

Autonomy

Just as there were three aspects of accessibility—to the islands, to wives' families, and to markets—the concept of autonomy has parts. The first aspect has to do with the freedom that islands gave men and their families to live as they would. The second aspect of autonomy relates to the choices available to the second generation as it came of age.

Autonomy for Families

The great charm of the coastal islands for many families was the independence they gave from outside interference. The quest for autonomy was responsible for Gabriola's early settler families arriving there in the first place. Not just Degnan and Gray, but numerous others were Nanaimo miners willing to forego a certain wage for the opportunity to be their own persons, dependent on their own resources.

This desire for autonomy was expressed in different forms. On Saltspring, where clusters of settlers existed, opposition to the island becoming legally "organized" in 1872 was most vehement at Burgoyne Bay among men with Indigenous wives and families. As stated in a local history published some eighty years later, these men

> have long since passed on, but their uncompromising fight to preserve their individual way of life, developed when the times

were not so good, has influenced the community ever since. The island is one of a rapidly decreasing number of places where in these days, a man may still live as a man, as he wishes "in peace, in dignity and without interference."[22]

A sense of autonomy also grew out of shared experiences typical of island life, as exemplified by the fears of the families settled around Active Pass. In similar fashion, Joseph Chapple, born on Gabriola in about 1870, "could recall childhood days when barricading of his home for protection from the wolves and cougars that ravaged the Island was a nightly task."[23]

Two very determined Portuguese men point up the relationship between coastal islands and the desire for autonomy. Joe Silvey and John Silva were, according to one account, sailors together on a Portuguese whaler, and when it reached Victoria sometime between 1852 and 1854, they jumped ship. After various adventures, they both turned to business. John Silva ran a fruit and vegetable store in gold rush Victoria; Joe Silvey, who by this time was becoming known as "Portuguese Joe," had a saloon in early Gastown on Burrard Inlet. They each found an Indigenous wife: John Silva a Cowichan chief's daughter who took the name of Louisa; Portuguese Joe Silvey, Squamish chief Kiapalano's granddaughter Khaltinaht.[24] As to how the men found their wives, Silva's daughter Margaret told the story of how "my mother always said he gave them two horses hitched and ready for working—two horses and about three sacks of spuds."[25]

The two men wanted more for their families. In 1873, John Silva purchased 237 acres at one dollar per acre around Village Bay, at the western entrance of Active Pass on Mayne Island.[26] Settling there, the couple had ten children.[27] In the interim, Portuguese Joe had settled down on the shores of the future Stanley Park, near where the totem poles and Brockton Oval now are, but became increasingly aware that, living there, he could not give his family the autonomy he wanted for them. So in 1881, Portuguese Joe Silvey, who had by now married a

Sechelt woman named Lucy following Khaltinaht's death, pre-empted 160 acres of Reid Island and moved his family there.[28]

Portuguese Joe and his family stayed put on Reid Island into the second generation, but in the search for autonomy, the Silva family made yet another move. The reason said to have caused the Silvas to leave Mayne Island for Gabriola was the persistence of Haida raiding parties.[29] According to their granddaughter:

> The Haida Indians kept coming through the passageway and they'd hoot and they'd holler and away they would come and they were a pretty fearful bunch and my grandfather kept sheep and he had goats and he had geese and stuff and these Indians would come through and they'd take about half of his stuff to feed their—I guess they didn't like to live on fish all the time!—and anyway my grandmother decided, "I am not living here," so she said to my grandfather, "I want to get out of here," and so she talked him into moving to Gabriola Island.[30]

In 1883, John Silva bought 133 acres of abandoned homestead land on Gabriola Island in an area that would become known as Silva Bay.[31] Their granddaughter recalled the Silva house.

> He built my grandmother a beautiful house there ... I saw their house ... you know how they used to put the plaster on the chicken wire, they put the plaster on, and it was beautifully plastered, all painted, and they had a fireplace downstairs and a fireplace upstairs and lovely [wooden] staircase ... he was a good carpenter and he had siding over the tops of the logs ... and he painted it, it was a beautiful house. He had lots of apple trees and pear trees and everything.[32]

For the Silva family, as for many of their island contemporaries, the search for autonomy had its desired outcome.

The autonomy that Gabriola and the other coastal islands gave was fundamental to their settlement. Through the end of the nineteenth century and even beyond, families of mixed ancestry were at Gabriola's core, particularly on the south end. Four of the early arrivals died before they really made a difference: Andrew McFarlane in 1863, Fletcher Ambrose in 1878, and Henry Heath and John Caufield the next year. Three others—William Jeffries, Thomas Jones, and Robert Dombrain—soon moved on. The remaining ten made Gabriola their home, not just for themselves, but for their wives and families, in many cases into the second generation and even up to the present day.

Autonomy for Children as They Came of Age

The second aspect of autonomy has to do with the options available to the second generation as it came of age. Across British Columbia, mixed-race children became by virtue of their birth trapped in racial rhetoric. Newcomers denigrated them as "halfbreeds" or "mongrels" who inherited the worst characteristics of each of their parents.

Some island couples had large families, others just one or two children. Such long-established Gabriola families as the Degnans, Edgars, McGuffies, Chapples, Martins, and Silvas each had six to twelve children. Their offspring were, at least to some extent, protected by their way of life. Where clusters of families grew up together, as on Saltspring and Gabriola, children might well make their lives so far as possible in their parents' shadow, continue to live on the island, and possibly intermarry. Jonathan and Helen Martin's son Jon married Charlotte Sampson, the mixed-race daughter of one of his father's shipmates on the 1849–1850 voyage of the *Norman Morrison* to Victoria, who had settled on the north end of Saltspring.[33] Thomas and Catherine Jones's son Azariah married Josiah and Jane Foster's daughter Emily. Even where sons headed off, as did Joe Chapple at a young age to work in the Nanaimo coal mines for the very good wage of $700 a year, they identified with their Gabriola origins. As his obituary put it, "he still called Gabriola 'home.'"

For offspring who did not intermarry, the sense of autonomy and self-confidence that coastal islands gave was fundamental to their choices of partners. Across British Columbia during these years, daughters had far more options than sons. A continuing shortage of newcomer females, combined with women's generally lesser status in society, made unions with newcomer men permissible. John and Louisa Silva's daughter married an American; Portuguese Joe Silvey's daughters, Josephine and Mary, Ontarians. Two LeBoeuf daughters "married white," to use the language of some newcomer descendants.

In general across British Columbia, mixed-race sons were perceived as sexual threats to newcomer daughters' virtue, and almost always, where they did not find mixed-race partners, turned to Indigenous women. However, among island offspring, not just numerous daughters, but also sons partnered with newcomers. Four of Jonathan and Helen Martin's eight sons married newcomers. So did two Degnan daughters, but also three Degnan sons. Mark Edgar made his life on his parents' Gabriola homesite with the daughter of a Welsh coal mining family from Nanaimo.[34] James, Louis, and John Silva all married Englishwomen.[35] These marriages of these sons speak to the self-confidence that the autonomy of coastal island life gave to them as well as to their sisters.

There was an important advantage in children selecting newcomer spouses having the same origins as their island fathers. To do so was to diminish their indigeneity at a time when visible mixed race was a stigma that was virtually impossible to overcome, no matter how hard individuals worked or how well they behaved. At the same time, the autonomy to choose took a son or daughter only so far. At age sixteen, Robert and Margaret Gray's daughter Jane married a twenty-eight-year-old Danish labourer, Henry Peterson, who after a few years in Nanaimo settled down to farm on Gabriola. Jane's brother James, who was so enterprising that he passed the provincial exam necessary to teach, even though he hoped to farm, wed the daughter of a Scottish couple living in Nanaimo before settling down on the family homesite. Whereas James Gray continued to be the model of respectability, even running the local post office, the rowdy Peterson brood was long perceived as the bane of the island's existence.[36] Whether it was cause or effect, at Jane Gray Peterson's death, her daughter described her on the official form not, as was usual for island families, by her father's origins and thereby as Danish, but as an "Indian."

Conclusion

What then do we make of this? Accessibility and autonomy, I've tried to show, were talismans for Gabriola and other coastal island families. Access to the islands themselves, to women' families, and to markets encouraged relationships' longevity, as did the sense of autonomy that islands gave to both the first and second generations. The various islands functioned, to a lesser or greater extent, as sanctuaries.

Notes

1 One of my principal sources is the manuscript censuses available for 1881, 1891, and 1901, which make it possible to trace individuals across British Columbia. I have also used church records, newspaper accounts, family recollections, and various other information located or made available to me, often through the generosity of descendants.

2 September 7, 1860, entry in Bishop George Hills diary, in Anglican Church, Ecclesiastical Province of British Columbia, Archives.

3 March 26, 1861, entry in Ebenezer Robson diary, BC Archives, PR-1654.

4 June Lewis-Harrison, *The People of Gabriola: A History of Our Pioneers* (Gabriola Island, BC: J. Lewis-Harrison, 1982).

5 Most information on the Degnan family comes from "Degnen Bay—Gabriola Island," typescript in BC Archives, Vertical Files.

6 "Magnus Edgar," typescript in BC Archives, Vertical Files.

7 "Gabriola Island," *Nanaimo Free Press*, May 1874.

8 Marie Elliott, *Mayne Island and the Outer Gulf Islands: A History* (Mayne Island: Gulf Islands Press, 1984).

9 Chris Arnett, *The Terror of the Coast: Land Alienation and Colonial War on Vancouver Island and the Gulf Islands, 1849–1963* (Vancouver: Talon, 1999). The Lamalcha (Lamachi) have since joined the Penelakut, a Hul'quimin'num First Nation.

10 Records of St. Paul's Anglican Church, Nanaimo, in BC Archives.

11 "Mary Chapple," *Nanaimo Free Press*, November 28, 1874.

12 Records of St. Paul's Anglican Church, Nanaimo, in BC Archives.

13 Phyllis James, "Incredible Grandparents," *Colonist* (Victoria), September 5, 1976.

14 Pat Turkki, "Family's Pioneering Spirit Lives on Today," *Sun* (Vancouver), May 30, 1987.

15 Allison Law in Lewis-Harrison, *People of Gabriola*, 68–69.

16 John Eastham ("Frisco Jack") in Lewis-Harrison, *People of Gabriola*, 86. Some in the family prefer "Easthom" with an "o," but Jack preferred the "a." Jack went to live with his grandmother after his father drowned in 1897.

17 "Degnen Bay—Gabriola Island," typescript in BC Archives, Vertical Files.

18 Lewis-Harrison, *People of Gabriola*, 197.

19 *Nanaimo Free Press*, September 19 and December 25, 1883.

20 *Nanaimo Free Press*, July 1893.

21 Lewis-Harrison, *People of Gabriola*, 152–53.

22 Eric Roberts, *Salt Spring Saga* (Ganges: Driftwood, 1962), 63, also 60–61.

23 "Jos. Chappel, 75 Years on Gabriola, Dies," *Vancouver Sun*, October 10, 1945.

24 Leo and Gaylia Nelson, "John Silva, William Blank, and Robert Shaw," March 7, 1975, typescript in BC Archives, MS. 242; "Josephine Silvey," typescript in City of Vancouver Archives.

25 Conversation with Margaret Hall Corbett, Quadra Island, July 29, 1982.

26 Land records, cited in Nelson, "John Silva, William Blank, and Robert Shaw."

27 Nelson, "John Silva, William Blank, and Robert Shaw"; also Jean Barman, *The Remarkable Adventures of Portuguese Joe Silvey* (Madeira Park, BC: Harbour, 2004).

28 W.C. Moresby to Minister of Lands, Victoria, October 22, 1929, in BC Archives, Surveys and land records, GR1088, box 1, file 5; and D.L. 35, Pre-emption record no. 31, as noted by Major J.S. Matthews on Elizabeth (Mrs. James) Walker and Alice Crakanthorp, conversation with Major J.S. Matthews, Vancouver, November 28, 1938, City of Vancouver Archives.

29 Nelson, "John Silva, William Blank, and Robert Shaw."

30 Conversation with Margaret Hall Corbett, Quadra Island, July 29, 1982.

31 Lands Department information, cited in Nelson, "John Silva, William Blank, and Robert Shaw."

32 Conversation with Margaret Hall Corbett, Quadra Island, July 29, 1982.

33 Information from Donald Martin, Santa Ana, CA, March 3 and 5, 2001.

34 British Columbia, Division of Vital Statistics, marriage registration, BC Archives, GR2962, no. 03-09-096726.

35 Conversation with Margaret Hall Corbett, Quadra Island, July 29, 1982.

36 Lewis-Harrison, *People of Gabriola*, 39–42, 61–63, 69, 105, 124; George H. Melvin, *The Post Offices of British Columbia 1858–1970* (n.p.), 42.

12

New Land, New Lives

Hawaiian Settlement in British Columbia

Here Barman details the genealogy and family histories of early settlers from Hawai'i, popularly referred to as Kanakas. Some crewed on sailing ships and either were stranded in the Pacific Northwest or chose to stay because colonization meant land had become scarce in their homelands. Others were recruited by the Hudson's Bay Company in the period before 1846, when the Canada-US border was set at the forty-ninth parallel. Then deprived of their civil rights in the United States, some chose to move north, and many of these men partnered with Indigenous women. Over time, life choices moved some into Indigenous communities (the Nahanee family of Squamish is a notable example), while others integrated into white society. Families often intermarried over time, contributing to their ethnic solidarity. Many descendants remember their ancestry and still today pass along stories to their children. In this account, Barman again taps into the living memories of the community, as well as the archival record.

By Jean Barman. Reprinted with permission from *Hawaiian Journal of History* 29 (1996): 1–32. Hawaiians' history in the Pacific Northwest is told more fully in Jean Barman and Bruce Watson,

Leaving Paradise: Indigenous Hawaiians in the Pacific Northwest, 1787–1898 (2006), and in Jean Barman, *Maria Mahoi of the Islands* (2004 and 2017).[1]

Between the late eighteenth and mid-nineteenth centuries a thousand or more, perhaps several thousand, native Hawaiians visited the west coast of North America as seamen, fur trade labourers, or independent adventurers.[2] While most returned home, a handful stayed behind. Patterns of Hawaiian settlement and family formation in British Columbia are distinct from those of Hawaiians elsewhere in the Pacific Northwest. Immediately to the south, Hawaiians were subjected to the legalized discrimination inflicted on Indigenous and Black people, whereas those who settled in British Columbia were accorded the same civil rights enjoyed by members of the dominant society. The consequence has been that, despite some racism based on physical appearance and Indigenous origin, descendants have not become segregated, or segregated themselves, but rather married and lived in ways similar to others of comparable socio-economic status.

Hawaiian men began to arrive on the west coast of North America almost from the time British sea captain James Cook visited the Hawaiian Islands, named by him the Sandwich Islands, in January 1778.[3] The islands quickly became a wintering and stopover point for European and American merchant vessels. Local men—sometimes termed Owyhees, an adaptation of Hawaiians, but more often called Kanakas, a Polynesian term meaning simply a human being or person—were taken on as crew members or recruited as labourers. The word "Kanaka" came to be used extensively in the Pacific Northwest, by others and by the individuals themselves, to mean ethnic origin and sometimes language.[4] Over time, the terms "Owyhee" and "Kanaka" have taken on negative connotations, and Canadian descendants prefer to be known as Hawaiians.

The first two dozen indigenous Hawaiians hired for the fur trade arrived in 1811, and thereafter they worked alongside Orkney Islanders and French Canadians as boatmen, blacksmiths, carpenters, farm workers, mill hands, and general labourers.[5] The Hudson's Bay Company acquired control over the entire Pacific Northwest fur trade in 1823, and from 1829 to 1850 the company had its own agent in Honolulu to oversee trade and recruit local men on two- or three-year contracts.[6] Virtually every fur trading post west of the Rocky Mountains had a contingent of Hawaiians, repeatedly praised for their reliability, cheerful disposition, and hard work.[7] A Catholic priest reported back from Honolulu in 1842, likely with a touch of exaggeration, that "more than 500 Sandwich Islanders" were "in the services of the Company" in the Pacific Northwest.[8] At the company's principal coastal fur trade post of Fort Vancouver, now in Washington state, the number of Hawaiians was large enough for them to be accorded separate quarters known as Kanaka.[9] Susan Kardas has counted up a total of 122 Hawaiians employed there between 1827 and 1860 out of a total paid labour force of 535.[10]

Although the fur trade had largely run its course by the middle of the nineteenth century, this decline did not necessarily signify Hawaiians' return home. Numerous men remained, at least for a time, after the expiry of their contract or following arrival on their own. Contemporary references, usually to unnamed individuals or to place names with the word "Kanaka" in them and therefore signifying the presence of Hawaiians, turn up from California northward through British Columbia.[11] Port Townsend, Washington, resident James Swan noted in 1859 as a matter of course how "a couple of Kanakas arrives from Smith Island," about six miles offshore, with a message concerning some belligerent Indians.[12]

Several reasons explain why some Hawaiian men considered staying on in North America. Visiting seamen brought news of deteriorating conditions at home, where indigenous Hawaiians were losing their autonomy and self-respect in the face of religious and economic exploitation by outsiders. Land on the west coast of North America was plentiful, unlike in the Hawaiian Islands, where newcomers had acquired control of much of the best land. One Hawaiian, William Naukana, is said to have returned home sometime in the 1850s only to find that family land had been appropriated for a sugar plantation, and so he came back to the Pacific Northwest.[13] Many of the men had families by Indigenous women and thereby acquired personal reasons for remaining in North America.[14]

For Hawaiians thinking about staying, discrimination and the denial of civil rights in the Oregon Territory may have driven some of them back home, others north to British Columbia. The brunt of American racism was against Black people, but Hawaiians were also targeted. Some were physically very dark, and they were all identified with the Hudson's Bay Company, viewed by American newcomers as the principal obstacle to the area's integration into the United States. A December 1845 act stipulated "That all persons who shall hereafter introduce into Oregon Territory any Sandwich Islander ... for a term of Service shall pay a tax of five dollars for each person as introduced." Any person employing Hawaiians and not returning them to the Islands was liable to an annual three-dollar tax.[15]

The agreement by Britain and the United States on an international boundary in 1846, and then the creation in 1848 of the Oregon Territory (comprising the future states of Oregon, Washington, and parts of Idaho, Wyoming, and Montana), brought matters to a head. A number of Hawaiians sought American citizenship and the right to vote in the territory's first election. As described in a Hawaiian newspaper, "some Hawaiians presented themselves before the proper officers, and desired to become American citizens, and be allowed to vote in the coming election of the 1st of June [1849], but the Governor did not feel authorized by the existing laws of the U.S. to allow them to do it."[16] They were excluded on the basis of federal legislation limiting naturalized citizenship to white males.[17] The 1849 Oregon census, titled "an enumeration of the inhabitants and qualified voters," did not count Hawaiians.[18]

In May of the next year, 1850, the US Congress passed a land grant act for the Oregon Territory.[19] In good part through the determination of the territorial delegate, Samuel R. Thurston, Hawaiians were excluded from applying for grants of public land or for ownership of lands already occupied. Thurston's argument, reflecting local sentiment, linked racial prejudice with the American dislike of the Hudson's Bay Company. Thus Thurston spoke out against a proposed amendment to the bill on the grounds that "it would give land to every servant of the Hudson's Bay Company, including some hundreds of Canakers, or Sandwich Islanders, who are a race of men as black as your negroes of the South, and a race, too, that we do not desire to settle in Oregon."[20] Thurston subsequently moderated his position, making clear that race was the fundamental issue:

After a decade working for the Hudson's Bay Company, William Naukana (1813–1909) settled on San Juan Island and, after it became American territory in 1872, he later settled on Portland and Saltspring Islands in British Columbia. Photo courtesy of William Naukana's great-granddaughter, Rosemary Tahouney Unger.

> Those foreigners in Oregon, who have left the company, or shall leave it, and prove their love of our country by completing their final oath of love and allegiance, should have an appropriation, and be taken into the fold of American citizenship—aye, sir, should have a donation of land; but I am not for giving land to

> Sandwich Islanders or negroes. I have no fears of defining my position here.[21]

Noting recent Oregon territorial legislation excluding free Black people from the territory, Thurston pronounced that "the Canakers and negroes, if allowed to come there, will commingle with our Indians, a mixed race will ensue, and the result will be wars and bloodshed in Oregon."[22] The bill, as passed, provided for land grants to "every white male settler or occupant of the public lands, American half breeds included."[23] Not only were Hawaiians in the Oregon Territory unable to acquire a land grant, be naturalized, or vote, they also could not purchase liquor or testify against whites in the courts.[24] The consequence, according to historian Janice Duncan, was that "by 1900 most Kanakas resident on the mainland had recognized the futility of seeing homes, security, and equality in the United States and retreated to their homeland where their abilities were respected and where the benefit of their experiences was eagerly sought."[25] The few who remained in the Oregon Territory "married into various Indian tribes and disappeared from local records."[26]

Hawaiians who went south or who came directly from Hawai'i to California for its gold rush of 1848 also encountered discrimination, there being lumped together with the Chinese as objects of disfavour. Not only were all foreigners, including Hawaiians, required to pay twenty dollars a month for the privilege of mining, but another, more general act of 1853 called for the exclusion of "Chinese or Kanaka carpenters, masons, or blacksmiths."[27] Concerned about the sudden departure of hundreds of young indigenous Hawaiians for California, and about population decline more generally, the Hawaiian government enacted restrictions on emigration at about the same time.[28] At least a few Hawaiians in California, unlike those in the Oregon Territory, did eventually become American citizens and vote.[29] A number of them enjoyed some success within the dominant society.[30]

In sharp contrast to those in the adjacent Oregon Territory, Hawaiians living in British Columbia possessed the same civil rights as did white males, perhaps due to the respect earned in the fur trade. So far as can be determined, their possible exclusion was never discussed. Whereas Chinese and Indians were virtually never listed in provincial directories and were enumerated only in cursory fashion in the censuses of the late nineteenth century, Hawaiians were included on a par with the province's white population. As a descendant has summed up,

> I think the difference for the Hawaiians was that they were considered to be Indians in the United States and not allowed to be citizens and the Hawaiians in British Columbia were treated as if they were whites—they were allowed to have citizenship. When British Columbia became a province, if you were a Hawaiian, you could be a citizen, you could vote, own land, you could do everything.[31]

Thus, when the San Juan Islands, long in dispute between the United States and Britain, were awarded to the Americans in 1872, a year after British Columbia joined Canada, a number of Hawaiian families who had settled there moved north.[32] A grandson has recalled the story passed down in his family: "the minute San Juan went to the United States, well they moved back to Canada to be under Queen Victoria."[33] The story recounted to white neighbour children about the Hawaiians who moved from San Juan Island to Saltspring Island in the Gulf Islands is similar: "About 18 of those Kanakas came over from, actually, they came from the San Juan Islands. They had wonderful names, there was Nawana, Kahana, all kinds of musical names."[34]

Despite the many Hawaiian names included in British Columbia voters' lists and other public records, the comparatively menial positions that Hawaiians occupied in the fur trade, their tendency to have a single name or just a nickname, and the facility with which names

William Naukana's close friend Johnny Palua (c. 1817–1907) settled adjacent to Naukana on Portland Island and married his second daughter, Sophie. Photo courtesy of Rosemary Unger.

were altered for ease of pronunciation make it extremely difficult to trace men of the first generation through their lifetimes.[35] The early Catholic marriage, birth, and death records described most Hawaiians only by some version of Kanaka, Owyhee, or the equivalent, such as "Pahapale Whyhee," "Charles Kanack," or "Honololo (Canac)," this clearly being how they were known.[36] The annual "Abstracts of Servant's Accounts" of the Hudson's Bay Company, giving wages and job descriptions, are the principal fur trade source where Hawaiians were systematically named. Even then there were usually only single names, often very similar in pronunciation—Kalama, Kalemaku, Kelenopale, Kaluaiai, Kamai, to give just a few.[37] Moreover, a name's spelling was sometimes so changed from instance to instance that it becomes impossible to know whether a single individual or several with similar names were being employed over a period of time. Some alterations have a certain pattern, such as the letters *K* and *T* being interchanged at the beginning of a name, but others were largely arbitrary, depending on the way a name was heard and then written down. By systematically going through fur trade records, Bruce Watson has been able to distinguish four hundred separate named Hawaiians employed across the Pacific Northwest between 1813 and 1858.[38]

These limitations mean that the Hawaiians who stayed behind can be linked back to Hawai'i only at the level of oral tradition. Most often, asserted ties go back to Hawaiian royalty. Thus, according to the son of a long-time Hudson's Bay employee at Fort Langley, "Peon Peon was a relative of the Kamehamas (Kings of the S.I.) and came to Ft Vancouver Wash in the Early Twenties [1820s] as the guardian of the Sandwich Islanders. Employed by the Hudson's Bay Co."[39]

William Naukana was "believed to have been a grandson of King Kamehameha I."[40] A member of the Nahu family of North Vancouver was described on his death in 1957 as "a grandson of Miyu, Hawaiian prince, who was expelled by his brother, King Kamehameha, after attempting to gain the throne."[41] Similarly, the Kalama family of Washington state has speculated about a relationship to "Queen Kalama, wife of Kemehameha III."[42]

Naming practices make it almost as difficult to link with assurance men employed in the fur trade or coming over as ship hands with the names of Hawaiians known to have settled in British Columbia. In the Pacific Northwest some Hawaiians also took a first name, usually Christian, although others continued to use a single Hawaiian name whose spelling, and even the name itself, might alter through time. Yet others were only called by Christian names, as was the case for the parents of the child baptized on Portland Island in British Columbia in early 1893 by a visiting Roman Catholic priest, whose names were given in the official register as "John and Cecilia (Canakas)."[43] The Catholic Church's records of baptisms, marriages, and deaths on the Gulf Islands, where many Hawaiians settled, were kept in Latin until 1946, meaning that spellings were systematically, and unsystematically, "latinized."[44]

Exemplary of the complexities of names and naming is a fur trade employee of the 1840s known in the Hudson's Bay accounts as Newanna.[45] The extant evidence suggests that it may have been the same man who settled on San Juan Island, and that it was very possibly his son, Joe Nohamo, who was hanged there in 1874 for the murder of three Europeans.[46] By that date, San Juan Island had been awarded to the United States, and young Nohamo's parents lived in Victoria's

"Kanaka Row."[47] An individual with the name of "Nuana (Kanaka)" turns up in the 1881 provincial voters' list as farming at Isabella Point on Saltspring Island.[48] By the time of the 1891 manuscript census, and then again in 1901, he had become William Nahana.[49] However, in the principal history of Saltspring, based on personal recollections, the same individual is referred to as Nawana.[50] As if that were not difficulty enough, the son who became the progenitor of the present-day family changed his surname sometime in the 1890s from Nuana to Tahouney, by which descendants are known.[51] To add even further complexities, these same descendants believe that the family name was originally Kahana and that it somehow became mispronounced as Nuana, Nahana, or Nawana.[52]

The difficulties of names and naming mean that even the precise number of Hawaiians who settled in British Columbia is impossible to calculate. Contemporary sources, including provincial voters' lists, land records, directories, Catholic church records, newspaper stories, and the manuscript censuses of 1881, 1891, and 1901, suggest that a hundred or more did so, at least for a time. In some cases, little more than a name survives to indicate an individual's presence, although in others family recollections, photos, and local histories make it possible to piece together the story of a family.

Several clusters of Hawaiian settlement existed by the late nineteenth century, primarily in coastal areas. The oldest was near Fort Langley in the Fraser Valley east of present-day Vancouver. In 1841, Oblate missionary Modeste Demers reported that "about twenty men are employed there at agricultural activities, of whom eight are Canadians, one an Iroquois, and the others Kanakas, inhabitants of the Sandwich Islands; all having wives and children after the fashion of the country."[53]

The men eventually took up land on the north side of the Fraser River near present-day Maple Ridge.[54] The settlement's core lay with Peon Peon or Peopeo, a Hudson's Bay employee from the 1820s who "married one of the Sub chiefs daughters."[55] Peopeo's older daughter, believed by Jason Allard, a long-time Hudson's Bay Company employee, to be "about one of the first to be born at the first Fort," married "a Sandwich Islander" known as Nahu, who worked as a river pilot. Her sister Sophie wed a Hawaiian named Ohule, and Peopeo's son, Joseph Mayo, worked alongside his father and Ohule as coopers at the fort.[56] When their contracts came up for renewal, some of the Hawaiians chose to go off on their own, so that by 1858 there was "a large body of Kanakas—a mixed race half Indian half Sandwich Islanders"—living in the vicinity of Fort Langley.[57] The Hawaiians' presence is attested by the son of a Hawaiian named Apnaut being elected to the Maple Ridge council in 1879.[58] In the late nineteenth century a cluster of Hawaiian families, including the Maoyors, Nahus, Apnauts, Chiers, Schells, and Wawakinas, lived in the Maple Ridge area.

Other Hawaiians sought paid employment in the sawmills on Burrard Inlet, the site of present-day Vancouver. A few families lived at Kanaka Ranch near what became Stanley Park, while the Nahus from Fort Langley were among those residing on Kanaka Row in Moodyville, today's North Vancouver, on Burrard Inlet's north shore. The Nahus became an important longshoring family in North Vancouver.[59] Among those working at Hastings Sawmill, on the south side of Burrard Inlet, was James Keamo, who, according to his son, arrived on his own, "just came for the trip, and stayed here."[60] Keamo's employer decided one day that for ease of pronunciation he should henceforth be called Campbell, which is precisely how all but a few dissident family members have henceforth been known.[61] Nearby New Westminster also attracted a number of recent arrivals from Hawai'i, single men with names like John Kahano, Joe Kanaka, and Kanak Moses, all born in the 1830s and 1840s, who may or may not have remained to rear families in British Columbia.

Yet other Hawaiians lived and worked in and around the capital city of Victoria, where they pre-empted land from the early 1860s.[62] Victoria's *Colonist* newspaper reported in 1860 on a fight in the city's "Kanaka Row," in which "Palew, a Kanaka, became enraged at one of his countrymen" and smashed all the windows in his house.[63] Three decades later, a Thomas Pellew was working as a moulder at Victoria's Albion Iron Works, perhaps the same man or more likely his son.[64] Another handful settled in the Nanaimo area, mostly working in the coal mines.

Reflecting their island heritage and undoubtedly a desire for an independent lifestyle, many if not most of the Hawaiians preferred to live on one of the many Gulf Islands dotting the British Columbia coast. Subsistence farming was combined with fishing and some logging or other paid employment in order to acquire the necessary cash to purchase necessities like sugar and flour from the local store. The Hawaiians became exceptionally self-reliant, planting some of the first and finest orchards on the Gulf Islands and growing and curing their own tobacco. According to a contemporary woman's description, her Hawaiian neighbour

> would cut a round off a log and bore a hole right down through the middle of it and he would crush the tobacco leaves and put the leaves down in the bottom, pour a little molasses on it and a tod of rum, more tobacco leaves and right up until he had got it crammed full. I suppose that would have to set for a while. He would split the log open and he would have his long tobacco stick which they cut and smoked when they needed a smoke.[65]

At least eighteen Hawaiians, some of whom had moved from San Juan Island, homesteaded and raised families on southern Saltspring Island. Numbers were sufficiently large for a visitor of 1885 to label that part of Saltspring "a Kanaka or Sandwich Islander settlement."[66] Other Hawaiians sought their own small island. William Naukana and his good friend and son-in-law Johnny Palua together pre-empted nearby Portland Island. Kama Kamai and Alexander Korney, the latter born in British Columbia of a father born in Hawai'i, opted for Coal Island, a few miles south of Saltspring. William Hamea lived first on

Saltspring and then, in the mid-1880s, homesteaded Russell Island just off Saltspring's south coast. Farther north, George Kamano settled on Harbledown Island after a stint working at Fort Rupert on northern Vancouver Island.

William Naukana's third daughter, Julia, posed with her husband, George Shepard, son of a Vancouver Island settler from the United States and an Indigenous woman. Photo courtesy of Rosemary Unger.

As had been the case with Peopeo at Fort Langley, all of the Hawaiians who can be traced produced families by Indigenous women or possibly the part-Indigenous daughter of a fellow Hawaiian. This pattern of marriage was in no way unique, paralleling the course taken by many other settlers of the first generation in response to British Columbia's long-time shortage of white women. As was the case with newcomer men more generally, some of the Hawaiians had several partners over their lifetimes, and had children by each. Mothers were sometimes no longer part of the family by the time children became conscious of their surroundings. One woman's comment has been repeated time and time again: "We don't know anything about it, we don't know who the woman was, we don't know where she was from except we think she was a Salish Indian. But we don't know, there is nothing there that we can go by. There are no records."[67]

The studio portraits and more informal photographs that survive of these early families, carefully posed and neatly dressed in Victorian or Edwardian fashion, underline the importance given to respectability and correct behaviour.[68] From the mid-nineteenth century to 1898, the time of the Hawaiian Islands' annexation to the United States, the

William Naukana's eldest daughter, Delia, posed in a studio portrait with her husband, George Napoleon Parker, and children. The photo was taken during an 1890 visit to Tacoma from the Gulf Islands. Photo courtesy of Rosemary Unger.

government of Hawai'i maintained consular offices abroad. The infrequency with which Hawaiian consuls at Victoria, Port Townsend, and Vancouver dealt with infractions of the law or cases of destitution by Hawaiian settlers testified to individual and family pride.[69] The sole British Columbia case coming to a consul's attention concerned a Nanaimo man known as "Kanaka Pete," sentenced to death in 1869 for killing his Indigenous wife and family on discovering her adultery. Twenty of Vancouver Island's leading citizens plus the Hawaiian consul unsuccessfully sought clemency for the condemned man due to the mitigating circumstances.[70]

Hawaiians, particularly those on Saltspring and nearby islands, appeared on voters' lists virtually from the time of British Columbia's entry into the Canadian Confederation in 1871, underlining how soon many took British citizenship and shifted their allegiance to Canada. Through naturalization, they publicly declared their intentions to behave, as did the members of the dominant society. The story passed down orally, perhaps with a touch of exaggeration, was: "Well our first elections here in B.C., the Hawaiians all voted. Because, when they came out to vote in them days, there were very few whites around you see. Well there was just as many Hawaiians that voted as were white people. Those that stayed in this country see, well they got their vote."[71]

A descendant has reflected, quite accurately, that British Columbian "Hawaiians were mostly Catholic" and "quite religious."[72] Perhaps this was due to the energetic and sustained Oblate missionary activity among the fur trade labourers, possibly to the influence of Indigenous wives and mothers already converted, but also very likely to their upbringings. In 1836 the Anglican minister at Fort Langley had remarked on Hawaiians' rejection of missionary efforts in favour of their own religion.[73] All but three of the more than two hundred Hawaiians by birth or descent located in the manuscript censuses for 1881, 1891, and 1901 gave their religion as Catholic, the three exceptions being daughters married to white Protestant settlers. George Kamano assisted the Oblates in conducting a mission on Harbledown Island off Fort Rupert in 1863.[74] Hawaiian families were a mainstay of St. Paul's Church on southern Saltspring, for which William Naukana donated the land and other Hawaiians supplied building materials.[75] The church's very first event was the baptism on December 27, 1885, of grandsons of William Naukana and fellow Hawaiian William Mahoi.[76] A hand-drawn map of St. Paul's cemetery, done by Naukana's youngest daughter, Matilda, in the early 1930s (before many stones were lost in the course of road widening), contains thirty to thirty-five members of the Hamea, Kami, Mahoi, Nawa, Nawana, Palua, and other families.[77] Hawaiian religiosity likely underlies the advice passed down to a grandson: "Don't feel bad when I go, I'm going to heaven. It is you folks that is going to be left with all the problems of the sicknesses the politics and all this and that."[78]

Although members of the first generation, both the Hawaiians themselves and their Indigenous wives, were mostly illiterate, their offspring, so far as geography permitted, attended local schools alongside neighbours' children. From 1874, when Emma Palua from Saltspring was sent away at the tender age of four, daughters of several families boarded at St. Ann's Catholic Convent School in Vancouver Island's Cowichan Valley.[79] Schooling continued to be prized. A treasured

Presentation of the Roll of Honour of Isabella Point public school on Saltspring to Johnny and Sophia Palua's son Willie, on the far left. Next to him is his teacher, and standing to the right of her in this 1905 photo is the Hawaiian known as Nawana and later Tahouney. On the far right is Nawana's daughter Mary, married to William Lumley, an Englishman, who is standing to the right of Nawana. Photo courtesy of Salt Spring Island Archives.

photo of 1905 celebrated the presentation of the Roll of Honour to a fifteen-year-old Saltspringer of the younger generation.[80]

Yet when the time came for marriage, many sons and daughters turned inward. As put by one woman, discussing the Mahoi clan, "they all married and intermarried."[81] William Naukana's second eldest daughter wed her father's friend and fellow Portland Island settler Johnny Palua, almost forty years her senior. The men Peopeo's daughters married were likely friends of their father. Often neighbours' children married each other, as with the Kamais and Korneys on Coal Island and the Naukanas, Mahois, and Nawanas on Saltspring. As had their parents, many descendants had two or more relationships in their lifetimes. One of those descendants has observed, "A lot of families married and separated and remarried."[82] Perhaps not surprisingly, only at the end of a long afternoon of conversation did two long-time friends realize that they shared common great-grandparents of mixed Hawaiian and Indigenous descent.[83]

All the same, marriage patterns in the second and subsequent generations were remarkably similar to those of other British Columbia settler families where the father came from elsewhere and the mother was Indigenous. In general, sons found it more difficult than their sisters to be accepted within the dominant society. Many sought out Indigenous women, and by the third, if not the second, generation had outwardly become Indigenous. The Fraser Valley Chiers, for instance, became one of the three major families on the Whonnock Reserve.[84]

The continuing paucity of non-Indigenous women in British Columbia gave daughters more options. A few wed another person of mixed race or a Hawaiian, but many married white men, and over time their families became absorbed into the dominant society. Maria Mahoi, half-Hawaiian and half-Indigenous, had seven children by a sea captain from Maine. She then married the son of an Englishman and a Cowichan woman and had another half-dozen children.

The best-known Hawaiian of the first generation in British Columbia, William Naukana, had six daughters by at least two Indigenous women, as well as, very likely, a son who died young. The eldest, Delia, first married a recent arrival from Hawai'i and then one from the Philippines; Sophie, her father's close friend Johnny Palua; Julia, the son of an American and an Indigenous woman; Mary Ann Naukana, a fisherman who had recently arrived from Denmark; and Annie, first a continental European and then a recent arrival from Hawai'i. The youngest, Matilda, first married a young Englishman and then a man of likely mixed race.

Gender has taken some families in different directions. A Cowichan woman had children by two former fur trade labourers, Eihu and Joe Nahanee, both of whom worked at Hastings Sawmill and, with the Keamos and several other Hawaiians, lived at Kanaka Ranch. Her son wed a Squamish woman and became the patriarch of the Nahanee clan,

Maria Mahoi, daughter of a Hawaiian fur trade labourer William Mahoi and an Indigenous woman. Mahoi had seven children by Abel Douglas, a whaler from Maine, and then another six by George Fisher, son of an Englishman and an Indigenous woman. Photo courtesy of George and Maria Fisher's great-grandson Karey Litton.

part of the Squamish Nation in North Vancouver, whereas the children of Eihu's daughter were absorbed into mainstream Vancouver.

If within two or three generations many Hawaiians were living outwardly as "Indian" or "white," this did not mean that they necessarily abandoned their distinctive identity. Unlike the American Pacific Northwest, where by the mid-twentieth century "many descendants of the early Hawaiians had lost the consciousness that they were part-Hawaiian," some sensitivity to origins has survived in family after family in British Columbia.[85]

Elements of culture acquired through the female line, such as the hula, did not transfer, due to the lack of women of the first generation to pass it on to their daughters. The only Hawaiian woman so far found to have had a family in nineteenth-century British Columbia was Teresa Aponi, who came to New Westminster in the 1860s with her half-Polynesian, half-Spanish husband.[86]

Language was another early casualty. Most families spoke English, possibly in combination with Chinook, the trading jargon long used across the Pacific Northwest. According to a granddaughter, "the wife of Grandpa Naukana spoke Indian and Chinook, but he wanted children to speak only English and Chinook, not Native Indian and not

The Eihu/Nahanee family of Kanaka Ranch in a 1903 family photo. Bill Nahanee, the progenitor of the large Nahanee clan prominent in the Squamish Nation of North Vancouver, is at the top left, with his wife bottom left holding one of their children. Nahanee's half-sister, Maggie Eihu, who twice married white Vancouverites, is four persons to the right; her daughters Irene and Edith are seated in the second row, second and third from left respectively. Photo courtesy of Jerry Nahanee.

Hawaiian."[87] All that survived of the Hawaiian language in most families, as exemplified in the recollection of a granddaughter-in-law, were words and phrases. There were "a lot of Hawaiian words that we used every day, just in our general conversations ... We always used to use these phrases. We didn't know the meaning of them and we didn't even know if we were saying them right ... When we went to Hawai'i on our first trip, we heard these words and began to put meaning to them." Their origin lay with this woman's mother-in-law. "They came down from her father. He taught her, I suppose. She picked it up from him and then she used to use them and then her children did likewise and used them."[88]

Descendants' retention of some sense of their Hawaiianness has been aided by the continued existence across coastal British

Maria Mahoi's children illuminate the role of gender in fashioning marital decisions and thereby place in British Columbia society. Her eldest son, George Douglas, half white and a quarter each Hawaiian and Indigenous, married Nettie Sparrow, who was half Indigenous and half white. Photo courtesy of George and Nettie's grandson, Ken Seeley.

Columbia of such place names as Kanaka Creek opposite Fort Langley, Kanaka Bluff on Portland Island, and Kanaka Bay on Newcastle Island off Nanaimo.[89] According to Saltspring neighbours, the Kanakas who settled nearby "brought their own flag with them over here, I believe, the Hawaiian flag." A love of music and a delight in playing stringed instruments passed down in many families: "They all brought their guitars with them. I think that you could have called this little Hawai'i along here."[90] Eihu, said to have been a teacher in native schools in Hawai'i before coming to the Pacific Northwest, treasured his Hawaiian-language bible, which was subsequently donated by descendants to the City of Vancouver Archives.

Well into the twentieth century, families on the Gulf Islands celebrated each autumn's harvest with a Hawaiian lu'au-style party, where food was roasted in a firepit dug in the beach. The party moved virtually intact from family to family, island to island. William Naukana and Johnny Palua would throw a lu'au on Portland. After a week or so, celebrants would go on to the Nawanas on Saltspring, then to the Kamais on Coal Island, to a Hawaiian family on Piers Island, and on to the Hameas and so on: "Well they sang and danced all winter until the time came to put in their crops."[91]

The elaborate wedding at St. Paul's on Saltspring of Maria Mahoi's youngest daughter, Mary Jane Fisher, half Indigenous and a quarter each Hawaiian and white, to a well-educated accountant from England, William Henry Roberts. Photo courtesy of Salt Spring Island Archives.

Physical appearance has created another enduring bond. The daughter of a Hudson's Bay officer on San Juan Island remembered how in her childhood she would frequently "meet a big kinky haired black-faced Kanaka ... [I]t seemed to me the woods were quite full of them going and coming, hither & thither, through the little trails in the woods."[92] Such distinguishing features as being "well made" and having brown eyes, a skin colour varying from light olive to darker shades, and wavy "brownish black" hair, to cite Captain James Cook's description from visiting there in the late eighteenth century, have appeared and reappeared in British Columbia families generation after generation.[93] Describing her husband, a Hawaiian of the third generation, a woman has recalled, "He looked like a Hawaiian. He had the complexion, the features, the whole bit. When we went to Hawai'i, the men folks down there would say, 'Hi bra, what island you from?'"[94]

The enduring bond of physical features is illustrated in this Saltspring Island school photo from the early 1930s. All pupils except the two girls on the right in the second row and the boy on the left in the front row were descended from Hawaiians. Photo courtesy of Salt Spring Island Archives.

Sometimes these characteristics have been cause for prejudice and discrimination, as with the woman who married a Kwakwaka'wakw chief only to find herself disparaged as "not fit to be his wife" because "only her mother was the part of her that was Indian," and her father was "from Honolulu or some place, and he was dark brown—almost black."[95] Physical features have also served as a bond uniting families and clans. The son of a man with "dark skin" who was born with his father's "eyes that go from dark green to gray" mused approvingly that it might come from the Hawai'i link.[96]

Perhaps several thousand British Columbians descend from Hawaiians, although the number may be considerably larger given that among just one extended family, the Nahanees of the Squamish Nation, some four hundred trace their origins back to a single man.[97] Although never a clearly defined community in the sense of having formal institutions, Hawaiians in British Columbia have valued their heritage. Stories passed down from generation to generation remain remarkably intact, in part perhaps because so many members of the first generation were illiterate, and subsequent generations have been for the most part ordinary British Columbians whose culture is as much verbal as written. Many who know very little about their precise family histories are nonetheless aware of their origins, and for the most part descendants take more pride in being Hawaiian than being Indigenous, due very likely to the greater respect accorded to Hawaiians historically. Particularly since the 1970s, some families have begun to visit Hawai'i, hoping, so far without success, to recover an actual as well as a spiritual link with families there. Operation 'Ohana, the Hawaiian government initiative to enroll all persons of indigenous Hawaiian ancestry into a cultural association based in pride in heritage, has been greeted with enthusiasm.

Attitudes are indicated by a somewhat spontaneous event in 1992. While individual families had gotten together from time to time, a first general reunion titled "The Hawaiian Connection" was organized by a descendant of Stanley Park's Eihu in conjunction with celebrations marking Canada's 125th anniversary. Although news of the event only spread informally, more than two hundred people turned up, representing virtually the entire British Columbia socio-economic spectrum from Indigenous leaders to a former provincial cabinet minister to ordinary men, women, and families. Most had never met before, but many discovered they shared the same stories and in some cases common ancestry. Dominant physical features created a special bond. One man quipped that, while looking for a parking space, he had seen his uncle nine times even though his uncle was long since dead. An elderly man who grew up in Victoria as "white" told of the shame he had felt as a boy whenever his visibly Hawaiian grandmother came to visit, and how he wished he had not denied her a place in his childhood. The editor of the province's principal Indigenous newspaper summed the event up as "a re-affirmation of ourselves."[98]

The Hawaiian contribution to the development of the North American Pacific Northwest extends far beyond early seafaring and the fur trade. The men who stayed behind in British Columbia were deemed citizens of Canada, and they have behaved as such. Their experience belies the myth that legal discrimination necessarily followed, historically, from distinctive physical features. Hawaiians and their families contributed in innumerable ways to the settlement of British Columbia. Their descendants continue to testify to the strength and durability of both the Hawaiian and Canadian fabrics.

Notes

1 My interest in this topic originated in a larger project funded by the Social Sciences and Humanities Research Council of Canada, for whose support I am grateful. Descendants in British Columbia have generously shared extant materials and family stories and encouraged me to write and publish. Particular thanks are due to Rosemary Tahouney Unger, Bea Shepard, Stan and Pauline Harris, and Gil Garrison for telling me about the Naukana and Nawana/Tahouney familes; to Mel Couvelier, Ken and Dale Seeley, Violet and Larry Bell, Karey Litton, Harry Roberts, Gladys Gardiner, and Ray and Duncan Harpur for telling me about the Mahoi family; to Norman and Mabel McPhee for telling me about the Eihu family; to Jimmy and Jerry Nahanee for telling me about the Nahanee family; to Carey Myers and Carolynne Sacht for telling me about the Kamano family; and to Tom and Leila Johnston for telling me about Teresa Aponi and her family. I also thank Bruce Watson, with whom I co-authored *Leaving Paradise: Indigenous Hawaiians in the Pacific Northwest, 1787–1898* (Honolulu: University of Hawai'i Press, 2006), for permitting me to draw on his biographies of Pacific Northwest fur traders, and Rodney Ohtani of Honolulu for his ongoing interest and encouragement. Freelance journalist Tom Koppel and I have shared information over the years as we have pursued our common interest in Hawaiians in the Pacific Northwest, his research culminating in the very readable *Kanaka: The Untold Story of Hawaiian Pioneers in British Columbia and the Pacific Northwest* (Vancouver: Whitecap, 1995).

2 Exact numbers of Hawaiians who worked abroad are impossible to calculate. One respected source puts those away from the Islands as rising from about two hundred in 1823 to four thousand in 1850. Unpublished, untitled manuscript by Romanzo Adams held at Department of Sociology, University of Hawai'i, 112, cited in Robert C. Schmitt, *Demographic Statistics of Hawai'i 1778–1965* (Honolulu: University of Hawai'i Press, 1968), 39. The figure of four thousand is likely taken from "Census of the Islands," *The Friend* (Hawaiian missionary newspaper, publishing 1843 to the present), November 15, 1849, 79. Various data are summarized in Richard A. Greer, "Wandering Kamaainas: Notes on Hawaiian Emigration before 1840," *Journal of the West* 11 (April 1967): 221–25. A Hawaiian publication of September 1844 considered that three hundred to four hundred were then employed by the Hudson's Bay Company in the Pacific Northwest, while another fifty had been hired in the past eighteen months as seamen on ships heading

in that direction. "Native Seamen," *The Friend*, September 4, 1879, places the total number taken on as seamen between January 1843 and May 1844 as 275, also including 57 to California and 114 on whalers. Others were taken to the east coast of North America. Janice K. Duncan, *Minority without a Champion: Kanakas on the Pacific Coast, 1788–1850* (Portland: Oregon Historical Society, 1972), 3.

3 Others were taken to the east coast of North America. Janice K. Duncan, *Minority without a Champion: Kanakas on the Pacific Coast, 1788–1850* (Portland: Oregon Historical Society, 1972), 3.

4 For contemporary usage of "Kanaka" as an ethnic origin, see household 670, district 190, Victoria, Johnson Street Ward, 1891 manuscript census of British Columbia, and household 5, Burrard, Vancouver, district 2, Vancouver City, 1901 manuscript census of British Columbia; as a language, see household 28, Vancouver, district 3, Saltspring Island, 1901 manuscript census of British Columbia. "Kanaka" is used as a synonym for Hawaiian "native" in "Native Seamen," *The Friend*, September 4, 1844, 79. Also valuable is the discussion in E. Momilani Naughton, "Hawaiians in the Fur Trade: Cultural Influence on the Northwest Coast, 1811–1875" (master's thesis, Western Washington University, 1983), 3–5.

5 Several American graduate theses have examined Hawaiians in the fur trade, notably Naughton, "Hawaiians in the Fur Trade"; Duncan, "Minority without a Champion," summarized in Duncan's *Minority without a Champion*, and "Kanaka World Travelers and Fur Company Employees, 1783–1860," *Hawaiian Journal of History* 7 (1973): 93–111; and Susan Kardas, "'The People Bought This and the Clatsop Became Rich': A View of Nineteenth Century Fur Trade Relationships on the Lower Columbia between Chinookan Speakers, Whites, and Kanakas" (PhD diss., Bryn Mawr College, 1971).

6 See Alexander Spoehr, "Fur Traders in Hawai'i: The Hudson's Bay Company in Honolulu, 1829–1861," *Hawaiian Journal of History* 20 (1986): 27–66. For an actual contract, see George Verne Blue, "A Hudson's Bay Company Contract for Hawaiian Labor," *Oregon Historical Quarterly* 25 (1924): 72–75.

7 This point is underlined in Duncan, *Minority without a Champion*.

8 J.B.Z. Bolduc, cited in Notice no. 5, January 1843, in *Notices and Voyages of the Famous Quebec Mission to the Pacific Northwest, Being the correspondence, notices, etc., of Fathers Blanchet and Demers, together with those of Fathers Bolduc and Langlois* (Portland: Champoeg Press for the Oregon Historical Society, 1956), 133.

9 See especially Kardas, "'The People Bought This'"; also Milton Bona, "Hawaiians Made Life 'More Bearable' at Fort Vancouver," *Fort Vancouver Historical Society* 13 (1972): 171; Naughton, "Hawaiians in the Fur Trade," 52.

10 "List of Kanakas (Owyhees) at Fort Vancouver," in Kardas, "'The People Bought This,'" 174–79.

11 For a broad sampling, see "Kanakas in British Columbia," in BC Archives, Vertical Files, and Naughton, "Hawaiians in the Fur Trade," 52–53, 71.

12 Lucile McDonald, *Swan among the Indians: Life of James G. Swan, 1818–1900* (Portland: Binfords and More, 1972), 56 58.

13 The story is recounted in Beth Hill et al., *Times Past: Salt Spring Island Houses and History before the Turn of the Century* (Ganges: Community Arts Council, 1983), 44; and in Thomas K. Ovanin, *Island Heritage Buildings: A Selection of Heritage Buildings in the Islands Trust Area* (Victoria: Islands Trust, 1984), 85. Both versions likely come from the Roland family, descendants of Naukana's youngest daughter, Matilda.

14 This point is made in Naughton, "Hawaiians in the Fur Trade," 30, 38–41.

15 Cited in Duncan, "Minority without a Champion," 121.

16 Samuel Chenery Damon, "Lower Oregon.—Population," *The Friend*, October 1849, 51.

17 Richard White, *"It's Your Misfortune and None of My Own": A History of the American West* (Norman: University of Oklahoma Press, 1991), 322.

18 Duncan, *Minority without a Champion*, 16–17.

19 For the entire debate, see House of Representatives, May 28 and 29, 1850, in *Congressional Globe*, May 30, 1850, 1075–80, 1090–96.

20 Debate of the House of Representatives, May 28, 1850, in *Congressional Globe*, May 30, 1850, 1079, col. 2.

21 Debate of the House of Representatives, May 28, 1850, in *Congressional Globe*, May 30, 1850, 1079, col. 3.

22 Debate of the House of Representatives, May 28, 1850, in *Congressional Globe*, May 30, 1850, 1079, col. 3.

23 Debates of the House of Representatives, May 28 and 29, 1850, in *Congressional Globe*, May 30, 1850, 1078, col. 3, and 1093, col. 1–2.

24 Duncan, "Minority without a Champion," 124.

25 Duncan, "Minority without a Champion," 7.

26 Norman Schlesser, "Kanakas in the Oregon Country," *Umpqua Trapper* (Douglas County Historical Society) 8, no. 1 (1972): 12–13, and his example of Makaine Owyhee family, 6, 8, 11. The Kalama and Kahana

families are described in Naughton, "Hawaiians in the Fur Trade," 31, 36–37, 54–56, and appendices; also see 30, 38–41. Bryce Wood, *San Juan Island: Coastal Place Names and Cartographic Nomenclature* (n.p.: University Microfilms International for Washington State Historical Society, 1980), 93–94, discusses descendants of the Hawaiian known as Joe Friday, after whom Friday Harbor on San Juan Island was named. Robert H. Ruby and John A. Brown conclude in *The Chinook Indians: Traders of the Lower Columbia River* (Norman: University of Oklahoma Press, 1976) that, at the expiry of their contracts, most of the Hawaiians who had families by Indigenous women simply abandoned them in favour of returning home.

27 Cited in Duncan, *Minority without a Champion*, 15; also Duncan, "Minority without a Champion," 106–7.

28 See David W. Forbes, *An Act to Prohibit Hawaiians from Emigrating to California "Where They May Die in Misery"* (1850; San Francisco: Paul Markham Kahn, 1986); also *The Friend*, March 1, 1849, 20, and November 15, 1849, 79.

29 Charles W. Kenn gives the examples of Edwin Mahuka, a "Native of Sandwich Islands," and Jim Crow, "another kanaka," both of whom were naturalized in 1871 and became registered voters in Sutter County in 1880. Charles W. Kenn, "Descendants of Captain Sutter's Kanakas," in *Proceedings of the Second Annual Meeting of the Conference of California Historical Societies*, ed. Richard Coke Wood (Stockton: College of the Pacific, 1956), 94–95, 96–97.

30 See *The Friend*, February 1861, 13; July 1, 1862, 49; February 2, 1863, 10; and August 1868, 69. Also see Kenn, "Descendants of Captain Sutter's Kanakas," 87–101; Charles W. Kenn, "Sutter's Canacas," *Conference of California Historical Societies* 2.2 (1955): 3–6; Charles W. Kenn, "Sutter's Hawaiians," *Honolulu Star-Bulletin*, February 11, 1956, 4–5; Richard H. Dillon, "Kanaka Colonies in California," *Pacific Historical Review* 24 (February 1955): 17–23; and Margaret A. Ramsland, *The Forgotten Californians* (n.p.: Jensen Graphic, 1974).

31 Conversation with Karey Litton, Victoria, June 19, 1991.

32 See the recollection of Lila Hannah Firth, "Early Life on San Juan Island," typescript, San Juan Library; interview with Miss B. Hamilton, Mrs. Ina Hamilton, and Mrs. A. Mabel Davis, 1965, BC Archives, tape no. 830.

33 Interview with Jack and Paul Roland, June 27, 1977, BC Archives, tape no. 3807.

34 Interview with Hamilton, Hamilton, and Davis.

35 Partial exceptions are reflected in David Kittelson, "John Coxe: Hawaii's First Soldier of Fortune," *Hawaii Historical Review* (January 1965): 194–98; Yvonne Mearns Klan, "Kanaka William," *Beaver* 38 (Spring 1979): 38–43; Margaret Nicholls, "Kamano—A Kanaka," *British Columbia Historical News* 24, 3 (1991): 12–15; and Jean Barman, "William Naukana," *Dictionary of Canadian Biography*, online.

36 Lists given in Naughton, "Hawaiians in the Fur Trade," 39–41.

37 Kalama: Fort Nes Perces, 1837–1840, middleman; Snake Party, 1840–1841, middleman; Fort Nisqually, 1841–1843, middleman; Fort Vancouver depot, 1843–1844, middleman or labourer, and 1844–1847, labourer. Kalemaku: Fort Vancouver depot, 1845–1846, labourer; New Caledonia, 1846–1847, labourer. Kalenopale: Fort Vancouver, 1844–1845, labourer. Kaluaikai: Fort Vancouver depot, 1845–1847. Kamai: Fort Vancouver, 1844–1845, labourer; Fort Vancouver depot, 1845–1846, labourer; New Caledonia, 1846–1847.

38 See Barman and Watson, *Leaving Paradise*.

39 Jason Allard, "Reminiscences," 10–11, in BC Archives, EC A1, 5A.

40 Ovanin, *Island Heritage Buildings*, 85.

41 "'Jumbo' Nahu," *Indian Time* (Vancouver) 3.2 (1957): 24.

42 Naughton, "Hawaiians in the Fur Trade," 37.

43 "St. Ann's Baptisms-Marriages, 1886–1896," held at St. Edward's Church, Duncan.

44 Records of St. Ann's Church, Duncan, and St. Paul's Church, Saltspring Island, held respectively at St. Edward's Church, Duncan, and St. Paul's Church, Saltspring Island. St. Paul's began maintaining its own records only in 1910.

45 Fort Vancouver depot, 1843–1846, labourer; Fort Vancouver, 1846–1849, labourer.

46 "Police Court," *Colonist* (Victoria), June 18, 1873; also May 27; June 7, 17–19, 21, and 25, 1873; October 10, 25 and 29, 1873; and March 7, 1874.

47 "'Joe': His Full Confession," *Colonist*, March 13, 1874.

48 "Salt Spring Island Polling Division," *List of Voters in the Several Electoral Districts in British Columbia in Force on the First of September, 1881* (Victoria: Government Printer, 1881), 152.

49 Household 160, 191 Vancouver (Cowichan), 1881 manuscript census of British Columbia; household 47, 3 Vancouver (Salt Spring Island), 1891 manuscript census of British Columba; and household 95, Vancouver, Victoria North, Saltspring, 1901 manuscript census of British Columbia.

50 Bea Hamilton, *Salt Spring Island* (Vancouver: Mitchell Press, 1969), 79–81.

51 Household 160, 191 Vancouver (Cowichan), 1881 manuscript census of British Columbia; household 47, 3 Vancouver (Salt Spring Island) and household 69, Victoria North (Saltspring), 1901 manuscript census of British Columbia.

52 Ovanin, *Island Heritage Buildings*, 85.

53 Notice no. 5, January 1843, cited in *Notices and Voyages*, 104.

54 Donald E. Waite, *The Langley Story Illustrated* (Maple Ridge: Don Waite Publishing, 1977), 14; and Jamie Morton, *Fort Langley: An Overview of the Operations of a Diversified Fur Trade Post, 1848 to 1858 and the Physical Context in 1858* (Ottawa: Environment Canada, 1980), 288–89.

55 Allard, "Reminiscences," 10–11.

56 Allard, "Reminiscences"; Morton, *Fort Langley*, 186, 269.

57 See the January 12, 1858, entry in Dorothy Blakey Smith, ed., "The Journal of Arthur Thomas Bushby, 1858–1859," *British Columbia Historical Quarterly* 21 (1957–58): 127.

58 Sheila Nickols, ed., *Maple Ridge: A History of Settlement* (Maple Ridge: Municipal Hall, 1972), 33; Waite, *The Langley Story Illustrated*, 102.

59 Conversation by Major Matthews, Vancouver archivist, with Herbert Nahu, April 1, 1940, City of Vancouver Archives, Add. Ms. 54.

60 Conversation by Major Matthews with Walter Keamo, April 18, 1952, City of Vancouver Archives, Add. Ms 54.

61 Conversation by Major Matthews with Mrs. Donald Robert Smith (granddaughter of Eihu, who lived at Kanaka Ranch), February 8, 1937; and with Walter Keamo, April 18, 1952, City of Vancouver Archives, Add. Ms 54.

62 "The Migration of Hawaiians," courtesy of Tom and Leila Johnston Lane.

63 "A Kanaka Row," *Colonist*, May 12, 1860.

64 Victoria directories of 1887 and 1895, cited in "Kanakas in British Columbia," in BC Archives, Vertical Files.

65 Interview with Hamilton, Hamilton, and Davis.

66 W.F. Tolmie to Henry Fry, Cloverdale, Victoria District, June 8, 1885, in BC Archives.

67 Conversation with Loretta Roland, Fulford Harbour, Saltspring Island, February 24, 1991.

68 For comparable photos from California, see Kenn, "Sutter's Hawaiians," 4–5.

69 This assessment is based on the correspondence in "Hawaii Officials Abroad," Foreign Office and Executive File, Hawaii State Archives.

70 Henry Rhodes, Hawaiian consul, to Governor Frederick Seymour, Victoria, March 6, 1869, enclosing petition; statement of Peter Kakua, Victoria, March 5, 1869; Henry Rhodes to Minister of Foreign Relations, Victoria, May 18, 1869, in "Hawaii Officials Abroad: Consul at Victoria." See also W.J. Illerbrun, "'Kanaka Pete,'" *Hawaiian Journal of History* 6 (1972): 156–66.

71 Interview with Jack and Paul Roland.

72 Conversation with Rosemary Unger, Victoria, June 22, 1990, based on research notes of Paul Roland.

73 Duncan, *Minority without a Champion*, 12.

74 Nicholls, "Kemano—A Kanaka," 12.

75 See photo in Hamilton, *Salt Spring Island*, 61; also interview with Hamilton, Hamilton, and Davis.

76 "St. Ann's Baptisms-Marriages 1859–1885," held at St. Edward's Church, Duncan.

77 Plan of graves in graveyard beside the church, courtesy of Rosemary Tahouney Unger.

78 Interview with Jack and Paul Roland.

79 "Pupils' Register Number 1, St. Ann's Convent, Cowichan, Vancouver Island, 1864–April 1929," Sisters of St. Ann, Victoria Archives, RG II, S 36, box 1.

80 See Hamilton, *Salt Spring Island*, 81.

81 Conversation with Vina Shepard, Victoria, June 27, 1990.

82 Conversation with Rosemary Unger, Victoria, June 27, 1990; see also Jean Barman, "Maria Mahoi," and "William Naukana," *Dictionary of Canadian Biography*, online; and Jean Barman, *Maria Mahoi of the Islands*, 2nd ed. (Vancouver: New Star, 2017).

83 Conversation with Bea Shepard, Vina Shepard, and Rosemary Unger, Victoria, June 27, 1990.

84 Charles A. Miller, *Valley of the Stave* (Surrey, BC: Hancock, 1981), 28–33.

85 Naughton, "Hawaiians in the Fur Trade," 75.

86 "The Hawaiian Connection: The Aponi Family," courtesy of Tom and Leila Johnston Lane. "The Migration of Hawaiians," 53, includes "Alepau, Wife and 3 children departing from Honolulu to Victoria on May 11, 1866." Mary Kaaiopioopio, buried at Anglican Christ Church Cathedral cemetery in Victoria on December 31, 1865, aged 43 (Christ Church Cathedral, Burial Records, on microfilm in BC Archives), was likely the wife of William Kaulehelehe, who came to Fort Vancouver in 1845, along with his wife, Mary Kaai, as a teacher, interpreter, and minister to the Hawaiian employees, and who later moved to Victoria (see Klan, "Kanake William"). There is no indication that they had any children.

87 Conversation with Rosemary Unger, June 27, 1990, based on information from her mother, Sophie Roland, daughter of Naukana's youngest daughter, Matilda.

88 Conversation with Loretta Roland.

89 For more precise geographical descriptions, see Naughton, "Hawaiians in the Fur Trade," 52–53.

90 Interview with Hamilton, Hamilton, and Davis.

91 Interview with Jack and Paul Roland.

92 Firth, "Early Life on San Juan Island."

93 John Barrow, ed., *Captain Cook's Voyages of Discovery* (London: Dent and Sons, 1906), 434.

94 Conversation with Loretta Roland.

95 Clellan S. Ford, *Smoke from Their Fires: The Life of a Kwakiutl Chief* (New Haven, CT: Yale University Press, 1941), 202–3.

96 Conversation with Dale Seeley, Campbell River, July 22, 1992.

97 Terry Glavin, "Legacy of Forgotten Hawaiians Seen throughout B.C. Coast," *Vancouver Sun*, May 25, 1991.

98 Maurice Nahannee, "Nahannee's Notebook," *Kahtou News* (Vancouver), August 1, 1992.

Navigating Schooling

13
Lost Nanaimo

Taking Back Our Past

The complexities of school attendance in British Columbia cut across gender, space and race. Incoming coal miners and their families from Britain in the 1850s stuck to their working-class traditions in that their daughters wed and their sons began work in the mines as young as twelve, although men were on average older when they married than the girls and young women. Although offered free public education, these families failed to take full advantage of it for many years. At the same time, the assumption of racial superiority common among the white elite meant that the presence of ethnically diverse others generally did not make it into early accounts of Nanaimo, although there were local Indigenous people, notably the Snuneymuxw, Iroquois men who had worked for the HBC, and Hawaiians among the population. Barman examines the 1907 memoir of Mark Bate, a businessman and mayor, as evidence that the existence of the Indigenous wives of many settler men was obscured. She notes how men with Indigenous wives removed themselves from the disdain of their neighbours by pre-empting land on Gabriola, Saltspring, and other Gulf Islands. Ironically, these families, in contrast to the descendants of the white mining families from Britain, were invested in their children's education, presumably realizing that it would be key to negotiating a social world essentially hostile to those with mixed ancestry.

By Jean Barman. Reprinted with permission from *Shale* 8 (June 2004): 16–26. Winner of BC Historical Federation's award for best article published in *British Columbia History* in 2006.

In my general history of British Columbia, *The West beyond the West*, I noted briefly the Hudson's Bay Company's (HBC's) relocation of its coal mining operations from Fort Rupert at the north end of Vancouver Island to Nanaimo in November 1852. I then went on to populate Nanaimo with the miners remaining from the failed Fort Rupert enterprise and with "some two dozen others and their families brought out from England" two years later on the *Princess Royal*.

There are twenty or so subsequent references to Nanaimo in my book, all of which relate to the mining economy, and to the coal miners' struggle for better working conditions. This is of course a topic that is very pertinent to the labour relations and political climate in British Columbia today. What I had done was construct Nanaimo's history from a contemporary perspective.

What I have since come to realize, and what I want to explore here, is the danger of this approach is that we may lose some aspects of the past simply because they do not accord with our present-day interests. We need to take back the past as it was, not as we would have it be. We need to learn to drive in two directions. Most often we use our present-day understandings as our vehicle for moving back in time. Far less often do we head in the other direction by taking the past on its own terms. When we do so, we are likely to encounter a lot of diversions and perhaps some dead ends. In other words, while the present leads rather easily into the past, or rather into the particular past toward which we choose to head, going from the "actual" past to the present is a far more difficult undertaking.

When we dare to take back the past on its own terms, we may well discover, in the much repeated opening lines of British writer L.P. Hartley's novel *The Go-Between*, published in 1953, that "the past is a foreign country, they do things differently [there]."

The history of Nanaimo, or, for that matter, of any other community in British Columbia, is, I suspect, not so neat and tidy as we would like, once we examine it as it was rather than as we would have it be. Looked at in this light, there are, I think, two important aspects of Nanaimo's early history that may have faded from view—an excess of tradition and the erasure of diversity.

By an excess of tradition, I mean that the societal values the *Princess Royal* families brought with them from England were so firmly held that they became, over time, more of a hindrance than a help to their making their way in the new world. By erasure of diversity, I mean that difference, particularly racial difference, was much more present in Nanaimo than the blip at the beginning made it out to be.

Each of these two propositions—an excess of tradition and the erasure of diversity—may sound contentious, but please bear with me as I try to make my case.

Early Nanaimo

Early Nanaimo is usually conceived, as I summarized in *The West beyond the West*, as having two stages. First the HBC; then the *Princess Royal*. As Richard Mackie reminds us in his book *Trading beyond the Mountains*, by the middle of the century the HBC had long since diversified away from furs—it had gone "beyond the mere traffic in peltries."[1]

The HBC began mining coal at Fort Rupert in 1849 to supply Royal Navy ships plying the Pacific coast. Three years later, mining operations were moved to Nanaimo for a variety of reasons, including the higher quality of coal to be found there; disputes with the northern Indigenous people over who actually owned the coal; and the HBC's inexperienced and inept management of its first coal mining venture.

It is generally accepted that the people of Nanaimo were from many different backgrounds up until the arrival of the miners and their families on the *Princess Royal* in November 1854. Indigenous people played a role in both the discovery of the coal and its extraction in the early days. The first schoolteacher, young Charles Bayley, recorded how, on his arrival in 1853, "the population of Nanaimo or Colville Town as it was named by the H.B.Co. was about one hundred and twenty-five composed of Whites, French Canadians, Iroquois, Kanakas [Hawaiians] and half Breeds, a motley crowd."[2]

In this view of the past, written as we perhaps would like to see it unfold from the perspective of the present day, the Nanaimo Bayley evoked was already giving way to another way of life on the model we associate with settler societies. The only element of diversity generally recognized as continuing was Chinese miners. Discriminatory attitudes toward them are well known, as is their material legacy in Nanaimo's Chinatowns.

What was celebrated from Nanaimo's first years, as was long proclaimed on the Nanaimo Museum website, was the "birth of the first white girl, Margaret," to the McGregors on March 16, 1853, and then "the first white boy born in Nanaimo," Alexander Dunsmuir, shortly after on June 2. These first white children came from among the families who had come on earlier vessels.

An Excess of Tradition

The seminal moment for early Nanaimo is most often considered to be the arrival in November 1854 of the *Princess Royal*. It was part of the agreement made in 1849 between the HBC and the British government that, in return for proprietorial rights to Vancouver Island, the

HBC would undertake to establish a settlement of resident colonists. It was also in the interests of the company to promote long-term stability. Accordingly, the HBC recruited intact mining families in Britain. Twenty-three men, twenty of them with wives and over half with children, came on the *Princess Royal* in 1854 to become, in the words of early British Columbia chroniclers G.P.V. and Helen B. Akrigg, "the true founders of Nanaimo."[3] While some of the arrivals briefly chased other opportunities, in particular the riches to be had from gold, none of them returned home. As one early resident enthused, "not one of the passengers who came out on the *Princess Royal*, and who were entitled to a return passage, in terms of their engagement, embraced the opportunity to go back."[4]

Rather, the *Princess Royal* contingent put their backs to the task. Faced with Charles Bayley's "motley crowd," they had to scramble for authority, and perhaps for that reason may have scrambled doubly hard to assert a way of life that was familiar to them from their lives in England. As argued by John Belshaw, "the miners' identity as miners went beyond the business of work and was something that the miners themselves were engaged in fashioning."[5] The priority given to recruiting mining families of good character almost ensured that they would seek to retain familiar ways. They followed these ways so fully in their new setting that tradition became a trap.

An excess of tradition had very real consequences for the second and subsequent generations. Thanks to Peggy Nicholls's meticulous research on the *Princess Royal* families, it is possible to get a fairly good sense of their priorities for their offspring.[6] It was assumed daughters would marry young, and that sons would go to work even younger.

The forty-two daughters of the first generation who can be followed into marriage in the Nanaimo area wed between twelve and twenty-seven years of age. Some of the latter were held back by virtue of having, as said about one of them, "to sew and to help care for the seven babies that followed her."[7] Even so, seven out of every ten daughters were wed by the time they were eighteen years old.

Sons followed their fathers into the pits. While I do not have overall data, Peggy Nicholls's examples suggest that they did so at an early age, much as they would have in England had they stayed there. The Ganner family arrived with two sons, to quote from the correspondence prior to their departure, "aged respectively abt 13 and 11 [who] have worked in the mines for some two or three years."[8] Similarly, ten-year-old John Hawkes went to work underground in 1863, coupling coal cars to be hauled by mules to the sorting bins.[9] His friend John Meakin was given the same task a year later,[10] as was George Sage in 1865 at the age of ten.[11]

Sam Thompson, who went to work in 1868, may have begun at the even younger age of nine, because his first job was to load coal cars for his father. Unlike the others, who earned seventy-five cents for an eight-hour day, Sam recalled receiving only board and pocket money.[12] Because another *Princess Royal* son, George Bevilockway, was considered a particularly good student, his entry into the mines was delayed until the age of fourteen in 1871. He confirmed the worth of his additional schooling by soon becoming an assistant manager.[13]

If sons went to work young, they did not necessarily immediately follow their sisters into marriage but tended to wait awhile. The twenty-five sons who can be traced from the *Princess Royal* contingent wed between twenty and thirty-seven years of age. Only half of them were married by their mid-twenties.

Once ingrained, the force of tradition was hard to break in Nanaimo. Attitudes toward schooling make the case. The new province of British Columbia, created in 1871, was determined to give children equality of opportunity by making schooling free and non-denominational. Viewed from the perspective of the present day, we might almost take for granted that families would make use of the opportunity. When we take the past seriously, on its own terms, we quickly discover that this was not the case, certainly not in a community like Nanaimo, bound to the traditions whence families came. The trap that tradition became precluded Nanaimo offspring from taking advantage of a public good intended to serve all young British Columbians.

Nanaimo families' attitudes were evident from early on. The first head of education in the province, John Robson, noted that on the day he visited the Nanaimo school in 1872, just eleven boys and sixteen girls were present, whereas the community likely contained about 175 children of school age. Numbers gradually rose, but twice as fast for girls, and Robson noted somewhat wryly two years later that "there are probably as many boys as girls in the town."[14]

The adherence to tradition gave Nanaimo children little motivation to either go to school or behave while there. Robson's report from the mid-1870s read: "When the school was visited, the senior classes in both departments were little advanced in their studies. The boys were noisy and disorderly." Robson was well aware of the reason: "A disposition on the part of many parents to send their children into 'the pit' at an early age is exercising a prejudicial influence on the rising generation by depriving them of the advantages of free school education."[15]

Cases of "truancy" were especially high in Nanaimo. In 1880–1881, for example, 23 cases were reported in the provincial capital of Victoria among 310 enrolled boys, whereas Nanaimo recorded 70 cases among 148 boys.[16] The relative proportions were one for every sixteen boys in Victoria; one for every two boys in Nanaimo.

In 1876, written examinations were held for admission into the new public high school established in Victoria, the first in the province. Whereas 54 out of 70 Victoria students who took the exam passed, not one of the 26 who sat for it in Nanaimo did so. The average score was 277 in Victoria, 139 in the other principal city of New Westminster, and just 53 in Nanaimo.[17] A year later, no one from Nanaimo even bothered to sit the high school entrance examination.

The head of the provincial system again despaired:

> It is a difficult matter to raise and maintain a high standard of attainment in the senior division [of the elementary school

> in Nanaimo] in consequence of pupils being withdrawn from school at a much earlier age than they ought to be. Parents should not under any consideration send their children into the mines, or give them employment above ground, till the before mentioned examination has been creditably passed.[18]

Over time, some Nanaimo boys did sit for the exam, but very rarely did the few who passed then bother to go on to high school.[19]

In 1886, a high school finally opened in Nanaimo itself. Attitudes toward it demonstrate the extent to which the traditions put in place by the first generation still held firm. Just twelve pupils enrolled. The problem lay, school authorities explained, in many being "engaged in pursuits by which they were enabled to support themselves or assist their parents."[20] In the late 1880s, growing racism led to Chinese miners being prohibited from working underground. The school inspector lamented the consequence: "Owing to the exclusion of Chinese from the mines, a great many of our boys left school to fill their places, and consequently deprived us of some of our best material."[21] The high school by this time contained nine boys and sixteen girls, whereas Nanaimo's elementary schools enrolled 430 children.

The only change came from the outside in the form of provincial regulations raising the entry age for mining. The earliest restricted boys under fourteen from working underground except with special ministerial permission. Only after the turn of the century were boys under fourteen completely banned from the pits. Even then they could still do clerical work above ground. A school official admonished Nanaimo parents at length in 1893:

> The great inducements held out to boys of thirteen to fifteen years of age to work in the coal mines naturally draws a large number from the school every year, and place the senior divisions at a great disadvantage. You will notice, by the list of pupils, quite a number of the boys of the age above mentioned

> have gone to work, thus carrying off the material that should go to the High School.[22]

This excess of tradition had unintended consequences. By the time Nanaimo parents realized the value of schooling, the damage was done from the perspective of provincial authorities. Helen Brown has written about the enormous efforts made in Nanaimo during the 1890s to improve the quality of schooling, but by then no one much was listening.[23] Provincial officials had despaired, and one of the consequences was large class size. Nanaimo's growth in population exacerbated the situation. Fifty, sixty, and more pupils were crammed into a single classroom. The only solution, the Nanaimo school board decided in 1899, lay in having "one half of these divisions attend school in the morning and one half in the afternoon."[24] Near the end of the year, sixty elementary children were moved into the high school building, which was still being underused.[25] By this time, some secondary education had become the norm in urban areas of British Columbia, but not in Nanaimo. Peggy Nicholls suggests, astutely, that one of the factors eventually moderating the situation was local teachers from Nanaimo, who understood the familial and job pressures being put on students.[26]

The Erasure of Diversity

Not only an excess of tradition, but also the erasure of diversity was a fundamental aspect of early Nanaimo's history. Virtually all of the men and women who put themselves in charge of settler society on Vancouver Island and across British Columbia shared similar attitudes toward diversity. Seeing themselves as white and on that basis inherently superior, they looked down on persons with darker skin tones. Indigenous people were to be disparaged, and all others who were perceived as not wholly white belittled. If not physically removed, they were at the least to be erased from view.

This perspective comes through loud and clear in the recollections of one of Nanaimo's most prominent early residents, Mark Bate, who arrived in 1857 at the age of twenty on a subsequent voyage of the *Princess Royal*. Within a dozen years, Bate was manager of the Vancouver Coal Mining and Land Company, which in 1862 bought out the Hudson's Bay Company. As well as running the company employing most Nanaimo residents, Bate was mayor for much of the time between 1876 and the end of the century. His reminiscences, published in 1907, provide one of the most graphic portraits of early Nanaimo to survive. They give us unusual insight into how the dominant view of its history was constructed by the men who had put themselves in charge.

Mark Bate's perspective on diversity has two components. The first is his determination to reduce the contribution of the HBC employees, who had, quite literally, built Nanaimo, into something of little consequence. Exemplary is his view of Narcisse Montigny, an HBC employee who arrived in Nanaimo in 1854 or 1855. According to Bate, "Montigny was an Axeman who supplied the Poles for House building, etc. etc. He was an uncouth, gruff, customer, who used to have lively times with the Iroquois, and others of his Tillicums. He left Nanaimo in 1858 for Fort Hope."[27] Bate's very visible sigh of relief that such persons departed and could thereby be erased from Nanaimo's history is even more evident in his description of three Iroquois he names as Lazaar Oreasta, Tomo Sakiowatti, and Louis Oteekorie who, in his words, "left Nanaimo prior to the termination of the Hudson's Bay Company's regime."[28] While acknowledging the contribution of the trio, and also of their fellow Iroquois Tomo Aumtony, to city building, he emphasized how Sakiowatti, for instance, was "a rather wild, quarrelsome fellow" who "was often mixed up with drunken carousals and brawls."[29] Mark Bate took great pride that, in the first census taken in February 1857, all of the 132 persons counted as living in Nanaimo were English, Scottish, and Irish, "excepting" five Iroquois, two each French Canadians and Hawaiians, and one Norwegian.[30]

The second, linked component of Bate's erasure of diversity relates to his attitude toward Indigenous people. Bate sharply differentiated between men and women among the "250 S'nenymos" who, according to his calculations, lived in Nanaimo in the 1850s.[31] Bate considered Indigenous women useful to city building, noting, for instance, how "a number of Indian women were employed carrying clay" to build the dam that provided the water power to run the first sawmill.[32] Bate was especially laudatory in his description of early work processes: "Coal was conveyed in canoes for shipment... thrown into a lighter made fast alongside a vessel, thence hoisted or shoveled on board. In this work of conveyance, the Indian women, as well as the men were engaged—the former, as a rule, earning the most wages, or goods."[33]

Bate's recognition of Indigenous women went only so far. As with his need to erase the HBC link, he was determined to hide from view another aspect of Nanaimo's early history. A long-time gender imbalance in the newcomer population across British Columbia encouraged relationships between Indigenous women and newcomer men. The 1857 census of non-Indigenous Nanaimo counted 58 males, 21 females, and 54 children. There were, in other words, two men in the newcomer population for every woman.[34] The situation did not much change. In 1870, there were 395 newcomer men compared to 206 women, or twice as many men as women.[35] Through the end of the nineteenth century, British Columbia as a whole counted two to three newcomer men for every newcomer woman.

Mark Bate, like most of his contemporaries, would have none of this. The unions that numerous men, in Nanaimo as elsewhere, formed with Indigenous women simply did not exist from his perspective. In his published recollections, Bate gave wives to all but one of the *Princess Royal* contingent and to four other men who came out on earlier vessels. These women he described in glowing terms. They were "faithful,"[36] "a good mother, a good house manager,"[37] "a kind-hearted, generous woman who delighted in 'doing a good turn.'"[38] They were all white women.

In sharp contrast, at least three Englishmen, three from the Orkneys in northern Scotland, a Welshman, a couple of French Canadians, and a couple of Iroquois who Bate mentions at length were described as if they were wifeless, when in reality they had Indigenous wives.[39] Bate could be enormously flattering about these men. He characterizes Englishman William Sampson as building up "a valuable Estate" on Saltspring Island, but as if he did so all by himself.[40] With James Stove from the Orkneys, who remained in Nanaimo, Bate described how he, "with much steady, persevering labour, made himself a home there which is today, with its alluringly pleasant surroundings, as pretty a spot as one could wish for."[41] Bate erased Stove's Indigenous wife, just as he did the others.

The only time Bate acknowledged a man having a family by an Indigenous woman was for the purpose of ridicule. A Welsh miner named Thomas Jones is described as "a run-away military man from Uncle Sam's domain" who died in 1864 and "was father, by the way, of Azariah Jones, known in town as the 'Dummy.'"[42]

Bate effectively erased Indigenous women from the history of Nanaimo. They could not, almost by definition, be faithful wives, or indeed wives at all. What is absolutely clear is that the Nanaimo Mark Bate and others erased did not disappear. Diversity was, rather, lost from view in the determination of the *Princess Royal* contingent and others to construct the Nanaimo of their aspirations.

An early glimpse of the diversity that marked Nanaimo comes from February 1860, when a Victoria newspaper reported that a twelve-year-old Indigenous girl, who had supposedly "already been the victim of a white man's passions under the guise of keeping house for him," was found dead in the home of a Nanaimo man named Weston. Not only was she discovered there, but the article also claimed that Weston's "Indian woman" had been feeding the dead girl liquor in order to secure her "possession" by another man.[43] Bate recalled William Weston, almost certainly the same man, only as "the village Constable, Nanaimo's first 'bobby.'"[44] Clearly, Bate kept in contact with

Weston, for he described Weston's death a couple of years before Bate was writing in 1907.

Another glimpse comes from a decade and a half later, December 1876, when the British Columbia Reserve Commission visited the Nanaimo area to confirm Indian reserves. As Cole Harris documents in *Making Native Space*, the commission's principal goal was to free up as much of the province as possible for newcomer settlement.[45] Thus, not unexpectedly, the three commissioners first consulted with Mark Bate in his dual capacities as mayor and manager of the town's principal employer, the Vancouver Coal Company. The commissioners next met with local Indigenous chiefs, when, to quote from the commission's report, "the evils of concubinage of their young women with the white men around were specifically pointed out."[46] The commissioners almost certainly admonished the Indigenous chiefs at Bate's request, given that no similar lecture was delivered to chiefs anywhere else on Vancouver Island or the Lower Mainland. In other words, Bate was well aware of the diversity he was determined to erase and sought, via the commission, to persuade Indigenous men to stamp it out by prohibiting their daughters from consorting with newcomer men.

We can also glimpse the erasure of diversity from the perspective of the men themselves. Despite all the attempts to ridicule and discourage such relationships, they persisted. The gender differential within the newcomer population virtually ensured that only some of the men at work in the mines would find marital partners of similar backgrounds to themselves. The relatively older ages at which *Princess Royal* sons married than did their sisters testify to the paucity of marriageable young white women. Girls as young as twelve were routinely courted, and sometimes persuaded into wedlock.

Numerous men working in Nanaimo opted for Indigenous women. Hawaiians and Iroquois did so as a matter of course, but so did at least four dozen English, Scots, French Canadian, and others who, in the language of the time, were white. The records of Nanaimo's St. Paul's

Anglican Church, Ebenezer Methodist Church, and St. Peter's Catholic Church make it possible to trace marriages, as do colonial and provincial records. Because of their survival, we gain an appreciation of how men did not so much seek to prostitute women for the short term, as with the Weston incident, but sought them out as life partners through church-sanctioned marriages.

Some men persevered in Nanaimo, though they were likely repeatedly made conscious of the way in which they had diverged from the accepted life course. As just one example, sixteen-year-old Orkney Islander James Malcolm was among the first group of prospective miners brought to Fort Rupert in 1851, then transferred to Nanaimo in November 1852. Within the year he was living with a local Indigenous woman named Emma. Their first child together was born at precisely the same time as the Dunsmuir son hailed historically as the first "white" boy. The HBC's head at Nanaimo informed his superior, James Douglas, in July 1853: "Two births have occurred in this Establishment since the *Cadboro* sailed in the cases of Mrs. Dunsmuir and the native wife of John Malcolm, labourer."[47] James Malcolm married Emma in Ebenezer Methodist Church in 1861. The Malcolms' eight children suffered the consequences of diversity, as with the Nanaimo schoolteacher's equation in 1880 of the Malcolm sons' behaviour with their skin tones: "The Malcolms are half-breeds and it is more difficult to deal with them as they are not looked after at home and they take the other boys away from school with them."[48] Given the high rates of truancy in Nanaimo, it seems likely that the Malcolm sons were only participating in a general phenomenon.

Numerous men responded imaginatively by erasing themselves. From 1859 it was possible to take up land on Vancouver Island and the nearby Gulf Islands by marking out up to 160 acres, registering the claim, taking up residence, and then paying a relatively small sum once the land was surveyed. While Nanaimo was given over to coal mining, nearby islands beckoned, including Gabriola Island, just five kilometres away.

The men who settled Gabriola were certainly not all from Nanaimo, nor did they all have Indigenous wives. But as June Lewis-Harrison describes in her book *The People of Gabriola*, a preponderance of early settlers fit both categories.[49] The first pre-emptor was Nanaimo carpenter Alexander McFarlane in January 1863. He was followed two months later by two and likely three Nanaimo miners, Richard Chapple, Thomas Degnan, and Thomas Jones, and over the next several years by at least a dozen men who, like their predecessors, had families by Indigenous women. Some of these men lived on Gabriola prior to taking up land, and numerous of them commuted to work in Nanaimo mines as they attempted to make their Gabriola holdings self-supporting.

Other men with Indigenous wives took other courses of action. Saltspring Island attracted a larger group of men with families by Indigenous women, including one-time Nanaimo resident Henry Sampson. Other men sought out an island of their own. Joe Silvey pre-empted smaller Reid Island north of Saltspring. Although he never lived in Nanaimo, for him as for many other islanders it was their market town.[50]

By losing themselves from view, families on islands gained greater opportunities to manage their children's upbringing. In the case of Gabriola, parents repeatedly made clear the value they attached to the school. In 1874, the provincial Superintendent of Education, John Jessop, described how there were "thirteen children in attendance, all half-breeds."[51] The designation was not, however, nearly as judgmental as it might have been in Nanaimo, for the Superintendent found much to praise. "Second class reading & spelling very good—All in first Reader last spring—First Reading Class making fair improvement … Children orderly & well behaved & making good progress."[52] Jessop enthused that the "parents also (in great contrast with other districts) are much interested in the school and careful to keep up the attendance."[53] Unlike those in Nanaimo, Gabriola parents took control of the school to the extent of complaining bitterly, a few years later, about a teacher who did not meet their expectations. As to the reason, the Superintendent noted how he "heard complaints of parents respecting the non-improvement of their children."[54] Gabriola parents saw in the school the best possibility for their children to acquire skills permitting them to negotiate their diversity.

Lessons Learned

The very different attitudes of Gabriola and Nanaimo families toward the principal state institution of the day, the public school, make little sense so long as we persist in viewing the past from the perspective of the present day. It is very hard to understand why parents would not take advantage of the opportunity for free education. Staying in school a year or two longer would not have lost Nanaimo daughters a husband or sons a job in the mines. It is equally difficult to comprehend why parents on Gabriola erased themselves from view rather than fighting for their rights, in line with today's priorities. It does appear that, yes, the past is a foreign country.

Parents' actions become comprehensible once we take the past on its own terms. An excess of tradition caused Nanaimo families to lose sight of the opportunities formal education might offer their children. Families marked by diversity were both erased by others and erased themselves.

The direction in which families headed, whether in Nanaimo or on islands like Gabriola, did not necessarily lead down a straight road to the present day. As Helen Brown has so well demonstrated, Nanaimo families had to work very hard during the 1890s and subsequently to diverge from the path they had set for themselves toward the educational mainstream. In similar fashion, it was only as negative attitudes toward race moderated in the dominant society in the later twentieth century that families who hid themselves away on islands could comfortably take pride in their distinctive identities.

By treating history not as a reflection of ourselves, but as a foreign country, we acquire a greater appreciation of why it is that individuals acted as they did. We need to learn to drive in two directions. By doing so, we can take back the past on its own terms to discover that, yes, they did do things differently there.

Notes

1 Richard Mackie, *Trading beyond the Mountains* (Vancouver: UBC Press, 1997), 218.
2 Charles Bayley, "Early Life on Vancouver Island," typescript in BC Archives, E/B/B34.2, 6–7.
3 G.P.V. Akrigg and Helen B. Akrigg, *British Columbia Chronicle, 1847–1871: Gold and Colonists* (Vancouver: Discovery Press, 1977), 78. I am grateful to Barry Humphrey for alerting me to this reference.
4 Mark Bate, "Closing Chapters of History of Nanaimo," *Nanaimo Free Press*, May 18, 1907.
5 John Belshaw, *Colonization and Community: The Vancouver Island Coalfield and the Making of the British Columbian Working Class* (Montreal/Kingston: McGill-Queen's University Press, 2002), 212.
6 Peggy Nicholls, *From the Black Country to Nanaimo, 1854*, 5 volumes, (Nanaimo: Nanaimo Historical Society, 1991–95).
7 Amanda Meakin in Nicholls, *From the Black Country*, vol. 5.
8 Ganner family in Nicholls, *From the Black Country*, vol. 4.
9 John Hawkes in Nicholls, *From the Black Country*, vol. 3.
10 John Meakin in Nicholls, *From the Black Country*, vol. 3.
11 George Sage in Nicholls, *From the Black Country*, vol. 4.
12 Samuel Thompson in Pearl C. Reynolds, "60-Year-Old Photograph Awakens Memories of Early Nanaimo," *Vancouver Sun*, March 25, 1944, p. 25 of Magazine section.
13 George Bevilockway in Nicholls, *From the Black Country*, vol. 3.
14 BC Department of Education, Annual Report (1874), 17.
15 BC Department of Education, Annual Report (1876), 94.
16 BC Department of Education, Annual Report (1881), 270–71.
17 BC Department of Education, Annual Report (1876), 128.
18 BC Department of Education, Annual Report (1877), 19.
19 BC Department of Education, Annual Report (1885), 313.
20 BC Department of Education, Annual Report (1886), 144–45.
21 BC Department of Education, Annual Report (1888), 199.
22 BC Department of Education, Annual Report (1893), 542.
23 Helen Brown, "Binaries, Boundaries, and Hierarchies: The Special Relations of City Schooling in Nanaimo, British Columbia" (PhD diss., University of British Columbia, 1999).
24 Nanaimo School Board, Minutes, meeting of September 2, 1899, also December 2, 1899, Nanaimo Archives (NA).
25 Nanaimo School Board, Minutes, meeting of December 28, 1899, NA.
26 Peggy Nicholls, conversation with the author, May 7, 2004.
27 Mark Bate, "The Men Who Helped to Build Nanaimo," *Nanaimo Free Press*, March 26, 1907.
28 Bate, "The Men Who Helped to Build Nanaimo."
29 Bate, "The Men Who Helped to Build Nanaimo." To be fair to Bate, many of his observations echoed those of HBC officials, as caught in their correspondence and journals. Bate had possession of the Nanaimo post journal at the time he penned his reminiscence. See the foreword to *Nanaimo Journal, August 1855–March*

1857, BC Archives, A/C/20.1/N15.2; and Nanaimo Correspondence, 1852–1853, BC Archives, A/C/20.1/N15.

30 Mark Bate, "Closing Chapters."

31 Mark Bate, "Reminiscences of Early Nanaimo Days," *Nanaimo Free Press*, February 9, 1907.

32 Mark Bate, "The Men Who Helped to Build Nanaimo."

33 Mark Bate, "Mr. M. Bate, Continues His Nanaimo Reminiscences," *Nanaimo Free Press*, February 16, 1907.

34 Mark Bate, "Closing Chapters."

35 Akrigg and Akrigg, *British Columbia Chronicle, 1847–1871*, 404.

36 Mark Bate, "Sketch of Geo. Baker and Other Pioneers," *Nanaimo Free Press*, April 6, 1907; also Bate, "The History of the Early Nanaimo Settlers," *Nanaimo Free Press*, May 4, 1907.

37 Mark Bate, "More Sketches of Old Time Nanaimoites," *Nanaimo Free Press*, April 13, 1907.

38 Mark Bate, "Sketch of Geo. Baker."

39 Described by Bate as wifeless when they had Indigenous wives were Orkney men Isbister, Paley, and Stove; Jones, who was Welsh; Englishmen Martin, Sampson, and Weston; French Canadians Fortier and Montigny; and a couple of Iroquois men.

40 Bate, "The Men Who Helped to Build Nanaimo."

41 Mark Bate, "How Chase River Came by Its Name," *Nanaimo Free Press*, March 30, 1907.

42 Mark Bate, "Closing Chapters."

43 Letter to the Editor, *Victoria Gazette*, February 22, 1860.

44 Mark Bate, "Interesting Early Nanaimo History," *Nanaimo Free Press*, May 11, 1907.

45 Cole Harris, *Making Native Space* (Vancouver: UBC Press, 2002).

46 Alex C. Anderson and Archibald McKinlay, Report of the Proceedings of the Joint Commission for the Settlement of the Indian Reserves in the Province of British Columbia, Victoria, March 21, 1877, in Department of Indian Affairs, RG 10, vol. 3645, file 7936, C-10113, Library and Archives Canada.

47 James William McKay to James Douglas, Nanaimo, July 17, 1853, in Nanaimo Correspondence, 1852–1853, BC Archives, A/C/20.1/N15.

48 John Mundell, teacher at Nanaimo, to C.C. McKenzie, Superintendent of Education, Nanaimo, March 18, 1880, in BC Superintendent of Education, Inward Correspondence, BC Archives, GR 1445.

49 June Lewis-Harrison, *The People of Gabriola* (Gabriola Island, BC: J. Lewis-Harrison, 1982).

50 See Jean Barman, *The Remarkable Adventures of Portuguese Joe Silvey* (Madeira Park, BC: Harbour, 2004).

51 October 3, 1874, entry in John Jessop Diary, BC Archives, GR 1468.

52 October 3, 1874, entry in Jessop Diary.

53 March 23, 1874, entry in Jessop Diary.

54 February 11, 1878, entry in Jessop Diary.

14

Families vs. Schools

Children of Indigenous Descent in British Columbia Classrooms of the Late Nineteenth Century

This essay contrasts two ideologies, one that supported common public schooling for all children, and the other that believed in the Social Darwinist idea that children's abilities were based on their "race." Barman reads the correspondence, letters, and diaries of John Jessop, an advocate of common schooling who was Superintendent of Education in British Columbia between 1872 and 1878. She notes how he stopped highlighting the racial backgrounds of his students in the public record just as he began focusing on them more often in his private writing. She argues that the maintenance of a public rhetoric of common schooling was undermined by a covert expectation that non-white students would not and could not succeed, a belief that became a self-fulfilling prophecy in provincial schools. She notes that the 35,000 letters received by the Superintendent of Education between 1878 and 1897 contained many openly discriminatory comments: white parents did not want their children to mix with their presumed social and intellectual inferiors.

By Jean Barman. Original title "Families vs. Schools: Children of Aboriginal Descent in British Columbia Classrooms of the Late Nineteenth Century." Reprinted with permission from *Family*

Matters: Papers in Post-Confederation Canadian Family History, edited by Edgar-André Montigny and Lori Chambers (Toronto: Canadian Scholars' Press, 1998), 73–89.[1]

By the time British Columbia joined the Canadian Confederation in 1871, an ideology of common schooling was firmly in place across much of North America.[2] Widespread public consensus existed that schools funded by the state should be common to all children in a community, providing them with a roughly equitable basic education regardless of class, gender, ethnicity, or race. The cluster of ideas that came together as common schooling was so pervasive in British Columbia that virtually no opposition existed to provincial legislation passed early in 1872 mandating non-sectarian common schools wherever a minimum number of children could be gathered together.[3]

The ideology of common schooling was not the only cluster of ideas contending for influence during these years. The ideology of racism was also taking hold. It was expected, indeed assumed within the dominant society, that persons who were non-white, non-Protestant, non-northern-European would perform less well, whatever the measure, be it in or out of school. Such persons were, as notions of survival-of-the-fittest growing out of social Darwinism attested, inferior by virtue of their race alone. The prophecy became self-fulfilling. As discrimination intensified, so generations of persons who did not physically mirror members of the dominant society ended up as adults almost entirely at the bottom ranks of Canadian society. As a wide range of scholars have demonstrated, the ideology of racism had enormous impact on Indigenous, Chinese, and Italian people, among others.

During the years of the late nineteenth century, when British Columbia's public school system was being implemented, the largest group of children caught between the two ideologies were those of mixed or sole Indigenous descent. At the time British Columbia entered the Canadian Confederation, its population was estimated at 36,000, dividing between 25,000 or more Indigenous people; about 1,500 Chinese, almost all of them adult males; some 500 Black people; and approximately 8,500 Europeans.[4] The public figures masked two other aspects of the population. The first was linguistic diversity. British Columbia during these years was a truly multilingual province, some children learning initially an Indigenous language or the trading jargon of Chinook, others French or a variety of Michif if descended from a fur trade labourer, Spanish if the offspring of a packer or gold miner from Mexico or South America, or any one of a seemingly infinite variety of tongues. The second was the growing number of persons of mixed Indigenous and non-Indigenous descent. From the beginning of the fur trade in the early part of the century, through the gold rush erupting in 1858, and into the next several decades, it was almost entirely men who had flocked to, and through, the Pacific Northwest. Many formed liaisons with local women enduring long enough for children to receive their father's surname and hence an intermediate status distinguishing them from their mother's people, even where fathers soon departed. Other men settled down with their families to become, very often, the first solely non-Indigenous settlers in a locality, and frequently were at the forefront in getting local schools established.

It was not just families of mixed race but also their Indigenous counterparts who valued formal education. As common schools opened across the far-flung province, there were, to quote an early teacher, "Indian children of school age in the immediate vicinity whose parents express a willingness to send to School," and in the years prior to the emergence of a federal policy on Indigenous education, they were often admitted.[5] The reasons some families made the request are suggested by the published annual reports of the Department of Indian Affairs, as in 1874: "The intelligence of the Indians of that province gives encouragement to the expectation that with liberal encouragement the Indians, who form so large a proportion of the population may, as they are not deficient in enterprise, be transformed into valuable members of the community."[6]

The ideology of common schooling gave families of mixed or sole Indigenous descent every reason to seek out their children's education. They were encouraged to consider common schooling as much for their children's benefit as it was for the benefit of all other children, whereas, unbeknownst to them, their children were being increasingly differentiated and even diminished. Had they been privy to the private as well as the public discourse, they would have realized that schoolteachers and administrators were equally, if not more, influenced by the coterminous ideology of racism. The interaction between the two ideologies virtually ensured that familial aspirations for children of Indigenous descent would be dashed by schools' practice. Instead of families and schools working together to students' advantage, schools became places where children of Indigenous descent were made ashamed of the bi/cultural identity/ies that they inherited from their parents.

The tension between the two ideologies can be detected almost as soon as common schooling began to be implemented in British Columbia under the province's first Superintendent of Education, John Jessop. Read together and contextualized, the public and private sources argue that by the time of Jessop's departure in the spring of 1878, the ideologies of common schooling and of racism had become joined.[7] The process was not necessarily self-conscious, premeditated, or deliberate in intent. No one set out to create a system of common schooling privileging some children over others. Rather, the attributes valued in common schooling were attributes increasingly identified with the white dominant society. The ideology of racism was in effect blended into the ideology of common schooling, even though in official documents the language continued to be inclusive and even welcoming.

John Jessop, an Ontarian who had for a decade been a vocal advocate of common schools on Vancouver Island, took on the job of

Superintendent of Education in the spring of 1872 with an explicit mandate "to secure the sound education of the young generally."[8] For the half-dozen years of his tenancy, as F. Henry Johnson has demonstrated in his biography, Jessop was a virtual whirlwind in his determination to put in place a system of common, or public, schooling on the Ontarian model.[9] In doing so he held almost total authority by virtue of long being the only paid administrator in the province's fledging Department of Education.[10]

Jessop's most effective strategy in turning dream into reality was his regular travels around the province. As well as personally determining just where sufficient numbers of children were in need of schooling, he was able to assess how well existing schools were operating. Jessop's personal travel diaries for the years 1872 to 1878 and his extensive correspondence offer an immediacy of reaction likely reflecting his views much more honestly than did the carefully crafted public reports that followed at the end of each year. Jessop's first visit, to the schools that had survived the financial uncertainties of the transition years from colony to province, began just a month after the legislation had passed and he was named Superintendent.

Jessop's diary entries and their public rendition in the annual reports at first largely corresponded, as reflected in the priorities for schools and for children that he drew out of the ideology of common schooling. Both schools and children were to be orderly, and here Jessop differentiated sharply between schools. On his first visit in the spring of 1872, and subsequently in print, Jessop wrote concerning Cedar Hill outside of Victoria: "Pupils orderly and attentive in their studies."[11] Nanaimo was denounced in his travel diary: "Everything dirty & disorderly—Teacher lacking energy & industry, order & discipline."[12] Publicly he wrote: "Children somewhat disorderly, and but little attention paid to teacher. Discipline and arrangement of studies very deficient ... School-room of the worst possible description."[13] About New Westminster, Jessop noted privately, "Scholars very orderly & quiet,"[14] and publicly, "School orderly and quiet."[15] The other two attributes of the ideology of common schooling that Jessop particularly lauded were discipline and parental support. His travels in the first half of 1874 brought familiar assessments in his diary, although, as the number of schools grew, comments in the annual reports became more summary and sometimes took on a didactic purpose. The public and private spheres remained very similar. For example, privately Jessop found "order and discipline satisfactory" at Metchosin;[16] publicly he emphasized how "the school is efficiently conducted" by an "industrious and painstaking teacher."[17] Nanaimo had not improved. Jessop observed in his diary in 1874, "School noisy and disorderly,"[18] and in his annual report, "There is an almost entire absence of proper discipline and order."[19] Jessop noted approvingly while on Gabriola Island, "Parents also (in great contrast with other districts) are much interested in the school and careful to keep up the attendance."[20] In the annual report he declared, clearly with a broader audience in mind, "Educational facilities are duly appreciated in this district; trustees and parents act in concert with the teacher, thus securing the best possible return for moneys spent for school purposes."[21]

Just as Jessop likely came to his position with his priorities in place concerning the ideology of common schooling, so he must have already reflected on the ideology of racism. In 1861–1864, while running a private school in Victoria premised on the Ontario common school model, Jessop had bowed to the threats of white parents to remove their offspring by excluding "coloured" children, recently arrived with their parents from California, from subsequent attendance.[22] Jessop was, however, in quite a different position in the early 1870s. Rather than operating a school for profit, he was in charge of a provincial system funded out of general revenue. Children of mixed Indigenous descent in particular were not nearly as easy a target for overt discrimination or exclusion as were children entirely of a different race than the dominant society, especially given that many fathers of these families, having come from the United States to escape racism, had become community leaders.

Only at the beginning of his tenure did Jessop comment publicly on children of Indigenous descent. In his first annual report he expressed surprise at their forming the majority in the scattered Interior settlements born of the Fraser and Cariboo gold rushes and, earlier, the fur trade: "There are 402 children, of all ages [of which] 287 are of school age, that is between 5 to 16; and 115 under five years. Dividing them into whites and half-castes, there are 105 of the former of school age, and 61 under; of the latter, there are 182 of school age, and 54 under."[23] As to specific schools, Jessop acknowledged such children's presence only in the former fur trade and gold rush town of Hope, noting: "Children neat and orderly—mostly half-castes."[24] Only once after this did Jessop publicly distinguish children as of Indigenous descent, and that was in his second annual report, 1873, where he described how "considerable difficulty has been experienced during the year in keeping some of the small rudimentary schools supplied with teachers," and gave as the reason: "Salaries in those districts are necessarily small; and as the pupils are few and merely beginning, and in many cases a majority of half-breeds, duly qualified teachers are not obtainable."[25] Thereafter, Jessop publicly described British Columbia's school children as if they were racially a single entity, leaving the inference that the ideology of common schooling had become sufficiently inclusive under his leadership "to secure the sound education of the young generally." Where differentiation occurred publicly, it was between schools as to their meeting Jessop's priorities within the ideology of common schooling of order, discipline, parental support, and later also cleanliness.

However, as references to race disappeared from the public record, they entered its private counterparts. Jessop's tours of inspection in the spring and summer of 1872 had revealed the large numbers of prospective students of mixed Indigenous descent, which he noted in his first public report. In his diary, Jessop at first did not note individual children as being of mixed race, possibly because he did not perceive that factor as necessarily distinguishing them from "the young generally," who were his mandate. For example, in "the district round Sayward's mill" on central Vancouver Island, he enumerated in June 1872 ten children of school age by surname: "Manly 2, Sheppard [*sic*] 3, B. Votre 2, F. Votre 2, Gabora [Gabourie] 1."[26] Whereas the two Manleys have come down in local lore as "probably the first white twins [born] in Cowichan," the Shepard, Vautrain and Gabourie children all had white fathers and Indigenous mothers.[27] Nonetheless, Jessop perceived them as part of a single whole from the perspective of the common schooling ideology, albeit possibly because he was unaware of their maternal parentage. Arriving a few days later on southern Saltspring Island, Jessop again did not note children of Indigenous descent, even though he personally "saw all the residents in the settlement." "Crossed over to Burgoyne Bay, Salt Spring—An interesting & fast becoming a wealthy little settlement extending three miles from Burgoyne Bay to Fulford Harbor entirely across the Island—There are 9 or 10 settlers already located—representing 20 or 21 children—of those about one-half are of school age."[28] Travelling westward on Saltspring, Jessop did identify some children and their teacher as "coloured," but without any sense of prejudice. Rather, it was the reverse. "Examination day with but three pupils in attendance—two little girls & one boy (coloured)—The boy working in Latin Grammar, having become so proficient in Eng. Grammar & Geography a year ago that those studies were dropped & Latin substituted … Teacher J.C. Jones (coloured) a graduate of Oberlin Ohio."[29] Jessop appended a list of surnames but did not note the several among them who were Black or of Indigenous descent. Moving on to Gabriola Island, he was similarly blind to race.[30]

In the spring of 1874, just as race disappeared from the public record, Jessop began privately differentiating children. Back on Saltspring Island in March, he again listed family surnames in his journal, but this time each was followed by the number of children and whether they were "half breed," "coloured," or "white."[31] He did the same for South and North Cowichan, Comox, and Wellington on

Vancouver Island, but then discontinued the practice for a time, even though numerous other children, as on Gabriola Island, were also of mixed race.[32] In Jessop's October 1874 tour of Vancouver Island schools, he similarly noted some children as of Indigenous descent, this time almost as a matter of course. He had, so it appears, come to perceive them as somehow different. Maple Bay in the Cowichan Valley: "Three half-breeds at the upper school."[33] South Cowichan: "Found six children in attendance four half-breeds." Burgoyne Bay on southern Saltspring: "Fourteen in attendance nine half-breeds & five whites."[34] Western Saltspring: "Found eleven in attendance all coloured & half-breed."[35] Thereafter, designations of children by race were selective, likely in part because Jessop no longer himself calculated total numbers of children but rather relied on trusted individuals in the localities, and in part because he became consumed over the cleanliness of classrooms and outhouses as another strand in the ideology of common schooling.[36]

Jessop was not, it must be emphasized, alone in distinguishing children as being of Indigenous descent. His voluminous incoming correspondence and his travels around the province gave him ongoing insight into attitudes that to some extent he may have been reflecting. Only for the last two years of Jessop's tenancy as Superintendent, 1876 and 1877, did he systematically note in his diary the surnames of individuals he visited to discuss local school matters and possibly stay overnight. Virtually all the surnames sufficiently distinctive to be identifiable belonged to members of the dominant white society, even in areas of British Columbia where schools enrolled mostly children of mixed race.[37] Indicative was Granville, on the south side of Burrard Inlet, where Jessop "called on Mrs. Alexander and Mrs. Miller," two long-time self-designated social leaders of its tiny white settler society.[38] Moreover, some of the individuals with whom Jessop talked informally, and from whom he likely received advice, were newcomers to British Columbia without the sustained contact with Indigenous people and persons of mixed race that some longer-lived white settlers had. In June 1877, Jessop wrote about Cheam in the Fraser Valley: "Order tolerably good, several newly arrived in country and many beginners in school. District prospering. New settlers with families constantly arriving from Britain. Spoke to children and visitors at close of school chiefly on behaviour and growing up young ladies and young gentlemen."[39]

Attitudes in the dominant white society toward children of Indigenous descent came to Jessop both through his travels and from incoming correspondence. Explaining low enrolments, the teacher in Yale referred in October 1872 to the "3 girls from Mr. Bailey's, ... the principal objection to their attending—if not the only one—is the presence of halfbreeds, so many of them," in the school.[40] As were schools in the province's other major urban centres of Victoria and Nanaimo, the New Westminster school had been divided by sex since British Columbia's years as a British colonial possession. Jessop became concerned in December 1876 about unequal numbers between classrooms, and at a trustees' meeting he suggested that "teaching labor should be equalized by drafting boys under seven into girls dept," only to have "objections raised to half breeds mixing with girls."[41]

Jessop's travel diaries, annual reports, and correspondence underline that all children frequently failed to live up to his hopes for them, but by virtue of his having already distinguished in his own mind the inferiority of children of Indigenous descent, he was made particularly aware of any perceived failings among them.[42] In general, it was the degree of adherence to his priorities of orderliness, discipline, parental involvement, and cleanliness, broadly defined, which served as the criteria. Noting in October 1874 that four of the six children in South Cowichan and nine of fourteen at Burgoyne Bay on Saltspring Island were of mixed race, Jessop went on to emphasize how "orderly" each of the schools were.[43] A teacher wrote the Superintendent in 1876 about a young Indigenous boy who "sent another boy to me to get a book as he wanted to learn to read ... I told him if he was so anxious to learn he could come to school as long as he behaved properly.

He has come ever since and is acquitting himself creditably both to himself and me." Moreover, "since then another Indian boy has come to me wanting to come. I permitted him to do so on the same conditions."[44] Jessop emphasized in response, "You are doing perfectly right in admitting Indian children so long as they are not taken [by force] & conduct themselves properly ... If they are troublesome or dirty the trustees must prohibit their attendance—Personally I am glad to hear of their attendance wherever circumstances will admit of it."[45]

Increasingly, Jessop's expectations for children of Indigenous descent diverged from those for "the young generally." Visiting Dog Creek in the Cariboo in May 1874, he observed: "Found only nine children of school age—all half breeds—of whom probably not more than five would attend school regularly if one were established."[46] At Granville, the future Vancouver, in June 1875: "The teacher's influence for good over the children, especially the half-breeds is very gratifying, but the children are hardly making satisfactory progress."[47] From Langley Prairie in the Fraser Valley in February 1876: "There was but two half-breeds attending in school—attendance since November next to nothing."[48] While not specifying that the children at Burgoyne Bay on Saltspring were largely of Indigenous descent, the thought likely crossed Jessop's mind when he assessed the school in March 1876: "Improvement not very decided—Attendance not what it ought to have been."[49] Again not putting down on paper children's race, Jessop commented later in the same month on the school at Moodyville, a sawmilling community on the north shore of Burrard Inlet across from Granville: "All very backward but quiet and orderly—Classes far behind where they ought to be." He added, "A change of teacher is required."[50] On his next visit to Moodyville, in December 1876, Jessop linked race and school achievement: "27 pupils in school nearly all half breeds and very backward." Jessop crossed over Burrard Inlet later in the day and on visiting Granville school made another direct comparison between race and achievement: "From 26 pupils in school only two in there of whom were half breeds. Heard all the classes without exception the children did remarkably well."[51] In May 1877, Jessop commented about the children in the various Nicola Valley schools that "all of them did remarkably well, the white children particularly."[52]

Jessop's growing ambivalence toward children of Indigenous descent extended even to Gabriola Island. In February 1876, he noted approvingly, almost as if it were a happy exception in his travels, "All half-breed but well behaved and apparently anxious to learn."[53] Back on Gabriola in December, he found the school "very quiet and orderly," although "improvement not as marked as in former occasions. Children not as much interested in their lessons. Attendance falling off in numbers." Jessop did not blame the teacher as he was wont to do in such circumstances. "The teacher Capt. Wake is evidently doing as well as he can," and he particularly commended "his influence for good over the half breed children."[54] Jessop returned to Gabriola in March 1877. Despite parental "complaints against Capt. Wake as teacher," Jessop praised his "moral influence." "Great pains taken to inculcate right principles." Although acknowledging "some of the parents desirous of a change," it was almost as if for Jessop the teacher's emphasis on morality overcame any lack of academic or personal qualifications.[55]

Jessop was again at Gabriola in February 1878, where, in a rare exception to the general rule, he stayed overnight with a family of Indigenous descent, possibly because there was no alternative. "Landed at Edgar's about five pm and stayed there all night."[56] Magnus Edgar, born in Scotland and a former fur trade labourer and coal miner, and his Indigenous wife, Ann, had a large family that may have provided a substantial portion of the school's enrolment.[57] Yet again, Jessop stressed, as he did nowhere else, the school's emphasis on right behaviour: "Teacher apparently painstaking and conscientious and exercising a good moral influence over the scholars." This was the case even though it was still the children's lack of academic progress that exercised parents: "Heard complaints of parents respecting the non-improvement of their children."[58] In no other British Columbia school did Jessop lay such emphasis, as recorded in his travel diary, on inculcation of morality, and, moreover, in apparent opposition to parents' desire for more rigorous academics.

Jessop's most explicit blending of the ideologies of common schooling and racism came on his June 1877 visit to the Langley Prairie School, where he "found 21 pupils, chiefly half-breeds and Indians." His overall assessment of the school was far more positive than was the rule with Jessop: "School orderly and quiet. Reading and spelling now middling. Fifth class did fairly. Arithmetic not at all creditable. Geography and grammar satisfactory." Yet Jessop was biting in his overall summary and did not mince words as to where he lay the blame: "Half-breed children very unpromising, dull and stupid and apparently incapable of learning."[59] The ideologies of common schooling and of racism had become joined.

Jessop's acceptance, at least tacitly, of the ideology of race had consequences far beyond their explication in his private journals. Jessop likely influenced teachers' attitudes, as well as being influenced by them. Some made a special effort to treat pupils equitably, whatever their race, as with the Granville teacher, who in September 1875 reported a white pupil's mistreatment of an Indigenous boy attending the school. Her letter concluded: "I love the children, black and white, are the same to me. I am an impartial Teacher. Act conscientiously and as long as I am able to impart instruction to them they shall all have it in equality."[60] Children of Indigenous descent were sometimes mentioned in teachers' letters without any indication of their race. In May 1878, the teacher at Lytton, Emily Crease, noted how "Jules McWha has studied it [a text on natural philosophy] and likes it—taking subjects he liked best. He is gone to join his father at Kamloops. I miss him."[61] The mother of Jules McWha, then about thirteen years old, was Cree; his father was an Irish immigrant.[62]

Teachers' attitudes emerge most clearly in their references to children's home lives. Language was a frequent theme. Many children of Indigenous descent, and some of those in the dominant society, did not know English when they came to school, and reactions varied. The speed with which children learned English could be cause for commendation. The new teacher on Gabriola Island wrote in August 1875 concerning his predecessor that "taking in the fact that they (the scholars) could scarcely understand any English when they commenced one must conclude that they have done remarkably well."[63] Given that fathers of early settler families on Gabriola came from Ireland, Scotland, Quebec, and the Azores, it may be that the children in question spoke French or Portuguese at home, and possibly an Indigenous language or Chinook.[64] The teacher at the long-time fur trade post of Stuart Lake in the central Interior reported in December 1877 that "the only difficulty I have to contend with is that more than one half of them [students] only speak the French."[65] Within two months he had become optimistic: "Eleven of them speak French only but it will not be long before they will be able to understand English. The remainder of them speak both languages."[66]

In other cases a lack of English directly affected children's treatment in school, quite apart from their having to learn the new language. Successive teachers at Moodyville almost assumed that children of Indigenous descent would be inferior personally as well as academically. The teacher in 1876 seemed surprised that this was not completely the case: "I find the children very careless and the majority backward although to be half breeds some of them are very nice children."[67] His successor wanted to know in February 1877 whether to distribute "merit cards," recently received from Victoria and already "a success" with parents, to all his pupils. Jessop had adapted merit cards from Ontario. Each contained "a scriptural exhortation to diligence and good conduct," followed by a statement "that the recipient was entitled to this reward of merit." Teachers were expected to award merit cards "daily to those pupils who had earned such through diligence, punctuality or good conduct," and "at the end of the term those pupils with sufficient merit cards were to receive a prize book suitably inscribed."[68] The teacher at Moodyville inquired of Jessop: "I wish to ask you if it is left to the discretion of the teacher as to who may receive them and who may not, as some of the Kanakas have parents who are unable to read English, and some of the half-breeds having parents who seldom see them."[69] The "Kanakas" mentioned by the teacher were indigenous Hawaiians who originally came to the Pacific Northwest as fur trade labourers or seamen and subsequently settled down with Indigenous wives.

With students of Indigenous descent, it was not only fathers, but also mothers who exercised agency, and this too concerned some teachers. The teacher at Yale grumbled in October 1872 how a pupil had "removed with her mother—an Indian woman—to Hope."[70] The teacher at Lillooet observed in the spring of 1876 how "the majority of the scholars is half-breed children of clootchmen [Chinook word for "Indigenous women"], some of whom are at present living with white-men, and some are not. Of the latter several have gone to Cariboo, and their children are not now attending, but very likely will recommense [*sic*] their schooling on their return. The children of the former will I think be permanent attenders."[71] Related to children's transiency was the assumption that they were not being properly controlled at home. The new teacher arriving on Gabriola in August 1875 reported to Jessop: "The Trustees told me I would have a rough lot to deal with & I find as I am most happy to say that though the children are wild by nature they are not at all incontrolable [*sic*]."[72] Home life may have accounted for differences in Nicola Valley student data from 1876 between white and mixed students. Numbers and attendance rates were almost identical but, when grouped by age, white students were generally at a higher grade level.[73]

Each common school has its own distinctive history in terms of how children of Indigenous descent fared, as with the first Okanagan Valley public school, which opened at Okanagan Mission in 1875 principally through the determination and sacrifice of families of Indigenous descent. Two of the school's three trustees had Indigenous wives. Children from across the valley, many the offspring of Indigenous women and fur trade servants or gold miners turned farmers, attended by living with local families, returning home only during the holidays. At first Jessop was optimistic about the school's progress, noting in his travel diary on visiting it in June 1876: "Considering that nearly all the children were ignorant of English when school was opened, wonderful improvement has certainly been made."[74] Visiting geologist George Dawson commented in 1877 that "there is a school with about 20 scholars [all halfbreeds] some of whom we met on our way to the mines, with lunches & books, neatly dressed."[75]

Over time, assessments became less complimentary in ways that almost inevitably rebounded on expectations put on children and thereby on their opportunities to learn. The teacher in 1883 reported: "With one exception the pupils are halfbreeds, & speak better Chinook & Indian than English, & those who have a French father speak French, Indian & Chinook at home, & English only when at school, consequently their written English is very inferior."[76] Children's obligations outside of the school became linked to their race. "Two more are obliged to reside at home & cook as their mother (a native) has been visiting her tillicums ["friends" in Chinook]." The same teacher noted the same difficulty with sending reports home as had the teacher at Moodyville: "There are several children in the first book [reader] to whom I do not give reports, some whose guardian is a native woman, uneducated."[77]

By the time Jessop left the position of Superintendent of Education in 1878, children of Indigenous descent had come to be perceived as less able to meet the priorities schoolmen drew out of the ideology of common schooling—in his case, order, discipline, parental support, and cleanliness. Their home lives were, as teachers repeatedly reminded Jessop, sometimes very different from those of members of the dominant white society. In the classroom they were carefully scrutinized, and any perceived failings were attributed to race as opposed to a range of factors likely also affecting other children. Increasingly they became viewed as clogs, incapable of responding to the advantages that common schooling offered them. Growing numbers of newcomers likely exacerbated the tendency to marginalize children of Indigenous descent and of other races than the dominant society. Rather than broadening the ideology of common schooling to encompass distinctiveness, schoolmen like Jessop found recourse in the ideology of racism, just as prominent as the ideology of common schooling during these years, or even more so.

The consequences, both immediate and long-term, were enormous for children of Indigenous descent, particularly since the blending of the two ideologies occurred in the private as opposed to the public sphere. During Jessop's superintendency, men with Indigenous wives and children of school age served as trustees in North Saanich, North Cowichan, and South Cowichan on Vancouver Island; on Gabriola Island and in Burgoyne Bay on Saltspring Island; and at Maple Ridge, Cache Creek, Nicola Valley, and likely also Moodyville on the British Columbia mainland.[78] Such men believed that common schooling was intended to be to their offspring's advantage, just as did their successors serving as trustees over the next years and decades. Annual reports continued to laud the ideology of common schooling as encompassing all British Columbia children in roughly equitable fashion. Jessop's final report as Superintendent of Education closed with the assertion that "school progress for the year is as satisfactory and perhaps more so than for any former period in our educational history."[79]

Over time, the differing expectations put on children of Indigenous descent and also on other non-white children accreted. In the next two decades, 1878–1897, the Superintendent of Education received approximately 35,000 letters from teachers, parents, trustees, and others, many openly discriminatory.[80] Children's everyday lives in the classroom were inevitably affected. So far as can be determined from surnames, virtually all of the approximately 120 students taking the high school entrance examination in 1878, shortly after the first high school in the province had opened in Victoria, were white.[81] Children whose surnames indicated Indigenous descent were virtually never publicly commended in the lists of students praised for behaviour, academics, or attendance in the published annual reports of the Department of Education.[82] Children of the dominant white society had become the norm, making it hardly surprising that, for children of Indigenous descent, schools increasingly became places to be avoided. Most, not unexpectedly, stayed as short a time as possible, only confirming the expectations that the ideology of race placed on them, and then led very ordinary lives, sometimes near the bottom of the socio-economic spectrum. In an autobiographical novel about coming of age at the end of the nineteenth century along the British Columbia border, the young heroine repeatedly laments her "breed" status, describing herself and like persons as "the social ostracized of two races."[83] For Mourning Dove, as for many thousands of other children of Indigenous descent, schools may not have been solely responsible, but they almost certainly played a role in the process whereby attitudes of inferiority were internalized. Rather than parents and schools working together in the best interests of children of Indigenous descent, it was parents vs. schools in British Columbia classrooms of the late nineteenth century.

Notes

1 I am grateful to the Social Sciences and Humanities Research Council of Canada for funding this research and to Clint Evans, Dana Whyte, Valerie Giles, and Roger Wiebe for exemplary research assistance.

2 The first definition of ideology in H.W. Fowler and F.G. Fowler, *The Concise Oxford Dictionary of Current English*, is "science of ideas." Ideology is used here to mean a cluster of ideas so widespread in their acceptance that they take on some of the characteristics and assumptions of certainty traditionally associated with a "science."

3 The Public School Act, given assent on April 11, 1872, is included as Appendix A in British Columbia, Department of Education, *First Annual Report on the Public Schools in the Province of British Columbia* (1872), 11–18. Initially, the minimum number of children was just seven aged between five and sixteen.

4 See Table 5 in Jean Barman, *The West beyond the West: A History of British Columbia* (Toronto: University of Toronto Press, 2007).

5 Alex Deans[?] to John Jessop, BC Superintendent of Education (SE), Langley, June 26, 1876, in BC SE, Inward Correspondence (IC), BC Archives, GR 1445.

6 Department of Indian Affairs, Annual Report (1874), 37.

7 By far the bulkiest source is the Superintendent of Education's inward and outgoing correspondence. The inward correspondence, on 14 reels of microfilm for 1872–1897 (GR 1445 in BC Archives), was systematically read by two UBC graduate students for letters meeting certain criteria as to substance. The overwhelming majority of letters, not unexpectedly, proved to be fairly routine. The Superintendent's responses, on 123 reels of microfilm for 1872–1919 (GR 450 in BC Archives), were retrieved as necessary.

8 "Duties of Superintendent," section 8(3), of the Public School Act, given assent on April 11, 1872, Appendix A in BC Department of Education, *First Annual Report*, 13.

9 F. Henry Johnson, *John Jessop: Goldseeker and Educator* (Vancouver: Mitchell Press, 1971).

10 In reporting to the Provincial Secretary in January 1874, Jessop lamented the time that "the routine work of this office" took "in view of the fact that no desk or messenger is employed." Jessop to Provincial Secretary, January 17, 1873, BC SE, Outward Correspondence (OC), BC Archives, GR 450; also Johnson, *John Jessop*, 83. Jessop had a Deputy Superintendent, Robert Clemitson, at least from June 1876, whose duties included inspection of interior schools as well as the supervision of Cache Creek Boarding School. June 7, 1876, entry in John Jessop Diary, BC Archives, GR 1468; and Johnson, *John Jessop*, 103.

11 May 25, 1872, entry in Jessop Diary; and BC Department of Education, *First Annual Report*, 4.

12 July 2, 1872, entry in Jessop Diary.

13 BC Department of Education, *First Annual Report*, 4.

14 June 14, 1872, entry in Jessop Diary.

15 BC Department of Education, *First Annual Report*, 4.

16 April 22, 1874, entry in Jessop Diary.

17 BC Department of Education, Annual Report (1874), 14.

18 March 20, 1874, entry in Jessop Diary. The remark referred specifically to the boys' division.

19 BC Department of Education, Annual Report (1874), 17. The remark also referred specifically to the boys' division.

20 March 23, 1874, entry in Jessop Diary.

21 BC Department of Education, Annual Report (1874), 16.

22 This point is made in Jean Barman, "Transfer, Imposition or Consensus? The Emergence of Educational Structures in Nineteenth-Century British Columbia," in *Schools in the West: Essays in Canadian Educational History*, ed. Nancy M. Sheehan, J. Donald Wilson, and David C. Jones (Calgary: Detselig, 1986), 241–64.

23 "Supplementary Report" to BC Department of Education, *First Annual Report*, 38.

24 "Supplementary Report" to BC Department of Education, *First Annual Report*, 36.

25 BC Department of Education, Annual Report (1873), 8.

26 June 25, 1872, entry in Jessop Diary.

27 Data on individual families come from my ongoing research, including the 1881, 1891, and 1901 manuscript censuses. On the Manleys, see E. Blanche Norcross, *The Warm Land* (Duncan, BC: Elizabeth Blanche Norcross, 1959), 100–101.

28 June 26–27, 1872, entry in Jessop Diary.

29 June 28, 1872 entry in Jessop Diary.

30 July 1, 1872, entry in Jessop Diary.

31 March 10 and 11, 1874, entries in Jessop Diary. Saltspring totals from March 1874, which did not include the island's principal Black community, were twenty-nine "half breeds," five "whites," and eight "coloured."

32 March 15, 16, 18, and 19, 1874, entries in Jessop Diary. Cowichan contained 29 "half-breed" and 24 "white" children, whereas all the 18 children at Comox and all but 3 of the 15 children in the coal mining community of Wellington were "white." They were "all half breeds" at Dog Creek in the Cariboo. May 18, 1874, entry in Jessop Diary. Jessop visited Gabriola on March 23, 1874.

33 October 5, 1874, entry in Jessop Diary.

34 October 6, 1874, entry in Jessop Diary.

35 October 7, 1874, entry in Jessop Diary.

36 For example, April 23, 1877, entry on Comox ("School room was dirty and everything disorderly") in Jessop Diary.

37 For example, June 5, 1876, entry from Nicola Valley in Jessop Diary. Also *passim*.

38 May 4, 1877, entry in Jessop Diary.

39 June 4, 1877, entry in Jessop Diary.
40 John Please, teacher at Yale, to Jessop, Yale, October 12, 1872, in BC SE, IC, BC Archives, GR 1445.
41 December 5, 1876, entry in Jessop Diary.
42 This topic is explored in Jean Barman, "Reflections on the Transition from School to Work in Resource Towns," in Rebecca Priegert Coulter and Ivor F. Goodson, eds., *Rethinking Vocationalism: Whose Work/Life Is It?* (Toronto: Our Schools/Our Selves, 1993), 10–27.
43 October 6, 1874, entry in Jessop Diary.
44 J[ane] E. Trenaman, teacher at Hope, to Jessop, Hope, October 25, 1876, in BC SE, IC.
45 Jessop to Trenaman, Victoria, October 30, 1876, in BC SE, OC, BC Archives, GR 450.
46 May 18, 1874, entry in Jessop Diary.
47 June 17, 1875, entry in Jessop Diary.
48 February 10, 1876, entry in Jessop Diary.
49 March 9, 1876, entry in Jessop Diary.
50 March 20, 1876, entry in Jessop Diary.
51 December 4, 1876, entry in Jessop Diary.
52 May 28, 1877, entry in Jessop Diary.
53 February 26, 1876, entry in Jessop Diary.
54 December 19, 1876, entry in Jessop Diary.
55 March 27, 1877, entry in Jessop Diary.
56 February 10, 1878, entry in Jessop Diary.
57 British Columbia manuscript censuses; and June Lewis-Harrison, *The People of Gabriola: A History of Our Pioneers* (Gabriola: J. Lewis-Harrison, 1982), 34–37.
58 February 11, 1878, entry in Jessop Diary.
59 June 8, 1877, entry in Jessop Diary.
60 Mrs. Catherine Cordiner, teacher at Granville, to Jessop, Granville, September 16, 1875; also L. Gold, to Jessop, n.d., in BC SE, IC.
61 Emily Crease, teacher at Lytton, to Jessop, Lytton, May 29, 1878, in BC SE, IC.
62 Data from British Columbia manuscript censuses.
63 O.M. Gregory, teacher on Gabriola Island, to Jessop, Gabriola Island, August 16, 1875, in BC SE, IC.
64 British Columbia manuscript censuses, 1881 and 1891; and Lewis-Harrison, *People of Gabriola*.
65 James Marion teacher at Stuart Lake, to Jessop, Stuart Lake, December 16, 1877, in BC SE, IC.
66 Marion to Jessop, Stuart Lake, March 1, 1878, in BC SE, IC.
67 T.H. Mathers, teacher at Moodyville, to Jessop, Moodyville, April 13, 1876, in BC SE, IC.
68 Johnson, *John Jessop*, 109.
69 Henry W. Hughes, teacher at Moodyville, to Jessop, Moodyville, February 16, 1877, in BC SE, IC.
70 John Please, teacher at Yale, to Jessop, Yale, October 12, 1872, in BC SE, IC.
71 Thomas Leduc, teacher at Lillooet, to Jessop, Lillooet, May 22, 1876, in BC SE, IC.
72 O.M. Gregory, teacher on Gabriola Island, to Jessop, Gabriola Island, August 16, 1875, in BC SE, IC.
73 A. Irwin, teacher at Nicola Valley, to Jessop, Nicola Valley, January 17, 1876, in BC SE, IC.
74 June 12, 1876, entry in Jessop Diary.
75 George Dawson, July 4, 1877, entry in Douglas Cole and Bradley Lockner, ed., *The Journals of George M. Dawson: British Columbia, 1875–1878* (Vancouver: UBC Press, 1989), 343.
76 R[ichard] S. Hanna, teacher at Okanagan Mission, to C.C. McKenzie, Superintendent of Education, Okanagan Mission, May 10, 1883, in BC SE, OC.
77 Hanna to McKenzie, Okanagan Mission, October 30, 1883, in BC SE, OC.
78 Lists of trustees, as reported in the Department of Education's Annual Reports, were compared with fathers in families of mixed race retrieved from the 1881 and 1891 manuscript censuses. Due to the common nature of some surnames or lack of contextual information, only a probable linkage was sometimes possible.
79 BC Department of Education, Annual Report (1877), 26.
80 The correspondence is extant in BC Archives only to that date; this statement is based on research assistants' thorough reading of this correspondence.

81 High School Entrance Examination Results, 1878, in BC SE, IC. It is possible from the surnames that three or four of the children had some mixed ancestry, but they were in each case less than half Indigenous.

82 This statement is based on a comparison of names in the annual reports with a list of over a thousand family surnames taken from the manuscript censuses of 1881, 1891, and 1901. With very common surnames it is of course impossible to determine with certainty who the children's parents were.

83 Hum-ishu-ma, "Mourning Dove," *Cogewea, The Half-Blood: A Depiction of the Great Montana Cattle Range* (Boston: Four Seas Company, 1927; reprinted Lincoln: University of Nebraska Press, 1981), 15.

15

Separate and Unequal

Indigenous and White Girls at All Hallows School, 1884–1920

The case of All Hallows School, run by an English order of Anglican nuns, provides some insight into the ways in which Indigenous girls were educated in a mission school that also taught upper- and middle-class white girls. Although during the first years of the school white girls were in the minority and the children shared classrooms, after 1910 they were strictly segregated. The white girls were prepared for marriage and, failing that, careers, while the Indigenous girls were trained at first for service in white homes. Interest in the academic progress of the Indigenous girls waned as the government decided they were not to be educated to integrate into the wider society but were to be "protected" at school until they could return to their reserves to marry Indigenous men. Until this point, they had progressed well and some excelled. The shift away from educating them in the same way as the white girls is blamed on "federal parsimony and white prejudice."

By Jean Barman. Originally "Separate and Unequal: Indian and White Girls at All Hallows School, 1884–1920." Reprinted with permission from *Children, Teachers and Schools in the History of British Columbia*, edited by Jean Barman and Mona Gleason, 2nd ed. (Calgary: Detselig, 2003), 283–302.[1]

During the first decade of the twentieth century, Indian, or Indigenous, education in Canada underwent re-evaluation. Previously, federal policy had been directed toward the immediate assimilation of educated Indigenous youth into the dominant socio-economic order. But, so the Department of Indian Affairs argued, most pupils were returning home to their reserves rather than settling down in white society. In 1910, the department's goal became "to fit the Indian for civilized life in his own environment" rather than "to transform an Indian into a white man."[2] The move away from assimilation altered the course of Indigenous history in Canada and so merits explanation. The federal government considered that educated young Indigenous people were themselves responsible for the change because of their unwillingness or inability to make the transition. A close examination of the policy shift within the context of a specific school admitting both Indigenous and white pupils, however, suggests that the failure of government policy became inevitable because of federal parsimony and white prejudice. The case in point is All Hallows School in British Columbia, in existence between 1884 and 1920.

Origins

All Hallows School developed as a result of similar interests shared by Christian missionaries and the federal government in the late nineteenth century. Almost as soon as the first white settlers arrived in British Columbia, the major denominations began demarcating spheres of influence for the purpose of Indigenous conversion.[3] The Anglican claim to the southwestern Interior was consolidated with the arrival from England of the first bishop of the diocese of New Westminster in 1880.[4] Bishop Sillitoe quickly became convinced that the establishment of schools was not only essential to carry out God's work among the three thousand "Indians" in the Yale district, but was also deeply desired by the Indigenous peoples. His travels about the mission showed him "examples enough of self-improvement under the present very limited opportunities to warrant the highest expectations" if the schools were begun.

> When we shall have been allowed to accomplish this, we shall have wrought a social revolution in the land, for we shall have elevated the people from the servile condition of hewers of wood and drawers of water and given them an equal chance in the race of life.[5]

To this end, the bishop enticed out from England both missionary clerics to establish a boys' school and Anglican nuns to work with Indigenous girls.

Unfortunately, by the time three sisters of the order of All Hallows arrived in British Columbia in October 1884, the diocese's finances were in disarray, the bishop's enthusiasms having far outstripped resources, which were limited to a small endowment and voluntary contributions from Britain.[6] The sisters had come on the understanding that financial support for a boarding school would be forthcoming, but instead found themselves isolated at Yale, "forced to take in washing to make ends meet."[7] The community, nestled in the steep mountains of the Fraser Canyon, had originated a quarter of a century earlier, during the gold rush, and had received its second life as a construction centre for the transcontinental Canadian Pacific Railway. Now it was "gradually decaying."

Despite their onerous conditions, the sisters immediately began a day school, but irregularity of attendance soon confirmed the absolute necessity of a boarding school.[8] The bishop proposed an expedient. Among projects proposed in his original spate of energy had been two church schools for white girls, intended to counter the non-denominationalism of the province's public system. Neither was self-supporting. If the sisters would commit themselves to take on this work, then funds granted by an English mission society for their capital costs could be used at Yale.[9] The sisters acquiesced, and white fee-paying boarders began to be accepted alongside Indigenous girls. Additional funds still had to be raised, however. Bishop Sillitoe turned to the Department of Indian Affairs, which he had first approached without success at the time of the sisters' arrival.[10] In June 1888, an agreement was concluded to subsidize up to twenty-five pupils and construction of a dormitory.[11] Thus All Hallows was established, with enrolments eventually reaching thirty-five Indigenous and forty-five white pupils, the latter almost all the daughters of Anglican families in the New Westminster diocese.[12]

Reasons for Attendance

Pupils were attracted to All Hallows for a variety of reasons. Many early white pupils were the daughters of Anglican clergymen who were sent primarily because All Hallows' religiously based instruction replicated what their parents, almost all of English origin, had themselves experienced. Other girls came for lack of alternatives. Almost half of the white pupils at All Hallows in the years for which enrolment data has survived—1899–1901, 1906, 1908–1909, and 1911—came from areas of British Columbia without a public high school, what one pupil has remembered as "small places."[13] Fathers were often establishment figures, such as the CPR or government agent, owner of the general store-cum-post office, or possibly the cleric or doctor. Some white girls came from very remote areas without even a primary school, their father a farmer, rancher, or mining engineer. Typical was the writer Charles Mair, who shortly after settling in the Okanagan Valley reported: "There is no school here as yet which is a draw-back, but there is a fine school at Yale, kept by lay-sisters of our church, and we shall send Mabel, and perhaps Bessie, there in spring."[14] In some cases, a paucity of alternatives was more a matter of perception. A young girl growing up on a ranch in the Kootenays remembered her first school being two miles down the valley, and her English mother deciding, a year later, that she "should not be taught by anybody whose grammar was all wrong." The alternative was All Hallows, where "the distinctiveness of their enunciations" suitably distinguished pupils from average "Canadians."[15] In time, All Hallows became fashionable and also attracted numerous daughters of prominent Vancouver families.

Since Indigenous youth were not yet legally compelled to attend school, they had to decide for themselves if they wanted a formal education. By the time of All Hallows' foundation, Indigenous people in the Yale district had experienced a quarter century of white contact. Thus, according to a contemporary, while few "parents can read or write (the mothers certainly cannot)," many Indigenous families accepted the utility of their offspring learning English, becoming literate, and acquiring some familiarity with white culture.[16] As one All Hallows pupil explained, she was sent "to learn White people's ways."[17] From the late 1890s, All Hallows had little difficulty attracting sufficient pupils and was compelled more than once to refuse applications for lack of room. To quote the order's magazine in 1897:

> The present difficulty is, not to secure children for the school, as in former years, when we had to go to the Indian Reservations to coax the parents into sending their children to school and the children into coming, but to find room for those who are desirous of admission.[18]

The local Indian agent reported in 1900 that members of the Yale band "take a good deal of interest in the education of their children and are anxious in this respect to see them on a par with their White neighbours." That same year a local chief expressed his pleasure to the sisters that Indigenous pupils were now "growing up together" with "the children of the white people." A decade later another elderly chief in the area "complained" to the local Indian agent that their "children were not taught enough": "We wish our children taught the same as the Whites. They go to school, maybe, five, six, seven years. They learn read [*sic*] a little. That's all. Not much use."[19]

In some cases the local Anglican cleric urged attendance. The Yale district contained about two hundred baptized Indigenous people. More than one family must have agreed because the request that their children attend the school came from a representative of the church. One Indigenous pupil recalled how the local cleric would regularly "pick up girls that wanted to go to school." Another, who in 1894, at the age of eight, joined her older sister and cousins at All Hallows, recalled, "Archdeacon Small, you see, was in charge of that part of the parish, and it was him that got these girls in and finally talked mother into letting me come."[20]

Family dislocation also brought numerous pupils to All Hallows. During Holy Week 1901, a "very pale thin child, with a care worn face," appeared on the school's doorstep, volunteering only that her name was "Tuchsia." Sometime later a telegram arrived from her mother, a former Indigenous pupil not remembered for her academic ability: "I sent my little girl to you pecause [*sic*] I am dying. Dake care of her, make her to pe goot." Among the Indigenous girls Tuchsia joined at school was "a loving soft dumpling" named Grace, who had arrived a year previous at age two on the death of her mother, also an ex-pupil, and who was still too young to understand that a few months later her father had been killed in a mine explosion.[21] The sole surviving school register, for the years 1910–1918, contains only partial information, but it indicates that many girls had only one living parent or that parents were separated.[22]

Another factor bringing Indigenous girls to All Hallows was lack of educational alternatives. According to the Department of Indian Affairs, only "in a few instances" across Canada did "Indian children attend the White children's schools." For a time exceptions existed in British Columbia, but in 1911 came the observation that "a very marked prejudice exists, I might say, generally among the Whites against association with Indian children." The next year pupils in at least one provincial school were told to discontinue attendance. The All Hallows' register for 1910–1918 notes only two occasions where a pupil had also attended a public school.[23]

Physical Separation of Pupils

The peculiar circumstances of All Hallows' creation appeared to offer a unique opportunity for Indigenous people and whites to learn to live together in an environment relatively isolated from the larger society. But such was not the case. Originally, a certain amount of contact existed. So long as only a handful of white boarders attended what was in essence an Indian school, they could not remain apart, nor did they. Indeed, in March 1888, Bishop Sillitoe commented approvingly that "no prejudice seems to exist among White parents against sending their children to the same school." Christmas 1889 was celebrated, to quote a participant, by "twenty of us Indians and Half-breeds, and only two young ladies," one of whom was "going to be Father Christmas, and she is followed by four Christmas spirits."[24]

Then came physical separation. Late in 1890, an anonymous letter appeared in the New Westminster newspaper "raising the question of mixed classes" at All Hallows. While denouncing the letter as "abusive and slanderous," Bishop Sillitoe in effect acquiesced, as evidenced by his statement that "there are certainly two classes of children in the Yale School." He went on to assure present and prospective white parents that the school's seven white boarders were, or would be, treated in a manner consistent with their station in life and thus were lodged separately: "Even in the play ground they only very occasionally mix with the other children." The visiting examiner that spring commented that "the school is, it may perhaps be well to note, having regard to racial and other prejudices, entirely distinct from the Indian Mission work of the All Hallows Sisterhood."[25]

Such arrangements continued. On Christmas 1895, as two of the seven white girls remaining at school alongside twenty-five Indigenous pupils reported somewhat wistfully, no common events occurred as had been the case a few years previously: "At midnight [on Christmas Eve] there was a celebration of the Holy Communion in the school chapel, to which the Indian children and about sixty Indians went. We were not allowed to go to this, but from our dormitory we tried to listen to the singing." Two days later, a party was held around "the Indian Christmas-tree."

> We were not allowed to go to it, only to peep in through the open door for a little while, but I will tell you what I saw ... The Indian children of the school stood on the platform at one end of the room singing carols. They all wore dark frocks and red pinafores and looked very nice.

A report to the order's Mother Superior in England summed up the new arrangements: "In accordance with the wishes of the English parents, the white children and the Indian do not mix." Eventually the only activity shared in common was the daily religious service. Even then, Indigenous and whites attended as two separate groups. As a thirteen-year-old white girl explained, "The seats are on either side, and the Indian school in red caps and pinafores sit on one side, and the Canadian school in White veils on the other."[26]

Pupil recollections confirm the entirety of separation. An Indigenous girl at school from 1894 to about 1900 said, "We didn't mix at all." However, to defend the sisters, whom she deeply admired, she put the case in favour of separation: "I think the sisters were very wise in keeping us separate because we didn't begin to have the nice things the other children had because our people couldn't afford it." The only

This 1886 photograph captures the first phase of All Hallows School in which Indigenous and white pupils were treated equitably and interacted in and out of the classroom. City of Vancouver Archives Out P697.1.

time she recalled talking with a white girl was once when they were both, for some reason, folding linen. According to a white pupil at All Hallows from 1909 to 1914, "Whites and Indians were never together, that I can tell you … We didn't think about mixing in those days." Another has summed up, "There was no contact at all." And another, "We weren't allowed to speak to them." A fourth white girl has made the same point: "We weren't allowed to look at the Indian girls, were not even supposed to look at them in chapel which was the only time we ever saw them."[27]

Physical Separation but Educational Parity

While the physical separation of Indigenous and "Canadian" girls put in place at All Hallows was significant enough on its own terms, its consequences would have been immeasurably compounded if accompanied by inequality. In All Hallows' early years, inequality remained relative, with parity existing to the fullest extent possible given the assumptions of the age. The churches believed, and the Department of Indian Affairs concurred, that Christianity and civilization were coterminous and, more specifically, that civilization was a white prerogative. To Christianize an "Indian" was to civilize him, and to civilize him was to socialize him into the dominant culture.

Thus Indigenous girls arriving at All Hallows at age five or seven or nine, familiar only with the world of their family and band, and probably knowing no English, were immediately thrust into a closely regulated alien environment. Family clothing had to be exchanged for garments provided by the school, consisting in winter of chemise and drawers of unbleached cotton, heavy red or grey flannel petticoat, long woollen stockings, high leather boots, dark blue serge long-sleeved dress, red pinafore, and red cloak for outside. New pupils had their own sleeping area in order "to acquire habits of cleanliness and order" before moving to a dormitory housing eight to twenty-five girls. Thereafter came a relentless routine, whose infringement brought such traditional European punishments as being "sent to bed early, put in the corner," or deprived of "Sunday pudding." Once in school, Indigenous pupils had little choice as to whether or not they wished to be "civilized."[28]

A second critical consideration of the nineteenth century held that status at birth was decisive in determining status in adulthood. A principal function of education lay in preparing individuals for their place in the socio-economic order as foretold by the conditions of their birth. Thus, in an English orphanage, also under the auspices of the sisters of All Hallows, poor white girls were "trained for domestic service, were confirmed, and were employed in performing the household chores of the main school whose pupils were also orphans but of the Upper Class."[29] Similarly, the Protestant Orphans' Home in Victoria, British Columbia, taught its female residents "to wash clothes, scrub floors, wash dishes and attend young children and all domestic work as a most important part of their education."[30]

White pupils at All Hallows at Yale, born into the middle or even upper class, had by force of circumstance to be suitably prepared to assume that lifestyle. On the basis of their birth, All Hallows' Indigenous pupils had not even attained the bottom rung of the white socio-economic order. Their education must therefore have as its first goal that achievement, which meant training not unlike that meted out to white orphans of the day. The federal Department of Indian Affairs concurred with the sisters' perception of pupils' probable class status, stipulating that "semi-industrial" schools like All Hallows provide "domestic training in cooking, housework, laundry, waiting, gardening and needlework."[31] In part for reasons of economy, All Hallows' pupils had always been expected to "assist in the domestic arrangements of the house." As the school grew through the admission of white boarders, the Indigenous girls, as part of their training, became responsible for all household duties, including food preparation.[32] As summed up by a white pupil, "They were the servants; they did the work."[33]

Consequently, Indigenous girls rose earlier than their white counterparts in order to do an hour of "House work" before the joint chapel service at 7:30. Whereas white pupils spent the hours from 9 a.m. to 3 p.m. wholly in the classroom, Indigenous girls interspersed classes with another hour of housework. While white girls went "up to dress for dinner," their Indigenous counterparts set the table and lit the lamps. At the end of the year on Prize Day, both groups received awards for academic performance and conduct, but Indigenous girls were also commended in such areas as "bread-making" and "laundry-work." The only work activities performed by All Hallows' white pupils appear to have been making their beds each morning after chapel and darning their stockings on Friday evening.[34]

Originally, inequality in work was offset by parity in the classroom. The concept of assimilation foresaw some opportunity for individual advancement beyond the bottom rung of white society. The potential in education was perceived as enormous, not only by Bishop Sillitoe but by federal authorities: "The Indian problem exists owing to the fact that the Indian is untrained to take his place in the world. Once teach him to do this, and the solution is had." Individual ability would make the difference, and some would do better than others. In 1892, the Department of Indian Affairs commented on "the prospects of being considered fit for promotion to schools of a higher type, seeming to act as a stimulus to the pupils to excel." Already "the Indian race of Ontario has its representatives in all the learned professions, as well as in every other honourable occupation," and "no doubt the same satisfactory results will in time follow" elsewhere in Canada.[35]

There is no question but that the sisters of All Hallows considered their Indigenous charges to be academically capable human beings. The external examiner of July 1887 spoke of

> the careful and successful teaching; of the readiness and accuracy with which my questions were almost invariably answered; of the quickness of apprehension and the clear understanding of the subjects treated of in the examination ... The children themselves seemed to brighten up and look pleased when I laid aside the books and appealed to their intelligence rather than to their memories.[36]

A year later the bishop himself held "a very rigid examination" to discover "the answers in all respects being equal, and sometimes superior, to anything that could be expected from White children of the same age."[37] From 1893, federal authorities required that Indigenous pupils be assessed annually. In British Columbia residential schools in general, over half the pupils were in the two lowest grades, just 14 per cent in grades 5 and 6. At All Hallows, 45 per cent were in grades 1–2 and fully 28 per cent in 5–6.[38] As summed up by a visiting Englishman, "Education goes on in much the same methodical routine as in England, only at Yale it is rather two schools under one roof."[39]

Individual pupils, Indigenous as well as white, made great strides. For example, "'Mary' came to us three years ago, not knowing her letters nor a word of English; she is now in the 'Third Canadian Reader,' and in the compound rules, weights and measures in arithmetic; she can also say the Church Catechism perfectly." During her holidays, Mary wrote a long letter to the sisters which suggests her progress:

> It was raining very fast when I got off the train. I got so wet, and my poor little dolly was wet too, because she had no hat on … Oh, Sister dear, if you can't find my Communion little catechism book, I got it here. It was inside of my Bible, that's why I didn't see it. If you wanted I'll send it to you. Now that is all I can say, so with best love, dear Sister, I remain your loving naught [*sic*] child.

Equally representative of the work is an essay, "About Music," by twelve-year-old Emma:

> God made everything, and He gave power to the birds to have music, and to the brook, and to the wind too. If you stand near the telegraph wires when the wind is blowing you will hear lovely music. Some birds have hardly any music. The pretty birds cannot have a nice music, because they have something pretty already; and the birds that are plain have a lovely music in their throats, because they have only dull feathers to cover them—they are not pretty outside. There is music in everything. Someone told me there was music too when everything was quite still, you could not *hear* [italics in original] that kind of music, but you could feel it in your heart.[40]

Talent was also encouraged in other areas. The bishop's mother-in-law reported with some astonishment in 1895 "that of the teachers standing before their classes, *two* [italics in original] were Indian girls, being in fact the more advanced pupils" who have become "efficient teachers, and are occupied in tuition five hours for five days each week." She received a note inviting her to an evening party organized by the "Indian girls" "quite by themselves ... the writing inside (one now lies open before me) such as no English maiden need be ashamed to own." To her pleasure, "among the attractions were a piano-forte duet, a piano solo (a well-known Mazurka, I have forgotten by whom). The execution of this last was a marvel to me; no mistakes were made, and the quick running passages given with light, easy fingering." A year later, Rosie, one of the Indigenous students, was encouraged to take, and passed, the Royal Academy of Music examinations alongside eight white pupils.[41]

Achievement did not necessarily come at the cost of complete alienation from traditional culture. Because the sisters also ministered to local Indigenous people, including many pupils' families, they were regularly invited to Christmas festivities and the spring Prize Day. Moreover, "whenever there is a service for the Indian adult congregation in the school chapel, and this happens about twelve times a year, the children are allowed to attend, and are taught to take their part in the portion of the service sung in the Indian language." When girls did go home for the summer, many, like Mary, wrote freely to the sisters about their adventures, suggesting a lack of strictures on behaviour.[42]

On the other hand, there is no question that pupils had to reconcile two cultures in their minds. Indicative of the dilemma is a long letter written to the sisters in 1900 by Mali, a pupil at the school from 1885 to 1897, who had just attended a potlatch, even though they had been forbidden by law since 1885. The letter is significant because Mali could accept both traditional Indigenous culture and Christianity, because she felt free to share her views with the sisters, and because they then considered it suitable to publish the letter in the school magazine.

> After an absence of many years, I went back to live among my people for a few months, and I saw again some of their

> customs which must appear to white people as very strange, and sometimes very wrong—but I think it is because they do not understand.

Mali went on to explain how the potlatch "is our way of praying for the burial of our dead ... I think you would call it etiquette, and the Indians are very particular about it." A lengthy analysis of the ceremony followed, and then Mali summed up:

> Potlatch is an old custom, and I do not think the Indians will ever give it up ... I think if some of our friends, I mean our *real* [italics in original] white friends like the Sisters and Miss Moody [a long-time teacher] would come, they would see for themselves; you cannot understand unless you see, and the Indians would be so glad, and there would be a chance to teach them more to be good Indians and Christians too, and not what they often feel, that to be Christians they must leave off being Indians and try to be like White people, giving up even what is harmless in their old customs.[43]

While no evidence exists that any of the sisters or Miss Moody took up Mali's invitation, it is clear from her letter that they were not unreceptive to discussion of differences between the two cultures.

Thus, while Indigenous pupils at All Hallows rapidly became physically separate from their white counterparts and were unequal in work duties, they were recognized through the turn of the century as possessing comparable intellectual capacity. Individual advance depended on individual ability and initiative, and many achieved much. As a knowledgeable observer of the national scene reported to the Department of Indian Affairs in 1904: "It is beyond doubt that Indian children have the capacity to learn and that the reason of non-success in education is not to be found in want of intelligence."[44]

With the passage of time, Indigenous and white students at All Hallows were not only schooled separately, but dressed distinctively in line with their supposed inferiority and superiority. By 1906, when this school photo of the white girls was taken, the transformation was complete. Image D-08486 courtesy of the Royal BC Museum and Archives.

Educational Inequality

Yet, despite demonstrated intellectual capacity, the paths of Indigenous children diverged from those of young whites both at All Hallows and across Canada after the turn of the century. At the time of All Hallows' foundation, public education had been relatively simple, with few children remaining in school more than half a dozen years. Gradually, public schools became more attractive. To remain competitive, All Hallows had to raise its academic appeal for white families, which it did by appointing a graduate of Queen's University in Ontario as "headmistress" in 1899. The results were soon apparent. In 1907, an All Hallows student came first in British Columbia and sixth in all of Canada in the entrance examination to McGill University. The next year another pupil received the first gold medal awarded in Canada by the Royal Academy of Music.[45]

The explanation for the growing inequality of Indigenous pupils must be sought primarily at the federal level. Disenchantment with the goal of assimilation can be dated from Clifford Sifton's assumption of ministerial responsibility for the Department of Indian Affairs. As his biographer has concluded, Sifton demonstrated during his ten-year term "an unvaryingly parsimonious attitude toward the Indian."[46] Up to that date it was generally accepted that, while residential education was expensive, it must be viewed "with relationship to the future interests of the country, as an excellent investment." Just a year into Sifton's tenure came the assertion in the department's annual report that "only the certainty of some practical results can justify the large expense entailed upon the country by the maintenance of these schools." The report went on: "To educate children above the possibilities of their station, and to create a distaste for what is certain to be their environment in life would be not only a waste of time but doing them an injury instead of conferring a benefit upon them."[47]

The die was cast. In retrospect it seems clear that the move away from assimilation would have less to do with the lifestyles of ex-pupils than with the inability of Sifton and, more generally, white Canadian society to accept Indigenous peoples even at the bottom rung of the dominant socio-economic order, much less as equal human beings. Indeed, Sifton's eventual successor stated as early as 1897: "We are educating these Indians to compete industrially with our own people, which seems to me a very undesirable use of public money."[48]

Supposed Indigenous "inability to mingle freely with White communities" became the pretext for a change in policy which was probably inevitable.[49] Sifton himself led the way: "I have no hesitation in saying—we may as well be frank—that the Indian cannot go out from school, making his own way and compete with the White man ... He has not the physical, mental or moral get-up to enable him to compete. He cannot do it."[50] The focus became "the danger ... of inculcating habits, tastes and ideas calculated to produce unfitness for and discontent with a subsequent environment from which the prospect of escape is most remote." A supposed concern to protect Indigenous youth from themselves was variously expressed in the public rhetoric. And "great caution has to be observed to avoid the danger of unfitting the pupil for the surroundings to which their destiny confines them."[51]

A decade and more of federal discontent with assimilation culminated in 1910 in a revised, more frugal policy intended

> to fit the Indian for civilized life in his own environment ... To this end the curriculum in residential schools has been simplified, and the practical instruction given is such as may be immediately of use to the pupil when he returns to the reserve after leaving school ... Local Indian agents should carefully select the most favourable location for ex-pupils [with] most careful thought given to the future of female pupils [in order that they be] protected as far as possible from temptations to which they are often exposed.

Since such temptations were perceived as emanating primarily from contact with white men of "the lowest type," this meant, in effect, young Indigenous women's exclusion from any independent role in white society: "If we can keep them on their reserves, in their homes, they will not be in the way of temptation." The problem with boarding schools' curriculums as they had previously existed was quite simply that "the girls are made too smart for the Indian villages."[52]

While raising the per-pupil subsidy, the new policy effectively restricted enrolments in existing schools through new health regulations requiring more space per child, and physical improvements whose capital cost had to be borne principally by the religious group operating a school. In the provision of new facilities, emphasis was on fairly simple day schools offering a little education to more children at far less cost to the federal government; the goal was less alienation from the culture to which pupils must now return. Any threat of young Indigenous people entering white society was effectively removed.

The changing federal attitude soon rebounded on All Hallows. The school's Mother Superior had early opposed any change in federal policy, writing to authorities as early as 1901: "Many people urge a shorter period of education and training as being more profitable both to the church and to the state by enabling greater numbers to pass through the school; but seventeen years experience has proved the great unwisdom of this advice."[53]

Yet the school gradually accepted the federal shift away from academic achievement, perhaps in part because a new Mother Superior arrived from England in 1907, less familiar with the school's traditional objectives. A white pupil even suggested that she was "second-rate," lacking her predecessor's "knowledge of *human* [emphasis in original] nature, not so good a judge of character."[54]

Up to that time, both the school magazine and the annual report sent to the Department of Indian Affairs stressed Indigenous pupils' intellectual growth and academic progress. Thereafter, neither did. The school magazine turned its attention to the activities of white pupils, whose social events alone merited four pages in 1908, compared with less than a page for those of Indigenous girls.[55] The greater academic accomplishments of white pupils also reflected more general shifts occurring in British Columbia. Expectations concerning mean length of schooling were rising, as evidenced by an increase in the number of public secondary schools across the province from four in 1900 to thirty-one a decade later and fully forty-nine by the First World War.[56] Thus, even as federal authorities were moving to curtail educational opportunities for Indigenous youth, white Canadians were raising academic standards for their own offspring.

The annual reports submitted by All Hallows to the Department of Indian Affairs similarly turned their attention away from Indigenous girls' academic accomplishments. In 1904 the report had stressed how they "compare very favourably with White children of the same age;

in fact, in several examinations where they have had the same papers, the Indian girls have gained the higher marks of the two."[57] Through the first decade of the century virtually all Indigenous pupils at All Hallows completed the allowable six grades, as evidenced by a total during these years of 31 per cent enrolled in grades 1–2, 35 per cent in grades 3–4, and 34 per cent in grades 5–6. From 1907, however, the emphasis in reports to federal authorities shifted to girls' acquisition of practical skills suitable for life on the reserve. The 1908 report highlighted the introduction of traditional cedar basket-making as "some practical handicraft which will stand them in good stead when returning to their homes."[58] No further mention was made either of classroom achievement or of pupils' preparation for external music or drawing examinations.

All Hallows accepted changing federal priorities and, publicly at least, the notion of almost inherent inequality between Indigenous and whites, inside as well as outside the classroom. In the years between 1910 and the closure of the Indian school in 1918, the proportion of Indigenous pupils reaching the two upper grades fell sharply to just 18 per cent, compared with 49 per cent enrolled in grades 1–2.[59] No longer was academic achievement a priority.

During these same years the factors leading to the eventual collapse of All Hallows' white school were also becoming apparent. The demand for exclusive private schooling that had been responsible for All Hallows' success encouraged more attractive alternatives, such as Vancouver's Crofton House School "with all city advantages culturally."[60] Yale had never offered much beyond the school itself; one visitor noted the "abandoned stores & dwellings" along "the old main street."[61] Public high schools were also being opened at more and more locations around the province. Then came the economic recession beginning in 1913, followed by the onset of war a year later. The fees of white girls had always subsidized the Indian school, and as the number of fee-paying white girls fell, so the Indian school's finances became increasingly tenuous.

In 1910, the federal funding policy for Indian schools was officially changed. More stringent health regulations meant that in order to receive full funding and so become financially viable, All Hallows had to raise at least $10,000 on its own to construct a new dormitory. Just half of the sum had been acquired by 1917. At that time, an English mission society that had recently established a boys' school at nearby Lytton offered to take over All Hallows' pupils. The sisters, emotionally exhausted from a third of a century of financial hardship in conditions of extreme physical isolation, gratefully accepted the proposal. Their Indian school was closed, followed by its white counterpart two years later in 1920. The sisters returned home to England.[62]

Lives of Former Pupils

All Hallows' significance extends beyond its lifespan as a school. In comparison to white girls at All Hallows, who easily melded into the upper ranks of the dominant society in British Columbia, principally as wives and mothers, the Indigenous pupils who attended had more complex decisions to make. Based on the number of Indigenous pupils annually admitted into grade 1, about 250 girls passed through All Hallows, remaining on average about three years. At a cost certainly of considerable alienation from traditional Indigenous culture, pupils were indoctrinated into Christianity, made conversant in the English language, given at least basic literacy, and familiarized with European methods of housekeeping and cleanliness. As well, in the words of one young pupil, "we were taught very nicely too [*sic*] behave ourselves, learn our manners and taught how to behave ourselves when we leave here and go out into the world."[63]

To prepare girls to "go out into the world" was a prime function of the school. From its earliest years, the sisters were committed to pupils becoming, if they so chose, "a very useful, permanent element of the working community of the Province."[64] Their practical training in household duties was intended to permit them to obtain the bottom rung of the white socio-economic order, while their academic achievement would presumably give some girls the possibility of rising further. For young white women of similarly modest background, few employment opportunities existed in the late nineteenth century. The work viewed as most viable for Indigenous girls was domestic service, which also allowed acquisition of additional familiarity with the dominant culture in semi-sheltered conditions.

In accord with general attitudes toward Indigenous peoples, Indigenous girls at All Hallows were by the beginning of the 1900s encouraged to follow up their school years with employment as a domestic servant. The practice was so lauded that this image of two former students was included as the frontispiece of the annual report of the Canadian Department of Indian Affairs for the year ended June 30, 1902. Library and Archives Canada.

As early as 1886, a pupil was sent out "into service" in Victoria. The report two years later was that not only was she performing her job but she had also been persuaded to teach Sunday school at the Anglican cathedral. Soon additional girls were placed into service, "giving satisfaction." In the autumn of 1899, an older pupil recorded being taken by Miss Moody to the provincial exhibition and having the opportunity to visit with Mali and Rosie, both nursemaids in Vancouver. Her one disappointment was not having time to accompany Mali to see the monkeys in Stanley Park, the incident suggesting that Mali, who had left the school two years previous, had already achieved some familiarity with the city. It is clear from the varying bits of evidence that survive that numerous Indigenous pupils went into domestic service, some of them becoming nursemaids or governesses, and at least one a nurse.[65]

On the other hand, the sisters were always quite content that their pupils should marry and thus "carry the leaven of Christian training into their Indian homes." As early as 1900, the local Indian agent was commenting that girls "who have been educated and who have taken up housekeeping show a marked improvement in their homes as compared with those of their less fortunate neighbours who have never received any education." Other girls married after several years in domestic service or some other occupation, not necessarily to Indigenous men: "Some have married respectable Englishmen and are comfortable settlers." Soon former pupils were sending "their little daughters to be brought up and educated in the old school which sheltered the childhood and girlhood of these young mothers."[66]

Other pupils returned directly home, in some instances to care for motherless siblings or invalid parents. Experience as a pupil-teacher was often put to good use, the Mother Superior noting in 1901 that "from more than one quarter pleasing testimony has been afforded as to the success of former pupils in carrying on this work after they have returned to their own people." Exemplary was Christina, an early pupil whose mother had died while she was at school. The cleric at Lillooet reported in 1900 that she was "going heart and soul into the teaching of the younger family."

> I spent Tuesday there and examined her pupils during the evening ... She has a regular system of marks, and gives conduct marks also, for the time out of school hours. You may well feel encouraged at finding your seed sown in the past, thus bearing fruit.[67]

For lack of information, it is impossible to be more than suggestive concerning the lifestyles chosen by All Hallows pupils during these early years, when federal policy favoured assimilation. Their choices were not easy, nor did they necessarily reach their goal. As Hallows' long-time teacher Althea Moody wrote in 1900:

> It is very probable that the results, of the first efforts in this direction, may not meet with marked success, but "Rome was not built in a day," and no work that is worth doing in this world succeeds all at once ... Still it is obvious that a thing has no chance of success until it is at least *begun* [italics in original]![68]

What is clear is that pupils from All Hallows, as well as from other schools, did for a time retain the option to choose their destiny. The reports of Indian agents in British Columbia reveal that many educated young women entered domestic service, while others became teachers in mission day schools around the province. In 1903 came the assessment that "among the younger Indians English is freely spoken, and their ambition to a greater extent inspires them with a desire to attain that condition which will put them on a level with the white man." The report a year later from the agent in the Lytton area was similar: "They dress well and live more like their white neighbours than was formerly the case. These improvements are more noticeable among those who have attended school." British Columbia's Indian agents agreed with Miss Moody in seeing pupils as a critical transition generation:

> The ex-pupils find their education so convenient in their ever-increasing intercourse with the Whites that there is no doubt that they will be anxious to see their children in turn acquire an education, and from these children better results may be expected.
>
> It is considered by many that the ultimate destiny of the Indian will be to lose his identity as an Indian, so that he will take his place fairly and evenly beside his white brother. It is only by systematically building from one generation to another

> that this will be accomplished. The ex-pupils merely form the second link in a chain between barbarism and civilization. Some of them are married and have children attending the schools, but they will only be the third link.[69]

However, that third link was not to be.

All Hallows' acquiescence to the federal shift away from assimilation paralleled its de-emphasis on academic achievement. In 1907, concern was expressed for the first time over "the dangers and temptations to which the Indian girl is specially exposed in our great cities." Increasingly, pupils' aspirations were directed homeward rather than outward toward the larger society. Not only was basket-making introduced; pupils were now taught, when doing laundry, not how to use appliances available if going into domestic service, but rather "to make use of such simple, homely contrivances as they would be likely to have to use in after-life, as, for instance, boiling their clothes in coal-oil tins to which wooden handles have been attached." In 1912 came almost a verbal sigh of relief that "very few, as a rule," were "choosing to go into domestic service." A year later the admission was voiced that only those "who had no homes, have lately been placed out in service," for we "prefer, when possible, to send them home."[70] Pupils from All Hallows, like Indigenous youth across Canada, had lost their freedom of action.

With the closing of All Hallows came another blow affecting many lives. For some girls, the school had been the only home they ever knew; for most of them it remained a centre of permanence to which they would periodically return and be refreshed. As a visiting English cleric observed, All Hallows "has produced amongst the pupils a deep spirit of loyalty, equally towards their teachers and their Alma Mater."[71] Numerous girls visited each Christmas and Prize Day, and many were regular correspondents. While the latter exchange continued, in some cases for decades after the school's closure, the living link disappeared. Not only was direct physical contact made impossible, but educational aspirations for many daughters were quashed.

Conclusion

During the third of a century that All Hallows was in existence, from 1884 to 1920, separation and inequality became the norm for young Indigenous students, not only there but across Canada. The Anglican church under whose auspices All Hallows was founded believed in the equal potential of Indigenous people given educational opportunities. The school's concern that pupils utilize their intellectual capacity as well as obtain work skills coincided with the policy of assimilation advocated by the Department of Indian Affairs during the late nineteenth century.

Despite a difficult transition to school life, many Indigenous pupils achieved much within a short time period, and some at least were able to reconcile differences between Indigenous and white culture within their own minds. A number ventured out into the dominant society, and while only scattered evidence survives, it seems fairly clear that a few at least chose to remain there either through occupation or marriage. Certainly, All Hallows influenced lifestyles, as is evident by the many who maintained contact and those who sent daughters back to the school. Most importantly, through the turn of the century the schooling provided at All Hallows maximized the opportunity for educated young Indigenous people to choose their destiny rather than having it imposed upon them.

Federal parsimony, together with white refusal to accept educated young Indigenous people into the dominant socio-economic order, redirected All Hallows' priorities. The school's original difficulty in securing federal funding makes clear that the Department of Indian Affairs was never overly generous with its support. Indeed, if assistance had come earlier, no "Canadian School" would have existed. Even with federal support, All Hallows was still expected to obtain additional funding to cover part of its expenses. In short, no federal expectation had ever existed that the conditions of Indigenous education ought, as a matter of course, to be made the most conducive means to achieve its goal of assimilation. For that reason alone, assimilation was never given a fair chance of success.

Much more importantly, the possible success of assimilation very rapidly became of itself an undesirable outcome. White Canadians did not want Indigenous youth entering their socio-economic order, even at the bottom rung. That such a threat was perceived is perhaps the best evidence that the assimilation policy was having an effect. To what extent Indigenous people would have been successful in white society if the federal policy in favour of assimilation had been allowed to continue is of course impossible to know. Contemporaries in British Columbia familiar with conditions among that province's Indigenous peoples believed not only that change was occurring, but also that its effect would cumulate with each successive generation. The principal opposition to assimilation did not come from Indigenous peoples but rather from the dominant society. First came the demand for physical separation in the classroom, then more general unwillingness to allow educated Indigenous youth into the workforce.

What is certain is that the federal reversal of policy in 1910 removed even young Indigenous students' option to enter the larger society with all its discrimination and prejudice. Their potential to mitigate some of that prejudice through the example of their own lives was taken away. Indigenous youth were forced back onto the reserve, and the dominant society was for a generation and more left comforted in believing that "Indians" were, after all, inferior. As one white pupil at All Hallows observed to me in passing, only at a school reunion in the late 1950s did she finally meet any of the school's Indigenous girls and discover that "the rules of the old days were rather silly."

Notes

1 The Sisters of All Hallows in Ditchingham, Norfolk, and especially Sister Violet, generously provided both hospitality and access to the order's archives. I am also grateful to Garth Walker, Archivist of the Anglican Archives, Diocese of New Westminster, for assistance in locating materials.

2 Department of Indian Affairs (DIA), Annual Reports (1900), 132–33; (1910), 273. The DIA's Annual Report contains a separate report from each funded Indian school, including All Hallows.

3 Boundaries are detailed in the *New Westminster Quarterly Paper* 12 (1884): 12–13.

4 Frank A. Peake, *The Anglican Church in British Columbia* (Vancouver: Mitchell Press, 1959), 62–68.

5 Recounted in Herbert H. Gowen, *Church Work in British Columbia, Being a Memoir of The Episcopate of Acton Windeyer Sillitoe, D.D., D.C.L., First Bishop of New Westminster* (London: Longmans, Green, 1899), 113–17.

6 Gowen, *Church Work*, 85–89, 122–24, 137–45; also *New Westminster Quarterly Paper* 6 (1885): 7–13.

7 *New Westminster Quarterly Paper* 2 (October 1884): 9, 19; and Sister Violet, *All Hallows, Ditchingham: The Story of an East Anglican Community* (Oxford, UK: Becket Publications, 1983), 37.

8 *Churchman's Gazette* (March 1884): 331, 335; Gowen, *Church Work*, 132–34; and *New Westminster Quarterly Paper* 2 (October 1884): 9, 18, 4; (April 1885): 23–27.

9 *Churchman's Gazette* (February 1891): 794–801; (August 1888): 340; (February 1889, Supplement): 580; (February 1890): 5; *New Westminster Quarterly Paper* 10 (June 1886): 11–13; (November 1888): 33; 67 (March 1896): last page; and *All Hallows in the West* (school magazine) 2, no. 3 (Christmas 1900): 63–64.

10 DIA, Annual Report (1885), 123; *New Westminster Quarterly Paper* 10 (1888): 25.

11 *New Westminster Quarterly Paper* 11 (March 1889): 27–28; *Churchman's Gazette* (August 1888): 539; *Work for the Far West* (1896): 10; *Churchman's Gazette* (1889): 587; and *Monthly Record* 4 (1889): 5.

12 *New Westminster Quarterly Paper* 11 (March 1889): 28, 65; (May 1895): 7; *Churchman's Gazette* (August 1888): 540; (February 1889, Supplement): 580; (February 1890): 5; (July 1890): 725; (August 1890): 730; (February 1891): 794, 801; *Monthly Record* 12 (August 1890): 6; *Over the Rockies* (April 1897): 15; (July 1900): 24; and *Work for the Far West* (1909): 18.

13 Interview with Mrs. Lorraine Pindemoss, Vancouver, February 12, 1980. Lists of white pupils included in *All Hallows in the West* 1, no. 2 (Michelmas 1899): 20–21; 1, no. 3 (Christmas 1899): 41–42; 2, no. 1 (Ascension 1900): 9; 2, no. 2 (Michelmas 1900): 31; 2, no. 3 (Christmas 1900): 56; 3, no. 1 (Ascension 1901): 12–13; 3, no. 3 (Christmas 1901): 76; 6, no. 8 (Ascension 1906): 519–20; 8, no. 11 (Whitsun 1908): 74–75; 8, no. 12 (All Saints 1908): 100–101; no no. (Christmas 1909): 16; no. 13 (Easter 1909): 15–16; no. 15 Canadian number (Midsummer 1911): 17–18.

14 Letter of Charles Mair to George Denison, Kelowna, December 5, 1892. I am grateful to Duane Thomson for access to this correspondence, in his possession.

15 Interview with Mrs. Doris Lazenby, North Vancouver, February 4, 1980; *Work for the Far West* (1908): 18.

16 *New Westminster Quarterly Paper* 65 (May 1895): 8.

17 Interview with Mrs. Clara Clare, Yale, 1964, by Imbert Orchard, BC Archives, Aural History Division, accession no. 400.

18 *East and West* (All Saints 1897): 516; (All Saints 1898): 564–65; and *Work for the Far West* (1901): 15.

19 DIA, Annual Reports (1900), 254; (1903), 271; (1904), 236; (1911), 381.

20 Interview with Mrs. Lavinia Brown, Lytton, October 4, 1983; and Clare interview. For the role of local clerics, see *All Hallows in the West* 1, no. 2 (Michelmas 1899): 23.

21 *All Hallows in the West* 2, no. 1 (Ascension 1900): 18–20; 3, no. 1 (Ascension 1901): 4, 19–20; Indian number 1 (Easter 1911): 8; 8, no. 11 (Whitsun 1908): 78; 1, no. 3 (Christmas 1899): 36; and *New Westminster Quarterly Paper* 4 (1885): 25–27. Until All Hallows' last years, Indigenous pupils were generally identified only by their first Christian name.

22 "Record of Indian Girls [at All Hallows and St. George's Schools], 1910 to 1922," then in possession of Rev. A.W. Harding, Lytton Hospital, Lytton. James Redford has determined that at two other British Columbia Indian residential schools, Methodist Coqualeetza and Catholic Kuyper Island, both co-educational, fully 45 and 50 per cent of pupils during these years had lost one or both parents. See his "Attendance at Indian Residential Schools in British Columbia, 1890–1920," *BC Studies* 44 (Winter 1979–1980): 48.

23 DIA, Annual Reports (1895), xxiii; (1899–1900), 256, 290; (1903), 317; (1907), 259; (1908), 270; (1910), 334, 340; (1911), 378; (1912), 395; (1913), 407; and "Record of Indian Girls," entries 157 and 166.

24 *Churchman's Gazette* (April 1888): 502; (August 1890): 729; *Monthly Record* 11 (July 1890): 6; and "Yale's Mission School," *Daily World* (Vancouver), July 5, 1890.

25 *Churchman's Gazette* (February 1891): 794–95; (August 1891): 842.

26 *New Westminster Quarterly Paper* 67 (March 1896): 19; *East and West* (Winter 1895): 375; *Work for the Far West* (1897): 14; and *All Hallows in the West* 2, no. 3 (Christmas 1900): 63; 3, no. 5 (Christmas 1901): 72.

27 Interviews with Mrs. Lily Rogers, Vancouver, March 7, 1980; and Mrs. Mary Hickman, Chilliwack, December 17, 1983; and Clare, Lazenby, and Pindermoss interviews.

28 Brown interview; *All Hallows in the West* 6, no. 8 (Ascension 1906): 544–46; Indian number, no. 1 (Easter 1911): 25; DIA, Annual Reports (1895–1896), 593–94; (1911), 390; (1913), 404, 409.

29 *East and West* (1886–1919); Sister Violet, *All Hallows*, 25.

30 Victoria Orphan's Home, Annual Report, 1886, quoted in Patricia T. Rooke and R.L. Schnell, *Discarding the Asylum: From Child Rescue to the Welfare State in English-Canada* (New York: University Press of America, 1983): 165.

31 DIA, Annual Report (1896), 394.

32 *Churchman's Gazette* (August 1890): 729; *Monthly Record* 4 (October 1890): 3; *New Westminster Quarterly Paper* 65 (May 1895): 7; *Work for the Far West* (1897): 15; *All Hallows in the West* 2, no. 3 (Christmas 1900): 64; DIA, Annual Reports (1909), 409; (1910), 516; (1913), 532.

33 Hickman interview.

34 *All Hallows in the West* 3, no. 3 (Christmas 1901): 71–73; 6, no. 8 (Ascension 1906): 518, 539; no. 12 (All Saints 1908): 91; Indian number, no 1 (Easter 1911): 18–19.

35 DIA, Annual Reports (1895), xxii; (1891), xii; (1892), xiii-xiv; also (1896), xxxvii.

36 *Churchman's Gazette* (August 1887): 433.

37 *Churchman's Gazette* (April 1888): 502.

38 DIA, Annual Report (1894–1897). Only schools in existence long enough to have pupils to have reached the upper grades were included in this calculation.

39 *Work for the Far West* (1897): 14.

40 *Monthly Record* (September 13, 1890): 8; and *Work for the Far West* (1901): 14. Letters were not edited for publication, and many girls did have trouble with English grammar. See *All Hallows in the West* 1, no. 2 (Michelmas 1899): 27–28. Pride in Indigenous pupils' academic accomplishments is evident in "All Hallows School," *Vancouver Daily World*, August 3, 1899.

41 *New Westminster Quarterly Paper* 65 (May 1895): 7–8; *Work for the Far West* (1896): 13; *East and West* (1894): 308; and *All Hallows in the West* 1, no. 2 (Michelmas 1899): 25; and 2, no. 3 (Christmas 1900): 64.

42 *Monthly Record* 13 (1890): 8; *East and West* (Winter 1891): 62; and *Work for the Far West* (1901): 14.

43 See, for example, *All Hallows in the West* 1, no. 2 (Michelmas 1899): 21–22; 1, no. 3 (Christmas 1899): 41; 2, no. 2 (Michelmas 1900): 33–34; Indian number, no. 1 (Easter 1911): 17 and 25.

44 "Inspector of Indian Agencies to Deputy Superintendent General," June 4, 1904, in DIA, School Files, v. 6001.

45 *East and West* (Ascension, 1907): 1066; *All Hallows in the West* 8, no. 12 (All Saints 1908): 96.

46 D.J. Hall, "Clifford Sifton and Canadian Indian Administration, 1865–1905," *Prairie Forum* 2 (1977): 128. See also Hall's *Clifford Sifton*, vol. 1: *The Young Napoleon, 1861–1900* (Vancouver: UBC Press, 1981): 127–28, 269–71.

47 DIA, Annual Reports (1894), xxi; (1897), xxvii; (1898), xxvii. For evidence that the shift came directly from Sifton, see Hall, "Sifton and Canadian Indian Administration," 133, footnote 32.

48 Frank Oliver in House of Commons debate, June 14, 1897, in *House of Commons Debates*, 2nd session, 8th Parliament (vol. 2), col. 4076, quoted in Hall, "Sifton and Canadian Indian Administration," 134.

49 See DIA, Annual Reports (1900), xxxiii; (1901), xxviii-xxix; (1904), xxvii, xxix; (1911), 388. No evidence exists in the DIA school correspondence files that Indigenous peoples themselves were ever consulted about the imposed change in direction.

50 House of Commons debate, July 18, 1904, in *House of Commons Debates*, 4th session, 9th Parliament (vol. 4), cols. 6946–56, quoted in Hall, "Sifton and Canadian Indian Administration," 134.

51 DIA, Annual Reports (1903), xxvi; (1905), xxxiii.

52 DIA, Annual Reports (1909), xxiv; (1910), 273–75; (1911), 347.

53 DIA, Annual Report (1901), 415.

54 "Notes of reaction-elaborated," in the Rev. Heber Greene papers, Anglican Archives, University of British Columbia.

55 *All Hallows in the West* 8, no. 12 (All Saints 1908): 96.

56 British Columbia, Department of Education, Annual Report (1914–1915), 20; and F. Henry Johnson, *A History of Public Education in British Columbia* (Vancouver: University of British Columbia, 1964), 61. Totals include both high schools and superior schools offering instruction through grade ten.

57 DIA, Annual Report (1904), 402.

58 DIA, Annual Report (1908), 416.

59 *All Hallows in the West*, no. 13 (Easter 1909): 25–26, 28. A similar decline to 18 per cent occurred at residential schools across the province. Even then the proportion was somewhat higher than at residential schools throughout Canada, where in the years 1910–1918, 53 per cent were enrolled in grades 1–2, and just 14 per cent in 5–6.

60 "Notes of reaction-elaborated" in Greene papers.

61 July 8, 1892, entry in Bishop George Hills diary, p. 55, in Anglican Church, Ecclesiastical Province of British Columbia, Archives. By comparison, across British Columbia just over a fifth of all Indigenous pupils enrolled in a residential school reached the two upper grades.

62 *East and West* (All Saints 1911): 2033; (Winter 1912): 30; (Winter 1913): 76; (Winter 1914): 19; (All Saints 1917): 26–27.

63 *All Hallows in the West* 1, no. 2 (Michelmas 1899): 27.

64 *East and West* (All Saints 1890): 33; *Monthly Record* 14 (October 1890): 3; and DIA, Annual Reports (1898), 390; (1900), 421.

65 *East and West* (All Saints 1888): 36; (Easter 1889): 31; (All Saints 1889): 31; (All Saints 1896): 466; (All Saints 1897): 515–16; *Churchman's Gazette* (August 1888): 539; (August 1891): 843; *New Westminster Quarterly Paper* 9 (March 1888): 15; *All Hallows in the West* 1, 3 (Christmas 1899): 47–48.

66 *New Westminster Quarterly Paper* 65 (1895): 8; *East and West* (Winter 1895): 380; (Winter 1903): 800; DIA, Annual Reports (1896), xxxviii; (1900), 255; (1903), 423; (1905), 367; (1908), 448; (1910), 517.

67 DIA, Annual Report (1901), 413; *East and West* (Winter 1899): 600; *All Hallows in the West* 1, no. 1 (Ascension 1900): 13.

68 *All Hallows in the West* 2, no. 2 (Michelmas 1900): 41–42.

69 DIA, Annual Reports (1908), 270; (1903), 317; (1904), 236; (1911), 374; (1913), 400. Rolf Knight argues that "the pinnacle of Indian labour and entrepreneurship within the broader economy [of British Columbia] was reached during the period 1890 to WWI." See his *Indians at Work: An Informal History of Native Labour in British Columbia, 1858–1930* (Vancouver: New Star Books, 1978), 185.

70 DIA, Annual Reports (1907), 407; (1910), 516; (1912), 501; (1913), 532.

71 DIA, Annual Reports (1903), 424; (1906), 443; (1912), 583; (1913), 352; *All Hallows in the West*, Indian number, no. 1 (Easter 1911): 28–29; and Clare interview.

16

Schooled for Inequality

The Education of British Columbia Indigenous Children

Declared to be educating Indigenous children to assimilate into mainstream society as equals, residential schools succeeded only in marginalizing them, destroying their cultures and languages, damaging their family relationships, and undermining their confidence. The system governing the schools was fundamentally flawed in ways that led to marked inequality in the treatment of white and Indigenous children. Four themes stand out: First, all Indigenous people were seen as the same, no matter what their culture or history. Second, although expected to complete the same curriculum as white children, Indigenous children spent far less time in the classroom because their labour was required to keep the schools running. Third, since the main goal of the religious denominations that ran the schools was Christian indoctrination, teachers were usually volunteers rather than professionals, and therefore generally untrained and of low quality. Finally, federal funding of both residential and day schools for Indigenous children quickly fell below provincial funding for public education, or the tuition at even modest private boarding schools, sometimes far below. Nonetheless, Indigenous pupils were excluded from public schooling where they could have done better and been closer to their families.

By Jean Barman. Original title "Schooled for Inequality: The Education of British Columbia Aboriginal Children." Reprinted with permission from *Children, Teachers and Schools in the History of British Columbia*, edited by Jean Barman and Mona Gleason (Calgary: Detselig, 2003), 55–79. The essay has been modestly edited to account for the presence in British Columbia residential schools of children of mixed Indigenous and non-Indigenous descent.[1]

The residential school has become a metaphor for the history of Indigenous education in British Columbia, as in Canada more generally. Any discussion of the broader topic must begin with, and centre on, the residential school, whose existence both curtailed and set the agenda for other educational options.

Residential schools' stark legacy assumes an element of tragedy when set in context. The schools' origins in the late nineteenth century lay in a federal policy premised on Indigenous peoples' assimilation into mainstream Canadian society: "The Indian problem exists owing to the fact that the Indian is untrained to take his place in the world. Once teach him to do this, and the solution is had."[2] By taking children away from the old ways and "civilizing" them into European ways, so the argument ran, "the Indian problem" would be solved in a single generation.[3] The initial goal of the residential school—and of its less favoured counterpart, the federal day school—was the absolute opposite of what occurred. Instead of becoming agents of assimilation, they served, so students' recollections attest, as vehicles for marginalizing generations of young men and women both from the Canadian mainstream and from home environments.[4]

Crucially, while residential schools were aimed at, and continue to be almost wholly associated with, Indigenous students, such was not the case in British Columbia. The phenomenon in that province also caught up children of mixed race, admitted by schools in part to meet enrolment targets, who were thereupon passed off to authorities, and treated in the schools, as being wholly Indigenous. Only in the early twentieth century did federal officials object, and then only partially so. As of 1911, the agreement individual schools signed with the Department of Indian Affairs (DIA) in order to obtain their necessary funding designated that "no half-breed child shall be admitted … unless Indian children cannot be obtained to complete the number authorized," and, if they were admitted, they were not to be federally funded.[5] In consequence, while this essay attends to children with Indian status, its insights also reference the many children having Indigenous mothers and non-Indigenous fathers who were similarly caught up in the schools.[6]

My purpose is not to assess the rightness or wrongness of the federal goal of assimilation, but rather to examine why that policy's principal vehicle, the residential school, became such a dismal failure with far-reaching consequences for the history of Indigenous education. The reasons for the failure had less to do with the actions of individual teachers or administrators than with a federal policy that legitimized and even compelled children to be schooled not for assimilation but for inequality. While teachers and administrators of goodwill were able to ameliorate the worst aspects of the system for their pupils, all of the individual goodwill in the world could not have rescued a system that was fundamentally flawed.

The inequality inherent in federal schools for Indigenous children rests in four complementary attributes of the system as devised and overseen by the DIA. The first was an assumption of the sameness of Indigenous peoples across Canada. Differences existing between tribes, bands, and individuals played no role in a federal policy that viewed Indigenous peoples solely as a singular "object" to be acted upon. In British Columbia, some Indigenous families were already sending their children to public school when federal policy intervened in the late nineteenth century to declare the residential school, and its lesser complement the day school, their sole educational options.

Second, despite a parallel curriculum between federal schools and the provincial schools that educated other Canadian children, Indigenous children attending residential schools were allotted less time in the classroom than were their non-Indigenous counterparts. The difference was particularly marked in the residential schools that formed the system's showplaces. Third, through the mid-twentieth century the instruction of Indigenous children occurred within the much older Western tradition of voluntarism, as opposed to the growing professionalism of teachers in the public schools across Canada. Indigenous schooling was carried on, with few exceptions, by Christian missionaries primarily concerned with saving souls, and only secondarily with literacy education. Finally, federal funding of schools for Indigenous children quickly fell below provincial funding levels for public schools. However fine a school's intentions, they became unrealizable. For these four reasons, as well as others, generations of British Columbia Indigenous children were effectively, if not always deliberately, schooled for inequality.

Assumption of Indigenous Peoples' Sameness

When British Columbia joined Confederation, it became subject to the provisions of the British North America Act that made Indigenous peoples "wards" of the federal government, subject to federally sponsored schooling, health care, and other services on their agreeing to treaties that surrendered traditional lands for much smaller reserves. The policy combined economics with racism. At the time the Canadian Confederation was created in 1867, Indigenous peoples still occupied much of the land on which newcomers hoped to settle. The rhetoric of the day, premised in biological determinism, assumed that persons who were non-white were inferior by virtue of their race alone, and thus incapable of using the land to best advantage or otherwise determining their own destiny. The British North America Act was consistent with this thinking. It made no attempt to distinguish Indigenous peoples in all their diversity and individuality, but simply reduced them to a single dependent status.

Schooling was initially viewed as something of a panacea by the new Department of Indian Affairs, which was charged with overseeing all aspects of federal policy. Using reasoning very similar to that gaining force in the United States, policy makers looked to "civilizing" Indigenous peoples "so as to cause them to reside in towns, or, in the case of farmers, in settlements of white people, and thus become amalgamated with the general community."[7] The residential school became viewed as the best means to achieve that goal, by separating the young from their families and thereby from the old ways.

> The Indian youth, to enable him to cope successfully with his brother of white origin, must be dissociated from the prejudicial influences by which he is surrounded on the reserve of his band. And the necessity for the establishment more generally of institutions, whereat Indian children, besides being instructed in the usual branches of education, will be lodged, fed, clothed, kept separate from home influences, taught trades and instructed in agriculture, is becoming every year more apparent.[8]

Two types of residential schools came into being in Canada: boarding schools for younger children and industrial schools for their older siblings. Not only did the latter put greater emphasis on occupational training, but they also tended to be larger and located farther away from pupils' home reserves. Over time the distinction between the two kinds of schools broke down, and they all became known as residential schools. Day schools were perceived by the DIA as less acceptable than either boarding or industrial schools, to be established only where circumstances did not permit their preferred counterparts.

For Indigenous peoples in British Columbia, the consequences of federal policy favouring residential schools were particularly poignant, for it removed an educational option already in place that might have given their children rough equality with white contemporaries across the young province. For a decade and more, British Columbia Indigenous children had been finding their way into provincial public schools alongside their neighbours and, to some extent, gaining acceptance there. Another narrative might well be constructed today about British Columbia Indigenous peoples had not federal policy intervened.

Part of the explanation for this situation lies in demographics and part in Indigenous peoples' circumstances of everyday life. At the time British Columbia entered Confederation in 1871, Indigenous peoples still formed the overwhelming proportion of the population. They totalled some 25,000 or more, compared to about 1,500 Chinese, almost all of them adult males, some 500 Black people, and approximately 8,500 whites. In many outlying settlements, Indigenous children were necessary to secure the minimum enrolment necessary for a public school's establishment and survival.

Indigenous peoples in British Columbia were, and are, among the world's most distinctive. Linguistic divisions were complex, economies self-sufficient, and cultures more developed, in many respects, than in any other part of the continent north of Mexico. Generational continuity was assured through ongoing, lifelong education premised on the young modelling their behaviour on that of their elders. There was, moreover, a long tradition of economic and social interaction with Europeans, initially in the fur trade and then during the gold rush beginning in 1858. The continued availability of such traditional staples as salmon, cedar, and game animals meant that British Columbia Indigenous peoples did not experience the wrenching despair and utter dependency that befell their prairie counterparts. As the DIA phrased it with particular reference to British Columbia, "The Indians have been from the earliest times self-supporting, and the advent of white population, which in the west caused the complete disappearance of the buffalo, did not occasion any serious change in their source of food-supply."[9] More than one settler was struck by how "the Indians differ *toto caelo* from the North West plains Indians. They are very well off."[10]

The published annual reports of the DIA repeatedly lauded British Columbia's Indigenous peoples. In 1880: "The Indians of British Columbia exhibit more enterprise than those of any other Province in the Dominion";[11] 1890: "The Indians of this Province, with but few exceptions, pursued their wanted course of manly independence, intelligent enterprise, and unflagging industry during the past year";[12] 1902: "Taking them altogether, the British Columbia Indians are remarkably industrious, enterprising, self-reliant, honest, sober and law-abiding. They are good neighbours, and friendly with the whites and with each other."[13]

Perhaps, then, it is not surprising that as public schools became established across the far-flung province in the 1870s and 1880s, Indigenous children were often among the earliest to seek to enroll alongside their settler neighbours. "There are a few bright-looking native children here. Would it be all right if I get them to attend the school?"[14] "There are numbers of Indian children that for whom no provision in the way of education has hitherto been made."[15] "There are three Indian ... children that wish to attend the school when it is established."[16] The Superintendent of Education was consistently supportive: "You are doing perfectly right in admitting Indian children so long as they are not taken [by force] & conduct themselves properly ... If they are troublesome or dirty the trustees must prohibit their attendance—Personally I am glad to hear of their attendance wherever circumstances will admit of it."[17] The Superintendent responded in 1886 to a query by some "parents of white children" about "Indian" children's attendance: "There is no authority given in the School Act to refuse them admittance. Since the inception of the present School system they have been admitted on an equality with other pupils."[18] Indigenous children's attendance was for the most part accepted without question, as a matter of course, perhaps because they were often not that different in actions and even appearance from their non-Indigenous contemporaries.

Indigenous families in British Columbia demonstrated a resourcefulness that would have served them well had not a federal education policy assuming their sameness across Canada intervened. Although only a handful of treaties were ever made in British Columbia, federal services similar to those in other provinces were gradually provided there as well. And despite repeated statements in the DIA's annual reports lauding the distinctiveness of British Columbia Indigenous people, they were treated no differently than their counterparts across Canada.

As the number of federal schools grew, it became increasingly difficult for Indigenous children to attend their local school. The shift began in about 1888. A teacher noted, concerning an "application to admit an Indian as a pupil," that the trustees "are of the opinion that the Dominion Government undertakes to provide for the educational interests of the Indians." To which the Superintendent responded:

> Although Indian children are considered to be wards of the Dominion Government, yet it has not been the custom to refuse them admittance to Public Schools whose attendance is not over large. Of course they are required to comply with the Rules and Regulations as to cleanliness, supplying themselves with books etc. In all cases refer such matters to the Board of Trustees.[19]

The Superintendent was less sanguine a year later, considering that "Indian children are wards of the Dominion Government, and are not presumed to be entitled to attend the Public Schools of the Province."[20]

Yet so many Indigenous children continued to attend British Columbia public schools that in the fall of 1891 the Superintendent of Education somewhat relented, stating in a circular that "the matter of attendance of Indian children is left entirely in the hands of the [local] Board of Trustees."[21] Responses from individual teachers and boards of trustees almost all supported Indigenous children's continued presence. A teacher wrote that they were "quiet, tidy and much more devoted to study than the average child";[22] another that "the rate-payers seem to be of the opinion that it is of advantage to the community if the young Indians who reside here was [*sic*] educated."[23] The secretary of a school board reported that "the present Trustees all think the privilege of getting a better education should not be denied them especially as their parents seem grateful for it."[24] Two years later, in the fall of 1893, the Superintendent ruled, "If a single parent objects to the attendance of Indian pupils, they cannot be permitted to attend."[25] To which one trustee responded indignantly, "It is desirable that in every locality the relations between Indians & settlers should be friendly but this ruling is not likely to secure it."[26]

While some Indigenous children continued to attend individual public schools up to the time of the First World War, and a few thereafter, they were the exceptions rather than the rule. Growing numbers of settlers meant that Indigenous pupils were no longer essential to most schools' survival, schools received no funding for Indigenous pupils, and federal policy discouraged their attendance. The moment of opportunity had passed. By 1900, British Columbia possessed fourteen Indian residential and twenty-eight day schools, enrolling 675 and 893 pupils respectively.[27] Two decades later, totals had risen to 1,115 children in seventeen residential schools and 1,197 in forty-six day schools; by 1940, 2,035 children were in fifteen residential schools and 2,025 in sixty-five day schools.

Into the mid-twentieth century, federal policy toward Indigenous peoples, adults as well as children, refused to acknowledge their distinctiveness within geographical areas or as individuals. They were treated as a single category to be dealt with as expeditiously and economically as possible. The initiative demonstrated by British Columbia Indigenous peoples, in political and economic matters as well as schooling, only served to label them as nuisances for refusing to conform into dependency.[28]

Time in the Classroom

Logically, the shift of British Columbia Indigenous children from provincial to federal schools should not have made any difference to them academically, for in 1895 the newly established School Branch of the Department of Indian Affairs laid down a uniform curriculum little different in form from its provincial counterparts. Indigenous pupils were to move between six "standards" or grades centred on readers similar to those being used in provincial systems.[29] Instruction was to be offered in writing, arithmetic, English, geography, ethics, history, vocal music, calisthenics and religion. It was anticipated that "the work done and results obtained ... [would] equal those of the common-schools of the rural districts."[30]

The new curriculum would have boded well for the proclaimed federal goal of Indigenous peoples' assimilation had not children been expected somehow to get through it in less time each day than was allotted their counterparts in provincial schools. While some flexibility existed in day schools, which were never that closely monitored by federal authorities, in residential schools only half of each day was usually spent in the classroom. Sometimes this occurred in segments. At one school, the hours of instruction ran 9 to 11:30 a.m. and 2 to 3 p.m.[31] Regardless of format, the total was two to four hours per day, compared with the five hours or longer that other Canadian children spent on the prescribed curriculum.

The reports on individual schools, included in the annual reports of the DIA, often implied longer hours of instruction, but accounts from individual schools almost always reveal a shorter time period. Personal testimonies are damning: "We went to school in the mornings about ten o'clock ... I would stay there till dinner time. Twelve o'clock."[32] "We spent very little time in the classroom. We were in the classroom from nine o'clock in the morning until noon. Another shift [of children] came into the classroom at one o'clock in the afternoon and stayed until three."[33] At a third: "We knew we had to do our chores, such as sweeping the dormitory, cleaning the washrooms, in the morning, and go to school half a day. We had our chores to do in the afternoon."[34] This pupil's daily round grew more onerous as he got older: "Our job was getting tougher. We went to school for half a day. One month you worked in the mornings and the next month you worked in the afternoons. We never went to school full-time until the last year, in grade eight."[35] In his discussion of the academic subjects taught in British Columbia Catholic residential schools, Oblate historian Thomas Lascelles concluded:

> Usually they occupied the students several hours a day, the remainder being devoted to training in practical skills such as farming, shoemaking and housekeeping, an arrangement which was not abandoned until the 1940s or 1950s when pupils began to spend full time on academic subjects, and to follow Provincial curricula more closely.[36]

Shorter time periods for classroom instruction existed despite many children's being forced to study in a second language. As part of their becoming "civilized," federal policy asserted that Indigenous children be "taught in the English language exclusively."[37] The languages that most boys and girls brought with them to school were almost always prohibited, even for private conversations between pupils: "Native languages were forbidden. English was the only allowable language."[38] "What I could never understand, we weren't allowed to speak our language. If we were heard speaking Shuswap, we were punished. We were made to write on the board one hundred times, 'I will not speak Indian any more.'"[39] "In my first meeting with the brother, he showed me a long black leather strap and told me, through my interpreter, 'If you are ever caught speaking Indian this is what you will get across your hands.'"[40]

The logic behind the limited time allotted to the formal curriculum was obvious to policy makers. While it was important that Indigenous children be made literate in English, it was even more critical that they acquire the practical skills permitting their entry into mainstream society, but only at its very lowest rungs. Although assimilation was a desirable goal, its achievement should not challenge the status quo. During the second half of each school day, boys learned how to do farm chores or some low-status trade such as shoemaking, girls to perform household tasks ranging from potato peeling to dusting to needlework. As a pamphlet widely distributed by the Methodist church put the case in 1906,

> The girl who has learned only the rudiments of reading, writing and ciphering, and knows also how to make and mend her clothing, wash and iron, make a good loaf of bread, cook a good dinner, keep her house neat and clean, will be worth vastly more as mistress of a log cabin than one who had given years of study to the ornamental branches alone ... The Indian must be educated along industrial lines. It should be along the line of the physical rather than the mental.[41]

However much federal rhetoric might have maintained the illusion of assimilation, the DIA was assuring failure in terms of Indigenous pupils competing socially or intellectually with their white neighbours. Whereas most pupils in provincial schools reached the upper elementary grades by the end of the First World War, the overwhelming majority of Indigenous children never got beyond grades 1 or 2. Up to 1920, four out of every five Indigenous boys and girls attending federal schools across Canada were only enrolled in grades 1, 2, or 3. This did not mean that they had been in the school so short a time period, but, more likely, that they were simply kept in the lower grades year after year for convenience's sake or because the level of instruction was so poor: "We only had two hours of classes when I went to residential school. We worked ... you had to get out as soon as you're sixteen. I didn't get much education, very little education."[42]

Indigenous pupils were, in any case, long prohibited by law from going beyond the elementary grades: "There was a rule at that time that Indians could not go past Grade eight. I do not recall many boys staying around long enough to protest the education that was being denied us."[43] "We had to stay in school until we were eighteen years of age to go as high as grade eight. And then no high school after."[44] Through the middle of the twentieth century, the proportion of Indigenous children in school across Canada who were in grades 1 to 3 stagnated at two-thirds or more. In sharp contrast, the percentage of their white counterparts in provincial schools who were enrolled in grades 1 to 3 fell by mid-century to just over a third, indicating that almost all non-Indigenous children were by then completing the elementary grades. Similarly, whereas the proportion of children of the dominant society reaching grade 7 or higher grew from less than one-fifth in 1920 to about one-third by 1950, the percentage of Indigenous children to reach grade 7 moved up from none in 1920 to 3 per cent a decade later and then to just 10 per cent by mid-century.[45] Father Lascelles summed up the situation in his observation: "The half-day academic program in effect until the middle of this century ensured that the children did not receive an education on a par with that given in the public schools."[46] Even thereafter, a boy at school during the mid-1950s recalled that "classes were from nine in the morning until three in the afternoon, but many times we were taken from class to work outside."[47]

Teachers and Teaching

The third attribute of federal policy ensuring that Indigenous children were schooled for inequality grew out of the remarkable symbiosis that developed between the federal government and the various religious denominations across Canada. Unlike the American education policy, where missionaries were subordinated to the federal government, in Canada they were left in charge. The major churches had already carved Canada up into spheres of influence for the purpose of Indigenous conversion, and they eagerly accepted the new challenge, subsidized by a federal per-pupil grant to existing schools and sometimes also by funding to build needed new ones. The DIA restricted itself to general oversight, which included annual reporting by each school and periodic visits by local officials, known as Indian agents.

While the Canadian policy was justified as suitably acknowledging a school system already underway, it was also an economy move, excusing the federal government from having to create and maintain its own institutions: "The department has fully recognized its inability to conduct such institutions as economically as can be done by denominations, and consequently it has endeavoured to have their management placed in the hands of the respective churches."[48] A student has recalled, "One day Sister Catherine told us in the classroom, 'We work so hard for you, we don't get any pay at all for looking after you Indians.'"[49]

By leaving schools' ongoing operation to missionary groups, the federal government relieved itself of direct responsibility for the provision, payment, or supervision of teaching staffs. In residential schools, teachers were most often missionaries principally motivated by commitment to Indigenous peoples' conversion. "We had prayers ten, twenty times a day and when we weren't praying, we were changing clothes for prayers. We prayed when we got up, we prayed before breakfast and after breakfast, and we prayed when we got to the classroom and when we were in the classroom. I lost count of how many times a day we prayed."[50] One pupil shrewdly observed: "Mr. Hall wasn't paid to teach us, I don't think. I think he was just paid as a minister."[51] At their best, teachers possessed, as one federal official phrased it, "infinite patience and tact, although without scholarly attainments."[52]

The situation was comparable between residential and day schools.[53] Although individual teachers were sometimes sympathetic to pupils' plight and so remembered by them, they were, with rare exceptions, untrained. A group of local parents informed the DIA in 1936 that "the Indians of our Band are quite willing and anxious to do their part in educating their children, but we are asking the Department to give us a capable Instructor who will take a deeper interest in the progress of our children."[54] Having considered the request, DIA concluded, "While he is not a trained teacher, and the children do not make the same progress as they might with a modern highly trained instructor, he is rendering good service to the Department in a variety of ways."[55]

The contemporary literature is replete with observations attesting to the poor quality of teaching. A pupil of the 1920s mused, "It is said by many that the teachers are not really teachers at all. They are not trained as the teachers are in the [local public] school."[56] Conversely, a sister teaching at the same school recalled being informed by the federal inspector of Indian schools that "there is no training for your situation anyway, just for public schools."[57] An anonymous comment in DIA's internal files, dated 1932, acknowledged that teaching positions were sometimes "merely posts provided for persons for whom billets had to be found."[58] The next decade the refrain was the same, that teachers "were often unqualified to teach. They used to just send old missionaries to the village to try and do the best they could."[59] The situation continued largely unchanged into the mid-twentieth century, in sharp contrast to the growing professionalism distinguishing teachers and teaching in the dominant society.

Where individuals' religious commitment conflicted with their role as a teacher, the former usually triumphed. A local Indian agent observed in 1912 that "there is a disposition to devote too much time to imparting religious instruction to the children as compared with the imparting of secular knowledge, which is perhaps not unnatural when the teachers are employed and selected by the various churches."[60] The pupil-teacher relationship outside of the classroom was often determined more by religious than by didactic considerations:

> If you passed them [the nuns] in the hall or anywhere, you're to stop and bow your head. They were really up on the pedestal ... They sure put themselves somewhere where you couldn't touch them. You couldn't reach them and you had to bow to them, ... it made me to a certain extent very bitter by the time I left school.[61]

Language sometimes compounded difficulties. Whereas Indigenous children were expected, once in school, totally to abandon their Indigenous tongue in favour of English, their teachers did not necessarily know the English language sufficiently well to speak it, much less teach it to others: "But them French teachers you know they don't really pronounce their sounds right. There was only Sister Patricia who was Irish."[62] The DIA acknowledged a possible conflict in its observation that "the dual system of control between the department on the one hand and the church on the other, each with their different ideals, the one requiring a secular education, and the other looking more to the spiritual instruction of the children, is almost somewhat anomalous."[63]

Underfunding

The fourth and perhaps most fundamental reason why Indigenous children were schooled for inequality lay in schools' low levels of federal financial support. Even taking into account the largely volunteer labour available as a consequence of schools' missionary ties, they were underfunded when compared with provincial institutions or even with the bare basics of survival. The per-pupil subsidy provided by the federal government assumed that much of the teaching would be volunteer, but even then it was inadequate to provide a minimum standard of everyday life, much less material conditions conducive to learning. The men and women who ran the schools were expected to scramble for donations simply to survive. Father Lascelles made an important link: "Crucial to the determined efforts [of Catholic residential schools to secure better qualified teachers], however, were dollars; dollars which were few and far between."[64]

The published reports of the DIA were very open in acknowledging the inadequacy of funding of residential schools, as in 1896: "The denominations interested in the last-named, owing to the smallness of the annual per capita grant, are forced to meet any shortage of the Government grant by contributions from outside sources."[65] A decade later the annual report stated bluntly that residential schools across the country were "all largely supplemented by the missionary societies."[66] Father Lascelles concluded that between 1915 and about 1950, "funding for the education of Indian children by the Department [of Indian Affairs] remained at a relative standstill."[67]

The half-day program adopted in most residential schools became little more than pupils' undertaking of the manual labour necessary for institutions' survival. From the early years, federal officials aspired to schools' "becoming self-supporting" through pupils raising crops, making clothes, and generally doing "outside work."[68]

> The longer half of our day was spent in what the brothers called "industrial training." Industrial training consisted of doing all the kinds of manual labour that are commonly done around a farm, except that we did not have the use of the equipment that even an Indian farmer of those days would have been using.[69]

The need for manual labour cut across the sexes, and many "an Indian girl washed, cooked, cleaned, and mended her way through residential school."[70] "We had to patch. We had to patch the boys' clothes. We had to wash and iron Mondays and Tuesdays. We had to patch and keep on patching till Saturday."[71] "We made all of the dresses and uniforms worn in the school, and socks, drawers, chemises, and aprons." The situation was, in this woman's view, even more detrimental for her male counterparts: "The bigger ones spent almost no time in class. Instead, they were cutting down trees and pulling up stumps, or else they were up before daylight feeding the horses and milking the cows." And long after he left Lejac residential school, one boy recalled, "I'm just a human bulldozer!"[72] "I was up at five-thirty every morning either to serve as an altar boy for Mass or to work on the farm, milking cows, working the garden, and so forth."[73]

From the perspective of some pupils, poor food, or too little to eat, caused most distress. "Hunger is both the first and last thing I can remember about that school. I was hungry from the day I went into the school until they took me to the hospital two and a half years later. Not just me. Every Indian pupil smelled of hunger."[74] Particularly difficult for pupils was their being expected to eat the barest of fare day after day while subjected to the smells and even the sight of the schools' staff dining far more sumptuously.

> After Mass we put our smocks over our uniforms and line up for breakfast in the hall outside the dining room. We can talk then because Sister goes for breakfast in the Sisters' dining room. They get bacon or ham, eggs, toast and juice. We can see when they open the door and go in for breakfast. We get gooey mush with powder milk and brown sugar.[75]

> "The food given to us daily was not of the best. I am saying the food for the staff was of better quality and more palatably prepared."[76]

> At school it was porridge, porridge, porridge, and if it wasn't that, it was boiled barley or beans, and thick slices of bread spread with lard. Weeks went by without a taste of meat or fish ... A few

> times I would catch the smell of roasting meat coming from the nuns' dining room, and I couldn't help myself—I would follow that smell to the very door. Apart from the summers, I believe I was hungry for all seven of the years I was at school ...we were on rations more suited to a concentration camp![77]

The comparison was not inapt: according to the wife of the commander of a First World War camp for German prisoners of war, they were provided only with "cheap" food, the allocation for food being limited to "approximately seventeen cents per person per day," or just over fifty dollars a year.[78]

The actual situation on the ground was that many Indigenous children fared less well than did prisoners of war. Up to 1910, boarding schools received from the federal government a grant of sixty dollars a year per qualifying pupil, which was intended to cover all costs, not just food. Industrial schools received double that amount, or even a bit more, but the consequence for all residential schools was what one administrator termed "frugal maintenance."[79] Moreover, because most schools, as part of their religious commitment to service, accepted additional children to the total allotted them by the DIA, federal funds were usually stretched over a larger pupil body than intended. Federal day schools in British Columbia received an annual federal grant of twelve dollars per pupil. The paucity of the amount becomes evident on comparison to neighbouring British Columbia public schools, whose budgets rose from an average of fifteen dollars per pupil at the turn of the century to double that amount by 1908.[80]

From 1900 to 1908, some industrial and boarding schools' statements of income and expenditure were published in DIA's annual reports. They make clear the extent to which schools struggled to make ends meet. Including donations, the annual income per pupil at the three British Columbia boarding schools whose financial statements were published for 1900 averaged $94. Of this total, $41 comprised the government subsidy, which in theory was $60 per pupil but in practice was much less due to the schools' greater enrolments than allotted by DIA. The remaining $53 of income per pupil consisted of donations, contributed primarily to further the schools' religious purposes. Housekeeping expenses alone, principally food, exceeded total federal funding at $44 per child. Physical upkeep of facilities added another $16 per pupil. Salaries for the minority of staff who received wages totalled $28 per pupil, and miscellaneous expenses ranging from school books to clothing $9 per pupil.[81] Financial statements for seven British Columbia boarding schools were published for 1908. Their average income per pupil was $87, of which $46 comprised the federal subsidy and $41 donations. Out of necessity, housekeeping expenses, including food, had fallen to an average of $38 per pupil. Physical upkeep was $13, salaries $21, and miscellaneous expenses $13.[82]

The parsimony of federal funding is particularly evident when comparison is made to private schools for children of the dominant society. At All Hallows, the only British Columbia boarding school enrolling both Indigenous and white female boarders, the latter's families were charged $160 a year in 1900.[83] At the turn of the century, even a relatively modest private day school had fees of $50 a year, roughly the amount on which the federal government expected Indigenous boarders to survive.[84]

Federal subsidies for Indigenous pupils were revised upward in 1910, but not to adequate levels. Moreover, "increased financial assistance" came at the cost of "greater demands" in the standard of buildings, care, and administration. For instance, the per-pupil subsidy for boarding schools was doubled from $60 to $125, but only after schools met rigorous new requirements demanding more space per pupil, better physical facilities, and far higher health and sanitation standards—no easy matter given that capital costs for upgrading were not integral to the revised policy.[85] By comparison, in 1912 an elite private school for white boys charged $470 a year for boarders, $150 for day pupils.[86]

Day school grants were raised in 1910 to $17 per child, but by then the comparable allocation per pupil in the British Columbia provincial system had reached $34.[87] As the reports of Indian agents repeatedly emphasized, teachers' salaries were a central issue for day schools often compelled to hire from outside of religious orders. "Complaint is continually made of the small amount allowed for a teacher. The teachers of the public schools receive at least $80 per month, with a long summer vacation, and have fewer scholars than the teachers of Indian day schools."[88] Another Indian agent noted that "the churches do not pay an adequate salary and trained teachers prefer to go to white schools, where social surroundings are always preferable to the isolated location among the Indians."[89]

Within a few short years, federal schools in British Columbia, and across Canada, were in even worse financial straits. A school inspector on the prairies reported in 1915 concerning residential schools:

> Although the per capita grant given by the department was increased about four years ago, the religious bodies, under whose auspices these schools are operated, find the grant to be inadequate to meet the advanced cost of foodstuffs daily in use in these schools. Moreover, contributions toward the support of such institutions are said to have been diminished, owing chiefly to the financial stringency caused by the war in Europe.[90]

Contributing to a deteriorating situation was some missionaries' growing interest in the conversion of Asians in Asia, viewed as more tractable and perhaps more glamorous than Indigenous peoples.[91] To some extent, Indigenous schools ended up with the leftovers, missionaries lacking the zeal and determination to put themselves in the front line of Christianity's advance.

Federal stinginess was not lost on contemporaries. The respected anthropologist Diamond Jenness undertook considerable personal observation across Canada during the 1920s prior to writing his landmark description of the country's Indigenous peoples. While damning the quality of teaching in many schools as "exceedingly poor," he was very concerned that missionaries not be blamed since "they lacked the resources and the staffs to provide a proper education ... It was not the missions that shirked their responsibility, but the federal government, and behind that government the people of Canada."[92] Yet as late as 1947, even as a Joint Parliamentary Committee was finally being established to probe Indigenous affairs, the federal government was spending $45 a year per Indigenous pupil in a federal day school, compared with about $200 that the British Columbia government allocated per pupil in a public school.[93] As Father Lascelles insightfully concluded, "Financial problems were one of the major handicaps the schools laboured under for more than half a century."[94]

The Indigenous Response and Changing Times

Perhaps the most fundamental critique of federal policy was its deluding of Indigenous peoples. Certainly, not all parents sought formal schooling for their offspring. Concerning "a large no. of children of the pure Siwash [Chinook word for "Indian"] persuasion between the ages of 5 and 16 in the district," an early British Columbia public teacher reported that "it will be a difficult matter to get them to attend school as their respected progenitors believe them to be as well off without book learning as with it."[95] Many an Indian agent reported that "parents see in education the downfall of all their most cherished customs."[96]

Still, many families accepted at face value what they were given every reason to believe was, despite its obvious tradeoffs, a genuine opportunity for their children. Indigenous parents in British Columbia sent their children first to public schools and then to federal schools, as one former pupil put it, "to learn White people's ways."[97] A woman born in 1931 remembered her mother's words: "You're going to have to learn to read and write because when you grow up you're going to have to get a job."[98] Other times it was fathers who made their children aware of changing times: "'It's going to get crowded in the valley in a few years,' he said … 'You kids want to get yourselves an education. Get a job. That way you'll be okay.'"[99] The deception wrought on Indigenous parents was deliberate. Pupils were repeatedly admonished against giving their families details of what went on in school and in some cases prohibited from doing so. As late as the 1950s, letters were routinely censored: "Sister Theo checks our letters home. We're not allowed to say anything about the school. I might get the strap, or worse."[100]

British Columbia families became frustrated as they realized that their children were being treated unfairly. The refrain was the same regardless of geographical area or particular circumstances. "Children are not taught enough." "We wish our children taught the same as the whites. They go to school, maybe, five, six, seven years. They learn read a little. That's all. Not much use."[101] "They just get nicely started—they just get their eyes opened the same as young birds and then they are turned out to fly. They don't get enough education for a livelihood nor are they taught a trade of any kind."[102] "The boys are not learning how to hunt and trap and set a net for fish … They are supposed to go to Lejac to be educated, but they are not in the classrooms. They are in the fields or the barns, and the girls are too much in the sewing room or the kitchen."[103] "We all apply to have [a day] school at our own place … Please look into matter soon as possible. We feed our children at home then."[104]

Not only were such voices unheard by federal policy makers, but individual parents faced tremendous obstacles when they sought to intervene in their children's best interests. Two examples from Vancouver Island are indicative. "I wanted my boys to go to high school, so I went to see the Indian agent, M.S. Todd, and told him so. He said to me, 'Nothing doing!' I asked him, 'Isn't it for everybody?' and he answered me, 'Not for you people.'"[105] A second father was forced to desperate measures so that his children "would be able to go to school a full term."

> The school at Village Island was run by the Indian Department and we used to have that schoolteacher for three months a year ... I went over to the Indian Office at Alert Bay and pleaded with the Indian agent to keep her on for another couple months. He told me that he had no authority to pay her for another month and that they had spent all that was allowed. So I went to the school teacher and asked if she would accept $50 to stay for another month ... So the next month Simon Beans paid her $50 to stay for another month. That's how hard it was.[106]

Parents who resisted federal schools altogether in favour of the local public school rarely succeeded. One exception was a North Vancouver parent who, having spent a decade in residential school, was determined that his children would not do so. Given that this was at the beginning of the Second World War, it may be that the system was beginning to crack. Alternatively, this father was particularly determined:

> We didn't want to send them to no boarding school because I was working and we wanted them at home. We had quite a time to have them accepted into the public school. We finally got them admitted. Priscilla and Barbara were the first Indian children to be accepted into the public school. I had to struggle with Indian Affairs, the North Vancouver School Board, the West Vancouver School Board to get my children in school ... I had to pay their tuition fee myself for two years to have my children go to the public school. I paid five dollars a month per child.[107]

It was not just adults but also children who became actors. In some cases, pupils through their own efforts mitigated the schools' worst characteristics, not just for themselves but for their fellow pupils. As one of them recalled about his time at residential school:

> Sometimes we used to help the ones who needed it. I always had that in my mind because I was brought up by my people, the teaching I got was to always try to help the other person … I used to take the lower class out who were having problems, go for a walk … I taught them about nature, making a bow and arrow, little canoes, to get their minds off problems.[108]

More often, pupils simply refused to cooperate as they realized that residential school was not what it purported to be: "The boys often rebelled and I didn't blame them. They were supposed to be in Lejac to get educated, but instead they were unpaid laborers, living on poor food and no more freedom than if they were prisoners in a jail."[109] Pupils protested treatment deemed unfair and discriminatory and, in cases of desperation, they ran away: "I ran away from the bus that was going to take me back to school and I hid in the bush until the priests and the police officers stopped looking for me."[110] "Some were successful and managed to reach their parents' traplines, but more often, they were caught by the Mounties, brought back and whipped."[111] Sociologist Celia Haig-Brown has argued that resistance was integral to everyday life in residential school.[112]

Over time, Indigenous peoples did effect change, but extraordinarily slowly. Unlike the United States, where federal policy began to encourage children into public schools during the interwar years, in Canada the symbiosis between state and church was too comfortable to be altered until it became absolutely impossible to ignore changing times.[113] Only after the Second World War did increased awareness of Indigenous peoples lead to the creation of a Select Joint Committee of the Senate and House of Commons, which in 1951 called for Indigenous peoples' integration into the Canadian mainstream. Although Indigenous education was still under federal jurisdiction,

Indigenous children were encouraged to attend provincial schools or a private school run by one of the religious denominations that had previously operated federal residential and day schools. Funding still came from the federal government, through tuition agreements negotiated with provincial governments or religious denominations. Early integration was often top down, with Indigenous children attending a local public school for grades beyond those available in an existing federal school: "Dorothy goes to classes at St. Mark's now, the Catholic high school in town. All the pupils in grade ten, eleven and twelve do. Father Pitt drives them in a yellow school bus every day."[114] Integration sometimes led to new forms of discrimination: "We still had to wear the residential school clothes and this made an obvious distinction between us and the other students who would taunt us."[115]

For individual Indigenous children, integration sometimes existed more in theory than in practice: "It was difficult going to [public] school, a lot of ideas and attitudes haven't changed much. Segregation is happening, not visibly but in the classes." At this school, Indigenous children were seated separately in the classroom, and it remained very much a "white man's school."[116] Other children continued to attend federal schools not that much changed from previous decades:

> We had a school that taught Grades One to Seven, with teachers hired by the Department of Indian Affairs. Some of them were good, but others were young and didn't give a hell. The villagers, the chief, and the councillors had no say in the qualifications or lack of them n the teachers who were hired—we just took what we could get.[117]

By 1970, three-quarters of the 13,000 Indigenous pupils in British Columbia were attending integrated institutions.

About the same time, in 1969, Prime Minister Pierre Elliott Trudeau issued a white paper, or policy document, calling for total

Indigenous integration into his "Just Society." He proposed to repeal the Indian Act and abolish Indigenous peoples' special status in Canada. The Indigenous response was overwhelmingly negative, a decade and more of growing awareness having awoken pride in heritage and culture. The white paper was withdrawn in favour of Indigenous self-determination moving toward Indigenous control over their own affairs. Band-operated schools, whose numbers have steadily increased across Canada, were intended to encourage pride in Indigenous languages and cultures alongside the necessary skills to participate in mainstream society.

The official shift in Indigenous education policy did not effect change immediately. As one band leader recalled about the 1970s: "We had to fight for every dollar and every bit of independence we could get for the education of our children. A policy of delay, delay, delay, was practised and is still practised."[118] The schooling of Indigenous children remains a federal responsibility, although tuition agreements with provinces, churches, and bands mean that children in British Columbia, like their counterparts across Canada, no longer have a single educational option. Indigenous children living on a reserve often attend a school operated by the local band, especially at the lower grade levels. Older children usually go by bus to the nearest public or Catholic parochial high school. Other families living on a reserve may have chosen to send their children from kindergarten on to a nearby public or parochial school. Most Indigenous children living in urban settings now attend school alongside their non-Indigenous contemporaries almost as a matter of course. Children in some urban areas also have alternative Indigenous-oriented facilities available to them. These shifts, as important as they are, only go part way. A paucity of Indigenous teachers, inadequate support for teaching Indigenous languages, and lack of appropriate Indigenous content in textbooks and in the classroom are only some of the difficulties yet to be resolved for the education of British Columbia Indigenous children to become truly equal to that of other British Columbia children.[119]

The Legacy

The education of Indigenous children remains unequal, and, although the residential school has disappeared from the Canadian educational landscape, its legacy endures. Federal policy resulted in practices whose consequences are still being lived across British Columbia and in the rest of Canada.

> If I had to pick one area where the federal government, through the Department of Indian Affairs, inflicted the most harm on my people, it would have to be in the field of education ... At the beginning of the white man's rule, Indigenous people were confined to reserves, most of them far away from schools. When the government was finally forced to do something about the lack of educational facilities, the solution was a partnership between church and state to set up residential schools. Children were removed from their communities and placed in an alien environment that almost destroyed their culture and their language; we call it cultural genocide.[120]

The personal accounts used to ground this essay have ranged through time and across British Columbia, but they have all told a similar story.

Half or fewer of the Indigenous children of past generations in British Columbia actually attended residential school, but numbers were sufficient for family life to deteriorate. A pupil has recalled her "inability to show love to my mom, brothers, and sisters."[121] Students of different sexes were almost always separated in residential school, and siblings in the same school often could not even speak to each other for months and years on end: "I never did get to know my brothers. We were kept away from each other for too long. To this day I don't know much about my brothers. I just know that they are my brothers."[122] "After a year spent learning to see and hear only what the priests and brothers wanted you to see and hear, even the people we loved came to look ugly."[123] "Some of the most damaging things that resulted from my experiences at residential school was lack of nurturing as well as being denied learning parenting skills."[124] The next generation reaped the consequences:

> Although my older brother and I didn't attend residential school, we didn't really escape it either as it visited us every day of our childhood through the replaying over and over of our parents' childhood trauma and grief which they never had the opportunity to resolve in their lifetimes ... I grieve for the gentle man in my father who was never allowed to grow, and I grieve for my mother who never had the loving relationships she deserved, nor the opportunity to be the mother I knew she could have been.[125]

Languages became a casualty. A father who spoke six languages in his job as a court interpreter deliberately refrained from teaching his children.

> He speaks lots of Indian languages, but he won't teach us. Mom won't either. She says the nuns and priests will strap us ... The nuns strapped her all the time for speaking Indian, because she couldn't speak English. She said just when the welts on her hands and arms healed, she got it again. That's why she didn't want us to learn Indian.[126]

The practice was widespread: "Because my parents also attended residential school they didn't see the value in teaching us our language. The Indian Agent told them not to speak to their children in Haida because it would not help them in school."[127] "It didn't matter that Carrier was the only language we knew—we were told not to use it and, if we did, wham! right now. I think now that it was the worst thing that happened to us."[128]

The self-fulfilling prophecy inherent in racism came to fruition as Indigenous peoples deemed to be inferior were schooled for inequality and thereby largely did end up at the bottom ranks of Canadian society: "The residential school (not just the one I went to—they were the common form of Indian education all across Canada) was the perfect system for instilling a strong sense of inferiority."[129] The reasons are not difficult to fathom:

> For many of us our most vulnerable and impressionable years, our childhood years, were spent at the residential school where we had always been treated like dirt and made to believe that we weren't as good as other people ... I find it hard to believe that these schools claim to have groomed children for success when we were not allowed to be normal children ... the constant message [was] that because you are Native you are part of a weak, defective race, unworthy of a distinguished place in society. That is the reason you have to be looked after ... That to me is not training for success, it is training for self-destruction.[130]

"I was frustrated about how we were treated, humiliated, and degraded, so I drank and took drugs to numb the frustrations of how my life had turned out."[131] And

> A lot of us left residential school as mixed-up human beings, not able to cope with family or life. Many of us came out with a huge inferiority complex realizing something was missing, but not knowing what it was. Many searched for love and support in the wrong way. Girls became promiscuous, thinking this was the only way they could feel close to another person. Never having learned to cope with the outside world, many turned to drinking and became alcoholics.[132]

For almost a century the federal government in Canada sought to control the lives and souls of Indigenous peoples. Outwardly espousing assimilation through education, the federal government neither took the leadership nor provided the financial resources to achieve any other goal than the self-affirming prophecy inherent in racist rhetoric. Religious denominations may have acted from the highest of motives, in their view, but lives were destroyed nonetheless. The logic behind the concept of the residential school was muddled at best, duplicitous at worst. The system's attributes made possible no other goal than Indigenous peoples' absolute marginalization from Canadian life—a goal that schools achieved with remarkable success.

Unable to consider Indigenous peoples as differing between time and place or capable of exercising control over their daily lives, federal policy deliberately bypassed the opportunity to integrate Indigenous peoples into the larger society at their own pace, a process which had begun at least in a small way in late nineteenth-century British Columbia. The Department of Indian Affairs may have saved a few dollars in the short run, but the cost was generations of diminished and even wasted lives. The past cannot be undone, but it can be better understood. Only then can the cycle of the residential school, and its dominance of Indigenous educational history, be broken: "The silent suffering has to end. It is time for the healing to start and the only way that will happen is if we acknowledge the past, face it, understand it, deal with it, and make sure that nothing like that ever happens again."[133]

Notes

1 Funding provided by the Social Sciences and Humanities Research Council of Canada made possible research on which this essay draws. I am grateful to SSHRCC and to Donna Penney, Clint Evans, Dana Whyte, Valerie Giles, and Roger Wiebe for their assistance.

2 Department of Indian Affairs (DIA), Annual Report (1895), xxi.

3 DIA, Annual Report (1895), xxi.

4 Personal testimony is used not to set apart individuals or schools but rather to demonstrate how federal policy constructed Indigenous pupils' experience of education similarly, regardless of individual or institution. The recollections used here, all of which are in the public domain, reference a variety of schools: All Hallows (Clara Clare), Christie (Francis Charlie), Kamloops (George Manuel, Shirley Sterling), Lejac (Lizette Hall, Mary John, Justa Monk), Port Alberni (Vera Manuel, Charlie Thompson), St. Eugene's at Cranbrook (Troy Hunter), St. George's at Lytton (Simon Baker), St. Joseph's at Williams Lake (Bev Sellars, Augusta Tappage), St. Mary's Mission (Mary Englund), St. Michael's at Alert Bay (Mabel James, Clayton Mack), St. Paul's at North Vancouver (Lois Guss), and Edmonton (Rosa Bell, Art Collison, sent from Haida Gwaii/Queen Charlotte Islands). Testimonies not otherwise footnoted are in Linda Jaine, ed., *Residential Schools: The Stolen Years* (Saskatoon: Extension University Press, University of Saskatchewan, 1993).

5 Copy of Contract between Department of Indian Affairs and the Management of Indian Boarding Schools, in DIA, Annual Report (1911), 440.

6 This topic is discussed at much greater length in Jean Barman, "Negotiating Interraciality in Three Early British Columbian Indian Residential Schools," in *Roots of Entanglement: Essays in Native-Newcomer Relations*, ed. Myra Rutherdale, Kerry Abel, and P. Whitney Lackenbauer (Toronto: University of Toronto Press, 2018), 181-208.

7 DIA, Annual Report (1887), lxxx.

8 DIA, Annual Report (1880), 8.

9 DIA, Annual Report (1910), 327.

10 Charles Mair to George Denison, Okanagan Mission, December 5, 1892, Mair Correspondence in possession of Duane Thomson and used with his permission. Italics in original.

11 DIA, Annual Report (1880), 3.

12 DIA, Annual Report (1890), xxx.

13 DIA, Annual Report (1902), 283.

14 Walter Hunter, teacher at Lillooet, to S.D. Pope, Superintendent of Education (SE), Lillooet, August 7, 1886, in BC SE, Inward Correspondence (IC), BC Archives, GR 1445.

15 Petition from a group of parents at Port Essington to Pope, Port Essington, August 27, 1888, in BC SE, IC.

16 O.N. Hughett, Secretary of Genoa Trustees Board, to Pope, Genoa, September 21, 1891, in BC SE, IC.

17 John Jessop to J[ane] E. Trenaman, Victoria, October 30, 1876, in BC SE, Outward Correspondence (OC), BC Archives, GR 450.

18 James Malpass, Secretary of North Cedar Trustee Board, to Pope, North Cedar, May 17, 1886, BC SE, IC; and Pope to Malpass Victoria, May 20, 1886, in BC SE, OC.

19 S. Shepherd, teacher at Yale, to Pope, Yale, December 12, 1888, in BC SE, IC; and Pope to Shepherd, Victoria, December 15, 1888, in BC SE, OC.

20 Pope to George Hopkins, Victoria, July 29, 1889, in BC SE, OC.

21 Pope to Samuel Cutler, Victoria, August 1, 1893, in BC SE, OC. The circular's date is inferred from M.E. Sheirs, teacher at Port Kells, to Pope, Port Kells, October 13, 1891, in BC SE, IC.

22 Sheirs to Pope, Port Kells, October 13, 1891, in BC SE, IC.

23 William McAdam, teacher at Port Hammond, to Pope, Port Hammond, November 2, 1891, in BC SE, IC.

24 Samuel Cutler, Secretary of Sooke Trustees, to Pope, Sooke, October 31, 1892, in BC SE, IC.

25 Pope to H[arriet] Young, teacher at Pavillion, Victoria, March 27, 1894, in BC SE, OC.

26 Cutler to Pope, Sooke, November 8, 1893, in BC SE, IC.

27 For historical statistics on British Columbia, see Thomas A. Lascelles, *Roman Catholic Residential Schools in British Columbia* (Vancouver: Order of OMI in BC, 1990), 95-98.

28 This argument grounds Paul Tennant, *Aboriginal Peoples and Politics: The Indian Land Question in British Columbia, 1849-1989* (Vancouver: UBC Press, 1990).

29 Reproduced in DIA, Annual Report (1895), 348-51; also Annual Report (1894), xxi.

30 DIA, Annual Report (1896), xxxvii.

31 Jacqueline Gresko, "Creating Little Dominions within the Dominion: Early Catholic Indian Schools in Saskatchewan and British Columbia," in *Indian in Canada*, vol. 1: *The Legacy*, ed. Jean Barman, Yvonne Hébert and Don McCaskill (Vancouver: UBC Press, 1986), 1, 96.

32 Jean E. Speare, ed., *The Days of Augusta* (Vancouver: J.J. Douglas, 1973), 18.

33 George Manuel and Michael Posluns, *The Fourth World: An Indian Reality* (Toronto: Collier Macmillan Canada, 1974), 64. According to Celia Haig-Brown's portrait of the same school, "no child attended school for longer than two hours a day." Celia Haig-Brown, *Resistance and Renewal: Surviving the Indian Residential School* (Vancouver: Arsenal Pulp, 1988), 61.

34 Verna J. Kirkness, ed., *Khot-La-Cha: The Autobiography of Chief Simon Baker* (Vancouver: Douglas and McIntyre, 1994), 30–31.

35 Kirkness, ed., *Khot-La-Cha*, 29.

36 Lascelles, *Roman Catholic Residential Schools*, 30.

37 DIA, Annual Report (1895), xxiii.

38 Lizette Hall, *The Carrier, My People* (Fort St. James: n.p., 1992), 81.

39 Speare, *Days of Augusta*, 7.

40 Manuel and Posluns, *Fourth World*, 64.

41 Thompson Ferrier, *Indian Education in the Northwest* (Toronto: Department of Missionary Literature of the Methodist Church, Canada, 1906), 17, 25. The Methodist Church was parroting federal rhetoric; see, for instance, DIA, Annual Report (1888), x, and (1897), 60.

42 Francis Charlie, quoted in Lascelles, *Roman Catholic Residential Schools*, 44.

43 Manuel and Posluns, *Fourth World*, 66.

44 Hall, *The Carrier, My People*, 81.

45 Data on Indian pupils taken from "School Statements" in DIA, Annual Reports; on pupils in provincial schools from *Annual Survey of Education* (Ottawa: Dominion Bureau of Statistics), renamed *Elementary and Secondary Education in Canada*.

46 Lascelles, *Roman Catholic Residential Schools*, 83.

47 Bridget Moran, *Justa: A First Nations Leader* (Vancouver: Arsenal Pulp Press, 1994), 51.

48 DIA, Annual Report (1896), xxxviii.

49 Hall, *The Carrier, My People*, 81.

50 Moran, *Justa*, 57.

51 Clellan S. Ford, *Smoke from Their Fires: The Life of a Kwakiutl Chief* (New Haven, CT: Yale University Press, 1941), 100.

52 Correspondence concerning Lejac School, 1910, cited in Jo-Anne Fiske, "Life at Lejac," in *Sa Ts'e: Historical Perspectives on Northern British Columbia*, ed. Thomas Thorner (Prince George: College of New Caledonia Press, 1989), 243.

53 The yearly reports submitted by individual day schools and extracted in DIA's Annual Reports often include information on teachers. See, for example the report for 1910, 328–41. For a later excellent insider account of a British Columbia day school, see Helen Raptis with members of the Tsimshian Nation, *What We Learned: Two Generations Reflect on Tsimshian Education and the Day Schools* (Vancouver: UBC Press, 2016).

54 Letter from Chehalis band following meeting of March 5, 1936, cited in Jo-ann Archibald, "Resistance to an Unremitting Process: Racism, Curriculum and Education in Western Canada," in *The Imperial Curriculum: Racial Images and Education in the British Colonial Experience*, ed. J.A. Mangan (London: Routledge, 1993), 101.

55 Inspector's response to letter from Chehalis band following meeting of March 5, 1936, cited in Archibald, "Resistance to an Unremitting Process," 101.

56 Bridget Moran, *Stoney Creek Woman: The Story of Mary John* (Vancouver: Tillicum, 1988), 53–54.

57 Quoted in Fiske, "Life at Lejac," 244.

58 Notation dated 1932, cited in Norma Sluman and Jean Goodwill, *John Tootoosis: A Biography of a Cree Leader* (Ottawa: Golden Dog Press, 1982), 157.

59 James P. Spradley, *Guests Never Leave Hungry: The Autobiography of James Sewid, a Kwakiutl Indian* (New Haven, CT: Yale University Press, 1969), 191.

60 DIA, Annual Report (1912), 399.

61 Mary Englund, quoted in Margaret Whitehead, *Now You Are My Brother: Missionaries in British Columbia*, Sound Heritage series no. 34 (Victoria: Provincial Archives of British Columbia, 1981), 64.

62 David Johnson, quoted in Whitehead, *Now You Are My Brother*, 50.

63 DIA Annual Report (1911), 374.

64 Lascelles, *Roman Catholic Residential Schools*, 42.

65 DIA, Annual Report (1896), xxxvii.

66 DIA, Annual Report (1906), 251.

67 Lascelles, *Roman Catholic Residential Schools*, 42.

68 DIA, Annual Report (1891), xiii.

69 Manuel and Posluns, *Fourth World*, 64.

70 Marjorie Mitchell and Anna Franklin, "When You Don't Know the Language, Listen to the Silence: An Historical Overview of Native Indian Women in BC," in *Not Just Pin Money: Selected Essays on the History of Women's Work in British Columbia*, ed. Barbara K. Latham and Roberta J. Pazdro (Victoria: Camosun College, 1984), 24.

71 Speare, *Days of Augusta*, 18.

72 Moran, *Stoney Creek Woman*, 44-5.

73 Moran, *Justa*, 51.

74 Manuel and Posluns, *Fourth World*, 65.

75 Shirley Sterling, *My Name Is Seepeetza* (Toronto: Groundwood Books, 1992), 24.

76 Hall, *The Carrier, My People*, 83.

77 Moran, *Stoney Creek Woman*, 39.

78 Gwen Cash, *Off the Record: The Personal Reminiscences of Canada's First Woman Reporter* (Langley, BC: Stagecoach, 1977), 23.

79 *All Hallows in the West* (school magazine of All Hallows School, Yale, British Columbia) 6, no. 8 (Ascension 1906): 538.

80 Comparisons were made for the school years 1899-1900 and 1907-1908. The two years compare Indigenous and rural public schools operating in close geographical proximity. In the case of 1899-1900, Alberni, Alert Bay, Comox, Quamichan, Saanich, and Somenos; for 1907-1908, Alert Bay, Bella Coola, Clayoquot, Hazelton, Lytton, Telegraph Creek, and Ucluelet. Comparative data extracted from British Columbia, Department of Education, Annual Report, Tables A and D; and DIA, Annual Report, "School Statement."

81 DIA, Annual Report (1899-1900), pt. 2, 14-15, financial statements for All Hallows, Port Simpson, and St. Mary's boarding schools.

82 DIA, Annual Report (1907-1908), pt. 2, 21-4, financial statements for Ahousat, Alberni, All Hallows, Port Simpson, St. Mary's, Sechelt, and Squamish boarding schools.

83 Calculated from financial statements in *All Hallows in the West*.

84 Advertisement in *News-Advertiser* (Vancouver), August 10, 1902.

85 DIA, Annual Report (1911), xxvi and 294-95.

86 University School, Prospectus, 1912, in St. Michaels University School Archives, Victoria.

87 Because no breakdown of financial support for individual Indian day schools is included following the 1910 revision, mean support per pupil across British Columbia is compared with mean cost in rural public schools operating in geographical proximity to an Indian day school—in this case, Alert Bay, Bella Coola, Clayoquot, Hazelton, Lytton, Masset, Similkameen, Telegraph Creek, and Ucluelet. Comparable data is extracted from British Columbia, Department of Education, Annual Report, Tables A and D.

88 DIA, Annual Report (1912), 408. For another example, see DIA, Annual Report (1911), 378.

89 DIA, Annual Report (1912), 399.

90 DIA, Annual Report (1915), 238.

91 This point is made in John Webster Grant, *Moon of Wintertime: Missionaries and the Indians of Canada in Encounter since 1534* (Toronto: University of Toronto Press, 1984), 191.

92 Diamond Jenness, "Canada's Indians Yesterday. What of Today?" *Canadian Journal of Economic and Political Science* 20, no. 1 (February 1954), reprinted in A.L. Getty and Antoine S. Lussier, ed., *As Long as the Sun Shines and Water Flows: A Reader in Canadian Native Studies* (Vancouver: UBC Press, 1983), 162.

93 Data comes from DIA, Annual Reports.

94 Lascelles, *Roman Catholic Residential Schools*, 83.

95 Thomas Leduc, teacher at Lillooet, to John Jessop, Lillooet, January 8, 1876, in BC SE, IC.

96 DIA, Annual Report (1888), 104.

97 Clara Clare, cited in Jean Barman, "Separate and Unequal: Indian and White Girls at All Hallows School, 1884–1920," p. 381n7, in this volume.

98 Ruth Cook, quoted in Dorothy Haegert, *Children of the First People* (Vancouver: Tillicum, 1983), 21.

99 Sterling, *My Name Is Seepeetza*, 125.

100 Sterling, *My Name Is Seepeetza*, 12.

101 DIA, Annual Report (1911), 381.

102 William Sepass, Stó:lo Chief, testifying before Royal Commission on Indian Affairs reporting in 1916, quoted in Archibald, "Resistance to an Unremitting Process," 100.

103 Moran, *Stoney Creek Woman*, 53.

104 Stoney Creek Council to DIA, 1917, quoted in Fiske, "Life at Lejac," 240.

105 Harry Assu with Joy Inglis, *Assu of Cape Mudge: Recollections of a Coastal Indian Chief* (Vancouver: UBC Press, 1989), 95–96.

106 Spradley, *Guests Never Leave Hungry*, 125–26.

107 Kirkness, *Khot-La-Cha*, 73.

108 Kirkness, *Khot-La-Cha*, 31.

109 Moran, *Stoney Creek Woman*, 44.

110 Moran, *Justa*, 10.

111 Moran, *Stoney Creek Woman*, 44.

112 Haig-Brown, *Resistance and Renewal*.

113 See Margaret Connell Szasz and Carmelia Ryan, "American Indian Education," in *History of Indian-White Relations*, vol. 4 of *Handbook of North American Indians*, ed. Wilcomb E. Washburn (Washington: Smithsonian Institution, 1988), 284–301; Irving G. Hendrick, "The Federal Campaign for the Admission of Indian Children into Public Schools, 1890–1934," *American Indian Culture and Research Journal* 5 (1981): 13–32; Margaret Connell Szasz, *Education and the American Indian: The Road to Self-Determination since 1928* (Albuquerque: University of New Mexico Press, 1977); and Guy B. Senese, *Self-Determination and the Social Education of Native Americans* (New York: Praeger, 1991).

114 Sterling, *My Name Is Seepeetza*, 41.

115 Art Collison, "Healing Myself through Our Haida Traditional Customs," in Jaine, *Residential Schools*, 38.

116 Sharon McIvor Grismer, quoted in Valerie Niehaus, "Mrs. Sharon McIvor Grismer," *Nicola Valley Historical Quarterly* 1, no. 4 (October 1978), 7.

117 Moran, *Justa*, 103, referring to 1971.

118 Moran, *Justa*, 156.

119 This assessment is necessarily simplistic; on the complexities see Archibald, "Resistance to an Unremitting Process," 93–107, 223–27; and the essays in Marie Battiste and Jean Barman, eds., *First Nations Education in Canada: The Circle Unfolds* (Vancouver: UBC Press, 1995).

120 Moran, *Justa*, 155–56.

121 Rosa Bell, "Journeys," in Jaine, *Residential Schools*, 13.

122 Bell, "Journeys," 10.

123 Manuel and Posluns, *Fourth World*, 67.

124 Charlie Thompson, "The First Day," in Jaine, *Residential Schools*, 129.

125 Vera Manuel, "The Abyss," in Jaine, *Residential Schools*, 115.

126 Sterling, *My Name Is Seepeetza*, 36, 67, 89.

127 Bell, "Journeys," 10.

128 Moran, *Justa*, 55.

129 Manuel and Posluns, *Fourth World*, 67.

130 Bev Sellars, "Against All Odds," in Jaine, *Residential Schools*, 131.

131 Collison, "Healing Myself," 39.

132 Lois Guss, "Residential School Survivor," in Jaine, *Residential Schools*, 92.

133 Sellars, "Against All Odds," 129. Sellars would later author the very powerful *They Called Me Number One: Secrets and Survival at an Indian Residential School* (Vancouver: Talonbooks, 2013).

Selected Works by Jean Barman

Books

Invisible Generations: Living between Indigenous and White in the Fraser Valley. Halfmoon Bay, BC: Caitlin Press, 2019.

Iroquois in the West. McGill-Queen's Native and Northern Series, no. 93. Montreal/Kingston: McGill-Queen's University Press, 2019.

Maria Mahoi of the Islands. Vancouver: New Star, 2004; new edition, 2017.

Abenaki Daring: The Life and Writings of Noel Annance, 1792–1869. Montreal/Kingston: McGill-Queen's University Press, 2016.

French Canadians, Furs, and Indigenous Women in the Making of the Pacific Northwest. Vancouver: UBC Press, 2014. Governor General's Gold Medal for Scholarly Research; Sir John A. Macdonald Prize, Canadian Historical Association, for best English-language book of Canadian history; Basil Stuart-Stubbs Prize for Outstanding Scholarly Book on British Columbia; K.D. Srivastava Prize for Excellence in Scholarly Publishing for best book published by UBC Press.

British Columbia: Spirit of the People. Madeira Park, BC: Harbour, for BC150 and the Province of British Columbia, 2008. Text written at invitation of provincial government honouring BC 150.

The West beyond the West: A History of British Columbia. 3rd ed. Toronto: University of Toronto Press, 2007. Canadian Historical Association Prize for best book on British Columbia.

With Jan Hare. *Good Intentions Gone Awry: Emma Cosby and the Methodist Mission on the Northwest Coast*. Vancouver: UBC Press, 2006.

With Bruce Watson. *Leaving Paradise: Indigenous Hawaiians in the Pacific Northwest, 1787–1898*. Honolulu: University of Hawai'i Press, 2006.

Stanley Park's Secret: The Forgotten Families of Whoi Whoi, Kanaka Ranch, and Brockton Point. Madeira Park, BC: Harbour, 2005. City of Vancouver Best Book Prize, 2006.

The Remarkable Adventures of Portuguese Joe Silvey. Madeira Park, BC: Harbour, 2004. Blanketed at Stanley Park launch of public sculpture honouring Joe Silvey and his two wives, 2015.

Sojourning Sisters: The Lives and Letters of Jessie and Annie McQueen. Toronto: University of Toronto Press, 2003. Canadian Historical Association Prize for best book on British Columbia, 2004; Lieutenant-Governor's Medal for best book on British Columbia history, 2004.

Constance Lindsay Skinner: Writing on the Frontier. Toronto: University of Toronto Press, 2002.

Growing Up British in British Columbia: Boys in Private School. Vancouver: UBC Press, 1984.

Edited Books

With Cheryl Suzack, Jeanne Perreault, and Shari Huhndorf. *Indigenous Women and Feminism: Politics, Activism, Culture*. Vancouver: UBC Press, 2010. Canadian Women's Studies Association Outstanding Scholarship Book, 2012.

With Mona Gleason. *Children, Teachers and Schools in the History of British Columbia*, 2nd ed. Calgary: Detselig, 2003. First edition co-edited with Neil Sutherland and J.D. Wilson, 1995.

With Marie Battiste. *First Nations Education in Canada: The Circle Unfolds*. Vancouver: UBC Press, 1995.

With Neil Sutherland and Linda Hale. *Contemporary Canadian Childhood and Youth: A Bibliography* and *History of Canadian Childhood and Youth: A Bibliography*. Westport, CT: Greenwood, 1992. Canadian History of Childhood Association's Founder's Prize, 1992–1993.

With Linda Hale. *British Columbia Local Histories: A Bibliography*. Victoria: BC Heritage Trust, 1991.

With Yvonne Hébert and Don McCaskill. *Indian Education in Canada*. Vol. 1: *The Legacy* and vol. 2: *The Challenge*. Vancouver: UBC Press, 1986 and 1987.

With R.A.J. McDonald. *Vancouver Past: Essays in Social History*. Vancouver: UBC Press, 1986.

Articles and book chapters (including those reprinted in this collection):

"Leaving Home for the Unknown: Pathways of Iroquois Recruited into the Early Nineteenth-Century Westward Fur Trade." *Iroquoia: The Journal of the Conference on Iroquois Research* 5 (October 2019), 7–28.

"The Many Ways of Seeing British Columbia." *BC Studies* 200 (Winter 2018–2019): 161–68.

"Negotiating Interraciality in Three Early British Columbian Indian Residential Schools." In *Roots of Entanglement: Essays in Native-Newcomer Relations*, edited by Myra Rutherdale, Kerry Abel, and P. Whitney Lackenbauer, 181–208. Toronto: University of Toronto Press, 2018.

"Beyond Chinatown: Chinese Men and Indigenous Women in Early British Columbia." *BC Studies* 117 (Spring 2013): 39–64. In appreciation for writing the essay, was awarded a Queen Elizabeth Jubilee Medal, 2015.

With Mike Evans, Gabrielle Legault, and Erin Dolmage. "Métis Networks in British Columbia: Examples from the Central Interior." In *Contours of a People: Metis Family, Mobility, and History*, edited by Nicole St-Onge, Carolyn Podruchny, and Brenda Macdougall, 231–67. Norman: University of Oklahoma Press, 2012.

"Sophie Morigeau: Free Trader, Free Woman." In *Recollecting Lives of Aboriginal Women of the Canadian Northwest and Borderlands*, edited by Sarah Carter and Patricia McCormack, 175–95. Edmonton: AU Press, 2011.

"Race, Greed, and Something More: The Erasure of Urban Indigenous Space in Early Twentieth-Century British Columbia." In *Making Settler Colonial Space: Perspectives on Land, Place and Identity*, edited by Tracey Banivauna-Mar and Penelope Edmonds, 155–73. London: Palgrave Macmillan, 2010.

"Indigenous Women and Feminism on the Cusp of Contact." In *Indigenous Women and Feminism: Politics, Activism, Culture*, edited by Cheryl Suzack, Jeanne Perrault, Shari Huhndorf, and Jean Barman, 92–108. Vancouver: UBC Press, 2010. The book received the Canadian Women's Studies Association Outstanding Scholarship Book Prize for 2012.

With Mike Evans. "Reflections on Being, and Becoming, Métis in British Columbia." *BC Studies* 161 (2009): 59–91.

"Cascadia Once upon a Time." In *Cascadia, The Elusive Utopia: Exploring the Spirit of the People of the Pacific Northwest*, edited by Douglas Todd, 89–114. Vancouver: Ronsdale, 2008.

"British Columbia in Jane Austen's Time." *Persuasions: The Jane Austen Journal* 29 (2007): 39–53.

"Writing Women into the History of the North American Wests, One Woman at a Time." In *One Step Over the Line: Toward a History of Women in the North American Wests*, edited by Elizabeth Jameson and Sheila McManus, 99–127. Calgary: University of Calgary Press, 2008.

"Erasing Indigenous Indigeneity in Vancouver." BC *Studies* 155 (Fall 2007): 3–30.

"At the Edge of Law's Empire: Aboriginal Interraciality, Citizenship, and the Law in British Columbia." *Windsor Yearbook of Access to Justice* 26, no. 1 (2006): 3–22.

With Jan Hare. "Good Intentions Gone Awry: From Protection to Incarceration at Emma Crosby's Home for Girls, 1874–1897." In *Beyond Good Intentions: Euro-Canadian and Aboriginal Relations in Colonial Canadas*, edited by Celia Haig-Brown and David Nock, 179–98. Vancouver: UBC Press, 2006.

"Aboriginal Women on the Streets of Victoria: Engendering Transgressive Sexuality during the Gold Rush." In *Contact Zones: Aboriginal and Settler Women in Canada's Colonial Past*, edited by Myra Rutherdale and Katie Pickles, 205–27. Vancouver: UBC Press, 2005. Canadian Committee on the History of Sexuality Award for best article on the history of sexuality in Canada published the past two years, 2006.

"Lost Nanaimo—Taking Back Our Past." *British Columbia History* 38, no. 3 (2005): 15–22, and *Shale* 8 (June 2004): 16–26. BC Historical Federation award for best article published in *British Columbia History*, 2006.

With J.I. Little. "'An Educator of Modern Views': The (Auto)biography of Margaret Ross, 1862–1943." *Historical Studies in Education* 17, no. 2 (2005): 337–61.

"Encounters with Sexuality: The Management of Inappropriate Body Behaviour in Late-Nineteenth Century British Columbia Schools." *Historical Studies in Education* 16, no. 1 (2004): 85–104.

"British Columbia's Pioneer Teachers." In *Children, Teachers and Schools in the History of British Columbia*, 2nd ed., edited by Jean Barman and Mona Gleason, 171–90. Calgary: Detselig, 2003.

"Deprivatizing Private Education: The British Columbia Experience." In *Children, Teachers and Schools in the History of British Columbia*, 2nd ed., 393–409.

"Growing Up British in British Columbia: The Vernon Preparatory School, 1914–1946." In *Children, Teachers and Schools in the History of British Columbia*, 2nd ed., 303–18.

"Reflections on the Role of the School in the Transition to Work in Resource Towns." In *Children, Teachers and Schools in the History of British Columbia*, 2nd ed., 363–75.

"Schooled for Inequality: The Education of British Columbia Aboriginal Children." In *Children, Teachers and Schools in the History of British Columbia*, 2nd ed., 55–79.

"Separate and Unequal: Indian and White Girls at All Hallows School, 1884–1920." In *Children, Teachers and Schools in the History of British Columbia*, 2nd ed., 283–302.

"Transfer, Imposition or Consent: The Emergence of Educational Structures in Nineteenth-Century British Columbia." In *Children, Teachers and Schools in the History of British Columbia*, 2nd ed., 13–35.

"Unpacking English Gentlemen Emigrants' Cultural Baggage: Apple Orchards and Private Schools in British Columbia's Okanagan Valley." *British Journal of Canadian Studies* 16, no. 1 (2003): 137–49.

"'Vancouver's First Playwright': Constance Lindsay Skinner and *The Birthright*." *BC Studies* 137 (2003): 47–61.

"Island Sanctuaries—Early Mixed-race Settlement on Gabriola and Nearby Coastal Islands." *Shale* 2 (March 2001): 1–13.

With Jan Hare. "Aboriginal Education: Is There a Way Ahead?" In *Visions of the Heart: Canadian Aboriginal Issues*, 2nd ed., edited by David Long and Olive Dickason, 331–59. Toronto: Harcourt Canada, 2000.

With Bruce Watson. "Fort Colville's Fur Trade Families and the Dynamics of Aboriginal Racial Intermixture in the Pacific Northwest." *Pacific Northwest Quarterly* 90, no. 3 (1999): 140–53. Washington State Historical Society Charles Gates Award for best article.

"Family Life at Fort Langley." *British Columbia Historical News* 32, no. 4 (Fall 1999): 16–23.

"What a Difference a Border Makes: Aboriginal Racial Intermixture in the Pacific Northwest." *Journal of the West* 38, no. 3 (July 1999): 14–20.

"Invisible Women: Aboriginal Mothers and Mixed-Race Daughters in Rural British Columbia." In *Beyond the City Limits: Rural History in British Columbia*, edited by R.W. Sandwell, 159–79. Vancouver: UBC Press, 1999.

"Vancouver's Forgotten Entrepreneurs: Women Who Ran Their Own Schools." *British Columbia Historical News* 31, no. 4 (1998): 21–29.

"Families vs. Schools: Children of Aboriginal Descent in British Columbia Classrooms of the Late Nineteenth Century." In *Family Matters: Papers in Post-Confederation Canadian Family History*, edited by Edgar-André Montigny and Lori Chambers, 73–89. Toronto: Canadian Scholars' Press, 1998.

"Taming Aboriginal Sexuality: Gender, Power, and Race in British Columbia, 1850–1900." *BC Studies* 115–16 (Fall/Winter 1997–1998): 237–66. Joan Jensen-Darlis Miller Prize, awarded by the Coalition for Western Women's History for best article on the history of women west of the Mississippi, 1999.

"Whatever Happened to the Kanakas?" *The Beaver: Exploring Canada's History* 77, no. 6 (1997–1998): 12–19.

"'I Walk My Own Track in Life & No Mere Male Can Bump Me Off It': Constance Lindsay Skinner and the Work of History." In *Creating Historical Memory: English-Canadian Women and the Work of History*, edited by Beverly Boutilier and Alison Prentice, 129–63. Vancouver: UBC Press, 1997.

"Lost Okanagan: In Search of the First Settler Families." *Okanagan History* 60 (1996): 8–20.

"Aboriginal Education at the Crossroads: The Legacy of Residential Schools and the Way Ahead." In *Visions of the Heart: Canadian Aboriginal Issues*, edited by David Alan Long and Olive Patricia Dickason, 271–303. Toronto: Harcourt, Brace, 1996.

"New Land, New Lives: Hawaiian Settlement in British Columbia." *Hawaiian Journal of History* 29 (1996): 1–32.

"Constance Lindsay Skinner and the Marketing of the Western Frontier." In *Canadian Papers in Rural History*, vol. 10, edited by Donald A. Akenson (1996): 81–116.

"'Oh, No, It Would Not Be Proper to Discuss That with You': Reflections on Gender and the Experience of Childhood." *Curriculum Inquiry* 24, no. 1 (Spring 1994): 53–67.

With Neil Sutherland, "Out of the Shadows: Retrieving the History of Urban Education and Urban Childhood in Canada." In *The City and Education in Four Nations*, edited by Ronald K. Goodenow and William E. Marsden, 87–108. Cambridge: Cambridge University Press, 1992.

"The West beyond the West: The Demography of Settlement in British Columbia." *Journal of Canadian Studies* 25, no. 3 (Fall 1990): 5–18.

"Birds of Passage or Early Professionals? Teachers in Nineteenth-Century British Columbia." *Historical Studies in Education* 2, no. 1 (Spring 1990): 17–36.

"'Knowledge Is Essential for Universal Progress but Fatal to Class Privilege': Working People and the Schools in Vancouver During the 1920s." *Labour/Le travail* 22 (Fall 1988): 9–66. Canadian History of Education Association's Founders' Prize.

"Accounting for Class and Gender in Retrieving the History of Canadian Childhood." Canadian History of Education Association *Bulletin* 5, no. 2 (1988): 1–27.

"Skimming Off the Cream: The Social Impact of Private Education in British Columbia, 1900–1950." *History of Education Review* (Australia) 16, no. 1 (1987): 51–60.

"The Preparatory School Abroad: From Britain to British Columbia." *History of Education* (London) 15, no. 1 (March 1986): 1–9.

"Ethnicity in the Pursuit of Status: The Behaviour of British Middle and Upper-Class Emigrants to British Columbia in the Late

Nineteenth and Early Twentieth Centuries." *Canadian Ethnic Studies* 18, no. 1 (1986): 32–51.
"Neighbourhood and Community in Interwar Vancouver: Residential Differentiation and Civic Voting Behaviour." *BC Studies* 69–70 (Spring–Summer 1986): 97–141.
"The Long Edwardian Summer of British Columbia's Gentlemen Farmers." *History Today* (London) 34 (April 1984): 9–15.
Biographies of William Naukana (vol. 13), William Curran (vol. 15), Maria Mahoi (vol. 16), and Constance Lindsay Skinner (vol. 16), in *Dictionary of Canadian Biography* online.

Index

Page numbers in **bold** indicate a photograph or other image; the letter *n* following a page number indicates an endnote.